Shaping the Future of
African American Film

Shaping the Future of African American Film

Color-Coded Economics and the Story Behind the Numbers

MONICA WHITE NDOUNOU

RUTGERS UNIVERSITY PRESS

NEW BRUNSWICK, NEW JERSEY, AND LONDON

LIBRARY OF CONGRESS CATALOGING-IN-PUBLICATION DATA

Ndounou, Monica White, 1976–
    Shaping the future of African American film : color-coded economics and the
story behind the numbers / Monica White Ndounou.
        pages cm
    Includes filmography.
    Includes bibliographical references and index.
    ISBN 978–0–8135–6256–8 (hardcover : alk. paper) — ISBN 978–0–8135–6255–1
(pbk. : alk. paper) — ISBN 978–0–8135–6257–5 (e-book)
        1. African Americans in the motion picture industry. 2. Motion pictures—
Economic aspects—United States. 3. Motion picture industry—Finance—United
States. 4. African American motion picture producers and directors. 5. African
Americans in motion pictures. I. Title.
    PN1995.9.N4N36 2013
    791.43'652996073—dc23   2013021946

A British Cataloging-in-Publication record for this book is available from the British
Library.

Visit our website: http://rutgerspress.rutgers.edu

Manufactured in the United States of America

For my family, ancestors and descendants

CONTENTS

ACKNOWLEDGMENTS

Studios don't give a damn how they make their money. It's business. History has said that African American movies don't translate. They have on occasion, but it's the exception rather than the rule.

—Casey Silver, chairman and CEO of Universal Pictures, 1998

As a scholar and as an artist with experience in directing, acting, and writing, as well as an avid film viewer who also happens to be an African American woman, I set out to determine if the above statement is true. What I discovered in the process has altered my approach to every aspect of my work. It has been an inspiring and at times overwhelming journey that continues in spite of the publication of this text. I am grateful for so much and so many, especially my family, friends, mentors, and students. My husband, Victorien, has been a consistent source of encouragement and inspiration, providing technical and emotional support through every incarnation of this project. Our fabulous children, Joshua and Jazmyne, have displayed the patience of saints throughout this process. My mother and role model, Esther Robinson Dixon, has also consistently reminded me to continue to stand and walk tall, regardless. Without all of you, and my siblings, I would be truly lost. To my grandmother, Jesse Mae White, your strength and courage inspire me. To my great-grandmother, Ella Mae Patterson, and grandfather, Bishop William White Jr., who joined the ancestors early on in this project: I miss you dearly and treasure your legacy.

This project had a number of inspirations but *Sankofa*, Haile Gerima's classic film and an oft-cited example in many preceding studies about African American film, is especially important. "Sankofa" is also an Akan proverb that means, "It is not forbidden to go back and reclaim what you have forgotten." The film and proverb have inspired this work, as have *Beloved* (1998), Jonathan Demme's cinematic adaptation of Toni Morrison's novel, and Spike Lee's *Bamboozled* (2000).

Although I began this project long before I started teaching film and theater courses at Tufts University, I would still like to acknowledge my students and colleagues. Your interest in this study and appreciation for its revelations has contributed to its current form. My teachers and mentors have been invaluable at every stage of development, especially Dr. Stratos Constantinidis, who has been honest and supportive every step of the way. I also want to thank Dr. Anthony Hill and Dr. Linda James Myers for their very helpful suggestions and support of early incarnations of the project. Dr. Mark A. Reid, Dr. Debra Walker King, Dr. Mikell Pinkney, Dr. Leah Rosenberg, Dr. Apollo Amoko, Dr. James Upton, Dr. Alamin Mazrui, Dr. Pam Monteleone, Dr. Sam Kimball, and Dr. James Smethurst, my teachers at various points in time, exposed me to the material that would later shape my scholarly and creative development. I would like to thank all the scholars, artists, and allies who helped inform this work, including those listed above and the many cited throughout this text. Special thanks to those scholars who have offered support and encouragement, including members of the Black Performance Theory Working Group, the ASTR Diasporic Imaginations Working Group, and the New England Black Scholars Collective (Soyica Diggs Colbert, Aliyyah Abdur-Rahman, Sandy Alexandre, Nicole Aljoe, Alisa Brathwaite, Kimberly Juanita Brown, Régine Jean-Charles, Stéphanie Larrieux, and Sam Vasquéz).

Most importantly, I would like to thank my editor, Leslie Mitchner, the staff of Rutgers University Press, copyeditors Adi Hovav and Eric Schramm, my assistant indexer, Katherine J. Swimm, and anonymous reviewers of this book, all of whom have guided my extraction of the fundamental elements from the original 876-page text. Creation is truly a collaborative effort, and I am in awe of the support the universe has provided throughout this process. This also includes the Jacob K. Javits Fellowship and The Ohio State University Presidential Fellowship. I sincerely appreciate the countless others who have provided familial support and encouragement.

Shaping the Future of
African American Film

Introduction

The Color of Hollywood–Black, White, or Green?

Many filmmakers still want to believe that there's not enough money spent on promotion, but it's been tried enough times, and tried recently enough, that the studios have seen that there is just very little interest from audiences abroad. It's not racism; there are a lot of American movies that don't work overseas–[that] don't travel.

—Steve Guila, president of Fox Searchlight, a division
of Twentieth Century-Fox, 2004

On April 20, 2012, director Tim Story's *Think Like a Man*, a cinematic adaptation of comedian Steve Harvey's self-help book, *Act Like a Lady, Think Like a Man*, debuted on over two thousand screens across the United States. Produced on a \$12 million budget,[1] *Think Like a Man* earned \$34 million in its opening weekend, holding the number-one spot for top-grossing movies for two consecutive weeks. Starring a predominantly black ensemble cast, including four black women in lead roles—rare for a studio-distributed romantic comedy—the production earned a total of \$92 million in domestic box office after eighty days in 2,052 theaters. The film helped Story replace Tyler Perry as the highest-grossing American black director. But despite the film's success in the United States, *Think Like a Man* was not shown in France. Distributors reportedly feared that a film featuring black actors in all the major roles and white actors in only minor roles would be perceived as lacking in diversity—notwithstanding that a number of Hollywood and French films with predominantly white casts were released in France in the very same year.[2]

Think Like a Man was not the only contemporary American film with a mostly black cast to receive little or no attention in international markets.[3] Even *Red Tails*, an action film produced by George Lucas, couldn't summon much interest on the international scene. Released in 2012, *Red Tails* is about the Tuskegee Airmen, a group of black pilots who fought in World War II. The film was written and directed entirely by African Americans in collaboration with Lucas and features a predominantly black male cast. Lucas, one of the most financially successful white directors and producers in American film, invested $58 million into the film's production budget and $35 million into distribution. Action films with male protagonists and/or well-known directors are often a winning formula at the box office. Accordingly, the film debuted at $19 million on 2,512 screens domestically where it played for 140 days for a total of $49.8 million. But *Red Tails* only received limited international distribution through Twentieth Century–Fox (in France), Capelight Pictures (Germany), and Momentum Pictures (Ireland and the United Kingdom).[4] The reported earnings for its limited international release are incomplete,[5] which makes it difficult to assess the film's overall outcome and challenge the perceived failure of black film in foreign markets. Considering such big-budget action films tend to make handsome profits in the international market, this data could prove useful in debates regarding the profitability of black films.[6]

While promoting *Red Tails*, Lucas revealed that he could not find any major studios that would back the film because "there were no major white roles in it at all."[7] In fact, studio executives described it as "not green enough," reminiscent of when a white distributor in Hollywood characterized Haile Gerima's 1993 film, *Sankofa*, which won several international awards, of being "too black."[8] Although *Sankofa* recouped production expenses when it earned $2.4 million domestically, paling in comparison to *Red Tails*' $49.8 million, both films had limited international distribution due to deeply embedded ideologies about race.[9] So why, when films with predominantly black casts have a clear record of economic success in domestic markets, is distribution so drastically limited in the international markets?

Hollywood studio executives insist that a lack of international demand drives their investment choices and overall reluctance to distribute or produce films about women and African Americans.[10] Considering the above examples, a more likely answer is studios' limited definitions of the international market and treatment of films with mostly black casts. While it is probably premature to say exactly how the onscreen narrative and the offscreen circumstances of these particular films will influence the future development of African American film, important insights can be gleaned by considering the past. By placing contemporary black films such as *Think Like a Man* or *Red Tails* into historical context, we can begin to see the various challenges these films face. In an industry that uses racial markers to categorize and evaluate its products, films with predominantly black casts are often labeled "urban" and, as a result, tend to fall outside the wide-release category. Regardless of genre, these films are perceived as niche films with limited market appeal. Such perceptions affect film conception, investment decisions, production, marketing, and distribution.

Still, history shows that films with black casts can earn nice profits in the domestic market. *Think Like a Man* is an excellent example. Further evidence can be found in economist Jordi McKenzie's finding, based on his study of 5,438 films released in the North American market from 1997 through 2007, that African American films generally outperform other types of films at the North American box office.[11] This stands in stark contrast to studio executives' misguided perceptions that black films are economic failures. Put another way, studio executives tend to invest in the production and broad distribution of films with predominantly white casts.

A closer look at one studio's film budgets and gross profits sheds light on racial disparities in investment patterns, further supporting McKenzie's findings. Screen Gems "focuses on films that fall between the wide-release movies traditionally developed and distributed by Columbia Pictures and those released by Sony Pictures Classics."[12] Although Screen Gems is a specialty studio, it provides a good example of industry-wide trends. Established in 1999, Screen Gems has produced fifty-eight films and distributed ninety-one films through 2013.[13] From 1999 to 2012, Screen Gems co-produced and distributed a total of forty-three films for U.S. theatrical release. Of those, fourteen have featured predominantly black casts. Comparing the gross receipts of films can be misleading when the production costs are not taken into consideration. The budgets for the black films were between $4.5 and $28 million, with most falling under $15 million. Screen Gems' remaining twenty-nine films featuring a predominantly white cast were produced with budgets ranging from $4.5 to $70 million, with most extending upward of $20 million. Screen Gems invests more money in the production of white films, which cost a total of $762 million to produce while only earning 39 percent on the investment in the domestic market. These films rely on the international market for significant revenues. Black films, on the other hand, only cost $187 million to produce and earned 184 percent on investment in the domestic market, most often without a significant foreign release.

The racial disparities are apparent in Figure 1 and Figure 2, as the return on investment for white films in the domestic market is clearly much lower than that of black films, for which revenues significantly exceeds the cost of production. Yet Screen Gems continues to produce a majority of predominantly white cast films in pursuit of foreign market revenues, which are a gamble in comparison to the consistency black films have demonstrated in the domestic market. Studio executives quoted throughout this book claim that it's not racism, it's only business. Yet we see a very different story in Screen Gems' investment patterns and outcomes. The racial disparities in Screen Gems' film budgets and

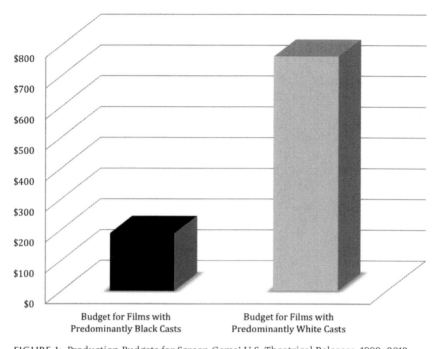

FIGURE 1: Production Budgets for Screen Gems' U.S. Theatrical Releases, 1999–2012

Sources: Figures from forty-three films co-produced and distributed by Screen Gems are averages of estimates from IMDB.com, The Numbers.com, and BoxOfficeMojo.com. For a list of all Screen Gems' films, see "Screen Gems [us]," http://www.imdb.com/company/c00010568/, accessed March 19, 2013.

earnings, which are intricately connected to distribution, are only the tip of the iceberg that threatens to sink the future of African American film.

Shaping the Future of African American Film considers how cultural politics affect the economics of African American filmmaking. In short, I argue that race-based economic principles guide investment decisions and distribution deals in the movie industry. Drawing on numerical data I collected on nearly two thousand films featuring black actors since 1980, this project illuminates critical sites of knowledge and empowerment at the intersection of race, culture, and economics. The raw data I reference throughout this book is too massive to include. But every step of analysis has been intriguing (if not at times overwhelming) considering how "numerically neutral" data can have real-life consequences for African American film and culture.

This book builds upon the work of other scholars, especially Jesse Algeron Rhines, Jacqueline Bobo, Mark A. Reid, S. Craig Watkins, Sheril D. Antonio, and Ed Guerrero. Their work cites and in some cases analyzes box office receipts of films with predominantly black casts and related films that have black themes.[14]

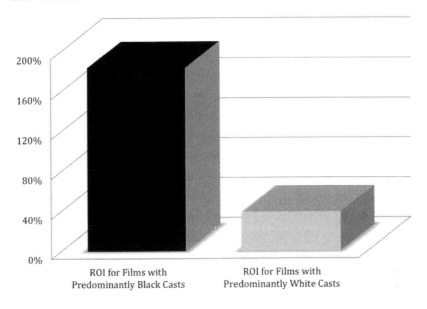

FIGURE 2: Domestic Return on Investment (ROI) for Screen Gems' U.S. Theatrical Releases, 1999–2012

Sources: Figures from forty-three films co-produced and distributed by Screen Gems represent averages of rounded estimates from IMDB.com, The Numbers.com, and BoxOfficeMojo.com. For a list of all Screen Gems films, see "Screen Gems [us]," http://www.imdb.com/company/c00010568/, accessed March 19, 2013.

According to Rhines, "Distribution is the greatest obstacle to broad-based success for African American feature filmmakers, film crews, and film cast members. From the early twentieth century until the present, the lack of enthusiasm that distribution companies, the overwhelming majority of which are controlled by whites, have shown for handling films controlled by blacks has meant a paucity of black entrepreneurial and employment success in the Hollywood film industry."[15] In this book, I expand upon Rhines's point about distribution to describe the integral role of race ideology in investment decisions and other Hollywood business practices such as casting and distribution deals. Unchanging racial and gender dynamics at the top tier of the Hollywood system increases the likelihood that the "matrix of domination," a term Patricia Hill Collins uses to describe the organization of intersecting oppressions in society, will continue to mutually reinforce the status quo.[16] Racism, sexism, religious discrimination, class bias, and homophobia thrive in these interlocking systems of oppression. For example, consider rates of employment in Hollywood: a 2009 report from the Writer's Guild of America finds "white males continue to dominate in both film and television sectors. Women remain stuck at 28 percent television employment and 18 percent film employment. The minority share of film employment has been frozen at 6 percent since 1999, while the group's share of television employment actually declined to 9 percent since the last report [in 2007]. Although women and minorities closed the earnings gap with white men in television a bit, the earnings gaps in film grew."[17] As the chapters of this book reveal, disturbingly similar patterns are also apparent when it comes to acting, directing, and producing.

This work is guided by an interdisciplinary set of methodologies drawn from adaptation and performance studies, cultural studies, feminist studies and economics. I provide a critical analysis of literature, plays, screenplays and films, language, line readings, and theater and film business practices. I also examine production processes, organizational history, and financial data to expose the racial underpinnings of economic outcomes of films with predominantly black casts as well as their cultural resonance. While there is a need to "obliterate this idea of black film being a genre"[18] in order to liberate it from the impediments of color-coded economics and their influence on content, production, marketing, distribution, and outcome, it is also critical to identify and nurture culturally nuanced cinematic languages that ensure the expression of black cultural values. Economics, form, and content are intricately connected, requiring intensive joint development of future films produced by and/or about people of color.

For the sake of specificity, I use racial markers throughout to describe people, cultures, and films. "Black" generally refers to Africans and people of African descent who have been dispersed around the world by the Atlantic slave trade and migration. African Americans, blacks in or from the United States, are members of this meta-community. Subject matter, worldviews, and film themes in what Paul Gilroy refers to as the black Atlantic reflect a range of narratives and styles that are often overshadowed by race ideology. As a racial category, whiteness frequently goes unmarked, thereby reinforcing its false universalism and marginalization of people of color. At times I distinguish between black and African American films as opposed to films featuring black or African American actors. The primary difference is not simply based on the cast or filmmakers' race (although it can be a factor, as discussed in chapter 1). I refer to an African American film as a film that disseminates African American worldviews and uses African American cultural storytelling techniques as a cinematic language that may or may not resemble mainstream standards or genres. Film scholars Richard Barsam and Dave Monahan refer to cinematic language as "the accepted systems, methods, or conventions by which the movies communicate with the viewer."[19] African American cinematic language refers to various technical and other devices filmmakers use to communicate African American experiences and perspectives. In other words, a film merely featuring black actors is less likely to incorporate a range of perspectives that appreciate the potential of black worldviews, subject matter, and themes.

Rather than redefining black film, which has been thoughtfully considered in previous studies,[20] my objective is to reevaluate the meaning of success and identify potential sites of empowerment for black films in economic and cultural terms. As such, I systematically unravel the economic and cultural implications of Hollywood's color-coded economics. As each chapter reveals, Hollywood (and related organizational systems and institutions that produce and distribute theater, literature, and film) employs racial categories to make investment decisions despite the fact that film executives continuously deny race ideology or racism's influence.

Escaping the Plantation: The Intervention of the Creole Model

Building on previous studies that expose race ideology in the film industry, I use the concept of creolization, a mixing process that occurs within culturally heterogeneous relationships evolving out of the plantation,[21] to identify and analyze the mutually reinforcing components of race, economics, culture, and gender in Hollywood. The creole model encourages theoretical and practical implementation of a variety of strategies across media by illuminating critical sites of empowerment in language, social conditions, business practices, narratives, and performances. Creolization accounts for post-emancipation cultural politics by acknowledging oppression, while also recognizing and promoting freedom in order to achieve autonomy. It is the critical next step for claiming self-ownership, which has been so frequently minimized, ignored, or insufficiently explored in critiques of the plantation arrangement.

In the plantation scheme, racial markers function to distinguish between the economic and social positioning of whites and blacks in a profit-driven system.[22] Whites are generally located at the top of the plantation hierarchy—they are the hegemonic center of Hollywood economic structures. As such, white male studio executives maintain the power to greenlight films, and they tend to favor films that will appeal to white audiences. According to Joe Pichirallo, the white producer of an African American film, *The Secret Life of Bees* (2008), "The bottom line is that the major studios want assurances that film projects have the potential to attract a significant white audience."[23] In other words, studios want movies with crossover appeal, which Rhines defines as "the potential of a film addressing nonwhite American concerns to secure a significant financial return from white American viewers."[24] As legendary African American playwright August Wilson has noted, crossover appeal evolves out of the literal and figurative plantation system in which enslaved Africans performed for their white owners' entertainment.[25] Gerima refers to this as "Hollywood's plantation arrangement" in which the relationship between African Americans and white Americans is rooted in a tradition of ownership, guidance, and responsibility.[26]

This arrangement directly influences African Americans' ability to access economic power and ownership, thereby limiting creative control and cultural production. Likewise, film scholar Ed Guerrero critiques the plantation genre, which Gerima refers to as the "plantation school of cinema." Starting with D. W. Griffith's *The Birth of a Nation* (1915), Guerrero outlines the social conditions that produced these narratives, demonstrating how the politics of plantation ideology is ongoing and varying.[27]

The first scholarly studies of black film appeared in the 1970s, over fifty years after *The Birth of a Nation*. These studies primarily identified the construction of images that contributed to a positive or negative profiling of black people.[28] Studies that followed, such as those by Thomas Cripps (1978), Phyllis Klotman (1997), Tommy L. Lott (1997), and James Snead (1995), are preoccupied with definitions about the nature and culture of African American films. There are also several studies, such as those by Manthia Diawara (1995) and Wahneema Lubiano (1997), which analyze the historical and social content of a limited number of black films. Collectively, these studies recognize remnants of the plantation as the structural foundation of power relations and art production in theater and film. Parallel patterns have been identified in American literature.[29] Ultimately, race ideology manifests across media, making adaptation and intertextuality critical tools for examining and counteracting these phenomena.

The American plantation economy continues to influence class structure in the entertainment industry in complex ways. Before looking at the entertainment industry, however, it is important to provide a foundation for how we think about class generally. In *The New Class Society*, sociologists Robert Perrucci and Earl Wysong examine class perception in American society. They argue that class structure and definitions of social class have been organized around two distinct traditions: production and functionalist.[30] "The production model . . . views class structure as organized on the basis of *relationships* people have with the means of production: people tend to be either owners of productive wealth, like factories, offices, malls, airlines, rental properties, small businesses, or non-owners—workers," very similar to the Marxist approach developed in the 1880s.[31] This single-factor approach limits full examination of the complex hierarchies and subcategories within this dynamic, especially when considering how slavery has significantly influenced blacks' access to wealth and ownership. Recent models find "classes are typically . . . based on a person's *location* in the production process—which also closely corresponds to the possession of wealth and the occupational roles people perform."[32] Yet this ignores race and gender, although it enables more nuanced discussion of hierarchies. The functionalist model, based on Max Weber's view of class stratification as complex and multidimensional, differs in that it takes into account the *prestige* associated with particular professions. It may factor in such things as advanced education or credentials in spite of income levels.[33] "Both models produce layer-cake images of class structure" and "emphasize the importance of occupation as a key factor in determining class occupation," albeit for different reasons.[34]

With four major features, Perrucci and Wysong distinguish their distribution model from previous models of class analysis. First, it takes an organizational approach to showing how the new class system is organizationally based and large organizations and their gatekeepers control distribution. Second, it argues that class location replicates the degree to which people possess combinations of four forms of generative economic and social resources—investment, consumption, skills, and social capital. Third, it explains how these organizations legitimate distributional processes and "the social inequalities that arise from them." Finally, it concludes that "American class structure is increasingly polarized by class inequalities."[35] While Perrucci and Wysong investigate the macrocosm of American society's complex class structure, the microcosm of the entertainment industry within it reveals how theatrical, literary, and film production reinforce race-based production models established in the plantation era: the creole model exposes race as a class location by investigating the collective positioning of blacks in Hollywood's organizations as well as the individual positions of specific industry players. It recognizes the role and power of these organizations, their gatekeepers, access to economic and social resources, and distributional processes. The creole model also exposes the inequalities organizations and gatekeepers reinforce in films as well as the interactions between the industry players behind the scenes.

We must also recognize Hollywood's various forms of institutionalized racism, which refers to "the combination of practices whereby blacks and other people of color as a group or class receive differential treatment within schools, housing, employment, health care, and other social institutions. Unlike bias and prejudice, which are characteristic of individuals, institutionalized racism operates through the everyday rules and customs of social institutions."[36] For example, rather than being picked up by the major American film distributors such as Warner Bros., Sony, Disney, MGM, Fox, Universal, or Paramount, films with predominantly black casts are more frequently produced and distributed independently or by minor distributors and specialty studios. In fact, Hollywood production and distribution of such films is shrinking, according to Tracey Edmonds, CEO of Edmonds Entertainment and COO of Our Stories Films. In 1993, when she entered the industry, there was "a plethora of distribution options for urban films and an assortment of studios to choose from. Now, we're pretty much limited to only two distributors, so it's very competitive, very difficult. It's also extremely competitive because you have all the filmmakers of color in the industry competing for only a couple of slots a year." This is also true in television, where BET, TBS, and more recently OWN are the only networks producing original, urban-cast shows.[37] Paradoxically, blacks are faring much better than many other people of color competing for the same few slots due to the black-white binary driving American racial discourse (discussed in chapter 1). The practice of fostering such competition amongst people of color may appear to be recent to Edmonds, but it is actually rooted in a very complex, ongoing system of race-based economics that evolved out of the plantation economy. This competition persists in spite of the clear patterns that point to the economic success of black films. In this book, I trace these class ideologies and operational procedures from the 1980s to the present to describe the precarious position of black cultural producers.

Hollywood History

A brief historical overview illustrates Hollywood's complex organization and evolving racial dynamics. Five major studios controlled Hollywood's golden age from the 1920s through the 1940s. Their top-down approach to dictating every aspect of production is known as vertical integration. Vertical integration virtually obliterates outside competition, ensuring film content and cultural values remain in the hands of a select few, which happen to be predominantly white

FIGURE 3: Vertical Integration in the Film Business

males. Although it did not address the cultural implications of vertical integration, the Supreme Court's 1948 Paramount Decree ended the monopolistic practice, which it declared to be a collusion that kept independent producers out of theaters controlled by the studios. As a result, the major studios divested themselves of theater holdings but maintained control over distribution,[38] a critical element of the filmmaking process and its influence on culture.

Although the positioning of blacks within Hollywood's golden era is beyond our scope, it is worth noting that the civil rights, Black Arts, and Black Power movements that followed interrogated the positioning of blacks in American society as well as their media representation. Our discussion primarily focuses on the 1980s to the present, but the late 1960s and early 1970s was a particularly difficult time for Hollywood. One way it recuperated is by appropriating selective elements of Melvin Van Peebles's major contribution to American cinema, *Sweet Sweetback's Baadasssss Song* (1971). This film sparked Blaxploitation, a subgenre of action film defined by its use of action sequences involving black protagonists pitted against white villains and other unsavory characters in violent situations. These films began to recede by the 1980s while the laissez-faire economic policies of the Reagan administration effectively reestablished vertical integration by allowing studios to merge with large media conglomerates.[39] Such corporate mergers persisted through the 1990s.

In addition to reviving vertical integration, corporate mergers also produced horizontal integration. Horizontal integration allows comparable businesses and companies to align and expand across the industry.[40] As a result of economic policies and industry practices over the past several decades, the current studio system's centralized control from the top down and across the entertainment industry creates a matrix of domination, overpowering potential outside influences. Through market synergy, which is the use of movie releases to simultaneously turn a profit in multiple venues, Hollywood studios resemble

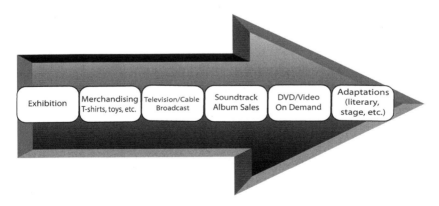

Exhibition | Merchandising T-shirts, toys, etc. | Television/Cable Broadcast | Soundtrack Album Sales | DVD/Video On Demand | Adaptations (literary, stage, etc.)

FIGURE 4: Horizontal Integration in the Film Business

a conglomerate monster with an insatiable appetite for revenue. The industry functions to create products and audiences that appreciate Hollywood's cultural values. Hollywood's contemporary economic structure therefore maintains continuous control of film content, form, and viewer experience.

The Power and Process of Adaptation

The creole model acknowledges adaptation as a critical site for exposing Hollywood's color-coded economics. Literary scholar Linda Hutcheon investigates adaptation trends in various forms including literature, stage plays, films, parodies, musicals, operas, and ballets as well as video games, reminding us that these various forms utilize distinct tools for storytelling.[41] She describes adaptation as (1) a formal entity or *product* transposed of a particular work or works, (2) a *process of creation* which involves reinterpretation and re-creation, and (3) a *process of reception*, making it a form of intertextuality that references preceding works.[42] In this way, adaptation serves as a product and a process of creation and reception, as well as a strategy for addressing various challenges influencing the development of black cultural production in theater, film, and literature.

Adaptation also refers to the adjustment to one's surroundings or circumstances, a survival strategy employed by enslaved Africans. Literally and figuratively, adaptation enables alternative approaches to storytelling across media. It represents opportunities to capitalize on horizontal integration, thereby increasing potential profits by telling a similar story in different forms. Both types of adaptation can contribute to developing African American film. Audience development and branding, which also has particular meaning in the plantation scheme, are critical. Slave owners branded black bodies like cattle to establish ownership.[43] The American Marketing Association refers to brands and branding as "a customer experience represented by a collection of images and ideas," including "a symbol such as a name, logo, slogan, and design scheme. Brand recognition and other reactions are created by the accumulation of experiences with the specific product or service, both directly relating to its use, and through the influence of advertising, design, and media commentary."[44] While racial markers complicate branding in the entertainment industry, adaptation allows for more strategic use of the concept of branding. Such tactics are exemplified by: (1) the acting styles (and directing) of Morgan Freeman and others; (2) the business savvy of Tyler Perry, Oprah Winfrey, and Will Smith; and (3) the cinematic language portrayed in work by a range of black filmmakers and allies. Adaptation, branding, casting, and genre animate the possibilities for developing the future of African American film.

By embracing the inherent intertextuality of black film, adaptation can enhance African American cinematic language, a term I use to describe the various technical devices, semiotics, narrative form, and content filmmakers use to communicate black and African American experiences. Cross-racial and international casting as well as genre revision also play an important role in this regard. The challenges and possibilities of cinematic adaptations (discussed in part 1 and part 2 of this book) suggest that acculturation occurs more often than interculturation. Hollywood's industry practices closely resemble those of plantation society's white ruling classes where those in power create dependency and encourage competition by maintaining control over language, mobility (social and physical), and resources—all in order to maintain the status quo and reinforce perceptions of black inferiority. This ideology is apparent in the shrinking distribution options for people of color in the studio system.

The Consequences of Crossover Appeal: Battling for "The Souls of Black Folk"

People of color and women who unquestionably accept the failure of black film are just as likely to perpetuate the ideology through imitation. For example, in a 1984 *New York Times* article, Ashley Boone, studio executive of *A Soldier's Story* (1984) and an African American, described his process for marketing and distributing this film. In the article, he boasts of distancing the film from its blackness to guarantee a box office return. According to Boone, marketing a black film is like marketing any serious movie without stars: "You stretch it over two to three months to overcome any quick description of the movie that could be derogatory—e.g. 'a black movie.' The first week people were saying to each other, 'There's a black movie playing.' The second week, they said, 'There's a good movie with a black cast.' And three weeks into the run, they said, 'Hey, there's a good movie.'"[45] Boone's strategy suggests that even calling a film black undermines its potential. With this knowledge Boone successfully exploits an existing model for marketing serious films. But he does not question the ideology that requires this distancing from blackness for economic success. Nearly thirty years later, a very similar idea was used to market *Think Like a Man.* These examples expose the consequences of categorizing a film as black versus distancing it from its blackness for profit.[46]

These consequences are simultaneously disrupted and heightened by double consciousness, which W.E.B. Du Bois refers to as the "two warring identities" of an American Negro. Early black feminist Anna Julia Cooper first introduced the concept in terms of being black and female in a society that valued neither. The concept is at the core of intersectionality, a feminist sociological theory that recognizes race, economic class, gender, sexuality, ethnicity, nation, and age as mutually constructing features of social organization.[47] Double consciousness and intersectionality have historically inspired blacks' varying responses to cultural production. For this reason, the practical strategies of empowerment devised by August Wilson, Haile Gerima, and various other African American cultural producers (and their allies) are just as noteworthy as the plantation ideology they resist. Indigenization, or secret acts of resistance, exhibited in the old plantation scheme are just as likely to occur in today's prevailing cultural institutions in the form of what I refer to as "performative indigenization." This refers to indigenization by actors and actresses in performance processes, though it can also occur with writers, directors, and powerbrokers behind the scenes. Performative indigenization cannot be fully appreciated without understanding the marginalized presence of minorities within the entertainment industry generally.

Films and filmmaking "function as a battleground for the clash between competing political players and their views of the world."[48] The National Association for the Advancement of Colored People (NAACP) understood this early on when they launched their first major protest against Hollywood upon the release of *The Birth of a Nation*, the groundbreaking, feature-length American film. Decades later, starting in the 1980s, the NAACP repeatedly investigated the roles that African Americans played within the industry as well as the roles they played onscreen. In 2000, the NAACP set out to "alleviate systemic discrimination against the exclusion of racial minorities in television." As part of their efforts, they collected testimony from witnesses describing all sorts of "unspoken exclusionary practices." They concluded that "it is inconceivable that anyone could deny the existence of racism in an industry that, after 50 years in business, cannot point to one black, Latino, or Asian-American who can greenlight a film, hire or fire a director or producer, or sign a development deal." Yet, as Carrie Rickey explains, most Hollywood executives—who are overwhelmingly white, male, and unwilling to have their names associated with comments about race—refute charges of racism by pointing to their black-themed films as evidence of equal opportunity. As we shall see, casting black actors and actresses and sporadically producing and distributing low-budget black-themed films is not enough to counteract the color-coded economics that drive industry profits. A closer look at budgets, distribution, reception, and box office receipts of these black-themed films provides clear evidence of the race ideology that drives these exclusionary practices.

The debate on race between the NAACP and Hollywood has not yielded substantial or consistent results. In a 2001 press conference lambasting Hollywood for its lack of diversity, NAACP president Kweisi Mfume detailed a long history of tension between blacks and Hollywood.[49] Mfume stopped short of calling for a boycott. Nevertheless, the NAACP annually bestows its coveted Image Award upon performers, television shows, films, and their producers. Their advocacy for more people of color in the industry and their efforts to remedy negative perceptions of black film is noteworthy, yet it severely underestimates the racist ideology that permeates the business. (Spike Lee lampoons the ongoing tension between the NAACP and Hollywood in *Bamboozled* when Dunwitty, the overtly racist white television executive, comments that a generous donation to the NAACP has quieted its dissent.)

Other more comprehensive approaches to articulate charges of racism focus on the economic basis of Hollywood studios' investment claims. Like the NAACP, African American studies scholar Wahneema Lubiano acknowledges that racial disparities exist but also identifies issues of market pressure and the need for more black investors and black people in powerful positions in Hollywood as contributing factors.[50] Likewise, journalist Sharon Waxman's investigation found that studio executives reject charges of racism but maintain that international market appeal influences their investment decisions. This is how films such as *Think Like a Man* and *Red Tails* are denied broad international distribution in spite of their success in the domestic market. These examples clearly demonstrate how crossover appeal to white audiences in the domestic market and nonblacks in the international market influences outcomes. When executives insist that "we can't give them what they don't want,"[51] they are not considering other thriving film industries in African nations such as Nigeria, Ghana, South Africa, Senegal, Benin, Egypt, Mali, and Gabon. The international production units of major studios such as Sony and Warner Bros. may finance local productions in European countries, India, and Mexico, but their general practices also ignore African diasporic audiences in Europe and the Americas with the massive output of films with predominantly white casts. If it is truly business and not racism, it would seem that expanding the business in these active markets and consistently recognizing black audiences would be a higher priority for Hollywood. This is not the case, even though these untapped markets are still viable and valuable.

The complications and contradictions of crossover appeal significantly influence Hollywood business practices and cultural production. Issues of ownership, the effects of international business partnerships, and political undercurrents shape the increasingly consolidated nature of content production and distribution. Sociologist David Brain defines cultural production as "the collective production of skills and practices which enable social actors to make sense of their lives, articulate an identity, and resist with creative energy the apparent dictates of structural conditions they nonetheless reproduce."[52] Cultural production generates cultural memory and preserves the methods for transmitting cultural values. Manipulating black culture through characterization, form, and narrative content significantly affects perceptions within and of the culture as well as the ways it is transmitted.

Another consequence of crossover appeal is cultural trauma. Sociologist Ron Eyerman refers to cultural trauma as a noun and a verb, in which the memory of slavery informs collective memory or forms of remembrance. Memories of slavery and related cultural trauma affect blacks as well as whites (albeit in different ways, which I discuss in the forthcoming chapters). Rememory, however, is of particular import to our investigation. Toni Morrison defines rememory as a thought picture from the past that emerges when a person returns to the site where a traumatic experience has occurred. As a storytelling technique, rememory represents one of many unique black contributions to American film. As a process, cultural trauma is mediated through various forms of representation and linked to reformation and reworking of collective memory.[53] Regardless of race, the process of confronting cultural trauma and the products that it produces are critical for identity formation and very much a part of the functioning of film.

Unfortunately, industry practices decrease the likelihood that films utilizing rememory and similar strategies will get produced, let alone distributed. Conversely, industry practices increase the likelihood of cultural amnesia, an individual and collective loss of consciousness of history and personal identity, particularly as it relates to the loss of a common frame of cultural references.[54] Cultural amnesia also refers to permanent or temporary loss of cultural memory by an otherwise cohesive ethnic group.[55] Cultural amnesia occurs when the ideology and economics of imperialism colonize and dominate smaller cultural markets by promoting a historical and theoretical exclusion that thwarts or slows the development of African American films. We see evidence of cultural amnesia when Afrocentric worldviews and cultural values are eroded in favor of crossover appeal.

Every culture has to combat definitions imposed by outsiders. Several European nations clearly recognize this. The British Cinematograph Films Act of 1927 established a quota for a requisite number of British films screened in British theaters. Recently, France has also attempted to resist the onslaught of American films, which currently capture 80 to 90 percent of continental Europe's box office.[56] This attempt to maintain a cohesive French identity by limiting the dominance of American films in France may explain but not excuse their selective distribution of African American films such as *Think Like a Man* and *Red Tails*. The bottom line is that African Americans have been unable to protect themselves from this matrix of domination through policy.

As a result, many resort to indigenization. For example, John Singleton obtains financing for his films by focusing on high-value elements such as action, violence, and the project's broad appeal, deflecting attention away from any intention to enlighten or change the general public's perception of African Americans.[57] To do so may invite preventive censorship, which occurs via the reliance on white male stars to generate (and guarantee) commercial interest in African American films domestically and abroad. This frequently foils blacks' ability to portray a broad range of experiences or use diverse genres and techniques to articulate them. Consider Reggie Rock Bythewood's *Biker Boyz* (2003). Investors loved this action film about the son of the leader of a legendary urban biker gang trying to retain his championship title, but they rejected Bythewood's proposed cast (he had already secured the agreement of several black stars, including Laurence Fishburne and Vivica A. Fox). Investors rejected the notion of an all-black cast for an action film, so Bythewood negotiated for a mixed cast. DreamWorks produced the film, which earned $22 million on 1,769 screens over ninety-four days. It came close to recouping the $24 million budget in the domestic market, but, like *Red Tails*, it did not have a significant overseas release, which is where most action films make their profits. This is in spite of the fact that Brendan Fehr and Kid Rock serve as the film's white points of entry. In this way preventive censorship also occurs through limited distribution of African American films to many of the audiences Hollywood so frequently ignores. The economic effects of preventive censorship through casting and limited distribution also contribute to the perceived inferiority of African American films.

A white point of entry, or "a sympathetic white character portrayed by a marketable, white actor who can endorse the film for a commercial guarantee,"[58] is risky business. It may increase the likelihood of broader domestic rather international distribution, but it also increases the dangers of cultural trauma and cultural amnesia because of the distortions to the narrative that promote white supremacy. Considering stars receive the highest portion of production labor costs, white actors whose role is in part to serve as white points of entry may be paid higher wages than others. The economic principles of industry practices are so infused with race ideology it is difficult to distinguish them from decisions based on neutral, numerical data. Economic factors and relationships affect the quantity and frequency of African American cinematic production in Hollywood.

Race ideology is embedded in established precedent and therefore influences distribution on multiple levels. Commercial genres and films cast with white male stars receive the broadest distribution; films that do not possess these elements get denied broad distribution. Hollywood's organizational structures and gatekeepers use race and gender as a class category in their distribution processes, and the location of black audiences, actors, directors, and producers within the system generally limits their access to resources and opportunities. As filmmakers, they experience difficulty accessing resources unless they are willing to accept the standard small budget, which can limit exploration of special effects so popular in commercial genre films and make casting of major black stars difficult if not impossible. As audiences, they have difficulty accessing the broadest range of films exploring black subject matter, which are frequently suppressed by limited or no distribution. As the NAACP reveals, people of color have been frequently denied access to institutions to develop skills, opportunities, or the social capital necessary for achieving the level of success comparable to those of filmmakers such as George Lucas. Yet there are anomalies, including Spike Lee, Tyler Perry, Oprah Winfrey, and Will Smith. As I discuss later in the book, these anomalies expose the complexity of racial disparities while also demonstrating important strategies for change.

Hollywood's organizational structures and processes legitimate distribution procedures and the social inequalities that arise from them through repetition, reliance on established precedent, and unwavering attachment to a bottom-line that privileges whites and males. Like race ideology, patriarchal capitalism is apparent throughout various aspects of the industry.[59] Hollywood's marketing and distribution models and their adoption by industry players ensure that women and minorities maintain unequal footing.

Distribution Dealings

Distribution paradigms are critical for examining the root causes of production and distribution patterns along with trends of cultural representation in film. Sociologist Patricia Hill Collins describes a distributive paradigm of justice that "focuses on allocating material goods, such as resources, income, wealth, or the distribution of social positions, especially jobs." This paradigm also occurs in the context of Hollywood's organizational practices, which "ignore social structures and institutional contexts that often determine distributive patterns." The onscreen narrative and offscreen circumstances of the large sampling of films consulted for this study expose Hollywood's operations within a distributive paradigm that views social justice-related aspects of economic empowerment and cultural production as "rights or bundles of static things, often in scarce supply, that are distributed to the most worthy."[60] This distributive paradigm is apparent in the most common types of distribution agreements assigned in Hollywood.

Various types of distribution agreements control film production in the United States. According to lawyer and author Shulyer M. Moore, the production/finance/distribution agreement, commonly referred to as a "PFD agreement," is one of the most common yet it is also very restrictive. Under such agreements, "a film company, typically a studio, hires a production company to produce a film, and the studio agrees to directly finance production and distribute the film. The production company is little more than a dependent agent of the studio, subject to the complete control of the studio on all aspects of production." Granting distribution rights to the studio in perpetuity throughout the world makes the studio the absolute owner of the film. The production company usually retains speculative interest in any net profits generated by the film.[61] PFD agreements can severely undermine creative control, making indigenization and other modes of capitalizing on Hollywood's structural imperfections viable if precarious forms of intervention.

In traditional distribution models, sometimes called the "all-rights deal," filmmakers have no control and no direct access to audiences. Under such agreements, distributors determine economic viability by the first film screening, which can then determine whether they proceed with distribution. Negative test screenings not only lose support, but distributors do not return the film to the filmmaker. The distributor also decides who distributes the film on video, which can be a major source of revenue for filmmakers even though sales have fallen in recent years as digital revenues are increasing. If the distributor has a digital division, they will automatically distribute it. If not, they will distribute it through an affiliated output company even if they are not the best company to distribute the film (as in the case of *Bamboozled*'s botched theatrical release and marketing campaign, New Line Cinema's inability to distinguish *Bamboozled* from their other films with predominantly black casts such as *Menace II Society* and *Set It Off* played a significant role in the film's initially negative audience reception and failure at the box office).[62] With an all-rights deal arrangement, the distributor is in control and may neither be interested in the filmmaker's knowledge of the core audiences nor how to reach them.

In addition, Hollywood accounting does not always benefit filmmakers or performers. As business reporter Derek Thompson explains, the practice of setting up a separate corporation for each movie they produce enables Hollywood studios to erase any possible profit. They charge the "movie corporation" a fee that exceeds the revenues of the film. For accounting purposes, the movie is perceived as a "money loser," which justifies studios' "no net profits" claims.[63] Filmmakers and performers can still be refused revenue for a film that unexpectedly grosses a huge box office, as in *Coming to America* or *Star Wars*.[64] Considering the limitations of traditional industry practices, it is imperative that all filmmakers and especially African Americans and people of color identify alternative methods of retaining creative control *and* control of distribution. These things can no longer be considered mutually exclusive. As the forthcoming chapters reveal, identifying and employing the most empowering distribution agreements are necessary for promoting the future development of African American cinema.

Peter Broderick, a distribution strategist, has identified emerging distribution models that benefit independent filmmakers from all backgrounds with a diverse range of films.[65] These models can directly benefit the development of African American film. More viable models have emerged since 2002, enabling independent filmmakers to bypass the gatekeepers and their traditional models, especially at critical points of the distribution and exhibition processes. Tyler Perry is a salient example of this. Perry retains control through hybrid distribution, which involves a savvy entrepreneurial process that other independent filmmakers are also employing more regularly. These innovators secure distribution through television, video distributors, internet companies, and Video on Demand (VOD) companies while retaining rights to sell DVDs through their own websites, at video screenings, through theatrical service deals, and through semi-theatrical release where the filmmakers tour the country with the movie themselves. This allows filmmakers to reach audiences directly online and at screenings, while the format allows filmmakers to continue to upgrade their product through the sale of related merchandise or even offering variations of improved or updated versions of the film. This process can not only generate revenue for the filmmaker but also extend the life of a project and identify a previously untapped market. At some point, the filmmaker may also decide to highlight the project's appeal to agents working in the traditional model for further distribution.

Hybrid distribution is a significant and viable solution to the crisis African Americans and people of color face in the film industry. It encourages the development of cinematic languages and cultural signs that are critical for exploring perspectives that tend to be minimized or ignored in mainstream Hollywood film. Hybrid distribution is most effective when filmmakers and collaborators identify a specific audience for the film *before* attempting to cross over to larger audiences identified by Hollywood studios. The internet and digital technology are fundamental tools for bypassing gatekeepers and reaching these audiences, as well as marketing and exhibiting the film to build audiences that support the work but also potentially the careers of filmmakers, performers, and similar films. This is an important reversal of the race-based economic principle of crossover appeal.

Alternatives to the PFD agreement that facilitate hybrid distribution include Negative Pick Up (domestic) and Pre-Sale (international) distribution agreements. The more complex Negative Pick-Up is similar to PFD agreements "except the film company, again typically a studio, agrees to pay a fixed price *upon delivery of the film* to the studio" instead of advancing the costs of production, which are generally covered by loans obtained with a completion bond guaranteeing delivery of the film to the studio.[66] The Negative Pick-Up (and the international Pre-Sale) can be more empowering than the PFD, although racial disparities in bank lending can be a factor. The Negative Pick-Up can provide access to studio resources without being subject to the same controls. In addition, studios may acquire "worldwide rights in perpetuity upon delivery of the film to the studio," but in some cases "rights are limited to a specified term or territory." In addition, "there may be an exclusion of certain ancillary rights," which are "film-related rights, soundtrack rights, music publishing rights, novelization rights, stage play rights and merchandising which generally include interactive games based on the film."[67] Output agreements, virtually a presale agreement for a number of indeterminate films, are also potentially empowering.[68] Other risky deals include Rent-a-System, in which "a producer licenses certain film rights to a film company" or studio for a limited term while "the studio avoids any risks related to the film."[69] In contrast to the more traditional PFD model, the Negative Pick-Up and Pre-Sale models represent viable alternatives wherein adaptation and horizontal integration can be used to enhance the development of African American films while innovating American cinema generally.

Hybrid distribution is the economic equivalent of the cross-pollination that occurs with hybrid and revisionist genres. Both require the adaptation of existing models to create new models in a constantly evolving process. All reflect the inherent intertextuality of black film and the possibilities of using intersectionality and adaptation to evolve economic and creative outcomes for the sake of cultures. As each chapter reveals, this is not only a viable alternative but a critical necessity for making black contributions to film production more accessible and better known.

Unfortunately, established precedent is a major problem for economic and creative models, especially when it comes to financing a project. "Seed money," typically provided by family, friends, and other non-Hollywood organizations, is the most common source of funding for black independent filmmakers such as Gerima. The more common "distributor financing" is more accessible to whites such as Steven Spielberg, though it can be culturally repressive as in the case of his adaptation of *The Color Purple* (discussed in chapter 3). At times, "funny money," which "seems to fall from heaven from some rich real estate or stock investor who is attracted by the sexiness of the industry,"[70] becomes available (Lee Daniels's *Precious: Based on the Novel Push by Sapphire* is a good example). But regardless of how a filmmaker obtains financing, the pitch process often compels filmmakers to cite the success of similar films. This can restrict African American innovation considering the history of films that have been deemed successful at the box office. This is how established precedent informs the fate of subsequent films.

The onscreen narratives and offscreen circumstances of each of the films discussed throughout this book show how using racial markers to justify economic investments is questionable, especially considering that the box office earnings of all films are unpredictable. In the case of Screen Gems' examples, African American films are not the dicey investments studio executives insist they are in comparison to mainstream white films. Most American films lose money due to an oversupply of films—roughly 600 to 700 per year—while only about 200 obtain a decent release allowing any return, much less a profit.[71]

Money and race matter from conception through release and reception of a film. As film scholar Sheril D. Antonio's study concludes, "Proof of profit, and not race exclusively, was more the motive for deciding which films would be made in the 1990s," thereby assuming more similar films would be made.[72] However, in 1998, studio executive Duncan Clark, head of the international theatrical department at Sony, remained unconvinced, insisting that the international market desires Americana but fails to relate to "that ethnic, inner-city, sports-driven region." Delores Robinson, an African American business manager and producer, notes that regardless of such economic success, studio executives fail to recognize the diversity of African American films.[73] Inner-city dramas, comedies, and sports films only represent a portion of the films pitched and produced by African American filmmakers. Unfortunately, they represent the most accessible commercial genres available to black filmmakers, which due to frequent repetition have spawned black comedy franchises and the hip-hop gangsta film cycle. The "color" of a film continues to be a determining factor regardless of a pattern of profits.

Indeed, the success of a single African American filmmaker can have a paradoxical effect on the inclusion of African Americans and African American narratives in Hollywood. Lubiano explains how the advancement of filmmakers such as Spike Lee marginalizes other African American filmic possibilities. For example, independent filmmaker Charles Burnett's film *To Sleep with Anger* (1990) portrays a black middle-class family threatened by an evil old friend.[74] The film's black southern folklore and occasional narrative disruptions through unconventional editing and cinematography exemplifies the possibilities for incorporating cultural perspective into the filmmaking process as an attempt to explore cinematic language. According to scholar Mark A. Reid, the film's failure at the box office is evidence of the disturbing truth that black avant-garde techniques are not welcome and do not sustain the interest of mainstream black moviegoers.[75] This situation forces studios to refuse to produce films similar in theme, structure, or content. Lack of frequent repetition and lack of broad distribution of these techniques creates a vicious cycle that prevents the likelihood that audiences will become literate in the cinematic vocabulary such films employ. This is particularly troubling considering accusations that Hollywood has appropriated the very themes, narrative forms, and aesthetics of African American filmmakers they claim are less marketable.[76]

Telling Stories

Each of the examples discussed in this book allow for direct and indirect comparison to the traditional Hollywood narrative. The storytelling processes of white Americans, typified by Hollywood films, are nicely exemplified by ethnographer Shirley Brice Heath's study of children's language development and cultural differences between two communities, one white and one black, set a few miles apart in the southeastern United States. Storytellers in the white community use formulaic conventions of storytelling to reaffirm group membership and behavioral norms. The stories maintain "a strict chronicity, with direct discourse reported, and no explicit exposition of meaning or direct expressions of evaluations of the behavior of the main character allowed."[77] This starkly contrasts with the African American community, whose stories are "highly creative, fictionalized accounts" that evolve out of reality, emphasizing individual strengths and powers. This anti-establishment emphasis demonstrates individuals overcoming constraints of conventional behaviors and institutions. Their stories are open-ended, fluid, and expanded upon by the audience. Many black and African American films exemplify similar traits in contrast to films with predominantly white casts that feature blacks. I refer to such examples throughout the book but not to infer that they are the only storytelling methods by white Americans and African Americans or to suggest this is the only study of such phenomena. Cultural values are as deeply embedded in the storytelling processes as in the stories themselves.

Coercing African Americans into making films that align with traditional Hollywood screenplay formats without encouraging experimentation is an ongoing problem with significant consequences. But there is still room for experimentation in narrative, cinematography, mise-en-scène, sound, and editing, all of which have yielded promising possibilities for developing African American film. The adaptation of black cultural traditions into various filmmaking techniques is discussed throughout the forthcoming chapters. For instance, the musical tradition of call and response inspires literary and cinematic innovation of narrative structure and cinematic techniques in films. Double consciousness likewise inspires strategies of resistance in conception, production, marketing, distribution, and reception.

As James A. Snead acknowledges, freedom from box office concerns, studio agendas, and censoring boards presents a range of creative options in independent films that is potentially widened rather than restricted. Because of, rather than in spite of, limited budget and exhibition, the adept filmmaker can exploit his or her marginal position to use sound and image to challenge established rules and codes.[78] New media and technology, hybrid distribution, and horizontal integration are now making it more likely that these efforts will be made available to audiences, reinforcing the need to explore these economic and cultural options simultaneously.

Overview

Divided into three parts, this book examines the cultural significance of what are considered to be economically viable narratives, techniques, and business practices in the film industry. The cultural capital of black film and its potential through horizontal integration and hybrid distribution are explored in chapters organized according to representative films ranging from the high- to low-grossing earning categories, which are also considered in relation to the films' budgets.

Part I reveals that the perceived failure of African American films is not only false, but contributes to the ongoing economic and cultural crisis African Americans have historically faced in theater and the filmmaking industry. Chapter I investigates creative and cultural models that have driven production and distribution in Hollywood. This chapter also explains how established precedent works across media as narrative patterns and racial representation become economic predictors for crossover appeal and successful box office. Critical analyses of *A Few Good Men, Driving Miss Daisy*, and *Convicts*—all cinematic adaptations of stage plays with predominantly white casts—reveal Hollywood and Broadway's preferred narrative form, content, and casting processes. These examples expose the oppressive circumstances that make performative indigenization for black performers and the oppositional gaze of black audiences a critical intervention in the comparatively least empowering positions in the paradigm. Chapter 2 locates the roots of black film in black theater, a necessary intervention that shifts the gaze from mainstream white plays and films as the only models for form, content, and economic viability. The marginal status of black theater represented by late nineteenth- and early twentieth-century performers Bert Williams and George Walker as well as the legacy of filmmaker Oscar Micheaux exposes ongoing patterns in contemporary cultural politics as well as the interconnectedness of entrepreneurship and creative content. Tyler Perry's *Diary of a Mad Black Woman* (2005) exemplifies how viable strategies can thwart the self-censorship in *A Soldier's Story* (1984) and the preventive censorship that undermined the distribution of *Bopha!* (1993).

Cinematic adaptations of black literature are featured in part 2, illuminating the publishing industry's role in the institutional framework through horizontal integration. Chapter 3 focuses on black women's literature and reveals the possibilities for developing culturally nuanced creative content that is also economically viable. The "Oprah Effect" exemplifies the power of branding and its relationship to black film and individuals in the industry. Critical analyses of *The Color Purple* (1985), *Precious* (2009), and *Waiting to Exhale* (1995) illuminate the perception and prominence of black pathology in broadly distributed, high-grossing films. Simultaneously, the processes and outcomes of each of the afore-mentioned films suggest that African Americans may no longer be as powerless in Hollywood as previously perceived. The historical narratives represented by *Beloved* (1998), *Panther* (1995), and *Once Upon a Time . . . When We Were Colored* (1995) in chapter 4 further highlight disturbing economic and distribution pat-terns, specifically the infrequency with which narratives with black heroes as opposed to warped historical narratives promoting white supremacy appear on screen. The influences of the master narrative, discussed in chapter 1, are apparent in the creative content, economic outcomes, and behind-the-scenes interactions of these films.

Part 3 begins with an examination of the valuation of black bodies in Hol-lywood, particularly in casting. Similar to Waxman's description of the finan-cial grid used by studio executives at New Line Cinema and other studios to estimate a film's value, the Ulmer Scale exposes important racial disparities. Chapter 5 explores how race, racism, sexism, and business become intricately intertwined yet hidden in the "neutral" numerical data that ensures black films remain on unequal footing. Several blacks and their allies effectively challenge these norms through entrepreneurship. Chapter 6 discusses this in greater detail in the context of original films, which are more frequently produced than cinematic adaptations. This chapter also considers the influence of franchises, film cycles, and the work of specific black directors. Previously noted creative and economic trends are reexamined with new discoveries for the possibilities of alternative distribution that can complement existing indigenization strate-gies. Black comedy franchises influenced by *Coming to America* and the hip-hop gangsta film cycle represented by *Boyz N the Hood* (1991) and *Set It Off* (1996) offer critical insights into economically viable models (and their potential pitfalls). The implications of this are detailed in an analysis of *Bamboozled*'s onscreen narrative and offscreen circumstances. The consistent marginalization of film-makers such as Haile Gerima and his films in favor of Tyler Perry or Spike Lee and other black filmmakers working in the studio system reveals how exclusive industry practices limit innovation for Hollywood generally and African Ameri-cans specifically. The sampling of films featured in this book shows how limiting creativity feeds the stagnant patterns in mainstream films.

In the concluding chapter, the importance of alternative filmmaking and business strategies for future development becomes clear. *Beasts of the South-ern Wild* (2012), *The Karate Kid* remake (2010), *Think Like a Man*, and *Red Tails* exemplify the promise and problems of recent films. The most economically viable adaptations, original films, film cycles, and franchises demonstrate the critical intersection between economics, race, and culture. Although Oprah Winfrey, Will Smith, Tyler Perry, and Spike Lee offer hope for strategic advancement in the existing paradigm, the current system still relies too heavily on crossover appeal to white and nonblack international audiences. As a result, the potential for creating an African diasporic distribution network using new media and digital technology to target black (and nonblack) audiences in North America and abroad not only becomes a viable option but a critical necessity. This is especially the case considering Michael Cieply's *New York Times* article "Coming Soon: A Breakout Year for Black Films," in which black filmmakers recognize the role of the independent-film circuit in sparking the independent and major distribution of ten black films, representing "an extraordinary cluster" of genres in the latter half of 2013. The circuit's creative support network served as a "laboratory of sorts for more prominent African-American-themed productions"[79] that have once again come to the attention of Hollywood studios due to recent successes. The expectation that the 2013 film season will yield future opportunities and consistent changes for blacks in Hollywood must be weighed with the reality that the recurring reabsorption of black film, narratives, filmmakers, performers, and audiences into the existing paradigm is not new. But the technology available to circumvent the stagnation that typically follows Hollywood's practice of reabsorption and eventual decline in support for black films can yield promising results. The 2013 film season can launch a new era of black film that does not rely on Hollywood's current operations yet benefits from the exposure. Maintaining and expanding the existing independent-film circuit and related networks is the most effective way to ensure the ongoing, consistent production, distribution, and variation in representation that truly reflects progress. Capitalizing on the technological revolution that will ultimately inform Hollywood's future does not resolve the negative effects of marketing and selling slavery and black cultural products through branding and merchandising. However, lessons learned from past successes and failures can guide future narrative and business development. Abandoning blackness in favor of crossover appeal is not the answer to the crises blacks have historically faced in Hollywood. As each chapter reveals, a collective, organized global movement that exploits the technological revolution while exploring the diversity and complexities of black experience along with intersectional identities is our best hope for the future.

PART ONE

Finding Freedom on Stage and Screen

I look at theater that is produced in some of the regional theaters and theater that is produced on that circuit as two different things. We shouldn't try to make them be the same things.

–Kenny Leon, director of three August Wilson Broadway productions, 2007

1

The Plantation Lives!

I'm constantly looking for good material, but most of what's out there is
not good because most screenwriters are only reading other screenplays.
They need to read books—they need to read real writing—and they need
to read more stage plays.

—Alfre Woodard, 2004

Academy Award–nominated actress Alfre Woodard's suggestion to look beyond
screenplays as a source for good material offers a useful although precarious
intervention in the future development of African American film due to the
critical interrelation between theatrical and cinematic production. Plays with
predominantly white casts and their cinematic companions examined in this
chapter illuminate the specific challenges of adapting African American drama
for the screen.

Exemplary of commercial theater, Broadway mirrors Hollywood in casting,
narrative, and reliance on the bottom line. Tracking economic data according to
source texts exposes greater frequency of adaptation and higher gross receipts
of productions with predominantly white casts as compared to those with predominantly black casts. In my research, I found no African American stage plays
adapted for film that exceeded $50 million in gross receipts until Tyler Perry's
cinematic adaptation of his urban circuit plays. Musicals are an exception,
however. Musicals are big business on Broadway and were especially prominent in Hollywood's studio era. Hollywood adaptations of musicals have made
a resurgence since 2000, proving that the genre remains economically viable.
For example, in 2006 the film adaptation of *Dreamgirls* had gross receipts of
$103 million domestically and $51 million internationally, eclipsing its production budget of $72.5 million. However, musicals are less significant to this study
because the majority of cinematic stage adaptations since the 1980s are of plays.[1]

This chapter focuses on the broad influence of productions with predominantly white casts on the development of African American drama onstage and
onscreen. In the current Hollywood scheme, black people tend to occupy the

role of actors and actresses playing marginal characters in original films and cinematic adaptations. Identifying critical sites of freedom and empowerment that counteract plantation ideology embedded in the narratives and permeating the industry provides the context necessary to fully appreciate the interventions recommended in the remaining chapters of this book.

The historical marginalization, dehumanization, and erasure of U.S. Latinos, Native Americans, Asian Americans, other nonwhite minorities, and blacks in mainstream white American theater and film have been the norm with the same basic results. A master narrative that reinforces white supremacy tends to operate within a standard narrative pattern that dominates the entertainment industry. This pattern presents in three parts and will no doubt be familiar to readers. The first part introduces the characters, goals, and conflicts. The second part is the turning point where dialogue, setting, or some other visual or sound techniques indicates important change. The last part is resolution.[2] This master narrative, with its literary roots, typically focuses on white male heroes with people of color and women in marginal supporting or minor roles.[3] In the master narrative, black people tend to appear as an Africanist presence. Toni Morrison defines this as metaphorical representations of blackness in imagery, characterization, language, and sounds, and various aspects of expression and existence.[4] Repeated use of classical Hollywood's technical elements and patterns of employing the Africanist presence has shaped audience expectations that affect reception of African American films, especially those that break the aesthetic contract.[5]

The Birth of a Nation (1915), an adaptation of Thomas Dixon's anti-black novels *The Leopard's Spots* (1902) and *The Clansman* (1905), helped establish the rules that were already gaining momentum in theater and short films, such as adaptations of Harriet Beecher Stowe's novel *Uncle Tom's Cabin* (1852). As Ed Guerrero explains, Hollywood's plantation genre is the quintessential master narrative spanning approximately sixty years, from 1915 through the mid-1970s. It significantly contributed to the creation and ideological functions of black representations, narratives, and images, now overdetermined by Hollywood's profit-making strategies.[6] While the plantation may not often be the visual setting of films produced since the 1980s, the ideology is insidiously embedded in casting and recurring narrative patterns. This affects the development of black film, especially African American film, in various ways.

As Hollywood established itself, blacks also established strategies of resistance, exemplifying the power of performance as well as the need for more empowering roles behind the scenes. Performative indigenization in various forms was the primary line of defense for black performers. Another strategy employed by black performers and audiences is the oppositional gaze, which bell hooks refers to as a critical gaze that looks to document resistance and struggle for agency.[7] These strategies exemplify a limited yet significant creole perspective, a more empowering approach to seeing and articulating black experience in Hollywood and American theater.

Hollywood's enduring resemblance to a plantation economy does not have to necessarily limit the possibilities of horizontal integration for developing African American film. However, it is important to acknowledge the impediments. A comparative analysis of the actual events that inspired the cinematic adaptations of *A Few Good Men* (1992), *Convicts* (1991), and *Driving Miss Daisy* (1989) exemplifies the potency of the master narrative and plantation ideology in different time periods and across media. Heavy reliance on established precedent and established profit-generating strategies mutually reinforce race ideology, undermining the potential for black theater and film to develop through casting, narrative form, and content, as well as marketing and distribution.

Plantation Matters

The untapped potential of black Americans' historical contributions to American theater and film becomes evident in their literal and figurative treatment on stage and screen as well as behind the scenes. Unmarked whiteness in addition to patterns of interracial interaction further reinforce racial hierarchies, making these plays dubious models for developing African American film. Normalized representations of whiteness are depicted in cinematic adaptations of plays such as *Down and Out in Beverly Hills* (1986), *Extremities* (1986), *Driving Miss Daisy* (1989), *Frankie and Johnny* (1991), *Convicts* (1991), *The Closer* (1990), *A Few Good Men* (1992), *A Bronx Tale* (1993), and *The Cemetery Club* (1993). Collectively, these works represent the most frequently produced narrative conventions and casting patterns in Hollywood and on Broadway. The lack of evolved representations of African Americans as individuals with emancipated consciousness, especially in their interactions with whites, in theater and film is symptomatic of the broader issue of plantation politics plaguing the development of African American characters and films past and present.

In many towns until the 1920s, films were shown in the same venues as plays, often an actual or designated opera house.[8] Since these films tended to use literature, stage plays, and theatrical performance as source texts, it is not surprising that they took on the same ideology and representation of blacks as the source texts. Treatment of African Americans in theatrical performances and narratives coincides with films produced by whites such as inventor and filmmaker Thomas Edison and William Selig, a former minstrel show manager. Selig produced *Who Said Watermelon* (1900), *Something Good—Negro Kiss* (1900), *Prizefight in Coontown* (1902), and *Wooing and Wedding a Coon* (1907), all of which reinforced derogatory representations of black people.[9]

Although film scholar Thomas Cripps describes Edison's films leading up to this period as "'relatively benign, vaguely anthropological shorts,'" political scientist and film scholar Cedric J. Robinson disagrees: "While it is true that some of Edison's racial vignettes were entitled *A Morning Bath* (1896), *Colored Troops Disembarking* (1898), . . . many more bore titles such as *The Pickaninny Dance* (1894), *Watermelon Contest* (1896), *Sambo and Aunt Jemima: Comedians, and Spook Minstrels* (all of the latter series produced between 1897 and 1904). Moreover, none of Edison's films, not even those which were reportorial, appeared to suggest the existence of black men like Lewis H. Latimer." Latimer worked with Alexander Graham Bell as a draftsman, improving Bell's patent design for the telephone.[10] Plays and films that follow established precedent continue to benefit from and carry out this limited and inaccurate representation of blacks in spite of alternatives.

Inspired by actual events that lend them authenticity, contemporary films such as *Driving Miss Daisy, Convicts,* and *A Few Good Men* share other features with their predecessors. Early racial melodramas are variations of the master narrative. They typically depict a battle between good and evil, between white Americans and African Americans, linking suffering to citizenship.[11] *The Birth of a Nation* focuses on two white families, northern and southern, on opposing sides in the Civil War. President Abraham Lincoln is prominently featured throughout the film, which depicts his assassination. Blacks appear as the requisite mammies, toms, coons, mulattoes, and bucks, significant only in relation to the white families. Loosely based on the life of Josiah Henson, *Uncle Tom's Cabin* is about a long-suffering black slave named Uncle Tom, his fellow slaves, and their slave owners. This nostalgic representation of the loyal black slave still feeds contemporary racial hierarchies. Diversifying the cast or focus does not automatically counteract the melodrama's master narrative. Both heavily adapted works cite actual events and rely on the Africanist presence to reassert the power and definition of whiteness. They helped to establish how interracial interaction on stage and screen would be depicted going forward, especially in historical dramas as discussed in chapter 4.

Uncle Tom's Cabin helped introduce the Africanist presence through stereotypes, including the mammy, the tragic mulatto, and Uncle Tom, which were then recycled and reinforced through works such as *The Birth of a Nation*, which also incorporates the image of the black brute. These films represent a long-standing tradition of American literature, theater, and film, becoming more racially coded and normalized over time. The plantation lives on in noticeable patterns of form and content in some of the most economically viable narratives in more recent films. Films such as *Convicts, Driving Miss Daisy,* and *A Few Good Men* draw inspiration from *Uncle Tom's Cabin*'s narrative content, characterizations, and interracial interactions.

"Tom Shows," multiple and frequent staging of Stowe's novel, were "the most widely produced play in the history of the United States, and despite the longevity of contemporary musicals, has yet to be surpassed."[12] Based on the best-selling novel of the nineteenth century, which sold 300,000 copies in its first year,[13] this racial stage melodrama incorporated the novel's pathos and abolitionist sentiment, clearly delineating the abolitionist position as "good" and the institution of slavery as "evil." It appears to have a progressive ideology, much like *Driving Miss Daisy, Convicts,* and *A Few Good Men,* but is structurally reinforced by white hegemony. Tom shows combine blackface, music, and minstrelsy to produce a spectacle with profitable results. The two most prominent versions of the play opened in 1852. George Aiken's version, which is considered the standard, closed on May 13, 1854, after 325 performances. The H. J. Conway version, which was the most popular, was created for the Boston Museum. Thereafter P. T. Barnum mounted a New York production, which directly competed with the Aiken adaptation. Tom show elements and their popularity continue to influence structure, content, and production patterns of stage plays adapted into films, particularly by excluding or marginalizing blacks.

Each film version of *Uncle Tom's Cabin* paralleled critical developments in filmmaking technology, economics, and racial politics. *Uncle Tom's Cabin* was adapted to film twice in 1903, 1910, 1913, and once each in 1914, 1918, and 1927. Every aforementioned version was made by white producers. The 1903 version was directed by Edwin S. Porter and was also one of the first full-length films (10–14 minutes at the time). In this version, white actors played the major black characters in blackface with black actors as extras.[14] J. Stuart Blackton's version, adapted by Eugene Mullin in 1910, represents "the first time an American film company released a dramatic film in three reels." It was also re-released in 1927.[15] Yet it is the offscreen circumstances of Harry A. Pollard's 1927 film adaptation that demonstrate how deeply embedded racial ideologies influence filmmaking. Charles S. Gilpin, a black actor best known for originating the title role in Eugene O'Neill's play *The Emperor Jones,* was to take the role of Uncle Tom. According to some reports, Gilpin engaged in heated debates with the director regarding the film and portrayal of Uncle Tom. As a protest, he returned to his job as an elevator operator rather than play a lucrative screen role that he felt would malign his people.[16] Other reports say the studio fired Gilpin due to concerns about "his aggressive reading of Tom and, according to gossip, to his drinking."[17] Regardless, production went ahead without Gilpin. Does a progressive ideology decrease the likelihood that producers question racist potential in production and reception of their films? This example suggests just that.

After originating the title role in O'Neill's *The Emperor Jones* in 1920, Gilpin went on to reprise the role in 1926. Black audiences remained divided over whether the play and performance improved representations of blackness. The actor's performative indigenization, also exemplified in his off-set attempts to avoid undermining the potential of black film, subjects, and worldviews, proved unable to fulfill the expectations of the audience's oppositional gaze. It is unrealistic to expect a single play, film, or actor's performance to completely repair or reverse the damage of early films such as *The Birth of a Nation* and *Uncle Tom's Cabin*. However, Gilpin's resistance against the master narrative perfectly exemplifies the historical double bind that the institutional framework creates for black people in Hollywood and on Broadway. American theater and film have relied on black subject matter and performers to innovate at critical historical moments, yet black subject matter and performers are frequently marginalized in the industry and the narratives.

Early Examples of the Paradox of Success

The rise of melodrama, evolving technology, and the emergence of the star system coincide with the rise of the Africanist presence in theater and film. As a result, traditional practices of adaptation and horizontal integration strengthened the bond between media, reinforcing plantation ideology within narratives and industry practices that coincide with the modernization of the American capitalist system around the turn of the century. American theater began to evolve in terms of subject matter as well as structure and organization of the entertainment industry. It was becoming big business controlled by capitalist entrepreneurs and financiers.[18] According to theater scholar Thomas Postlewait, modern advertisers learned their trade from late nineteenth- and early twentieth-century theater entrepreneurs such as P. T. Barnum, B. F. Keith, Flo Ziegfeld, and the Shubert brothers, among others.[19] As independent venture capitalists, Barnum and Ziegfeld are best known for producing and delivering a profitable product for the audiences they created. Barnum's productions included museum and carnival displays featuring African Americans and Native Americans.[20] The display of "circus Africans," which began as early as 1810, was meant to portray the animalistic nature of Africans.[21] Reportedly an abolitionist, Barnum used "deceit and exaggeration, deception and disguise to make his fortune . . . [developing] techniques of advertising and exhibiting"[22] that are the foundations of contemporary marketing strategies that continue to inform audience expectations.

There is a complex tradition of using black bodies to build white wealth throughout entertainment history. This tradition is further complicated by the way in which blacks have historically used the opportunities made available to them. Ziegfeld, a white producer and the creator of the Ziegfeld Follies, made history when he hired Bert Williams, a black American actor, to join the ensemble. Williams's iconic portrayal of the Jonah man, a comic darkie figure in blackface, represents a highly significant trend in black performance. He did not see his character as inferior due to his blackness but rather as a human being with a philosophy and pathos often misunderstood by those who looked down on him. Later in his career black audiences were also divided on whether or not his work was progressive. Nevertheless, Williams's Jonah man is another example of performative indigenization, enjoyed by black and white audiences who remained unaware of his inspiration. Williams's performing partner, George Walker, explains,

> In 1893, natives from Dahomey Africa were imported to San Francisco to be exhibited at the Midwinter Fair. They were late in arriving for the opening of the Fair and Afro-Americans were employed and exhibited for native Dahomians. Williams and Walker were among the sham native Dahomians. After the arrival of the native Africans, the Afro-Americans were dismissed. Having had free access to the Fair grounds, we were permitted to visit the natives from Africa. It was there, for the first time, that we were brought into close contact with native Africans and the study of those natives interested us very much. We were not long in deciding that if we ever reached the point of having a show of our own, we would delineate and feature native African characters as far as we could, and still remain American, and make our acting interesting and entertaining to American audiences.[23]

Their story provides clear evidence of the practice of putting blacks on display as wonders and curiosities as well as the ways in which blacks revised and resisted those practices.

Williams and Walker developed a carefully nuanced approach to humanizing the minstrel character. The duo featured Africa in their productions *In Dahomey* (1902) and *Abyssinia* (1906). Their revised yet controversial representations of Africa and Africans proved to be lucrative and innovative as *In Dahomey* became the first all-black production on Broadway. It also introduced a tradition of black American representation of Africa and Africans in an attempt to counteract popular perceptions, providing the vital contrast through performative indigenization both on set and off. Williams's performative indigenization paradoxically contributed to his stardom and led to his typecasting. His stint on Broadway and short-lived film career helped dictate the range of characters African Americans could play on Broadway and in Hollywood for years to come. This is an early example of how black resistance strategies were reabsorbed into the same oppressive institutional framework they challenged.

In addition to the Barnum and Ziegfeld models for advertising, Keith and E. F. Albee created a vaudevillian version of the Theatrical Syndicate, a network of businesses that was in essence a monopoly of legitimate theater.[24] These networks integrated all aspects of entertainment much like the current studio system. Despite the fact the Theatrical Syndicate lasted only about fifteen years due to competition with the Schuberts, the mainstream system developed by the first venture capitalists in American theater and film never truly changed. Race ideology in its origins persists in narrative structure, characterizations, and interracial interactions, all of which are apparent in film imagery and advertisements.

Consider, for example, the posters for *The Birth of a Nation* and *Uncle Tom's Cabin* (see image 1 and image 2). These posters foreground white actors and actresses, while black characters appear on the margins or in fragments if they appear at all. Fast-forward to the 1980s and we see little change. In the poster for *Driving Miss Daisy* (image 3), a 1989 cinematic adaptation of an off-Broadway play, we see the disembodied faces of Morgan Freeman and Jessica Tandy. Freeman, an African American actor, plays the role of Tandy's character's chauffeur—a servant role.

Early films established precedents for black representation in advertisements, production processes, and narratives. One need only peruse film pages on IMDB.com to see how these patterns persist in posters, DVD covers, and related images that advertise films with predominantly white casts. Whether or not they portray servants, blacks tend to be absent from these images. If they do appear, they are in the background or on the margins as whites occupy the center foreground. These images inform audience expectations, suggesting blacks are only significant in relation to whites. Such audiences are less likely to seek out or appreciate films with predominantly black casts without central white characters. These expectations inform mainstream film production processes, outcomes, and critical reception of films with predominantly black casts.

Current theater models reflect similarly disconcerting trends. While Broadway maintains a level of historical prestige, since the mid-1970s Chicago has become known as "the best damn theater city in the country."[25] A 2005 study of Chicago theater published in *Time Out Chicago* found that primarily white professional theater ensembles dominate the theater industry, developing works that are less likely to reflect local diversity.[26] Even though Chicago's population of African Americans, Latina/os, and white Americans is nearly evenly split, the professional theater scene is predominantly white with an occasional ethnic character added to meet diversity initiatives.[27] In New York City in 2010, 51.4 percent of the population was African American and Latina/o, yet the professional theater scene there is also predominantly white.[28] Regardless of the demographics, white hegemony renders people of color invisible. Mainstream American theater has become more racially exclusive even as the business and the country have become more racially diverse.

The Birth of a Nation (1915) film poster

Uncle Tom's Cabin (1927) film poster

The funny, touching and totally irresistible story
of a working relationship that became a
25-year friendship.

MORGAN
FREEMAN

JESSICA
TANDY

DAN
AYKROYD

The Comedy That Won A Pulitzer Prize.

WARNER BROS. PRESENTS
A ZANUCK COMPANY PRODUCTION MORGAN FREEMAN JESSICA TANDY DAN AYKROYD
"DRIVING MISS DAISY" PATTI LUPONE ESTHER ROLLE EXECUTIVE PRODUCER JAKE EBERTS EDITED BY MARK WARNER PRODUCTION DESIGNER BRUNO RUBEO DIRECTOR OF PHOTOGRAPHY PETER JAMES, A.C.S.
MUSIC BY HANS ZIMMER BASED UPON THE PLAY BY DAVID BROWN SCREENPLAY BY ALFRED UHRY BASED UPON THE PLAY BY PRODUCED BY RICHARD D. ZANUCK AND LILI FINI ZANUCK DIRECTED BY BRUCE BERESFORD

Driving Miss Daisy (1989) film poster

The structure and practices of funding and distribution networks in the Chicago model marginalize ethnically diverse audiences, writers, and performers. In Chicago, theaters that are not members of the League of Chicago Theatres are not counted in local figures for measuring audiences and cannot access economic and cultural resources that members share.[29] The majority of theaters located in communities of color are not members of the League. As a result of this system of member theaters and nonmember theaters, actors from diverse backgrounds express frustration with typecasting and limited professional opportunities while casting directors complain that actors are unprepared and undeveloped,[30] thereby perpetuating a cycle of invisibility and perceived failure that is difficult to combat.

Rather than investigating the ideology behind exclusive definitions of audiences, Parsi and Piatt conclude that the lack of diversity is an issue of segregation, rather than a practice of racism. Such determinations underestimate the role of race in the economics of theater and film. Without actually investigating the industry practices that perpetuate racist ideology, the outcome renders minority audiences invisible, describes diverse actors as incapable, and posits culturally diverse narrative forms and content as undesirable. In short, the status quo is preserved. The plantation ideology driving these assumptions does not change and has long-term consequences for the distribution of funding for theatrical and cinematic productions.

Patricia Hill Collins's description of the distributive paradigm, a theory viewing social justice as rights or bundles of static things in scarce supply, effectively relates to standard business practices that historically produce the master narrative in the organizations that make up the institution of American theater.[31] Blacks, nonwhite minorities, and women are frequently minimized and ignored by industry gatekeepers. Their perceived absence and failure as cultural producers is used to justify the economic decisions that contribute to the vicious cycle. These patterns of distribution contain African American cultural production in theater and film by maintaining the dominant group's control over the ideas, values, and representation of the larger society, all of which has dramatic cultural implications.

For instance, in his keynote address at the Mid-America Theatre Conference in 2007, Lou Bellamy criticized the displacement of African American directors with growing practices of hiring white female directors for African American plays. He suggests that African American participation is necessary for cultural nuance, as accomplished by performers like Bert Williams. Current practices ensure that "a white point of entry" will be embedded in African American-authored productions regardless of the racial makeup of the cast. Likewise, in 1996, African American playwright August Wilson identified cultural imperialism and the lack of funding for black theater as the major culprits plaguing the development of black theater in the mainstream. He referred to white theater critics like Robert Brustein as cultural imperialists due to their tendency to impose their cultural values, expectations, and practices on all ethnic groups in American theater. This exemplifies a lack of consideration for cultural worldviews and cultural transmission processes of other ethnic groups.[32] In sum, past expectations continue to inform investors and critics' notions of what constitutes an economically viable narrative and praiseworthy performance in theater and film.

Plantation Genre

A play or film does not necessarily have to feature a central white male protagonist and Africanist presence packaged in the form of racial melodrama infused with patriarchal capitalism in order to be economically viable. Yet a project is still less likely to be funded or broadly distributed if it does not somehow include these elements. A comparative analysis of three projects, all of which are to some degree based on real events, illustrates this point. *A Few Good Men, Convicts,* and *Driving Miss Daisy* are the types of plays that would be staged in theatrical organizations like those in Chicago or on Broadway in order to meet diversity initiatives. They tend to serve as white star vehicles and as such embody the characteristics of early theater and film narrative structure, interracial interaction, and visual imagery. The onscreen narrative and offscreen circumstances of each of these works and their evolution from event to play to film expose how studio investment practices negatively affect the development of African American film.

Each text fits the master narrative, predictably rendering African Americans in one of the following ways: (1) as absent or invisible, (2) as supporting characters merely present for the development of central white characters, or (3) as extras in stories that suggest racial tension can be absolved not through social justice but through blacks forgiving and serving the needs of whites. However evolved, they contain traces of the same race ideology apparent in early cinematic adaptations such as *The Birth of a Nation* and *Uncle Tom's Cabin*. We see the same pattern across an even larger sample of films (see table 1). Even when alternative narratives and points of views are potentially more lucrative, mainstream American theater and film tend to revert to the same hegemonic master narrative.

A Few Good Men, a military courtroom drama based on real events, is an excellent contemporary example of masked plantation ideology. The film's lead character is a young white lawyer, Lieutenant Daniel Kaffee. He is assigned to defend two marines, Corporal Harold Dawson and Private Louden Downey, who are on trial for the murder of fellow marine William T. Santiago. Santiago's death is attributed to a failed hazing incident. The play had its premiere at the

TABLE 1.

White-Authored Southern Plays Adapted for the Cinema

Title (Author)	Cast	Broadway Productions	Tony Awards	Cinematic Adaptation	Oscars	Estimated Budget (millions)	Domestic Gross (millions)	Screens	Days
*Driving Miss Daisy (Alfred Uhry)	Predominantly white (Morgan Freeman as major black character in subservient role in play and film)	2010	1 nomination (Best Actress)	1989	9 nominations (including for Morgan Freeman, Best Actor); 4 Wins (including Best Picture & Best Adaptation)	$7.5	$106	1668	180
The Best Little Whorehouse in Texas (Larry L. King)	Predominantly white (no notable black characters)	1978 Revival 1982 Revival 2006	6 nominations, 2 wins 1 nomination	1982	1 nomination (Best Supporting Actor)	$28	$70	1435	91
The Miss Firecracker Contest (Beth Henley)	Predominantly white (Alfre Woodard, supporting role in film)	2013	n/a	1989 (as Miss Firecracker)	n/a	Unknown	$1.8	211	17
*Crimes of the Heart (Beth Henley)	Predominantly white (no notable black characters)	1981	3 nominations	1986	3 nominations	Unknown	$22	685	45

Title (Playwright)	Cast	Broadway Production(s)	Tony Awards	Film(s)	Oscar Awards		Box Office		
The Trip to Bountiful (Horton Foote)	Predominantly white (no notable black characters)	1953, 2013 (predominantly black cast)	1 win (Best Actress), 1 win (Best Actress: Cicely Tyson)	1985	2 nominations, 1 win (Best Actress)	Unknown	$7.4	118	164
Convicts (Horton Foote)	Predominantly white (James Earl Jones and Starletta DuPois in supporting roles, with other blacks in minor roles and as extras in film)	None	n/a	1991	None	Unknown	$0.013	1	13
Steel Magnolias (Robert Harling)	Predominantly white (no notable black characters)	2005	None	1989, 2012 Television Remake with all-black cast	1 nomination (Best Supporting Actress)	Unknown	$84	1,372	131

Sources: Summaries, cast, and Oscar information are taken from IMDB.com. Broadway production history and Tony Award data are from IBDB.com. Figures are averages of estimates from IMDB.com, The Numbers.com, and BoxOfficeMojo.com.

*Pulitzer Prize winner

Heritage Repertory Theatre at the University of Virginia in 1989. Later that year it opened at the Music Box on Broadway, where it ran for 449 performances.[33] By this time, Hollywood had already purchased the rights, intending to reduce much of the dialogue to "visual images." The film had the largest non-sequel December opening ever, debuting at $15 million.[34] Presented on 2,201 screens for approximately 178 days, the film grossed an estimated $141 million. As one of the highest-grossing cinematic stage adaptations made since 1980, the film exemplifies the economic signs of visual pleasure[35] and epitomizes the master narrative's contemporary form.

Specifically, *A Few Good Men* reflects the problems of racial reconciliation imagery in contemporary versions of the master narrative. The white male hero, Kaffee (Tom Cruise), interacts throughout the film with a supporting cast of marginalized figures. The two marines on trial are Dawson, an African American (Wolfgang Bodison), and Downey, a white American (James Marshall). Private Downey is portrayed as less mentally acute than those around him, a reversal that makes the racial dynamics appear to be progressive. The murdered private, Santiago (Michael DeLorenzo), is Latino. Kaffee's legal team features two white Americans, one a Jewish man, Lieutenant Sam Weinberg (Kevin Pollak), and the other a woman, Lieutenant Commander JoAnn Galloway (Demi Moore). The play incorporates a kind of diversity not frequently seen in many mainstream plays, yet the minority and female characters end up reinforcing rather than challenging the master narrative. The film, on the other hand, leads audiences to believe it transcends existing models of interracial interaction as well as racial and gendered representation through sophisticated camera movement, frame composition of character interactions, and seemingly universal themes repeated throughout: loyalty, code, and honor.

Racial melodrama and the Africanist presence are found throughout the film. The race of the defendants and victim are not mentioned, even in the courtroom where they are tried before an African American judge (J. A. Preston). Declining to acknowledge race in an attempt to overcome a history of racism is apparent in the onstage/onscreen narrative as well as the behind-the-scenes circumstances that produce those narratives. For instance, the race of both the judge and Dawson are unspecified in the play, but they have consistently been cast as African Americans in stage productions and also described as such in the screenplay. This suggests that racial profiling may be even more salient in the film version than it is in play. Simultaneously ignoring race while selectively using it exemplifies the paradoxical treatment African Americans receive in mainstream white American theatrical and cinematic productions.

This is further illustrated in the characterization of nonwhites as accomplices in the racial reconciliation dynamic that is embedded within the master narrative. Dawson's Africanist presence and his interactions with Kaffee convey a more subtle yet powerful narrative of racial reconciliation. He illuminates Kaffee's initial deficiency and serves as the vehicle to Kaffee's eventual development into the narrative's hero. Kaffee's development symbolizes an emerging ideology that will displace outmoded interpretations of loyalty, code, and honor represented by Colonel Nathan R. Jessup (Jack Nicholson), the high-ranking officer who authorized the Code Red, the hazing that killed Santiago. A similar pattern can be found in the 1991 film *Convicts,* which I discuss later in this chapter. The repetition of these patterns reinforces perceptions that nonwhites are only significant in relation to whites.

In *A Few Good Men,* the juxtaposition of Dawson and Kaffee in the play and screenplay becomes even more powerful in the film itself. In the screenplay, Kaffee is "*15 months out of Harvard Law School, and a brilliant legal mind waiting for a courageous spirit to drive it. He is at this point in his life passionate about nothing . . . except maybe softball.*"[36] Dawson is "a handsome, young, black corporal. Intense, controlled and utterly professional."[37] Dawson's passion is the Marine Code, as he "*would rather die than breach military protocol.*"[38] Dawson embodies the values Kaffee believes his father would respect, but Dawson's blackness makes these values threatening to societal expectations. He exists primarily to teach these values to Kaffee so that Kaffee can occupy his destined, authoritative position. In order for this to occur, Dawson is demystified and therefore discredited as a potential leader.

This pattern of black characterization permeates contemporary variations of the master narrative and can be seen in other present-day films such as *Safe House* (2012), starring Denzel Washington and Ryan Reynolds. Set in Cape Town, South Africa, the film concerns rookie CIA agent Matt Weston (Reynolds). Mercenaries attack the safe house Weston operates when rogue veteran CIA agent Tobin Frost (Washington) is captured, taken to the safe house, and interrogated. Together, Frost and Weston escape the attack and attempt to get to another safe house. Frost admits to treasonous crimes yet tries to evade authorities and the persistent mercenaries who eventually kill him. Weston proves his patriotic heroism by overcoming his more experienced charge and exposing a conspiracy in the process.

Plays and films with predominantly white casts often turn to criminalizing black characters. The hierarchy of race relations is often reinforced via narrative or visual techniques. Such techniques help ensure that the focus remains on the white male hero (and star) even if the black character has admirable qualities. For example, the trial reveals Dawson's substantial service record: he received two "Exceptional" evaluations prior to his last one, in which he received a "Below Average." He had a perfect ranking after Infantry Training School, but more than half his class had been promoted to full corporal while Dawson had not advanced.[39] Dawson becomes increasingly criminalized in the film adaptation of

A Few Good Men. As such, playwright and screenwriter Aaron Sorkin's narrative misses an opportunity to interrogate the role of hegemonic limitations within the military system via Dawson's dubious lack of advancement. Instead, the film narrative reinforces the system when Kaffee, Dawson's defense attorney, says: "Corporal Dawson's been charged with a number of crimes, why wasn't he charged with firing at the enemy without cause?"[40] This new, criminalized characterization of Dawson was added in the process of adaptation in order to establish Kaffee's development as a trial lawyer. Kaffee's development over the course of the film and Dawson's increasing criminality are inextricably linked via narrative, characterization, and cinematography. Dawson typically shares the frame with Kaffee or his colleagues whenever he appears, thereby visually articulating his significance as being solely in relation to whites. In this way, he is guaranteed to never become the actual focus of the narrative. Repetition of these narrative and visual patterns reinforce the perception that blacks are not capable of occupying the stage or frame outside the presence of whites.

Other elements expose the film's reliance on the Africanist presence to develop the white hero. Kaffee's ability to obtain justice for Santiago as well as his ability to gain Dawson's respect shows that he is able to live up to his father's legacy as a prominent civil rights attorney. As a flippant military lawyer in the post–civil rights era, Kaffee reasserts his right to rule by obtaining respect from supporting characters, all of which are more qualified than he is in one way or another. Lieutenant Commander JoAnn Galloway outranks Kaffee. She is a stronger investigator, but a poor trial lawyer. She is reduced to being the love interest that drives Kaffee to become the lawyer she cannot be. Weinberg has a longer tenure in the military but equal rank with Kaffee. He is considerably more knowledgeable about the military and the law but is reduced to being Kaffee's sidekick, punctuating his jokes. As these examples demonstrate, the marginalization of ethnic minorities and women is a critical component of the master narrative so prevalent in theater and film.

The film's outcome is primarily pleasurable for audiences who identify with Kaffee, due in part to cinematic techniques that employ frequent close-ups and camera movement to convey Cruise's awesomeness in the role. He wins the case as well as the romantic affection of Galloway, his superior officer. Dawson and Downey are found not guilty but are dishonorably discharged. While Kaffee views the outcome as a clear victory, Dawson does not feel the same way. As a marine, he feels disgraced. Santiago receives justice with the arrest of Colonel Jessup. However, he never completely materializes as a character with any substance, family, or community. As is so frequently the case with these marginal, ethnically diverse characters, the effects of Santiago's experience are never fully explored.

Santiago's marginalization in this narrative is highly significant in light of the circumstances that inspired the film. There are varying accounts regarding playwright and screenwriter Aaron Sorkin's inspiration. He claims Kaffee is "entirely fictional and was not inspired by a particular individual," although four white male lawyers claimed to have been the basis for the character, including Walter C. Bansley III, who was singled out by various media outlets. Sorkin admits he got the idea for the story from his sister, a young military lawyer who represented one of ten marines facing assault charges in a hazing case at Guantanamo Bay in the 1980s.[41] According to some reports, ten marines decided to inflict punitive retribution on a marine named William Alvarado for writing a letter to his congressman complaining about the Marine Corps. The marines bound Alvarado in order to shave his head. From this point the available reports conflict. Some suggest that Alvarado choked to death on a stocking they stuffed in his mouth.[42] Others indicate that he survived the incident.[43] There were also inconsistent reports regarding charges brought against the defendants. Journalist Dave Altimari reported that all ten marines were brought up on homicide charges. Seven decided to take dishonorable discharges and three pled innocent. When the mystery of the Code Red was finally unraveled, the trial concluded with one man's innocent verdict and the guilty verdicts of the other two. In contrast, Bill Glauber reported that "seven of the attackers accepted 'other than honorable' discharges," with one eventually upgrading to honorable. Three others refused to plea, one of whom was found not guilty of aggravated battery but guilty of simple assault, a misdemeanor that carried a thirty-day jail sentence. Both reports concur that the defendants had already served the sentence awaiting trial.

If we are to consider Altimari's account, Sorkin altered the story for creative and legal reasons. Altimari found that Sorkin's play follows the real-life case with only two divergences: the trial takes place in Washington, D.C., instead of Cuba, and a female investigator was added to be Kaffee's love interest. However, Altimari overlooked other notable changes. The number of assailants was decreased from ten to two. Accounts of the actual event do not specify the racial dynamics of the case, but the victim's name implies Latino ancestry. Sorkin's decision to maintain the seeming ethnic identity of the victim is apparent in the play and the film, although it is never addressed. Regardless of which account he considered, Sorkin could have focused the story on the female lawyer, the Latino victim, or the African American defendant rather than the white male defense attorney. Even when there is an opportunity to tell a story from diverse perspectives, *A Few Good Men* typifies the tendency in mainstream theater and film to privilege the white male point of view.

In order to situate the event from Alvarado's viewpoint, Sorkin would have had to deeply question the power structure of the military and society. He would have had to investigate Alvarado's complaint from all aspects of his identity, including his ethnic heritage. Situating the story from the perspective of the defendants would have also challenged Sorkin to explore the event from the less-empowered position of those whose fate are in the hands of others. History suggests that Broadway and Hollywood are often unwilling or unable to engage alternative perspectives. Most often, they cite economic reasons and audience expectations as the reason. Regardless, the end result is the same: the privileging of a master narrative that reinforces white male hegemony. The outcome of the film and play reinforce perceived economic viability of white, male-centered narratives. Thus, subsequent, similar narratives are more likely to rank highly on Hollywood scoring systems and financial grids, and are thereby most likely to secure financing and distribution. *A Few Good Men* is only one example of the tendency to marginalize ethnic minorities and women. This practice invariably affects the development of African American film.

Convicts and *Driving Miss Daisy* also exemplify troubling patterns. As stated earlier, these films are also based on true events and only deviate from the master narrative slightly if at all. They are nostalgia films, which function to provide "an escape from reality and the attempt to return to a presupposed golden age."[44] Neither goes as far back as slavery, though both return to a pre–civil rights era in which blacks were expected to be subservient to whites. The paradox of nostalgia is that it encourages a peculiar condition in which memory fuses with desire to create a pain that is very nearly pleasurable.[45] While nostalgia allows for the dichotomous experience of pleasure and pain, it also introduces the possibilities that pleasurable experiences for some members of an audience may be painful for others.

Convicts demonstrates how the pain or displeasure of black audiences in response to derogatory depictions may be transferrable to crossover audiences who under different circumstances may find pleasure in the work. In this case, pleasure is more likely for a crossover audience that laments the loss of the plantation and the golden age of the Old South. *Convicts,* set on Christmas Eve 1902, centers around Horace Robedaux, a thirteen-year-old white American boy who lives and works on Mr. Soll's plantation, which is operated by the use of convict labor. Ben and Martha, a black couple that lives on the property and runs the general store, descend from slaves owned by Soll's family. They chose to stay and work on the plantation even after emancipation. As Soll slips in and out of reality due to his increasing dementia, Horace tries to collect six months' worth of pay from him in order to purchase a headstone for his father's grave.

Convicts is the second play in a nine-play cycle written by white screenwriter and playwright Horton Foote. The plays are based on his family's life in the South. The plays represent a grieving process; they deal with death, the loss of childhood, the loss of innocence, and the loss of the southern lifestyle.[46] *Convicts* was a theatrical success before it was adapted into a film. Although it was not produced on Broadway, it was produced off Broadway and in regional theaters. Foote's Broadway and Academy Award pedigree also helped justify adaptation. Although the film only earned $13,311 at the box office, its failure did not limit Foote's options in Hollywood. He went on to write for film (*Of Mice and Men* [1992] and *Main Street* [2010]) as well as television. Foote's overall success exemplifies his hard work and talent but also the opportunities provided to white men in theater and film that are frequently limited or denied to others due to race or gender.

As a subtle racial melodrama, *Convicts* represents how the Africanist presence is constructed in the racial reconciliation narratives, which is meant to be nostalgic but fails. The film seeks to evoke nostalgia through narrative, characterizations, and technical elements yet fails to elicit the technical gloss required to mask racialized discourse embedded in every frame of the film. The narrative reflects the innocence of a young boy whose experience is not colored by race. It is driven by the tragic loss of his father and his social-class status as a poor laborer, a position generally inhabited by African Americans who are either domestic servants, sharecroppers, or convicts under the employment of white landowners. Horace, juxtaposed against Soll, is supposed to represent an emerging ideology that does not privilege whiteness above blackness. Yet the very structure of his character as an emerging hero who is destined to rule is developed in contrast to the black characters. In nearly every interaction with them, Horace is portrayed as ultimately more intelligent, a notable contrast to their lack of education and much like the dynamic between Dawson and Kaffee in *A Few Good Men*.

Similarly, the presence of black characters serves to establish Soll's social-class position as a plantation owner. In this case, Ben and Martha's ties to the land and their ancestors are juxtaposed with Soll's inability to maintain connections with his own family or others with whom he interacts. Like Dawson, Ben and Martha are presented as noble characters but are only significant in relation to the white characters. Foote's character structure reflects his own encounter with a former black slave on his great-great grandfather's plantation. It was this stumbling upon a "living, suffering human being" at a local grocery store that helped make real for him the previously abstract nature of slavery.[47] The former slave Foote describes is not exactly the same stereotype as those represented in the fictional yet historically inspired films *Uncle Tom's Cabin* and *The Birth of a Nation*. But Foote's description of the former slave as a "human being" still pales in comparison to the revised trope Gerima introduced in *Sankofa*. Black people never truly become the focus of Foote's work, nor are any of Foote's narratives told from the perspective of a black character (although black actors have interpreted Foote's lead characters in performance, such as the 2013 Broadway production of *The Trip to Bountiful*).

The ubiquitous presence of slavery, the memory of slavery, and the Old South permeates American theater and film, at times limiting its treatment. For instance, Foote's play cycle is a grieving process inspired by his mother's death. He insists that looking to the past is not out of nostalgia, "but to figure out something for myself" and separate what is permanent from what is not.[48] The autobiographical nature of the stories is reflected in a lot of the plays, produced around the same time as *Convicts*. Other white playwrights and contemporaries of Foote grappled with the veritable end of the Old South versus exploration of the post–civil rights New South. Many focused on the past or completely ignored black experiences in the Old or New South in their work. Most of these plays appeared on Broadway and/or have been adapted into films. Some like *Convicts* did not transition well. These works represent the types of narratives most frequently produced on Broadway and in Hollywood. The definition of the South is limited as a result. Douglas Turner Ward, an African American playwright (*Day of Absence* [1965]) and director of the Negro Ensemble Company's *A Soldier's Play*, acknowledges, "The definition of a 'Southern' play takes on wider meaning in the context of drama written by blacks."[49] Ward's work demonstrates how inclusion of black characters, voices, and worldviews alters perceptions of the South as well as definitions of American theater and film.

Convicts is a distinct variation of racial melodrama set on the plantation. It mentions race but does not focus explicitly on arguing for or against the rights of blacks or whites. The image of the "happy slave" that lacks a complex identity or desire for freedom is only slightly more nuanced than previous depictions. According to Guerrero, the reversal of this plantation formula began in the 1970s with films like *Mandingo* (1975) and arguably *Roots,* which offers a more nuanced, contested view of traditional nostalgic representation of slavery and the plantation.[50] Films such as *Convicts* have alternative models but tend to revert to traditional formulas, a recurring problem in cinematic and theatrical production.

Art historian and film scholar Arnold Hauser explains that crossover audiences do not react to films in terms of their artistic content but to impressions in which they feel reassured or alarmed. Their artistic interest is only in whether they find the subject matter attractive.[51] As such, the way a film is experienced frequently depends on the point-of-entry character, which is traditionally a white male. Structurally, *Convicts* and *A Few Good Men* are very similar in that they both position a white male at the center of the narrative, with women and ethnic minorities on the margins. For women and minorities who are seduced into identifying with the white male perspectives that dehumanize women and minorities, the visual experience becomes uncomfortable or even painful. Others may attempt to identify with the marginal characters who spend less time on screen and therefore offer less access into the narrative. This displeasure is even more intense in *Convicts* because the film lacks the technical gloss that makes identification with the white male protagonist so seductive in films such as *A Few Good Men.* Without the consistent use of elaborate costumes and music to support the narrative, the hegemonic foundation of the master narrative is exposed. Whatever its appeal, *Convicts'* gross receipts compared to other similarly located cinematic adaptations of stage plays released during the same decade suggest that even crossover audiences rejected the film. The film's inability to mask the race ideology embedded in the narrative likely contributed to its rejection and limited distribution.

The film privileges whiteness, which is also depicted as dysfunctional. There is no romantic imagery of the graceful southern belle and the dapper southern gentleman, contradicting the visual pleasure of previous plantation films. Characterizations contribute to this displeasure, exposing a national consciousness through Soll's attitude toward race in general and blackness in particular. Just as Dawson's criminality is enhanced in the cinematic adaptation of *A Few Good Men,* Soll's racist attitudes increase over the course of the film, suggesting that film emphasizes race more explicitly than the stage. In the play, Soll describes convicts as cheap labor, suggesting they are more trouble than they are worth; then, hallucinating, he spots a bear and shoots at it.[52] The bear represents his fear of blackness and the paranoia that accompanies his racist attitudes.

Soll's hallucinations are manifestations of his anxiety, which is inextricably tied to race. Like Horace, Soll fears death. While Horace fears death in abstract terms, which is typified as normal or universal, Soll fears death by Negroes. This fear manifests itself in his dementia, which is used to justify or explain his dysfunctional behavior. In this way, the text excavates the subconscious fear and repulsion of blackness that has been historically and deeply embedded in the national psyche. The lynching of a reported 3,589 blacks, including 76 women, between 1882 and 1927 provides clear evidence of the nation's fear of blackness around the turn of the century.[53]

On a more technical note, *Convicts* illuminates how crossover audiences can reject racist narratives while at the same time highlighting some potential strategies for future filmmakers. With its straightforward use of cinematography, sound, editing, and mise-en-scène, the film leaves an alarming impression without the technical gloss to mask its fallacy. Technical gloss is a critical tool for disseminating the master narrative (e.g., *A Few Good Men*). As such, its strategic use may also be an important strategy for the future development of African American film.

On the contrary, the success of *Driving Miss Daisy* points to the pitfalls of making a film using technical gloss to disseminate the master narrative. Some critics describe the film as an enduring story about prejudice and healing race relations via an elderly white Jewish woman's twenty-five-year relationship with her black chauffeur. The play, written by white playwright Alfred Uhry in 1987, won the Pulitzer Prize, and the film adaptation went on to earn nine Oscar nominations. The film ultimately earned approximately $106 million at the box office. Like Foote's play and its cinematic companion, Uhry's play and adaptation attempt to dramatize his childhood memories of the South. As products of the 1980s generation of white playwrights writing about the South, he is also processing these memories through something playwright Larry L. King refers to as the "memory machine." Although King does not define the term, theater historian Marvin Carlson's *The Haunted Stage: The Theatre as Memory Machine* examines the concept in the dramatic text, performer's body, production elements, and the actual site of the performance: "Theatre, as a simulacrum of the cultural and historical process itself, seeking to depict the full range of human actions within their physical context, has always provided society with the most tangible records of its attempts to understand its own operations."[54] Carlson refers to "ghosting" as a process of "using memory of previous encounters to understand and interpret encounters with new and somewhat different but apparently similar phenomena . . . [which] is fundamental to human cognition in general and it plays a major role in theatre, as it does in all the arts."[55] The process of returning to the South in order to understand its changes is less problematic than the ways in which the return tends to reinforce racial hierarchies by focusing on white characters or inserting a white point of entry into black narratives. As table 1 illustrates, many of the products of the memory machine on stage and in film of the 1980s and early 1990s focus on white perceptions of the South, many of which appear to be nostalgic for the bygone eras of slavery or Jim Crow.

Driving Miss Daisy's unique approach reaches the same conclusions as *Convicts:* whether the South is Old or New, black people are primarily significant in terms of their relationships with whites, and that relationship is usually subservient. Both are nostalgia films, although *Driving Miss Daisy* is a variation of the master narrative as it foregrounds a white, Jewish, female protagonist who is much older than traditional leading female characters. Like *A Few Good Men,* this is another case where what appears to be progressive requires interrogation. The narrative's incorporation of the Africanist presence, racial reconciliation narrative, as well as the agency or lack thereof in African American performance represents critical sites of investigation. This is especially important due to the fact that black actors are historically cast in supporting roles in such frequently produced works.

Both onstage and in the film, Morgan Freeman plays the black chauffer, Hoke Colburn. Freeman's performance evidences a continuous tradition of African Americans engaging in performative indigenization, exemplifying the potential for using the adaptation process from stage to film to enhance the performance of complex black characters and subjects. His work represents a more contemporary example of African Americans' historical attempts to combat representation in one of the only roles they could occupy in the mainstream

American entertainment industry for the first half of the century: as actors in subservient or comical roles.

Performative indigenization represents one of the many significant contributions black Americans have made to theater and film. The strategies in many ways exhibit the ghosting Carlson describes. Through various techniques, black actors have tried to make sense of the plantation ideology that so heavily influences reception of their performances. Paradoxically, to succeed means to offer such a believable performance that the characterization reinforces the very ideologies the performer wants to resist. Still, I argue that the cultural nuance that performative indigenization inspires and illuminates is still a viable option for altering existing circumstances. The increased frequency with which black characters are treated with these techniques and the amount of focus they receive in contrast to white characters, especially in racial reconciliation narratives, can positively influence the cultural literacy of audiences and the reception of black film in general.

Historically, strategies of performative indigenization have been employed through dialogue, facial expressions, and physical movement, often in spite of what the script dictates. Like Freeman, Charles Gilpin was known for making revisions in his performances. According to actor, director, and theater scholar David Krasner, Gilpin reportedly changed racist references of "nigger" to other terms and even adjusted dialogue to appear more natural in terms of his speech patterns, much to the chagrin of the playwright. Similarly, Freeman adjusts nearly all of the dialogue in the screenplay to reflect his natural speech patterns as an African American from the South. In this way, he returns to a critical site of cultural memory to combat misrepresentation in the script and stage directions. He edits the disjointed, racially marked language Uhry imposes on the southern black characters (though not the southern whites).

There are several scenes in *Driving Miss Daisy* that exemplify patterns of performative indigenization. For example, there is a scene where Daisy uses a segregated restroom while Hoke pumps gas on their way to an out-of-state family event. As they continue to travel and darkness falls, Freeman's Hoke wears a concerned but calm expression. He delivers his lines, quietly but firmly explaining that he has to pull over and excuse himself because he was unable to use the restroom at the service station. When she denies him this he says, "Yassum," takes a breath and tries to continue, his face void of emotion. Then he says, "Nome" and removes the metaphorical mask. He pulls the car over to the side of the road, turns around in his seat, and speaks to Daisy.

There are minor changes from play to screenplay, but the most significant changes are from screenplay to film, indicating Freeman's role in enforcing the alterations. In Uhry's screenplay Hoke says:

Hoke (Morgan Freeman) addressing an offscreen Miss Daisy in *Driving Miss Daisy*

> Yassum. *I hear you.* How you think *I feel havin' to ax* you when can I make my water *like I some damn dog?. . . I ain' no dog and I ain' no chile* and I ain' just a back of the neck you look at while you going wherever you want to go. *I a man, nearly seventy-two years old, and I know when my bladder full* and I gettin' out dis car and goin' off down the road like I got to do. *And I'm takin' the car key dis time.* And that's the end of it![56]

But in the film Freeman's Hoke says:

> Yassum. *I heard what you said.* Now how you think *I feel having to sit up here and ask you* can I go make water *like I'm some child?. . .* Well I ain't no child, Miss Daisy. And I ain't just some back of the neck you look at while you going wherever you got to go. *I'm a man. I'm near about seventy-two years old. And I know when my bladder full.* I'm a get out this car and go on off back over yonder somewhere and do what I got to do. *And I'm a take the key with me too.* Now that's all there is to it. [*He looks back at her throughout but not directly at her when he says he's taking the keys.*] (emphasis added)

The changes convey a difference in dialect as well as emotion and ideas. Freeman maintains Uhry's pronunciation of "yes ma'am" as "yassum" and "no ma'am" as "nome," but he then proceeds to turn the remainder of the monologue on its ear. It becomes a heartfelt expression to Miss Daisy rather than the rant it appears to be in the play and screenplay. Altering the language also adjusts the tone of emotions and ideas, thereby exemplifying the critical function of language and dialogue.

Freeman's revised dialogue also reflects an important shift to a black cultural worldview. Altering "I hear you" to "I heard what you said" represents a change in verb tense. Past tense marking is very common in black American speech.[57] The change also represents a shift from hearing her to hearing what she said, which exemplifies an analytical shift in his response that reinterprets what she says to him as a display of bad manners and racism. The phrase "sit up here and ask you" is also a form of image making indicative of African American English.[58] It reflects Caribbean Creole's serial verb in which two or more verbs appear in the same clause with a single subject (i.e., "He picked up and went to town").[59] Replacing the word "dog," which appears consistently throughout the play and the screenplay, with the word "child" humanizes Hoke's reference to himself and challenges Daisy's attempts to infantilize his character. By seizing freedom and empowerment in his use of language in the dialogue, facial expression, and physical movement of his character, Freeman provides a model for emulation in performance.

Unfortunately, the final scene of the film undermines the progressive resistance Freeman displays throughout the film. In the final scene, Hoke appears as loyal and subservient to Miss Daisy, reinforcing the master narrative Freeman challenged in his performance. There are not enough frames in the film to counteract these images and fully convey the humanity Freeman infuses into his performance. Scenes in which he opens doors for her and guides her safely from one location to the next, or in the final scene when he feeds her pumpkin pie on Thanksgiving rather than spend it with his own family, overwhelm the power of his earlier resistance. Freeman did not fail in his performance, as many critics of the film suggest. The film and filmmakers failed him by not

Hoke feeding Daisy (Jessica Tandy) pie in *Driving Miss Daisy*

realizing the liberating potential of his performance. Instead, his performance was absorbed to meet the needs of the master narrative.

As a result, Freeman's performance is now read as stereotype. Freeman has expressed regret that this wise, old, dignified black man became an iconic, bracketed, identifiable character that is bound by expectations.[60] Freeman succeeded in resisting the limitations of the narrative and creating new possibilities, but many audiences failed to read the signs.[61] Many lack the cultural literacy to recognize subtle shifts in verbal and body language. Acculturation of nuanced black cultural performances can end up reinforcing the dynamics of the very power structure that those performances intend to resist.

Conclusion

Driving Miss Daisy, Convicts, and *A Few Good Men* collectively exemplify the most common limitations that African American actors face in mainstream theater and film. Hollywood and Broadway procure black performers to keep up appearances of a progressive America while many of the shortcomings we have faced as a nation persist behind the scenes. Enlisted as supporting characters in narratives about predominantly white American mainstream experiences, the economic success of racial reconciliation narratives in turn affects the production potential of subsequent films. Each time a play or film with a predominantly white cast performs exceptionally well, it reinforces the perception that plays and films with predominantly black casts are uncompetitive. This is in spite of evidence to the contrary that reveals productions featuring predominantly black casts are economically viable. When white American films fail, the production potential of subsequent films with mostly white casts is not affected. When an African American film fails, the production potential of subsequent African American films and/or films with mostly black casts are very directly affected. As a result, African American films are haunted by the success of the master narrative, especially films with predominantly white casts featuring African Americans in smaller roles.

It is critical to access creative control and locate "good material" beyond these narratives. Freeman's performance in *Driving Miss Daisy* reflects one of the least empowered positions one can occupy in the industry: as the actor without star power or entrepreneurial intervention. African Americans become products, packaged and sold for international and domestic audiences that do not consider the concerns of people of color valuable or valid. Still, African Americans and their allies are challenging this through the practice of performative indigenization. In the next chapter I consider the influence of black theater on black film by showing how Freeman and others translate star power and theatrical success into opportunities behind the camera.

2

Insurrection!

African American Film's Revolutionary
Potential through Black Theater

Did . . . [studio heads] give me a certain amount of freedom? I took a
certain amount of freedom [laughs].

—Morgan Freeman on *Bopha!* (1993)

Plays with predominantly black casts are less likely to be adapted into films.
This is in part because adaptations of plays with predominantly white casts have
been more lucrative. Those plays with predominantly black casts that have been
adapted to film tend to receive comparatively lower budgets and less distribution than their white-cast counterparts, shedding new light on the complications of filmmaking in a racialized world. This chapter explores some of the
potent possibilities residing in black theater's intersection with black film. Specifically, plays such as *A Raisin in the Sun, A Soldier's Play, Bopha!,* Tyler Perry's
Diary of a Mad Black Woman, and *The Color Purple* demonstrate the potential of
black theater, film, and literature to work in concert to capitalize on each medium's benefits. These plays represent the first steps toward using the release of
black narratives on multiple platforms (i.e., horizontal integration) via hybrid
distribution as strategies in the development of African American film.

The following analysis of several source texts and films along with an examination of the offscreen circumstances of each duly exposes the emerging, evolving, and paradoxical positioning of African Americans within the economics of
black film. Key elements of dramatic structure and staging as well as the politics
of adaptation in narrative, cinematography, mise-en-scène, editing, and sound
demonstrate how cinematic language can reflect, revise, or repress certain cultural worldviews. Each outcome sheds light on critical sites of empowerment in
opposition to Hollywood's plantation arrangement. They also help shed light on
several strategies for developing African American film generally.

Micheaux's Legacy

One cannot fully appreciate the intersection of black film and black theater without first discussing Oscar Micheaux, arguably the most successful African American filmmaker of the first half of the twentieth century. Micheaux drew on a variety of sources for his films including real events, his own novels, other films such as *The Birth of a Nation,* and white-authored plays such as Eugene O'Neill's *The Emperor Jones.*[1] In this way, Micheaux is a clear example of how theater and other adapted source materials influenced the development of early black film.

The legacy of black theater has influenced black film, primarily through the ingenuity of resourceful blacks and allies working across media and asserting creative control whenever and however possible. As such, Micheaux represents a critical legacy for African American film. He made and produced forty-four films in thirty years, twenty-four of which were features.[2] He also penned at least ten novels released over three decades.[3] While film studies scholar J. Ronald Green stresses that many critics panned Micheaux's films as being "racked by uneven talents and close budgets," he also argues that the "poor production values" and "the aesthetics of poor cinema" apparent in Micheaux's work reflect the concept of "twoness" introduced by W.E.B. Du Bois.[4] Green takes film scholar and critic Thomas Cripps to task for describing Micheaux's films as having "an amateurish, almost naïve artlessness," particularly in relation to Hollywood production values. Green explains, "Black African art and African American music were important in breaking the arrogant hegemony of decadent classicisms after the turn of the century. Black filmmaking might have helped bring life and reality to Hollywood classicism a few years later. It could still do so today."[5] Just as with Bert Williams's and George Walker's contributions to innovating black theatrical performance and genre of musical comedy, Micheaux's work represents the early potential of black subject matter and worldviews in film. The case studies in this chapter further illustrate this point, also showing how industry practices suppress such possibilities even as blacks continue to resist in various ways.

For example, the Lincoln Motion Picture Company, the first group of organized black filmmakers and producers, rejected Micheaux's submission of his autobiographical novel, *The Homesteader* (submitted with the condition that he direct). As a result, Micheaux entered independent film production, highlighting the need for creative control. Micheaux's hands-on approach to ensuring the accessibility of his films is of particular import. According to Jesse Rhines, an African American studies scholar, Micheaux was more entrepreneur than artist, addressing distribution by bicycling or hand-carrying separate prints to individual theaters around the country. Rhines explains,

> He would show his movie to a house manager, along with the script for the next feature to be made. Sometimes he would be accompanied by his star actors and actresses. Micheaux would then begin to haggle with the

manager for rental fees and length of play in the theater in an attempt to secure an advance against the film's return. By late spring Micheaux would be back in New York to film the script as its producer, director, and often even cameraman. He would edit during the summer, and by fall he would be on the road again bicycling his film from theater to theater and promoting it as he went along. And the system was successful. Even with limited, generally low-income audiences, he was able to make a feature film every year for two decades without a grant, subsidy, or monopoly, an achievement subsequent filmmakers would envy.[6]

In addition to the cinematic models he helped establish via the content of his work, Micheaux helped to establish an important precedent for black entrepreneurship in film.

Similarly, stage performer Bert Williams wrote, directed, and produced film shorts in which he starred. He mentored actor/screenwriter/film producer/filmmaker Spencer Williams. Following in Micheaux's footsteps, Williams transitioned from being a comedic performer in all-black cast independent films to writing, directing, and producing race films such as *The Blood of Jesus* (1941).[7] The religious drama concerns a man who accidentally shoots his devoutly religious wife. Voiceover, gospel music, and blues music punctuate the narrative. Produced on a $5,000 budget, "it is possibly the most successful" of all the race movies made during this period.[8]

A Raisin in the Sun: How to Cross Over without Losing Your Soul

In 1959, less than a decade after Micheaux's death, Lorraine Hansberry's *A Raisin in the Sun* premiered on Broadway. The play continues to serve as a significant cultural and economic model for black theater and film production in the American entertainment industry. As the first Broadway production of a play by a black woman, Hansberry's *A Raisin in the Sun* exemplifies a culturally nuanced model of black theatrical and cinematic storytelling with economic viability. A line from poet and playwright Langston Hughes's poem "A Dream Deferred" inspired the play's title. The play focuses on the Youngers, a black working-class family with middle-class aspirations for education, a business, and home ownership—in essence, the American Dream. The stage musical adaptation premiered on Broadway in 1973, running for 847 perfomances. The stage play's cinematic companion received theatrical release in 1961, and a more recent version appeared on television in 2008. The play was revived on Broadway in 2004. In addition to being anthologized as the quintessential example of African American theater, it receives frequent staging throughout the United States and has been translated into over thirty languages on six continents.[9] Often described as "universal," *Raisin* is the epitome of a predominantly black theater and film production with crossover appeal. Like August Wilson's less frequently adapted works, the play manages to "feed the spirit and celebrate the life of black America" while also entertaining diverse audiences.

Due to its crossover appeal, the nuance of Hansberry's play was originally lost on some critics. In the 1960s, poet and playwright Amiri Baraka heavily criticized Hansberry's play as representing the "passive resistance phase of the movement," focusing too much on "moving into white folks' neighborhoods, when most blacks were just trying to pay their rent in ghetto shacks." After seeing a revival nearly three decades later, Baraka had this to say: "[In the 1960s] we missed the essence of the work—that Hansberry had created a family on the cutting edge of the same class and ideological struggles as existed in the movement itself and among the people. What is most telling about our ignorance is that Hansberry's play still remains overwhelmingly popular and evocative of black and white reality, and the masses of black people dug it true."[10] *Raisin* exemplifies a method of achieving a universal (not read as white) message that can cross over without losing its cultural resonance. It is a viable model for examining aspirations for upward social mobility that does not demonize black people in the lower or middle class.

But Hansberry finds her own play flawed in that it lacks a "big fat character who runs right through the middle of the structure, by action or implication, with whom we rise or fall."[11] She refers to this flaw as a dramaturgical incompletion, which I suggest may actually be a reflection of Afrocentric worldviews. While Hansberry may not provide a big fat central character, she does offer varied and multidimensional characters, including a revised representation of the African in America. Asagai, as a "real revolutionary-in-the-making,"[12] and one of the suitors of aspiring doctor Beneatha Younger, is an African intellectual who sharply contrasts with the savage imagery of Africa so frequently portrayed in American theater and film. He improves upon Williams and Walker's more nuanced yet controversial representation of Africans, thereby paving the way for Akeem, the African prince-hero in the 1988 film *Coming to America* (see chapter 6). Also, the African concept of self emphasizes the interconnectedness of individuals with one another across time and generations. It is possible that neither Walter Lee nor Mama Younger emerges as the protagonist in *Raisin* because all their fates are so intricately connected, a reality that lends to the play's power. An ensemble piece rather than a star vehicle in which a central protagonist emerges may be the most effective approach to expressing some African American worldviews. While Hansberry added several scenes to the screenplay to correct the aforementioned "flaw,"[13] the frequent restaging of the play and its two cinematic companions reveal the potential for adaptation to further develop a narrative in theater and film that appeals to a broad, multi-ethnic audience.

Black Theater's Legacy and Emerging Potential

As Micheaux helped to pave the way for Hansberry, so Hansberry helped to pave the way for Ntozake Shange's *for colored girls who have considered suicide / when the rainbow is enuf* (1976). Like *Raisin*, this play represents a significant milestone for black women in theater, particularly on Broadway. Shange staged the work in a bar outside Berkeley. Stage and film director/producers Oz Scott and Woodie King Jr. later optioned the project and presented a modified version at the Henry Street Settlement's New Federal Theatre in April 1976. Later, theater producer and director Joseph Papp transferred it to his New York Shakespeare Festival's Public Theatre. In September 1976, the play opened at the Booth Theatre on Broadway, where it ran for 876 performances. After great economic success with his original stage plays and their cinematic adaptations, Tyler Perry wrote, directed, and produced the film adaptation of *for colored girls* in 2010.

Shange's choreopoem[14] epitomizes the comparatively few African American–authored stage dramas to grace the Broadway stage, with August Wilson representing the pinnacle of such works within the past thirty years. Unfortunately, Wilson's works are not the focus of this chapter because none of his plays have been adapted into a major, feature-length film distributed in movie theaters (although there are rumors of a pending adaptation of Wilson's *Fences* directed by Kenny Leon). This is, in part, due to Wilson's insistence on having a black director for his work. Perry, on the other hand, has adapted six of his original stage plays into major feature-length films, maintaining broad distribution of videos of the stage plays he writes, produces, directs, and in which he appears. Perry's fierce creative control across media is not unlike Micheaux's.

Despite the fact that none of his plays have been adapted into a major feature-length film, Wilson had an influential part in the economic development of African American cinema. Many influential African American film actors matriculated into the mainstream through Wilson's work or through training with his collaborating director, Lloyd Richards. This includes but is not limited to such luminaries as Angela Bassett, Phylicia Rashad, Laurence Fishburne, Courtney B. Vance, Charles S. Dutton, Alfre Woodard, and Delroy Lindo, among others. Wilson's work in general has garnered a great deal of critical acclaim. In contrast, Perry's approach has led to economic success but not critical acclaim, increasing his cultural capital by enlisting many of the aforementioned actors to appear in the cinematic adaptations of his stage plays. The appearance of accomplished black actors in works such as his adaptation of *for colored girls* lends his work a degree of credibility that it might otherwise lack.

Perry's *for colored girls* merges three distinct approaches to black commercial theater production and exhibition in the United States: independent, mainstream professional (Broadway and the regional theaters), and the urban theater circuit. Mainstream white American professional theater on Broadway and in Chicago considers each of these approaches as marginal at best, yet they demonstrate how a play written for a predominantly black audience "crosses over" on stage and eventually on film. As a result, these approaches expose the plantation ideology that underpins the mainstream entertainment industry. Combined, these approaches reveal the potency of black subject matter in theater and its potential for African American film.

Adapting Black Professional Theater: *A Soldier's Play / A Soldier's Story*

Black theaters and culturally or ethnically diverse theaters tend to have a short life span due to inconsistent financial support and management issues.[15] The rise, fall, and resurgence of the Negro Ensemble Company (NEC) typify the evolution of black professional theater companies, especially those that operate as nonprofit organizations.[16] Co-founded in 1967 by playwright Douglas Turner Ward, producer/actor Robert Hooks, and theater manager Gerald Krone, the NEC received its initial funding from the Ford Foundation. But by 1972, the Ford Foundation grant was exhausted and the resident company disbanded. With staff cutbacks, cancelled training programs, and deferred salaries, the NEC faced the eminent demise countless black theater companies have faced since the African Grove. Instead of closing, the company decided to produce one play per year. The success of Joseph A. Walker's *The River Niger* (1972), the first play selected following this decision, proved to be the company's salvation. It was the first NEC production to move to Broadway, where it remained for nine months, and it won the Tony Award for Best Play, embarked on a national tour, and revived the company for the next decade. The NEC has produced more than two hundred new plays since 1967 with more than four thousand cast and crewmembers. Currently, foundation, government, and corporate supporters along with patrons and individual supporters keep the company afloat.[17] Making it to mainstream venues on Broadway or in Chicago that cater to predominantly white audiences and achieving critical acclaim through mainstream white institutions that evaluate according to established precedent would be a critical component to changing perceptions of black theater's viability. While *The River Niger* was a success by any measure, it was *A Soldier's Play* that ensured the NEC's future.

In order to fully understand the context in which the NEC operated and the example set by *A Soldier's Play* and its cinematic companion, it is important to highlight the role of the League of Resident Theatres (LORT) in theater generally and black theater specifically. The LORT is the largest professional theater organization in the United States. The organization trains members and supports the business of theatrical production. Although black professional theater has and continues to receive financial and other forms of support from various sources, historically, few have been members of the LORT. As a result, professional black theater has not benefitted from the organization's invaluable resources. As of 2010, the lack of a consistent black presence in the league's seventy-six member theaters located in every major market in the United States further maintains the plantation arrangement, privileging whites in organizational structure and selection of material.[18] As a result, racial disparities on Broadway and in Chicago persist throughout professional theater. Very few plays that originated in these predominantly black professional theaters are adapted into films, which is what makes the NEC's successful transition to the mainstream so significant.

Black professional theaters exist in a liminal space, on the margins of the mainstream. They provide a home to nurture talent as well as a venue for exploring and testing a narrative's development and appeal to black audiences. Historically, black theater has been an empowering space for developing black drama for a predominantly black audience even in cross-cultural collaboration. Even with mixed audiences, maintaining focus on the cultural group repre-sented and on the broad range of material that entails, the outcome can be culturally resonant and economically successful. In this way, black theater can create, test, and develop narratives for African American cinema, which are often targeted at white audiences even before they are produced. This stage-to-screen model increases possibilities for measuring and documenting immediate public response to a story, characters, and various other elements. A successful adaptation also becomes a source of funding as well as a marketing tool for sub-sequent theatrical or film productions, as with the NEC.

A Soldier's Play, written by Charles Fuller, opened at Theatre Four in New York City in 1981. It is a murder mystery involving the death of a black army sergeant in a small military town on the Gulf Coast during World War II. Captain Davenport, a black officer, travels from Washington, D.C., to investigate the mys-terious death and in the process exposes racism in the military structure as well as intra-racial conflicts within the black unit. Fuller uses flashbacks and detec-tion devices to tell the story. The African American cultural storytelling tech-niques in the play—including Davenport's direct address to the audience and the blending of past and present through lighting cues and overlapping dialogue—end up becoming watered down in an attempt to follow established Hollywood precedent. The film omits direct address by not incorporating voiceover narra-tion or interactive camerawork. Reducing the interconnectedness of time to the limbo scene (discussed below) along with Davenport's altered characterization ensures that the play's story and characters more closely resemble the master narrative in spite of the play's broad appeal.

Evidence of crossover appeal typically means that a production will be more attractive to Hollywood studios and Broadway producers. By the time the play won the Pulitzer Prize, it had achieved record ticket sales, rave reviews, and documented crossover appeal off Broadway. The NEC was already in negotiations to move it to Broadway, and Warner Bros. had purchased the film rights with white director Norman Jewison at the helm and Fuller's conditional involvement.[19] The film, retitled *A Soldier's Story,* was released in 1984. It cost $6 million to produce with a marketing budget of $3.5 million.[20] The film went on to receive enthusiastic reviews as well as an Oscar nomination for Best Screenplay after earning approximately $22 million on 581 screens for 157 days. In comparison to other successful films, the gross receipts may seem unimpressive. Yet when compared to the production and marketing budget they are extremely remarkable, representing the moderate yet consistent economic success of African American films. (Such patterns of smaller budgets, limited distribution, and modest earnings can be found in a number of other films, including *Bopha!, Panther, Once Upon a Time . . . When We Were Colored,* and *Sankofa.*) *A Soldier's Story* earned more than twice its budget and a roughly $12.5 million profit. However, its success did not drastically increase the number of African American stage plays adapted into films. The success of black-themed films is too often dismissed as an exception rather than recognized as evidence of a viable market and product; that is, unless they reinforce pathological perceptions of blackness, black-themed films are not seen as profitable.

Narrow definitions of success and limited perceptions of economic viability of black themes have a resonating effect on black theater and film. While black professional theaters lack access to LORT resources, they produce work of a comparatively higher quality than the urban theater circuit. The NEC recruited top performers in the original cast of *A Soldier's Play:* Adolph Caesar played Sergeant Waters, Denzel Washington played Private Peterson, and Samuel L. Jackson played Private Henson. These casting choices continue to positively affect the theater's growth. Additionally, talented designers such as Felix E. Cochren (set designer), Judy Dearing (costume designer), Allen Lee Hughes (lighting designer), and Regge Life (sound designer) contributed to the cultural transmission process, supporting African American perspectives in the narrative rather than repressing them.

Fuller's "limbo" concept offers an ideal example of how to effectively dramatize African American cultural perspectives. The stage is "*a horseshoe like half-circle*" with several platforms at varying levels. Stage right represents a military office and stage left represents the barracks. The rear of the horseshoe is a bare platform that "*can be anything we want it to be—a limbo if you will.*"[21] Some critics read limbo as Fuller's indication of blacks' social position, but even more as the elusive truth within a racist society.[22] The concept and staging of limbo via the set design, lighting (use of bluish gray lighting to depict the past), sound (music and overlapping dialogue between scenes), and other elements made it possible to dramatize, witness, and compare past and present simultaneously onstage. Collaboration between seasoned director, skilled designers, and an exceptionally talented cast in *A Soldier's Play* more effectively dramatizes an Afrocentric cultural worldview than *A Soldier's Story* does.

A significant shift in the relationship between theater practitioners and the audience during adaptation further illuminates how cultural perspectives are conveyed in dramatic structure and staging. The generic structure of the popular detective mystery engages detection devices and audience interaction, encouraging call and response. Similarly, Captain Davenport's narration and direct address to the audience maintains the intimate relationship but also encourages the dramatization of double consciousness. In scenes with Captain Taylor and other white adversaries, Davenport maintains his composure as he tries to solve the murder. In his direct address to the audience he reveals his true feelings about the racial humiliation he experiences in silence. These devices empower black audiences, inspiring catharsis by confirming the reality of racism while strategically combating it. Infusing cultural values like double consciousness and call and response to articulate black intra-racial experiences as well as encounters with racism empowers black audiences rather than minimizing or ignoring them in order to avoid offending white audiences. Black professional theaters such as the NEC provide a space for writers, directors, actors, and designers to experiment in this area, assessing black audience reception in real time much like Wilson and Richards on the regional networks leading to Broadway. New advances in social media may offer additional methods for direct interaction with audiences.

But black professional theaters face a host of funding challenges. In order to ameliorate those challenges, August Wilson decided to premiere *Jitney,* the first play he wrote in a series of ten plays called the Pittsburgh Cycle, at the Crossroads Theatre in New Jersey in the spring of 1997. At the time, the Crossroads Theatre was the only African American member of the LORT.[23] Unfortunately, *Jitney* did not receive as much coverage as the only play from Wilson's ten-play cycle to premiere in a black professional theater, though many theaters continue to benefit from staging subsequent productions. Will Smith's Overbrook Entertainment produced *Jitney* off Broadway in 2001 (it went to London but not Broadway). In his speeches to the Theater Communications Group in 1996 and the National Black Theater Festival in 1997, Wilson recognized the anomaly of his triumph, the power of his brand, and the racial disparities of funding.[24] As the most prominent black voice in mainstream American theater, his unparalleled success as a playwright and the lackluster outcome of his only play to debut in a black theater further demonstrate that when the concerns of black artists and audiences conflict with funding agencies, black theatrical production suffers.

Similarly, Fuller's involvement in the film adaptation of *A Soldier's Play* could not prevent the repression of Afrocentric cultural perspectives. The murder mystery shifted from the examination of "the impact of racism on black people's interactions with one another" to a focus on racial reconciliation between blacks and whites during World War II, which did not happen. Such revisions overlook the realities of African American experiences, disregarding lynching, police brutality, and the race riots and upheaval that occurred when black veterans returned from war. Indeed, they came back to the same second-class citizenship they endured before the war. In this example, we can see very clearly how, when African American narratives are made to cross over to white audiences, they end up internalizing the plantation ideology so heavily promoted in mainstream white American theater and film.

Adhering to established precedents such as linear narrative, invisible editing, stereotypical black representation, and racial reconciliation without critique is dangerous and limiting. Specifically, Davenport's narration gets omitted from the film. It could have been included as voiceover in the film to dramatize double consciousness. The film's use of cuts or fades to transition into flashbacks rather than consistent dissolves to communicate simultaneous influence of past on present and future misses an opportunity to capitalize on cinematic vocabulary and Afrocentric worldviews. Reverting to established precedent undermines the development of more nuanced film language, not just for African Americans but also for Hollywood. Maintaining plantation ideologies and hierarchies embedded in industry practices increases potential for cultural amnesia by promoting false memories of racial reconciliation and historical events. These clashing elements exhibit the multiple ways in which African American culture conflicts with Hollywood narrative.

There are other instances of how *A Soldier's Play* was depoliticized for the purposes of creating crossover appeal in the cinematic adaptation. For example, Davenport's initial appearance in the play differs significantly from the screenplay. In the play, Davenport is self-assured, sharply dressed, friendly yet professional with flair.[25] In the screenplay, he is described as "a black man . . . wearing dark sunglasses, and is slumped down in his seat sleeping, his officer's cap tilted forward over his forehead. He stirs, then awakens with a start, looks around sleepily then suddenly embarrassed as he realizes he has reached his destination," having also realized that the bus driver called him a boy.[26] The character's revised introduction plays on the stereotypical representations of black people in cinema as he is literally sleeping on the job. It also emphasizes the racism displayed in black/white interaction, which significantly increases throughout the film. Indeed, the increased presence of white actors over the course of the film visually and ideologically reflects the shift in focus from the effects of white racism on black intraracial interaction to the racial implications of black/white interaction. Despite Fuller's role as screenwriter, he was not able to prevent this ideological shift. While theater and film are both highly collaborative media, the outcome of this film suggests filmmaking is a more complicated process for African Americans due to established precedents and dynamics in Hollywood. Fuller's collaboration with cinematographer Russell Boyd, director Norman Jewison, film editors Caroline Biggerstaff and Mark Warner, and numerous others could have allowed for more nuanced use of technical devices.

Another example of how the adaptation process dilutes Afrocentric worldviews is the minimization of the concept of limbo from play to film. While limbo was eloquently articulated in the stage production, it only appears in one scene in the film. The scene begins with Private Wilkie recounting to Captain Davenport his memory of Sergeant Waters's dislike for Private C. J. Memphis. The camera cuts to the bar, visually depicting Wilkie's memory by staging the flexibility of space and time. C.J.'s guitar-playing reflection appears in the mirror as Waters describes his hatred for southern Negroes. The reflection conveys Waters's disdain as a manifestation of his self-hatred. Waters stands beside Wilkie just before Wilkie and C.J. fade into the dark background while Waters remains isolated in the dark frame, telling his story: "We were in France during the First War, Wilkie. We had won decorations, but the white boys had told all the French gals we had tails. And they found this ignorant colored soldier. Paid him to tie a tail to his ass and parade around and make monkey sounds . . . called him 'Moonshine, King of the Monkeys.' And when we slit his throat, you know that fool asked us, what he had done wrong?" As Waters nears the end of the story, C.J. and Wilkie slowly dissolve into the frame. C.J. reappears as a reflection in the mirror as the close up widens into a medium shot including all three men in the frame. C.J. appears in the background of the frame, emphasizing his ghostly quality. The images of the three men dissolve out at different rates, representing different moments in time. This scene exemplifies the possibilities for African American cinematic language that is initiated through theatrical staging and then transferred into film. Paradoxically, this particular theatrical device, reduced to a single scene, expresses an Afrocentric worldview of interconnected time, a worldview that originated in the stage version. The device's reduction in the film is only one example of how African American perspectives and Afrocentric worldviews are eroded in filmmaking processes.

In the film, the ending overlooks the plight of the black military unit in lieu of Davenport's assimilation (due to his rank and class) into the racially stratified military. The film's ending also indicates a shift in viewpoint, a historical revision, and evidence of false racial reconciliation narratives. The stage play ends as Davenport, the last man standing, delivers a "fitting eulogy" for the men destroyed by the event. He reports Private Peterson's and Private Smalls's incarceration and the entire unit's death in battle against Hitler. Staging typically involves Davenport in a single spotlight on a darkened stage to emphasize his singular survival, followed by a brief exchange in which Captain Taylor admits he was wrong and will have to get accustomed to Negroes being in charge. Davenport's characterization and previous interactions with the audience underscore his reply: "Oh, you'll get used to it—you can bet your ass on that. Captain—you will get used to it." In the screenplay and the film, Davenport's flippant retort remains the final line of dialogue. Yet the context of their preceding exchange subtly changes as Taylor admits he was wrong and Davenport replies, "So was I" before joining Taylor in the jeep. The monologue from the play is replaced in the screenplay by a caption that is superimposed over the image of the black soldiers accompanied by music and the sound of their cadence call. The caption reads: "The 221st Chemical Smoke Generating Company, all its officers and enlisted men, were wiped out in the Ruhr Valley during a German advance in heavy fog."[27] Immediately following Davenport and Taylor's exchange, Fuller's script recommends cinematography, sound, and editing to illustrate the tragic end that befalls the men.[28] The script suggests that even if Taylor changed his mind about the inferiority of blacks, his newfound ideology would have no influence in the United States, where racial tension continued to run high after the war. Yet the film ends with Davenport and Taylor, wearing MacArthur sunglasses, riding together in a military vehicle. The mise-en-scène and cinematography suggests that they now see the world similarly and are moving in the same direction. Throughout the film, Davenport's middle-class values are aligned with perceivably mainstream white middle-class values (see chapter 6). With Taylor in the front passenger seat and Davenport in back, they are chauffeured in a jeep in the midst of the black GIs marching off to war. The final image of the film, a hilly road with the advance of soldiers, omits the sobering caption Fuller's screenplay prescribes. The film's ending significantly changes the moral of the story, which becomes less about intra-racial interaction and more about interracial reconciliation.

The offscreen circumstances of the adaptation of *A Soldier's Play* further highlight the racial politics of success in Hollywood. Specifically, expectations created by the star system likely contributed to Fuller's transforming this ensemble piece into a star vehicle for Howard E. Rollins Jr., in an attempt to attract his crossover fan base from the film adaptation of *Ragtime* (1981). Based on E. L. Doctorow's 1975 novel, the cinematic adaptation focuses on a young black pianist, an upper-class white family, and a Jewish immigrant in early 1900s New York City. Racial tension, violence, infidelity, and nostalgia for racial reconciliation narratives are prominently featured throughout. There are conflicting reports regarding the film's gross receipts, ranging from $11 million to $17 million, and no available figures regarding its budget. *Ragtime* was nominated for eight Oscars, including for Rollins as Best Supporting Actor. His critically acclaimed characterization of Coalhouse Walker in *Ragtime* lent the necessary star power to warrant Hollywood's investment in *A Soldier's Story*.

It is fairly easy to get a copy of the film version of *A Soldier's Story,* whereas it takes some work to find a recording of the original staging of the play. It is therefore not surprising that the film now tends to serve as the inspiration for later stage productions.[29] Reviews, documented audience responses, and creative choices in revivals display the signs of cultural amnesia, forgetting one's own culture due to the heavy influence of an outside, dominant cultural perspective. This is particularly apparent in the use of music in theater and film. Hollywood and Broadway's traditional use of black music tends to conflict with the organic musicality of the cultures represented by more culturally nuanced uses in African American plays, films, and literature. For example, Big Mary was not in the original play. Her character was added to the film adaptation and played by Grammy Award–winning singer Patti LaBelle. A 2005 revival of the play in Pittsburgh included Big Mary, further illuminating the power of film to supplant written text even when the play's script is the original source. The addition of Big Mary as a new character in stage productions embellishes the narrative with additional musical numbers much like her inclusion the film, the film's emphasis on C. J. Memphis's singing and guitar playing, and the film's sound track.

Big Mary is just one example of how increased musical presence in a film or a play has the potential to attract larger audiences. Music helps foster crossover appeal, especially when featuring a famous singer or popular style of music. One need only consider the rising prominence of the sound track from 1970s Blaxploitation films through 1990s hip-hop gangsta films,[30] as well as patterns of casting music stars like Fantasia Barrino in *The Color Purple* musical, Beyoncé Knowles in *Dreamgirls,* and other singers/rappers turned actors. The addition of music also helps make taboo subjects more palatable: lesbian relationship (*The Color Purple* film and musical, discussed in chapter 3), inner-city violence (hip-hop gangsta films, discussed in chapter 6), and interracial romance in the segregated South (*Memphis,* Broadway musical 2009–2012).

In cinema, sound contains three major components: dialogue, music, and sound effects. Music establishes historical context, shapes space and emotional tenor, defines character, and distances audiences.[31] Appropriation of black music in mainstream master narratives such as *Driving Miss Daisy* conflicts with its use in works such as *A Soldier's Play,* where music conveys experiences with hegemonic domination. Adding Big Mary to *A Soldier's Story* undermines the message in order to entertain. It increases the musical content of the play while upstaging the culturally nuanced use of music to construct C.J.'s character as a black southerner in the source text. The music is a survival mechanism, speaking the unspeakable, especially for those who have historically had no voice. Added scenes and songs embellish entertainment value for crossover appeal. This strategy is also apparent in nostalgia films such as *Convicts* and *Ragtime,* both of which use music as the Africanist presence defining whiteness.

This pattern is also apparent in films set in the South, which compels the inclusion of scenes featuring black church choirs singing gospel music. Guerrero refers to one famous example as the "same tired juke-joint-church polarity" depicted in Spielberg's *The Color Purple*. Walker's novel articulates and celebrates the eventual triumph and independence of black "womanist" values[32] that are completely undermined in this scene of the film. Blues and gospel music supplants the source text's core ideology by cross-cutting between Shug singing the blues in the juke joint and an unidentified soloist in the church choir. Accelerated montage merging scene and audiences (juke joint and church) as well as the reconciliation between Shug and her preacher father contradicts the novel's core thesis. It also exemplifies Hollywood's depoliticizing practice of using music or melodrama underscored with music to erase or overshadow any underlying critical discourse challenging hegemony.

Incorporating black music in Hollywood narratives serves several functions. It increases possibilities for horizontal integration with a music sound track. In addition to attracting crossover audiences, it is often used in master narratives to attract black audiences seeking content that reflects some aspect of their lived experience. This is yet another example of the intricate connections between creative choices and economic influence, as well as possibilities of employing horizontal integration in more strategic ways.

While a single film (or play) may not have the power to completely erase or significantly alter collective memory, a combination of elements can have a considerable effect. This brings us back to the point about the accessibility of the film and its influence over subsequent stage performances. In order to combat cultural amnesia, audiences would need exposure to the play, especially productions that maintain Afrocentric worldviews. White Australian Jo Bonney's 2005 off-Broadway revival of *A Soldier's Play* at the Second Stage Theatre, starring Taye Diggs and James McDaniel, refocuses the audience's attention back to those unique elements of the play that were lost in adaptation. Theater critic Michael Feingold astutely highlights how collaboration among theater designers, technicians, and the cast, Bonney's staging, and the lighting design helped merge past and present even more fluidly than the original. According to Feingold's review, events are depicted within a continuum where the enlisted men's interactions with Sergeant Waters in the past, Captain Davenport's interrogations with the men, and duels with Captain Taylor represent an ongoing pattern rather than parallel events as they appear onscreen. This exemplifies the changing shape of narrative depending upon the medium. Feingold also notes how this production emphasized the military as a microcosm of society, investigating the problem through the strata of race and class.[33] This was a deviation from the original, which appeared to be more of a study of what can happen in individual cases. Revivals do not have to mirror the original. They have the freedom to adapt alternative perspectives rather than repressing them. It is unclear if the film's limitations inspired Bonney's detailed focus on these elements and reformation of the narrative. Regardless, the staging allows audiences to see the interconnectedness of past and present.

Contemporary social climate and events at the time of staging or of a film's release play a critical role in audience reception and box office receipts of recent revivals. This is particularly challenging for African American and other black films that address issues of institutionalized racism, sexism, or other modes of oppression. Reviews of *A Soldier's Play* revivals in 1996 and 2005 indicate that perceived long-term progress tends to diminish the timeliness or relevance of the project. As theater critic Ben Brantley notes, "Audiences who saw the original staging of Fuller's play or its film adaptation may discover it less easily categorized than they remember."[34] Critic Elyse Sommer's review of a 1996 off-Broadway production, staged at Theatre Four where the original premiered, suggests the play could appear to be "dated" because the army is now integrated and because of the accomplishments of "retired general and still-possible future presidential candidate Colin Powell." According to the review, the ghosting achieved by producing the play in the original space is less the reason for its relevance, asserting "history, forcefully dramatized, is never dated."[35] Likewise, Christopher Rawson's review of a 2005 New Horizons Theatre production in Pittsburgh, Wilson's hometown, finds that the intra-racial politics within the group appear less surprising to contemporary audiences, who are more aware of class divisions and colorism (a form of internalized racism that privileges lighter skin color, straight hair texture, and other European features in contrast to African features).[36]

Similarly, a number of reviews and commentary related to Bonney's 2005 revival consciously link the historical themes of the play with Hurricane Katrina. David Rooney's review echoes comments by actors Diggs and McDaniel, who acknowledged the relationship of the themes in the play with their experiences, citing the Hurricane Katrina tragedy as evidence.[37] Reviews in each case found the productions represent a useful act of cultural recovery, reminding audiences and critics about the reality of segregation in the armed forces in World War II. Here we can clearly see how historical context significantly affects believability and relevance. Linking real events to the play's historical significance engages the individual and collective memory of both performers and audiences.[38] The original concept evokes memories of the failed promises of World War II for African Americans' quest for citizenship and autonomy and resulting tragic effects on individuals and communities. The Katrina aftermath reminded the nation and the world of the continuing ramifications of socioeconomic disparities. Without an event like Katrina, the film selectively memorializes the promise but not the failure of the American Dream; the story thus loses its immediacy for crossover audiences. As a result, audience perception and participation in revivals of the play are severely handicapped unless the production can be linked to a contemporary event, as in the case of Hurricane Katrina and its aftermath. This process potentially corrects the damage that cultural transmission processes sustain through adaptation choices that tend to limit perspective and reinforce racist ideologies.

Producing a work that critically engages history and has the potential to be marketed in relation to contemporary events is one of many strategies black theater offers African American film. This differs significantly from standard race-specific marketing, which emphasizes race but ignores racism and reinforces hegemonic norms in the form of crossover appeal. In contrast, strategic, politicized marketing can acknowledge the effects of race and racism. The point here is to recognize the racial dynamics that influence film treatment, distribution, and exhibition. Profit potential is intricately tied to distribution, which plays a major role in the erosion of cultural storytelling processes, values, and cultural perspectives. Black-cast films are more likely to receive studio financing if they mirror the ideology presented in films with predominantly white casts that feature African Americans. Black professional theater could serve a greater role in developing black film narratives. Still, the case of *A Soldier's Story* exemplifies the danger of using the accepted master narrative and Hollywood cinematic language without conscious variation. The consequences of defying plantation ideology by exploring the possibilities for culturally nuanced storytelling are chillingly apparent in the case of *Bopha!*

Defiance: *Bopha!*

In the fall of 1986, the Lincoln Center for the Performing Arts in New York City hosted Woza Afrika!, a festival of plays presented by South African companies. *Bopha!*, which means "arrest" in Zulu, was the second production in the festival. *Bopha!* takes place in apartheid-era South Africa. The play concerns a black South African policeman (Njandini) who struggles between his loyalty to his family, community, and commitment to his job. He and his son (Zwelakhe) end up on opposing sides of school and community protests as he comes of age. The plot is intended to illuminate the influence of apartheid on families: the black policeman, his son, and brother (Naledi), who is forced to become a policeman when he is arrested for unemployment.

Seven years later, in the fall of 1993, the film adaption of *Bopha!* appeared on American screens, starring Danny Glover. The film was directed by Morgan Freeman in his directorial debut, and Arsenio Hall served as executive producer. How did a play about apartheid written by a black South African playwright make it to Hollywood? What is the role of imported art? And what can the play's journey across media and across continents tell us about race and politics in Hollywood?

Under apartheid in the 1980s, black South African professional theater was primarily supported through affiliation with the Market Theatre, a predominantly white institution funded by donations from the private sector. This interracial organization did not receive state funding until the post-apartheid 1990s because its very existence and mission resisted apartheid's ideologies and policies.[39] Without international connections and private-sector support, this interracial organization would not have had the resources to contribute to the development of black South African theater.

Heavily rooted in township theatrical tradition, the Market Theatre attracted black audiences for its expression of the new militancy that evolved after 1976, which was missing in other outlets. For liberal white audiences and investors, such works proved the institution's commitment to nonracial theater. Their international exposure proved commercially appealing as well as politically evolved, making the institution and its investors attractive to anti-apartheid supporters abroad.[40] The Market Theatre benefitted from its inclusion of black artists and audiences much in the same way that white theater organizations in the United States can receive diversity funding for staging at least one play that features black actors. The intersection between politics, economics, culture, race, and art production are more visible in South Africa's apartheid regime than in the United States and other racially stratified countries.

The Market Theatre would benefit the careers of numerous black artists, including Percy Mtwa and Mbongeni Ngema. Mtwa and Ngema founded the Earth Players when they collaborated on their township drama, *Woza Albert!* The Earth Players is a theater group that consists of four black actors. They utilize a more traditional township mode with *Bopha!,* portraying roles that examine a particular problem in the township as opposed to the militant view in Ngema and Mtwa's other collaborations.[41] Mtwa later wrote *Bopha!* for the Earth Players after Ngema went on to found Committed Artists. The Market Theatre took on the Earth Players' production of *Bopha!* Matsemela Manaka, another local artist supported by the Market Theatre, would go on to co-produce the 1986 Woza Afrika! festival at Lincoln Center. Although it did not originate in the Market Theatre and has a longstanding cultural tradition in the townships, black South African theater began to thrive as a business when it gained an international audience, especially through theater festivals such as Woza Afrika! Festivals expose black drama to international and crossover audiences as well as to potential investors that can promote tours, offer transfers to commercial theaters, and open the doors to cinematic adaptation. The Market Theatre provided access to the mainstream American theater industry and Hollywood through the Woza Afrika! festival, leading to subsequent performances in the United States and abroad. This history shows clearly how the development of independent theater companies through the Market Theatre specifically and black theatrical production in South Africa generally had a significant influence on the development of black theater and film in the United States.

Co-produced by Lincoln Center and New Playwrights' Theater, the Woza Afrika! festival exhibited the economic viability of South African themed plays for an American audience. Matsemela Manaka collaborated with Victor H. Palmieri (president of the Beaumont-Newhouse board), Miles Rubin (industrialist fundraiser for art projects), and program director Duma Ndlovu. The festival cost approximately $400,000 to produce. Funding came in the form of grants from the Ford and Rockefeller foundations and ticket sales.[42] The production's success resulted in New Playwrights' Theater showing a net profit for the first time in several years.[43] Once again, the inclusion of black cultural production economically and critically benefits a predominantly white institution. In addition to increased ticket sales, the Woza Afrika! festival also earned the producers a $10,000 Lucille Lortel Award for Outstanding Achievement Off-Broadway. Earnings, reviews, and subsequent productions throughout the United States and abroad brought significant prestige to other black South African plays, further benefitting their position in the studio system. In some instances, the mutual benefits of black inclusion in predominantly white institutions outweighed the threat of acculturation, at times providing opportunities for interculturation through interracial and international collaborations and coalition.

Ngema's *Asinamali!* and Mtwa's *Bopha!* were both featured at the Woza Afrika! festival. They are positive examples of strong economic outcomes for black South African drama in the United States: *Asinamali!* moved to Broadway and *Bopha!* to Hollywood. Investors first learned about these projects at Woza Afrika! and came at the invitation of executive director Ndlovu. Warner Bros. invested in *Asinamali!*'s transfer from Roger Furman's New Heritage Theater in Harlem to Broadway's Jack Lawrence Theater. The geographical transference from a symbolically black space (Harlem) to the Great White Way (Broadway) epitomizes the process of crossing over for black narratives and productions. Still, the Woza Afrika! festival served the function of increasing the visibility of black cultural productions.

Asinamali! was the first black South African play to run on Broadway, thereby establishing it as a model for emulation. It was selected because it solicited similar responses between black and white audiences.[44] Whether they originate in the United States or other parts of the world, all black productions are ultimately measured by their ability to appeal to white audiences. Black audiences gain visibility with production and promotion of black culture, but they are most significant when their reactions can be aligned with that of white audiences. This complicated power dynamic is even more apparent in works such as *Bamboozled*, in which Spike Lee suggests black audiences' responses to film and television can influence white audiences. Using the Woza Afrika! festival as a way of measuring audience interest and response, *Asinamali!* also marketed its Broadway premiere.

Unlike *Asinamali!*, *Bopha!* did not appear on Broadway. It did, however, find new life on the silver screen. When the play was featured in the Los Angeles Arts Festival in 1986, newcomer producers Lawrence Taubman and Lori McCreary saw it and later pitched the project to Paramount, which invested $11.58 million in the film.[45] The Earth Players' stage production was also featured in a PBS documentary before it was adapted into film. In general, the further a black play moves from its original, literal, and figurative location, the broader the potential audience. The bigger the audience, the more money there is to be made. Economic viability via crossover appeal thus has a paradoxical effect on the development of black theater production.

A comparative analysis of budgets of films with predominantly black casts illuminates this paradox. *A Soldier's Story* had a $6 million dollar budget in 1984, as did *Boyz N the Hood* in 1991. *Driving Miss Daisy* had a $7.5 million budget in 1989. However, in 1992, *A Few Good Men* had a $40 million budget, further evidence of how films with predominantly black casts tend to be devalued in comparison to whites. While *The Color Purple*'s $15 million budget in 1985 exceeded that of *Driving Miss Daisy* four years later, it is still considerably lower than the average $20 million budget for Hollywood films. Films such as *Bopha!* are less likely to receive large budgets and therefore broad distribution in comparison to films with predominantly white casts because they are not generally expected to appeal to white audiences. This film exposes the consequences of these practices.

Bopha! deviates from established precedent to create what could become an emerging genre tailored to African American cultural worldviews. Its exhibition on twenty-six screens for seventeen days is not consistent with its $11.58 million budget or the distribution of other films that received smaller budgets such as *A Soldier's Story* and *Boyz N the Hood*. In theory, *Bopha!* should have been shown on twice the number of screens as these films. Due to limited distribution and a short run, it earned between $179,962 and $212,483 overall (on opening weekend, $90,000 on twenty-six screens).[46] It was expected to do much better in early stages of development that led to greenlighting. Critical elements changed in adaptation, illustrating the promise and potential for revolutionary filmmaking and exposing the master narrative as Hollywood studio executives' preferred form.

Morgan Freeman was initially approached to play the lead role in *Bopha!* but he declined. When he expressed interest in directing films and started looking for projects, *Bopha!* was the only script he was offered for his debut behind the camera.[47] Freeman still found ways to resist studio practices by revising the narrative according to insights from the local people, altering the generic structure from melodrama to tragedy, and by changing the ending from Micah's survival and reconciliation with the black community he polices to his death at the hands of an angry mob. Playwright Percy Mtwa filed and lost a lawsuit against Paramount, expressing disappointment with the way his story was interpreted.[48] Paradoxically, Freeman's approach yielded a positive outcome for African American film's development while further illustrating the complications of creative control for authors of adapted works. By changing the ending Freeman challenged the status quo, thereby exposing the plantation arrangement of the studio system.

A limited viewpoint of conflicting race relations under apartheid is superficially developed in Mtwa's play. The film, however, transforms this comic-infused township theatrical structure, which merges street theater, mime, song, and dance, with the oral storytelling traditions of the African village communities from which it emerges. Screenwriters Brian Bird and John Wierick develop a dramatic structure that emphasizes the tragic elements of the father/son conflict, showing how the system dictates their fates and restricts their freedom in spite of perceivable alternatives. Mtwa's initial intention was to make a statement about the innocence of the human race.[49] *Bopha!*'s transformation exemplifies the intricate connections between form, content, and ideology.

The influential relationship between black South African drama and African American theater is evident in the stage production. According to poet, playwright, director, and producer Duma Ndlovu, the play's use of comedy, props, face paint, and quick-change artistry all reflect black township conventions as well as the influences of colonialism and the American Black Power movement, culminating in an artistic and political theater.[50] The process illuminates the *necessity of revolt*, not necessarily *explorations of how to revolt*. This is best exemplified in the father/son conflict, which is unbalanced in the play, demonizing Njandini by association with white villains and opposition against his brother and son who revolt against their family's professional legacy as policemen. In the end, they convince Njandini to join the revolution, thereby tipping the scales.[51] The political undertone built into the work is present but limited. Freeman's filmmaking processes reflect those of other black filmmakers such as Oscar Micheaux, Haile Gerima, Melvin Van Peebles, Spike Lee, John Singleton, and Reggie Rock Bythewood.

Bopha! emerges from a cycle of film dramas with South African themes produced in the 1980s and 1990s, which I refer to as apartheid films. These films, which include *Sarafina!* (1992), *A Dry White Season* (1989), *Cry Freedom* (1987), and *The Power of One* (1992), fared generally well at the box office. Studios and critics believed *Bopha!* had little chance of revealing anything new about the story of apartheid when released in 1993.[52] While other critical historical moments and white personalities are frequently produced and reproduced, black-themed films and subject matter are less likely to be afforded this opportunity.

Apartheid films, including *Bopha!*, share several formulaic elements. They consistently manufacture scenes of protest and violence against black South Africans as they march and sing songs of protest. Even *Safe House* (2012) features a brief protest scene in an urban setting. *Bopha!* incorporates the traditional protest scenes but deviates from the formula through the poetics of liberation. Theater director and writer Augusto Boal defines the poetics of liberation as the revision of stories and performance methods to feature the perspectives of the oppressed in order to liberate the artist and the audience through a more in-depth critique of the system. This powerful and empowering approach exposes and decenters dominant viewpoints inherent in the most frequently produced films with predominantly white casts. As noted in chapter 1 in regard to narratives, apartheid films maintain a white point of entry through either a white actor or a black actor with proven crossover appeal to white audiences. Apartheid films also include an Africanist presence, exchanging African American or black British representation for black South Africans. The Hollywood formula for racial melodramas is the chassis for the apartheid film.

The poetics of liberation are processes by which the chassis is meticulously remolded in order to focus on perspectives of the oppressed. Boal distinguishes his poetics of liberation from Aristotle's *Poetics* in Boal's emphasis on the critical performer/audience relationship and his challenging the status quo. In *Bopha!*, the poetics of liberation are exemplified in the theatrical staging of the play and effectively translated into cinematic elements. For instance, both works embody Boal's concept of newspaper theater, in which daily news items are transformed into theatrical performance (including newspaper projections onstage and newspaper props with headlines that support the film narrative). Providing different versions of the story increases possibilities for assessing the situation. According to Boal, Aristotle's catharsis substitutes dramatic action for real action, imposing dominant values on spectators. Boal alternatively suggests that catharsis can be achieved without relying on the character but through the actions of the spectator.[53] The danger of ignoring black audiences in order to achieve crossover appeal is implied in Boal's resistance strategy.

Freeman uses adaptation to accomplish the poetics of liberation through cinematic devices. Mise-en-scène, sound, and narrative are employed in ways that significantly accentuate the original play structure while embracing the essence of resistance embodied in its content and purpose. These techniques reinvent existing formulas out of political consciousness and artistic necessity. This produces a new genre that I call black Atlantic tragedy. The concept of the black Atlantic tragedy is meant to recognize the perspective of the oppressed so

frequently minimized and ignored in existing genres. It combines the convention of Hegelian tragedy (colliding, equally opposed justified positions) with the
cultural production practices in the black Atlantic, a meta-community linked
by the transatlantic slave trade as described by Paul Gilroy. A black Atlantic
tragedy is not just a revisionist apartheid film. To call it such would privilege the
predominant apartheid film formula as the norm, thereby minimizing the innovative genre as a mere variation. Rather, black Atlantic tragedy's complex rei-
magining of intra-racial, interracial, and international interactions challenges
the more commercial racial melodramas. Black Atlantic tragedy requires audiences to contemplate the ways human freedom may be limited or fate dictated
by interlocking systems of oppression. This genre and its formulaic conventions
are relevant within a cultural continuum whether or not it is recognized by
Hollywood or other predominantly white nations and cinematic histories. As
the circumstances surrounding *Bopha!* and others examined throughout this
book reveal, African Americans empower themselves and the possibilities of
film and filmmaking by naming and defining genres and exploring formulas
using a cultural lens. The fact that many African American films do not easily
fit into existing genres exposes the various problems with and limitations of the
current structure of the mainstream entertainment industry.

Invention and implementation of a new genre requires collaboration. A
creative team implements a variety of alterations in the adaptation process to
accommodate as well as resist limiting generic conventions established with
previous films. In the case of *Bopha!* some alterations followed convention. For
instance, the screenwriters transformed the nontraditional family (father, son,
and uncle) into a more nuclear family unit (father, son, mother), anglicized
Njandini's name to Micah, and reinserted and enhanced the role of Rosie, the
policeman's wife. They also increased and expanded the white roles by making Captain Van Donder/Van Tonder a more liberal version of the white man
conflicted by apartheid (Marius Weyers). His role is balanced out by DeVilliers
(Malcolm McDowell), a white, extremely violent Special Forces officer. This shift
toward more standard definitions of the nuclear family and the expansion of the
roles of the white characters at first appear to align with the master narrative,
or "Ozzie and Harriet" in Africa, as Freeman referred to it.[54] Yet the filmmakers also expanded the role of Pule Rampa (Malick Bowens), a black rebellion
leader, ensuring the focus remains on black experiences under apartheid. These
revisionist elements reflect a significant amount of genre experimentation that
broadens the scope of apartheid and its effect on families.

Casting choices, character relationships, and depictions of violence complicate the narrative, exhibiting performative indigenization on- and offscreen.
Studio practices, such as Paramount's insistence that the major parts go to big-
name stars, limit the opportunities for South African actors who frequently lose

parts to African Americans. In this way and others, African Americans are often complicit in reinforcing western hegemony. But casting African Americans Danny Glover and Alfre Woodard in *Bopha!*'s lead roles also revealed strategic use of ghosting: the same pair had played Nelson and Winnie Mandela in HBO's *Mandela* (1987). Thus via casting, Freeman was encouraging more complicated readings of the film, not only for those familiar with *Mandela* but also with Glover's offscreen activism (along with Woodard and several other black American actors and artists, he has championed causes such as the co-founding of Artists for a New South Africa in 1989, as well as mathematics education and anemia awareness in the United States).

Other expressions of indigenzation are apparent throughout the adaptation process. Paramount and screenwriters Bird and Wierick wanted to enhance the action,[55] while playwright Mtwa expressed great concern that they were "laying on the violence and losing the innocence."[56] The script's mounting violence initially functions as a form of cross-pollination, infusing elements of the action film with racial melodrama, which is characteristic of apartheid films. Freeman and his collaborators deliberately use escalating violence to explore the possibilities and consequences of revolution, embodying Boal's poetics of liberation and thereby emphasizing the necessity of rehearsing for revolution through performance and social activity. As a result, *Bopha!* reveals how narrative structure and characterization can both limit and promote an emancipated consciousness in film.

In spite of Mtwa's concerns, Freeman's filmmaker/audience relationship mirrors performer/audience relationships in theater and in the cultural tradition of African American storytelling, which has its roots in various African cultures. When performing Hoke onstage in *Driving Miss Daisy*, Freeman consulted his black friends about their interpretation of his performance due to excessive praise from white audiences, suggesting he was encouraging nostalgia for the good ol' South.[57] As a director, Freeman used similar strategies for making *Bopha!* He and his team interviewed black police officers, their wives, and children in South Africa and Zimbabwe, where the film was shot.[58] This corrected many of the liberties taken in the first drafts of the script for "an easygoing family drama with no tension at anytime in the picture."[59] His strategy to keep his eye on the family drama and acknowledge the potential blind spots in his perception of the subtleties of South Africa is noteworthy. His approach exemplifies an emancipated consciousness that gets captured in the film in two primary ways: the characterization and performance of Rosie Mangena and the ending of the film. Through Rosie, the audience is better equipped to see the opposing positions of Micah and Zweli (Maynard Eziashi). Rosie's love for her husband and her son prevents her from choosing sides and prevents the scale from tipping too far in favor of either position. Although Woodard has fewer scenes and dialogue than Glover and Eziashi, her expanded role significantly enhances the politics of liberation in the film. Two critical scenes demonstrate this. One occurs in the market when the local women refuse to sell her groceries in protest of their children's arrest. In another, she lies in the dirt after the Mangena home is torched during a riot. Frequent close-ups of her imploring eyes and the intensity of her performance throughout the film make her a compelling point of entry.

The tragic ending is one of the most powerful aspects of the story because it deviates from formulaic conventions of melodrama, stimulating the audience's intellect and emotions. The community kills Micah after he sheds his uniform and joins them at the burial of several students killed by the police. The funerals evolve into a rally leading up to another riot against the police. Freeman and Glover explain Micah's death as his redemption.[60] It can also be read as the community's attempt to dismantle the power structure he represents by implementing a new paradigm with more choices and opportunities. Their attack against Micah, when read as a rehearsal for the impending conflict with the approaching police convoy, evidences an emancipated consciousness with limitless possibilities. Yet Micah's murder can also be problematic as a form of black-on-black violence in response to white oppression, a counterproductive release of anger rather than an act of resistance. Freeman's earlier use of the poetics of liberation makes the first interpretation much more likely because it empowers viewers to see the complications and contradictions of conflicting cultural worldviews. Micah's death is tragic because it is at once justified yet inhumane, calling into question the tactics of the black community rather than simply depicting them as victims. As a result, Micah's death, one of the ultimate revisions of the melodramatic element, serves to challenge the system rather than reinforce it. This differs significantly from Hollywood racial melodramas, especially the apartheid films that preceded it.[61]

Hollywood's inability or unwillingness to accommodate a revolutionary narrative in form and content is apparent in the offscreen circumstances following *Bopha!*'s completion. Paramount's reaction to the new ending and several reviews reflected a desire to see the resolution of apartheid as opposed to the struggle for freedom.[62] This suggests a preference for reconciliation narratives as seen in *Driving Miss Daisy, A Few Good Men, Convicts,* or *A Soldier's Story.* Critics Ed Guthmann and Bill Keller found the protagonist unbelievable and the narrative unrecognizable for post-apartheid South Africans in spite of Nelson Mandela's endorsement of the film.

But what ultimately led to the film's economic failure was limited distribution. According to film critic Leonard Klady, Paramount expected the film to score in urban ethnic areas,[63] but it couldn't because distribution was so limited. Mtwa's failed lawsuit against Paramount lacked the power to affect the distribution in this way. The film's exhibition on twenty-six screens for seven-teen days does not jibe with the original budget of $11.58 million. Paramount supported all the alterations to the "Ozzie and Harriet in Africa" version of the script used to greenlight the film, except for Micah's death. This suggests that the studio's commercial prospects for the film changed as a result of the ending.

Rather than the pattern of race reconciliation so frequently portrayed in Hollywood films, what they got was the implication that violent resistance against apartheid would continue. The pending revolutionary conflict in *Bopha!*'s final freeze-frame starkly contrasts with the closing images in *Driving Miss Daisy* in which Hoke feeds Daisy pie on Thanksgiving rather than spending the holiday with his family. Freeman's alterations to *Bopha!* illuminate ideologi-cal influences on genre and ways in which an emancipated consciousness can revise, expand, and create new ones. Paramount's refusal to encourage revision reflects the importance of film endings as well as how creative and ideological restrictions contribute to Hollywood's narrative and technical stagnation.

The film's limited distribution also exposes how race intersects with cre-ative choices, cultural perspective, and economic potential. *Bopha!* exposes the complex role people of African descent play within the industry. African Ameri-can influence on the representation of black Africans requires careful vigilance in order to avoid reinforcing western hegemony. Black directors may have more influence than actors and actresses in films with predominantly white casts, but they still contend with unresolved distribution issues. The studio dictated the director and influenced numerous other decisions, including the struc-ture of the narrative and its distribution. However, the filmmakers' literal and

Bopha! (1993): Zweli (Maynard Eziashi) in pending conflict with South African police

figurative distance from the studio during the production process actually provided them the space to examine oppressive systems such as apartheid.

The film and filmmakers' accomplishments serve as a revolutionary model for emulation and a rehearsal for a cinematic revolution. The choice to shoot in Zimbabwe as opposed to South Africa yields other significant opportunities for film production. Although violence in South Africa made the insurance premiums too high to shoot there, the rural townships in Zimbabwe closely resembled those in the eastern cape of South Africa. Also, the screenwriters, actors, and director were able to travel to South Africa to conduct research. Shooting in such close proximity to the country allowed access to South African nationals for consultation, including many who were affiliated with the African National Congress. *Bopha!* also provided jobs in Zimbabwe, which was in the midst of economic recovery at the time of filming. Employing political consciousness and economic empowerment at various stages of the process enhanced the project's offscreen success. The local economy as well as the political and cultural landscape benefitted from the film's production in spite of the studio's decision to kill the film's distribution.

Contrary to popular belief, studios give a damn how they make their money, preferring to rely on the vetted master narrative and standard racial melodramas rather than relying on the star power of black actors and directors to carry a film, especially a film that deviates from established norms. Creolization in combination with an internationally and racially diverse cast may not have been enough to ensure broad distribution, yet these elements can still serve as strategies for intersectional appeal that do not privilege whiteness but acknowledge the diversity of a global audience. *Bopha!*'s cast and crew came from the United States, South Africa, England, Australia, and Zimbabwe. The film was also a collaboration between principals new to their roles, as producers (Taubman and McCreary), executive producer (Hall), and director (Freeman). Because studio funding equals studio control, alternative access to distribution beyond the reach of the studios is critical for future development. Such possibilities for developing alternative definitions of audience and distribution networks are best explained by the less critically acclaimed work of playwright and filmmaker Tyler Perry.

Tyler Perry: Charting New Territory?

While he has accumulated his share of criticism, there is no arguing that Tyler Perry earns a very successful living in the entertainment industry. Born in New Orleans, Perry staged his first production in 1992 at the age of twenty-two. Perry invested $12,000 in the show, which drew only thirty people in its opening weekend. With the help of an investor from the original audience and self-promotion at area black churches, Perry persisted in producing the play. By the late 1990s and early 2000s, Perry was selling more than $150 million in tickets, videos, and merchandise connected to his urban circuit shows.[64]

The urban circuit can be traced back to the chitlin' circuit of the 1920s. The Theatre Owners Booking Association (TOBA), the predominant organization for managing black vaudevillian talent and venues during the 1920s and 1930s, represents the first attempts to organize black theaters into regional chains. Though marginal, the chitlin' circuit proved to be lucrative. The urban theater circuit is today's incarnation of the chitlin' circuit. It reaches a heretofore-untapped market of predominantly black theater patrons. As such, Perry's work reveals an important intersection between the urban theater circuit and African American film.

The lucrative urban theater circuit remains marginal to the mainstream framework that prioritizes white institutions on Broadway and in Chicago above black professional theaters such as the NEC. Therefore, the urban theater circuit represents more nontraditional avenues for financing black theater. Although Henry Louis Gates Jr. reports that drug dealers invest their earnings from criminal activity into contemporary chitlin' circuit productions,[65] urban theater has become much more established in recent years so that many artists are now capable of self-financing. Unlike black professional theater and black South African theater, urban theater circuit practitioners sustain productions by controlling costs and reinvesting ticket sales and merchandising revenues to support subsequent productions. Black theater and film can similarly support one another in ways that are mutually beneficial.

Perry's journey from urban circuit to cinema exposes the potential power of circuit strategies to gain audiences. Specifically, collaboration between black artists in theater and film, the black church, and other organizations that support the concerns of people of color can offer benefits across the board. Consistently organizing collective audiences to support black plays locally, nationally, and internationally can help thwart existing reliance on crossover appeal. T. D. Jakes's *Woman Thou Art Loosed* is a perfect example of this. Jakes, an evangelical preacher, approached Perry to adapt his bestselling book of the same name into a musical. With Perry as director, it earned $5 million in five months onstage in 1999. (While Perry didn't have a direct role in the film adaptation, the production was eventually adapted into a film starring Kimberly Elise, who also starred in *Tyler Perry's Diary of a Mad Black Woman* [2005].)[66] Perry's collaboration with Jakes highlights the power of the church audience to determine a project's success.

Perry is an exceptional representative of successful branding. Regular appearances (often playing multiple characters) in his own plays better enabled him to establish his brand.[67] Indeed, individual creation, development, and

ownership are key factors when it comes to the success or failure of black theater and African American film. Playwright Charles Fuller's inability to prevent
alterations to *A Soldier's Story* allowed racial reconciliation narratives and other
black stereotypes to get reinforced. Likewise, diminished distribution thwarted
Morgan Freeman's efforts with *Bopha!* In contrast, Perry translates his theatrical
process into film by writing, producing, and directing even if the original work
isn't his own.

By 2000, Perry had become a brand name, ensuring each play's success.
According to Terryl Calloway, a New England promoter of several chitlin' circuit productions, some urban circuit plays have grossed more than $20 mil-
lion, more than many Broadway plays.[68] Perry's ability to build his brand means
that success is no longer a matter of marking the black body to establish white
ownership or marking/endorsing black bodies within predominantly white narratives to uphold whiteness. As a marketing tool, branding establishes black
cultural producers' ownership of manufactured products. This very lucrative
model of the writer, director, producer, and, in Perry's case, actor demonstrates
strategic branding's long-term success and transferability between media.

Perry's success offers several lessons for the future. As of this writing, Perry
has put on eleven stage plays, which have earned more than $200 million. He
has reinvested this money into subsequent films such as *Diary of a Mad Black
Woman*.[69] He continues to use his name—his brand—in his film projects, which
enables him to distinguish his work from others and prevent imitators benefiting from his niche. His efforts behind the scenes represent a viable, sustainable
business model, especially for black independent film. The future of African
American film relies in many ways on developing a narrative outside of mainstream theater and film venues as well as finding empowering ways to use exhibition and distribution networks.

Hollywood's vertical and horizontal integration continues to enforce a
nearly impenetrable matrix of domination that Perry manages to evade. His
production companies (Diary of a Woman Productions, Inc. and the Tyler Perry
Company) produced *Diary* along with support from black-owned company Reu-
ben Cannon Productions and BET Pictures (no longer black-owned as of 2003).
Perry's distribution deal with Lionsgate, a reputable company known for supporting independent films, enabled him to receive broad distribution outside
the Hollywood majors. This also provided him a significant degree of creative
control denied to Fuller as screenwriter of *A Soldier's Story* and Freeman as director of *Bopha!* Perry's strategic positioning outside the studio system allows him
more ownership of his product and more control over distribution. But the creative aspect and cultural outcome of the project require exploration.

In comparison to more developed works by writers such as Hansberry,
Shange, Wilson, and Lydia Diamond, who authored a stage adaptation of Toni

Morrison's *The Bluest Eye,* urban theater circuit plays in general are incomparable. This is not to argue the tenets of high versus low culture but to acknowledge the paradoxical nature of circuit productions. However limited the comparison, chitlin' circuit plays have a set formula and narrative structure that can be difficult to reproduce. Diamond, who was commissioned to write such a play, shared her experience when she spoke on a panel at Roxbury Community College in the fall of 2009. She explained that the plays contain a standard combination of elements: "Basically melodrama, with abundant comic relief and a handful of gospel songs interspersed" with themes such as gang violence, crack addiction, teenage pregnancy, deadbeat dads, and other problems of everyday life that are of immediate concern for the target audience of working-class, often religious, black audiences.[70] While dealing with issues of immediate concern to their audience, the plays risk reinforcing negative profiling of black people for cultural outsiders. In the case of the stage productions, ignoring a potential white audience is liberating and lucrative. Targeting a specific segment of black audiences for the plays and films yields profits. However, mass production of these projects means that they eventually reach a broad audience, exposing these works to cultural outsiders. With Perry's growing crossover appeal and status on the *Forbes* 2011 list of highest paid men in Hollywood,[71] he and his films have become the primary example of African American film and representation of African American culture in Hollywood. The historical tendency to narrow African American storytelling and cultural transmission through a singular, often black male perspective (most recently and consistently represented by Spike Lee until 2005, when Perry emerged) constrains further development and promotes the essentializing of black culture. Nevertheless, the urban theater circuit model offers valuable insights for the future development of African American film.

Urban theater circuit writers and producers have an intimate relationship with their core audiences that many black writers trying to make it to the mainstream rarely achieve due to American theater industry practices. Professional black playwrights' livelihood and longevity often depends on critics and mainstream white professional theater commissions, though the production itself relies on an imagined audience of people of color for cultural resonance. Given industry practices, black playwrights have talked about how difficult it is to stage work for predominantly black or Latino/a audiences without the necessary economic resources from the mainstream white establishment.[72] Writers and marketing strategists advertising these productions often find themselves in the awkward position of assuring crossover audiences that the work is universal in spite of its predominantly black or Latina/o cast. Under these circumstances, black playwrights working in mainstream professional theater are less likely to share the same intimate relationship that urban theater circuit writers have with their audiences.

Perry demonstrated this intimacy with the opening of *Tyler Perry's Diary of a Mad Black Woman* in January 2001 to full houses in New Orleans. The play's ending changed each night. Through commentary on his website and post-show talkbacks, Perry decided to commit to the film ending in which Helen leaves Charles. Younger women in the audience disagreed with older women, who insisted Helen should stay with Charles after he professes his love for her, apologizing for domestic and emotional abuse and infidelity. Since the narrative's primary themes focus on family and forgiveness, the younger women's response to the ending suggests a need to redefine these values in a more accessible narrative that acknowledges the challenges that contemporary women face in comparison to previous generations. As this example demonstrates, African American cultural values are constantly evolving.

The video production of the stage play documents the project's dramatic structure, staging, and audience reception. The DVD incorporates wide angles, close-ups, and medium shots, filmed more in the style of a sitcom or soap opera. This is particularly apparent when Perry uses a close-up of Madea's hand punching figures into a calculator to emphasize the cost of domestic violence. Transitions between scenes offer black and white replays of previous scenes underscored by Helen's voiceover to help the audience follow the narrative.

The play's simplicity has positive and negative implications. Each scene's structure is technically basic: lights rise, dialogue and blocking ensue, lights dim for songs, lights fade to black for the transition between scenes. The low-tech style is easy to reproduce even in a church with little equipment. Music underscores each transition as well as moments throughout the play, both diegetically and nondiegetically. As a gospel play, which has been compared to minstrel traditions due to its stereotypical representations and crudely structured narratives, *Tyler Perry's Diary of a Mad Black Woman* is reminiscent of early musical comedies pioneered by Will Marion Cook and Bob Cole as well as George Walker and Bert Williams. Yet *Diary* lacks the sophistication and awareness of Langston Hughes's *Simply Heavenly* or *Tambourines to Glory,* the first gospel play. Still, Perry's work and urban theater circuit plays in general have a place in black theater traditions even if it is tangential to more sophisticated explorations in professional black theater. To discount the urban theater circuit is to reinforce dominant ideologies of theater and culture.

The urban theater circuit provided Perry an unlikely pathway into Hollywood, enabling him to challenge existing expectations. His ability to hijack the box office in *Diary*'s opening weekend and sustain momentum with each subsequent film made Hollywood take notice and begin to recognize the value of Perry's audience base. In an attempt to tap into this market, without investing in a film with a predominantly black cast,[73] producers cast Perry as the lead in *Alex Cross* (2012), in what one producer has referred to as the new, international

Tyler Perry franchise.[74] Critics slammed both Perry's performance and the film, which earned back only $25 million of its $35 million budget. In spite of this failure, Perry continues to effectively manage his business and brand, outperforming other filmmakers in terms of output while still developing in terms of craft.

Until his 2010 film adaptation of Shange's *for colored girls*, Perry had not shown himself to be well versed in cinematic language. In the film, he ineffectively attempts to employ various strategies that Lee Daniels used in *Precious* (2009), a film I discuss in greater depth in chapter 3. In other films, Perry speaks to his audience in a cinematic dialect. Cinematic dialect can be a variation of Hollywood's cinematic language or African American cinematic language, which consists of distinct narrative, visual, and aural terminology as exemplified in the work of Kasi Lemmons, Julie Dash, Haile Gerima, Spike Lee, Melvin Van Peebles, and others. It is just as important in terms of cultural expression to speak directly to audiences in a familiar language that uses recognizable cinematography, editing, sound, and mise-en-scène.

The most sophisticated ventures in *Diary* are in narrative and sound. Perry's stories are often cluttered with clichés and multiple intersecting plot points. Much as *A Soldier's Play* does, he relies on music to convey worldview and entertain. He also incorporates an element of Africanist presence that plays well for his core, church-going audience and has crossover potential due to its prevalence in mainstream white films that feature black actors. He capitalizes on gospel music and preaching as each narrative contains a scene in which a preacher or related character delivers an inspiring message to the protagonist. This act of defiance against Hollywood studios, which he insists has attempted to repress his religious views,[75] helps maintain his audience. These scenes also provide a way for him to incorporate gospel music diegetically into scenes, a core element of his plays. This facilitates his use of horizontal integration by being able to sell a music sound track separately (many of the songs he composes himself, such as "Father Can You Hear Me?" in *Diary*). Perry effectively translates his stage play strategies into film in a way that Fuller was unable to accomplish as a screenwriter. The influence of Perry's work on and off the set cannot be discounted even if some audiences and critics find it polarizing.

In *Diary*, director Darren Grant, cinematographer David Claessen, and editor Terilyn A. Shropshire experiment with cinematography and editing, conveying a sense of rememory. When Helen returns to the mansion to care for her estranged husband following his shooting and resulting paralysis, she explains in voiceover that every room holds a painful memory. Previous scenes in which she experiences domestic abuse, isolation, or loneliness appear as images of her present situation and past abuse dissolve into one another throughout the sequence. This is the most sophisticated use of the medium in the entire film, reflecting the ways in which memories of the past are confronted and examined by black filmmakers such as Kasi Lemmons, Haile Gerima, Melvin Van Peebles, and Spike Lee.

The play and film adaptation of *Diary* share several elements which in turn reveal various intersecting points between Perry's core black female audience and crossover white audiences. He maintains the use of voiceover, basic narrative, Helen's virtue, gospel music, flat characterizations, pop culture references (through singing styles, iconic figures, quoting of pop culture and especially black movies and game shows), life lessons, jokes about stereotypes ("all black people know a crackhead" and "all black people got a Uncle named Peaches"), imitation of black celebrities, the characterization of Madea, proclamations combating stereotypes of black men, and the gospel song during the big finale ("Father Can You Hear Me?"). These elements bring up two significant points. First, Perry's work, like much of black film generally, is highly intertextual. Second, these elements of crossover appeal reflect a significant overlap between the tastes of Perry's core black female audiences and the crossover white audience.

The core audience is clearly delineated at the end of the DVD recording of the play, where black women praising the show are interviewed. This marketing campaign was later used for the film, which also included testimonies from white audience members who praise Madea. This is a significant example of crossover processes that still privilege the initial intended audience. In this way, Perry used the same barometers as Columbia Pictures (*A Soldier's Story*) and Paramount (*Bopha!*) to measure the potential success of his work. In other words, studios look for similar responses between black and white audiences to determine crossover potential and, ultimately, economic viability.

Perry, in fact, privileges his crossover audiences while maintaining a level of familiarity with his core audience. For example, he includes fewer references to differences between black and white women, which may be less alienating for white audiences. Charles's mistress in the play, a dark-skinned, petite black woman, becomes a light-skinned Latina by the name of Brenda (Lisa Marcos) in the film. Brenda represents the spitfire Latina, a stereotype that is also included in *Meet the Browns* (2008). Positioning this Latina opposite Kimberly Elise in the film adaptation of *Diary* actually increases the likelihood of reading Elise's character as darker than the actress actually is. This echoes the longstanding practice from the minstrel tradition of emphasizing the desirability of mulatta types over darker-skinned black women. Making the mistress Latina in this case adds a cross-racial and cross-cultural layer that extends the film's context and thereby broadens the audience base. Like Hollywood studios, Perry's strategy involves incorporating colorism and the racial politics of casting for profit.

In the film, Perry participates in the longstanding tradition of cross-dressing, which is also part of the minstrel tradition and is a prominent feature of black comedy franchises. He has been highly criticized for misrepresenting black women and reinforcing stereotypes of black culture. Nonetheless, Perry provides the sort of "vital contrast" Bert Williams insisted upon in his own work by ensuring his audience sees him out of the Madea costume. In Perry's attempt to avoid being caricatured as Madea, he also plays Bryan, a lawyer and husband of a crack addict. Performing male and female characters increases Perry's range of influence on black representation in the film. Unlike Bert Williams's carefully nuanced approach to providing vital contrast through representations of the African and African American, Perry's work does not exploit the subversive capabilities of black comedy to their full extent.

Perry's enterprise demonstrates black theater's potential for cultivating successful African American film. Considering changes in adaptation, it is clear that Perry uses the DVD audience as a focus group to guide his adaptation choices. Scenes and moments that garnered positive reactions in the play made it to the film (like the calculator moment). Developing narratives for, near, by, and about black audiences in the work before adapting it into film makes strategic use of call and response and the integral storyteller/audience relationship embedded in African American culture. Whether imagined or actually present, black audiences of varying classes, cultures, and national backgrounds are integral to creating culturally nuanced works. Perry translates this into economic success.

Perry has made other noteworthy advancements in terms of narrative content and business models. In theory and practice, his business savvy challenges the studio system. Production budgets for his films generally range from $6 million to $12 million rather than the $20 million typical of a low- to mid-budget Hollywood film. By cutting expenses and time in half, Perry makes his investors a 120 percent return. There's no better evidence of Perry's economic viability than the growth of Lionsgate's annual revenues in direct correlation to the growth of Perry's enterprise. As a result of his economic success, Perry exemplifies an alternative position for the black independent filmmaker, which has historically been the worst position to occupy in terms of resources.

In Perry's case, crossover appeal is less important because his economic success clearly proves that his predominantly black, working-class, disproportionately religious, and largely female primary audience is an asset rather than a liability. Perry's accomplishment is somewhat similar to other filmmakers discussed in subsequent chapters. All rely on black audiences to some degree. This isn't to say that black audiences are a homogenous group. Mixed reception of these works within black communities indicates a great deal of diversity. Still, Perry's predominantly black target audiences enabled him to go mainstream. While many white audiences patronize these films, filmmaker Spike Lee as well as theater and film scholars fear the potentially negative long-term effects of Perry's empire including rapid and frequent reproduction of the same harmful images that reinforce white supremacy, but with a predominantly black cast.

Perry's success and paradoxical contributions demonstrate how African Americans can operate independently from Hollywood. At the same time, he has created his own studio system of vertical integration: the majority of his productions are personal projects he writes, directs, and produces himself. Although Perry served as executive producer for Daniels's *Precious* and has adapted Shange's *for colored girls,* he has only recently started to invest in other filmmakers. Two examples include Angelique Bones and Isaias Casteñeda's *Season of Death: Chasing the American Dream* (2011) and Tina Gordon Chism's *We the Peeples* (2013), the latter of which flopped upon release. Ultimately he has created a system of production that prioritizes his own polarizing work, revealing that people of color can also reinforce plantation ideology through individualistic, capitalist business practices that enable one dominant voice to speak for all black people and cultures.

A concentration of control with someone who appears to lack awareness or concern for the historical misrepresentation of black people for white audiences can have dangerous implications. Fortunately, Perry often works with actors and actresses who are astute and able to convey the depth of humanity of their characters. Still, Perry's performances and writing often undermine their influence much like Freeman's nuanced characterization of Hoke in *Driving Miss Daisy* is overshadowed by narrative, characterization in the script, cinematography, and editing. Perry's collaborations with Oprah Winfrey and other black cultural producers and allies may yield further opportunities to increase his awareness of these potential pitfalls as he continues to develop his approach to the craft.

The paradoxical emancipation Perry represents is exhilarating and unpredictable. His cycle of films will eventually run their course, especially if they show no signs of evolution. Still, Perry's career reveals some of the key elements necessary for both economic and cultural success. A story has to honestly and accurately reflect the concerns of the people it represents. Casting and marketing are critical. Black film does not have to rely on crossover appeal to white audiences for survival. Effective storytelling targeting core black audiences can attract audiences across the color line, especially when they are provided easy access to the material.

Perry has in essence developed a model for production that exposes the limitations of Hollywood's vertical and horizontal integration for African Americans. It also reveals the system's weaknesses, given that there was no preventing Perry from rising to the top, not even terrible reviews from major outlets.[76] Perry's institutional framework is difficult to subvert (benefiting him but not necessarily other African American theater practitioners or filmmakers). Yet, as the above analysis demonstrates, much can be gleaned from his empowered and powerful position at the intersection of the theater and film industries.

Conclusion

Collectively, the examples discussed in this chapter exemplify the powerful potential of black theater to grow African American film. Each of these examples represents three specific ways a "black" or "African American" play moves from the margins to the mainstream and eventually to adaptation. They also illuminate ways that black theater can test the viability of cinematic narratives that prioritize the concerns of black audiences, which is necessary considering the pattern of revisions revealed in this chapter.

As a playwright and screenwriter of black productions on the stage and on the screen, Fuller represents a step toward an empowered role for black people in the entertainment industry. Freeman reveals how the black actor can translate limited power in performance into star power in other roles in front of and behind the camera. Power is fluid and can be used strategically. As a director, Freeman empowers his actors to share creative control, taking liberties the studio would not allow. He represents a useful creative model that is more empowered than Fuller, but a weak business model that relinquishes all ownership to the studio, thereby diminishing the film's influence in the form of limited distribution. Together, the examples of Fuller and Freeman reveal that working under contract with a studio disempowers black artists and may account for the perceived failure of African American films.

Perry offers an alternative business model that successfully challenges direct studio control over black narrative construction and dissemination. Yet the Perry model is flawed due to its heavy reliance on historical stereotypes of black people and culture without in-depth inquiry. His work reinforces the master narrative but with a predominantly black cast. Perry's uncritical approach to black stereotypes combined with the full extent of his creative control exposes the dangers of the existing dynamic. Discerning artists can also proactively use theater venues, however marginal, to contribute to the development and accessibility of black narratives across media. Relying exclusively on white mainstream institutional resources or acclaim is no longer the only pathway to success. The potential and power represented by the business acumen driving the urban theater circuit provides a useful model for selecting narratives with predominantly black casts from stage drama and literature for cinematic adaptation.

The plays discussed in this chapter demonstrate important lessons for the relationship between African American film and theater. Specifically, TOBA's black regional theater network in the early part of the twentieth century, existing black audiences on the chitlin' circuit, and contemporary professional and community theaters offer inspiration for greater collaborative efforts between theater practitioners and filmmakers through adaptation. Further developing existing audiences in both media, as Perry has done, can achieve success but with more diverse representation of cultures. Possibilities exist for using theater houses to screen films denied a studio theatrical release by creating a network of theaters that also stages plays or even college campuses with screening capabilities. When these venues, works, and audiences are provided opportunities and resources to develop and filmmakers take advantage of hybrid distribution deals that allow for greater freedom in sharing the work, possibilities increase. Such processes can begin by coordinating simultaneous staging or reading of a play at various venues across the country in order to reach a larger, targeted audience. New technology such as digital production and distribution and social media websites offers artists an ability to reach a broader audience simultaneously, allowing for direct dialogue with the audience as well as an opportunity to revise projects before they get translated into film. Issues of cultural amnesia that emerge in the evolution from page to screen to stage, discussed in greater detail in the next chapter, can be reduced with better strategic use of the symbiotic performer/audience relationship.

PART TWO

Black Pathology Sells [Books and Films]?

You have a major void with a movie, which is: You don't have a reader, you have a viewer, and that is such a different experience. As subtle as a movie can be, as careful and artful as it can be, in the final analysis it's blatant because you see it. You can translate certain things, make certain interpretations, create wonder, certainly there can be mystery, but the encounter with language is a private exploration.

–Toni Morrison, 1998

3

Playing with Fire

Black Women's Literature/White Box Office

In all honesty, white people care when white heroes are centrally involved. Politics is a hard sell, ethnic politics is a harder sell, and ethnic politics without a white box office draw is damn near an impossible sell.

−Mario Van Peebles, quoting a studio executive, 1995

Given the racial dynamics of the entertainment industry, films by and about black women are poised to fail. Yet since 1980, there have been three cinematic adaptations of books by black women, all with black female protagonists, that are among the highest-grossing of all African American film dramas. Based on budget/gross ratios, number of screens, and length of time in theaters, the success of *The Color Purple* (1985), *Waiting to Exhale* (1995), and *Precious* (2009) suggests that, like black theater, black literature can have a positive influence, both economically and artistically, on the development of African American filmmaking. Black women's literary adaptations in particular are a critical site for exploring development of African American film because they illuminate culturally nuanced cinematic language and economic strategies that can be applied to future films. These three particular films also represent works whose source texts were highly successful in their own right (all three spent time on the *New York Times* best-seller list).[1]

But economic success is not without controversy. Too often, crossover concerns displace black female protagonists and audiences. Understanding how black cultural producers and allies respond to these challenges can shed light on potential strategies for future filmmaking and marketing of African American films. If we simply assume that black pathology sells, we end up overlooking the potential influence of black women in African American film.

95

The Oprah Effect

Few have achieved the power and influence of Oprah Winfrey, a black woman whose success defies logic in a racialized society and has raised the bar for the possibilities for African Americans in Hollywood. By taking ownership of her brand, she has helped to define black ownership in the entertainment industry. Oprah epitomizes unprecedented power and influence in television, film, literature, and theater, paradoxically threatening to create a skewed perception of black women's empowerment at the intersection of economics, culture, and artistic production. Indeed, her commendable accomplishments easily overshadow racial and gender disparities across the entertainment industry.

Winfrey is an anomalous media giant in an industry dominated by white men. She is not the only black entrepreneur and media mogul significantly shaping the future of African American cinema, but her active and diverse range of participation and influence on some of the highest-grossing films featuring African Americans since the 1980s can't be ignored. Some have dubbed this "the Oprah Effect."[2] Oprah's core audience of women spends more than $7 trillion a year, further illustrating the economic benefits of targeting female audiences.[3] Oprah's media empire includes her flagship television program, *Oprah*, Harpo Films, OWN TV, Harpo Creative Works, Oprah's Book Club, *O Magazine*, *O at Home*, Oprah and Friends Radio, and Oprah's Angel Network. She thereby symbolizes the mutually reflexive potential of developing star power and entrepreneurship to realize full individual and collective potential of African American film.

Oprah's far-reaching influence is evident across all three works discussed in this chapter. She was involved in each project in some form and it would be difficult to argue that her involvement didn't have a role in their success. *The Color Purple* actually preceded the so-called Oprah Effect, though it can be argued that her role in the film helped lay the groundwork for her later success. Quincy Jones, the film's executive producer, saw Winfrey on her local TV show in Chicago and told director Steven Spielberg that she would be perfect for the role of Sophia, a woman who pays the price for refusing to pacify white people's wishes. Winfrey, already taken with the book by Alice Walker, had hoped to play the role in the film before she even knew of Spielberg's plans. Her involvement with *The Color Purple* turned out to be beneficial for both the film and her career.

Oprah had a hand in the success of *Waiting to Exhale*. The book and film brought author Terry McMillan to the attention of mainstream white audiences who were unfamiliar with her first two novels, *Mama* and *Disappearing Acts,* which were promoted by black organizations. The cast appeared on *Oprah* three weeks prior to the film's release.[4] The film went on to nearly recoup its entire budget in its opening weekend, further illustrating Oprah's unprecedented success at branding unknown or lesser-known products and businesses.

Oprah teamed up with fellow media mogul Tyler Perry to serve as executive producers for *Precious*. The two represent a handful of African Americans poised to compete with some of the major media conglomerates that control African American film production. He credits her with his success, following her advice to use writing as catharsis to overcome his troubled childhood and other challenges. He has appeared on her show numerous times promoting his plays, films, and studio in Atlanta, and recently inked a deal to produce programming for OWN network.[5] Each example has some connection to Oprah or the Oprah Effect. The box office returns demonstrate the economic viability of films featuring black female protagonists.

The Power of Womanist-Centered Aesthetics

For Hollywood to invest in a black film means proving sufficient crossover appeal to white audiences, in turn displacing black protagonists and audiences. How have black cultural producers responded to this challenge? One such response involves womanist-centered aesthetics, which features prominently in each of the source texts included in this chapter. Each text is, to borrow the words of Alice Walker, committed "to exploring the oppression, the insanities, the loyalties and the triumphs of black women," whom she calls the most fascinating creations in the world.[6] Although this womanist-aesthetic and philosophy is at times eroded in the films to achieve crossover appeal, such contributions by, for, and about black women can help reconcile tension between economic success and cultural values.

The Color Purple, which was Walker's fifth book and sold four million copies in 1982,[7] is part of a trilogy of novels including *The Third Life of Grange Copeland* and *Meridian*. Each investigates similar themes of black women doubly oppressed by racism and sexism. The story unfolds between the early 1900s and the mid-1940s as Celie, a young black girl in Georgia, is repeatedly raped by Pa, her stepfather, who she believes is her biological father. She conceives two children with him, whom he takes away at birth. Pa eventually forces Celie into a loveless and abusive marriage with Mister (also called Albert), who is in love with a famous blues singer named Shug Avery. Through her relationships with her sister Nettie, daughter-in-law Sophia, and her eventual lover and friend Shug, Celie discovers the meaning of self-love and empowerment. After years of abuse and heartbreak, Celie leaves Mister, starts a business making pants, and eventually reunites with her children and her sister when they return from Africa where they had served as missionaries in a village.

The publication and cinematic release of McMillan's *Waiting to Exhale* followed that of *The Color Purple* by a decade. *Waiting to Exhale* tells the story of four contemporary professional black women and their experiences with love, life, and personal development. After eleven years of marriage, Bernadine's African American husband, John, casually informs her that he intends to leave her for Kathleen, his white secretary. Bernadine struggles to care for their two children and regain her sense of self throughout the divorce proceedings. Concurrently, Savannah, her former college roommate, struggles to advance professionally as a television producer while caring for her elderly mother. In search of a romantic relationship that can evolve into marriage, she is similar to Robin, head underwriter at an insurance firm. Also extremely unsuccessful in maintaining romantic relationships resulting from her superficial taste in men, Robin struggles to support her parents because her father suffers from Alzheimer's. Gloria completes the group of friends as owner of the only African American hair salon in Phoenix. She is also the single mother of a teenage son named Tarik. Of the four women, she is the only one who is overweight and the least experienced with romantic relationships. This contemporary exploration of black women and their relationships with black men infuses elements of black comedy and black middle-class representation.

Set in Harlem in 1987, Sapphire's *Push,* the source text for *Precious,* explores the historical present in a way that appears to be in conversation with *The Color Purple* and *Waiting to Exhale.* Published in 1996, the book tells the story of Claireece "Precious" Jones, a teenage incest survivor who is physically, emotionally, and sexually abused by her parents, resulting in the birth of two children. Longing to escape her abusive environment and poverty, she fantasizes about having an appearance that meets mainstream beauty standards, a loving relationship with an attractive young man (referred to as Tom Cruise in the film), and a life in a world of luxury. After transferring to an alternative school, she encounters a teacher who helps her learn her self-worth. The story ends as Precious finds out she is HIV positive. The story merges several themes, including dysfunctional relationships among black people, particularly within the family, that also appear in *The Color Purple* and (to a comparatively lesser degree) in *Waiting to Exhale.*

These texts capitalize on the inherent intertextuality of black literature and film. Each project's unique exploration of sisterhood and the intersections of racism, sexism, and class oppression in different time periods "revise[s] the philosophies, representations and narrative underpinnings of previous texts."[8] They signify on the fairy-tale formula in ways that expose the formula's limitations. As literary scholar Steven Swann Jones notes, these are fairy tales "in that they have ordinary protagonists who encounter magic on their quests, in tone and in other regards." Jones adds, "Not all fairy tales do appeal to all cultural groups; while the various cultural communities on the European continent share a large number of basic tale types, the same cannot be said for African, Native American, Asian or Oceanic people. While most of the communities in these regions have tales that could generally be considered fairy tales . . . these tales are recognizably different from the class of tales in the European tradition that we have come to call fairy tales."[9] Therefore, it is not surprising that the process of applying cultural nuance to mainstream, fairy-tale formulas has become a significant strategy for merging commercial appeal with cultural values.

These texts and their subversion of traditional formulas reiterate the possibilities of black literature informing African American cinematic language. For example, Walker wrote *The Color Purple* as a series of letters. This narrative style creates an interactive relationship between reader and text, encouraging intimate identification with the character.[10] Likewise, Sapphire uses Precious's journal to create the voice and tone of the novel. Directors Steven Spielberg and Lee Daniels employ voiceover narration in their adaptations, which, along with close-ups, aids in the intimate relationship between audiences and the protagonists, who are perceived as ugly, stupid, undesirable, and unwanted. Daniels's approach in *Precious* is highly symbolic of the ways in which African American literary traditions can inform the development of African American cinematic language, whereas *The Color Purple* exemplifies the economic possibilities of adaptation and horizontal integration.

The black female protagonists in each film are intended to appeal to female audiences across color and class lines on the basis of women's issues. In other words, these films demonstrate the potential for attracting audiences by embracing various aspects of identity rather than creating crossover appeal exclusively on the basis of race. Black women's intervention in economic and cultural enterprise to develop African American film illuminates the possibilities of intersectionality as a strategy for success.

Historically, stories by and about black women have not been as lucrative as the mainstream master narratives examined in chapter 1. These works have succeeded against the odds to achieve significant economic success. They are not commercial genre films (unless *Waiting to Exhale* is considered a romantic comedy), yet they all incorporate elements of crossover appeal to nonblack audiences. Not only do they share an Oprah connection, but they reflect similar patterns of achieving crossover appeal through de-politicizing the source-text narratives, demonizing black men, promoting sisterhood, and emphasizing music. *Precious* avoids some pitfalls and achieves crossover appeal through other elements that are mostly progressive yet still problematic. Each text, screenplay, and film indicates how womanist aesthetics can effectively inform cinematic language.

The Inner Workings of the Publishing Industry

Because each of the films discussed in this chapter began as a book, it is important to trace each book's journey. The entertainment industry, whether theater, film, or publishing, runs on exclusionary practices that disempower authors and audiences of color. There is an undeniable interconnectedness between theater, publishing, and film. Specifically, this interconnectedness was made possible through conglomeration, the absorption of subsidiary companies or divisions into larger media corporations. Harcourt Brace Jovanovich, owned by the Education, Media and Publishing group, published Walker's *The Color Purple* in 1982. Since 1985, the paperback has received mass publication through Pocket Books, an imprint of Simon and Schuster. Simon and Schuster is a part of the CBS Corporation, with holdings in broadcast and cable television including but not limited to Showtime and The CW.[11] Viking Penguin published McMillan's *Waiting to Exhale* in 1992. The Penguin Group is owned by Pearson, an international media company.[12] Vintage published Sapphire's *Push* in 1996. Vintage is a division of Random House, which has a movie production arm. Bertelsmann, a private German media corporation, owns Random House.[13] None of the companies that published these works is black-owned (as of publication of this book) but they all have published numerous authors that have made the best-seller list and/or won the Pulitzer Prize, among other honors. Absorption of black women's literature into these mainstream media corporations is a complex practice that has major implications for the future of African American literature and film.

Nontraditional routes to publishing, including self-publishing, gaining publication deals through blogs, celebrity status, and other means offer some authors a way to circumvent more traditional (often exclusive) avenues. Traditional publishing deals, however, often result in comparatively limited ownership and earnings in contrast to self-publishing of e-books in recent years.[14] Because unpublished African American authors are at a great disadvantage in terms of having their work published or promoted in these outlets, many turn to self-publishing and self-promotion.[15] In fact, Oscar Micheaux developed a publishing company in the early 1900s in order to distribute his books before he started directing and producing films. Much like August Wilson's collaborative efforts with Lloyd Richards and playwrights on the urban circuit, African American authors have a history of finding ways to circumvent exclusionary industry practices. Their efforts expose the necessary correlation between creative work and entrepreneurship for black artists regardless of the medium. Without African American cultural literacy, the gatekeepers in theater, film, and publishing are less likely to recognize the value of and values in an African American artist's work.

McMillan's first book, *Mama*, was published by Houghton Mifflin in 1987, but, still a relative unknown, she took to self-promoting her work. She subsequently won the Doubleday New Voices in Fiction Award and was introduced to a white literary agent, Molly Friedrich, who continues to represent her.[16] Like agents in the entertainment industry, most literary agents are white. It is therefore significant that the success of *Waiting to Exhale,* her third novel, encouraged mainstream publishers to gamble on African American writers, thereby leading to the entry of more black literary agents into the publishing industry.[17] Literary agents assess and develop writers, market their work, and negotiate contracts, frequently earning an estimated 10 to 15 percent of author earnings.[18] Diversity in the industry's workforce potentially increases the possibility for greater diversity among authors, audiences, and narratives. *Waiting to Exhale* spent thirty-eight weeks on the *New York Times* best-seller list and forty-three weeks on the *Publisher's Weekly* list. By 1996 the book had sold 650,000 copies in hardcover, and Simon and Schuster paid $2.64 million for paperback rights and Twentieth Century–Fox $1 million for screen rights.[19] This is quite a feat considering African American authors have rarely made it to the best-seller list until recently. Indeed, the best-seller list reflects the commercial success of a book and increases the likelihood that it will be adapted into a film, which can also increase book sales. The simultaneous appearance of McMillan (the only black author in the twentieth century other than Bill Cosby to have two best sellers),[20] Walker, and Toni Morrison on the *New York Times* best-seller list in 1993 signaled a significant shift in mainstream trends. For the first time, African American women's literature was no longer at the margins. This is especially true for McMillan's novels, which illuminated a heretofore-untapped market of African American readers, much like Perry's work in African American theater and film. Work by and about black women that appeals to black and crossover audiences in literature and film is potentially empowering for black artists and audiences, especially women from diverse backgrounds.

Intersections of Culture and Economics in Womanist Aesthetics

Onscreen narrative and offscreen circumstances of these films elucidates two critical problems. First, the paradoxical, liminal positioning of black women in Hollywood due to white and male dominance is exemplified by the fact that each film was directed by a man. *The Color Purple,* in particular, represents a Hollywood production pattern in which white male directors helm films with predominantly black casts when the reverse happens less often. (Spike Lee lampoons this practice in his film *Bamboozled.*) August Wilson has argued that black directors understand the potential threats to the dissemination of cultural values. Yet even a film such as *Waiting to Exhale,* directed by Forest Whitaker, the African American (and Academy Award–winning) actor in his first outing behind the camera for a theatrical release, suggests that dangers persist due to the prevalence of the master narrative. Lee also demonstrates this in *Bamboozled* by showing how the black writer Delacroix, who is initially engaged in indigenization, begins to collaborate in the same madness he had criticized.

Race and gender alone do not qualify or disqualify artists to write or direct black or women's films as much as sensitivity, awareness, and conscious deviation from the master narrative. White director John Sayles wrote and directed *The Brother from Another Planet* (1984), which concerns The Brother (Joe Morton), a mute alien who is nearly indistinguishable from the Harlem residents he hides amongst while evading the white outer-space bounty hunters (John Sayles and David Strathairn) who attempt to capture and return him into intergalactic slavery. The film is an excellent example of a nuanced exploration of black experience using the commercial genre of sci-fi. The film earned $3 million on a $300,000 budget, thereby proving that culturally nuanced narratives can be profitable regardless of the race of the writer or director. Second, high profile figures such as Oprah Winfrey, often cited as evidence of equal opportunity, and the economic success of films starring black actresses such as Academy Award nominees Whoopi Goldberg, Angela Bassett, Gabourey Sidibe, and Mo'Nique, compound such misperceptions. However, in addition to the liminal position of black women, these texts reveal how literary textual devices might further develop African American cinematic language.

According to poet and artist Thulani Davis, African American women writers of the 1990s use a style that more closely resembles the mainstream than previous generations of writers represented by Morrison and Walker.[21] Instead of writing entire novels in dialect such as Walker's *The Color Purple* or with experimental styles such as Morrison's *Beloved,* novels such as McMillan's *Waiting to Exhale* use traditional linear narratives that feature primarily standard English, incorporating dialect or colloquial language in the dialogue rather than throughout the text. This linear style is more similar in structure to master narratives produced in mainstream, white American literature, theater, and film. Moreover, the context shifted from in-depth social critiques of marriage (*The Color Purple*) and slavery (*Beloved*) to more covert critiques of racism and sexism. Davis determines that the quest for materialism and the "buppie" lifestyle has become the primary concerns of black women writers of the 1990s.

At first glance, Sapphire's *Push* appears to be a departure from the style represented by McMillan's text. However, it merges generational techniques by incorporating experimental styles and dialect with more contemporary concerns and representations of the buppie lifestyle from the perspective of an impoverished black teenager. In this way, Sapphire's and McMillan's novels reflect an evolving consciousness of the concerns of black women in literature. They assume readers' familiarity with earlier texts and choose to focus on the next step of self-actualization, which they recognize is tied to class.[22] The relationship between class and self-actualization is also apparent in *A Raisin in the Sun, A Soldier's Play, Diary of a Mad Black Woman,* and *Bopha!,* albeit in very different ways. This shift to incorporate class in the narratives has had a significant effect in terms of recognizing a broader range of black experience in production, reception, and distribution of African American literature and has in turn affected African American film generally.

While the texts discussed in this chapter are arguably more representative of academically appreciated African American literature, another approach to portraying African American experience in literature has also emerged with paradoxical results. More recently, the publishing industry has benefitted from the mass production of erotic novels written by black authors. "Ghetto lit"— "poorly written, black-oriented titles—novels that depict wall to wall crime, sex, violence and hip hop ghetto-fabulousness"—is a highly lucrative enterprise for large and small publishers.[23] These titles offset the expenses of publishing the more serious literature that tends to be overshadowed in the process. McMillan and African American editor and author Nick Chiles[24] chastised the industry (McMillan cited Simon and Schuster specifically) for the proliferation of ghetto lit. McMillan finds such trends harmful to black consumers, pointing out that diversifying an industry driven by hegemonic racial and gendered ideology matters little if the ideology remains intact.[25] Ironically, McMillan's novels helped pave the way for the publication of these works by mainstream publishers. The explicit sexual details provided in Sapphire's novel also reflect this shift, for which she has been criticized as well. A closer look at the challenges of adaptation illuminates the complexities of her work and the dangers for the future of African American literature and film.

African Americans continue to be marginally positioned in mainstream theater, publishing, and film. As authors, their works are disseminated and controlled by large corporations that selectively identify black audiences based on economic benefits to their corporations and at major costs to black cultures. More specifically, these practices affect cultural transmission through storytelling in its various forms: oral, literary, cinematic, theatrical, musical, and dance, among others. Their selective tastes and patterns of publication define what is deemed an acceptable story both in terms of themes and format. Nevertheless, literature can inform cinematic language in various ways, primarily through cinematic translation of literary devices.

Literary scholar Henry Louis Gates Jr. and psychologist Allyssa McCabe, among others, convincingly argue that African American cultural storytelling methods, particularly oral, are closely tied to literary traditions. Gates explains, "Whereas black writers most certainly revise texts in the Western tradition, they often seek to do so 'authentically,' with a black difference, a compelling sense of difference based on the black vernacular."[26] McCabe's study of African American children's oral storytelling recognizes variations in cultural traditions by highlighting similarities to jazz compositions: beginning (theme), middle (improvisation on the theme), end (return to the theme).[27] "African-Americans children's and adolescents' written narratives," she notes, "frequently contain many stylistic devices . . . [that] might be said to mirror features of African-American novels on best seller lists, novels such as Toni Morrison's *Jazz* (1992)."[28] The interactive relationship between storyteller and audience in jazz music and oral storytelling has been adapted into written works like children's narratives and best-selling novels, thereby revealing potential for adapting similar strategies in cinema.

Cinematic vocabulary that effectively translates concepts such as double consciousness, the African concept of self, or the interconnectedness of time while representing an evolving consciousness of blacks can be translated from literary elements that examine a range of issues from black perspectives. Each film demonstrates how a novel's first-person narration translated through voiceover can effectively convey double consciousness and related internal thoughts of a character that can contradict or support onscreen images. *Waiting to Exhale*'s use of collective voiceover narration in the film also effectively links the four women, further emphasizing themes of sisterhood, family, and community at the core of each of these source texts. Additionally, the manipulation of the fairy-tale formula in each source text represents opportunities to redefine established norms by revising the standard Hollywood narrative structure or characterizations. The visual aesthetic of the text on the page apparent in *The Color Purple* and *Push* also represents opportunities to use the credits, subtitles, title cards, and shots of writing to underscore narrative and character development. Literature that has succeeded in conveying such complex concepts may provide more effective tools than the mainstream works discussed in chapter 1.

As a result, films adapted from novels offer significant insight into these oral and literary storytelling methods and their potential for producing an economically viable cinematic translation. Black theater and literature offer tools for cinematic innovation, especially to counteract racially constructed formulaic conventions. Unfortunately, alterations made during the adaptation process, especially in the case of black women's literature, too often rely on appealing to white audiences for economic purposes rather than intersectional appeal, which could achieve a similar economic outcome. This undermines exploration of the human condition in favor of selling black pathology.

Novels and their cinematic companions from 1980 to the present are significant for two reasons: the unprecedented number of literary cinematic adaptations and the emerging boom of black women writers.[29] In terms of literary production, the 1990s resemble the Harlem Renaissance and Black Power era except for the fact that the bulk of literary luminaries of those decades were male.[30] It is common for filmmakers to take liberties with cinematic adaptations of literary texts, a process in which several elements of the narrative may be lost in adaptation processes. These texts revise philosophies, representations, and narrative underpinnings of previous texts,[31] thereby capitalizing on the inherent intertextuality of black literature and film. The cultural significance of patterns of selected alterations is critical for understanding the success and failure of African American films.

Precious: Don't Throw the Baby Out with the Bathwater

Despite charges of pathology, *Precious* is one of the best recent, broadly distributed examples of an African American novel's potential contribution to African American cinematic language. The film is a collaborative effort of African Americans: Sapphire (author), Geoffrey Fletcher (screenwriter), and Lee Daniels (director). The onscreen narrative and offscreen circumstances that produced it can serve as a model for emulation, with revision, of course.

For better or worse, key decisions and specific actions throughout the adaptation and production of *Precious* contributed to the overall success of the film and the book. While *The Color Purple* and *Waiting to Exhale* were adapted into films within three years of their publication, it took thirteen years to adapt *Push* into *Precious*. Recognizing that filmmaking is a collaborative process, the director's role in this case is of particular import. Lee Daniels approached Sapphire for the film rights, prompting her to see Daniels's films *Monster's Ball* (2001), which he produced, and *Shadowboxer* (2005), which he directed. She later agreed to sell him the film rights under the condition that adaptation would not begin until five years after the book had been published. Sapphire wanted to give the book a life of its own before it was adapted for fear that a poorly adapted film would harm the book.[32] In addition, giving the book time to circulate prior to adaptation served to build an audience, not just for the book but also for a potential film, and allowed the story and subject matter to take priority.

Recognizing that she had essentially signed away creative control of the film to Daniels, Sapphire was surprised when he consulted her throughout the adaptation process. Such an arrangement is not often the case. Walker served as an on-set consultant for Spielberg's *The Color Purple* for which Menno Meyjes, a white male, penned the screenplay. McMillan served as co-screenwriter for Forest Whitaker's *Waiting to Exhale* in partnership with veteran white male screenwriter Ronald Bass. However, McMillan had no power to prevent gratuitous sex scenes from replacing more emotional scenes, such as Robin's interactions with her father who suffers from Alzheimer's. Like Walker, McMillan's presence suggests collaboration but on unequal footing compared to that of Sapphire and Daniels. In all these examples, the effect of black female authors relinquishing creative control to white and/or male directors has been to shift emphasis from more serious issues in the source text to more simplistic gender conflicts in black heterosexual relationships.[33]

Sapphire's and Daniels's actions reflect a willingness to serve the best interest of the work through collaboration and mutual respect. Their attempt to maintain the source text's worldview, which originally drew audiences from various backgrounds, is noteworthy for several reasons. First, both identify as queer, and while both represent liminal identities in Hollywood and in black communities, their collaboration suggests a willingness to recognize the potential hegemonic effects on their interactions. More collaboration like this is needed for the cultural success of black literature and drama adapted into film.

In addition, *Precious* is proof that privileging the story over concerns of crossover appeal or even charges of selling pathology can lead to economic success. The goal is to tell the best possible stories from the broadest range of perspectives consistently and over long periods of time, even though this may require the production of films with unsavory characters and sensitive subjects. Using intertextuality and various other cinematically transferrable literary devices can help. Although the story is the key, the acquisition of capital to tell that story is still a very important factor.

Fundraising for a film such as *Precious* is a particularly daunting task. Independent films are already at a disadvantage and the challenges are only compounded for black independent filmmakers due to the perceived failure of African American films. Thus many black independent filmmakers have begun turning to wealthy African Americans as sources of funding, which have increased in recent decades. For example, Earvin "Magic" Johnson has used his wealth from careers in sports and business to build movie theaters in largely black neighborhoods and invest in ventures such as AspireTV, a cable television network targeted at African American audiences. Another example is a program created by Jeff Friday, head of the American Black Film Festival (ABFF), to train professional athletes to become producers in an effort to fortify production of black film.

In the case of *Precious*, various other elements decreased the likelihood of significant funding and distribution, including a female protagonist (also black); portrayals of incest, domestic violence, HIV, and poverty; and institutional critiques of these realities. To finance *Precious*, Daniels initially approached screenwriter Geoffrey Fletcher, an African American who has wealthy family members. After reviewing Fletcher's work, Daniels recruited Fletcher to adapt the novel, fearing his own personal identification with the story would negatively affect adaptation. Instead of funding the film Fletcher agreed to write the screenplay, and Daniels solicited the film's total estimated budget of $10 to $12 million elsewhere. He received approximately $12 million from Sarah Siegel-Magness and her husband, Gary Magness, a wealthy white couple from Denver. Tom Heller, one of the film's producers, cold-called Sarah in regard to financing another film, *Tennessee* (2008). The couple invested

$5 million in the film, which became another business venture for Sarah, daughter of the founders of Celestial Seasonings (also entrepreneur and founder of So Low, a high-end women's clothing line), and her husband, Gary, the head of a Colorado-based investment firm (his parents founded Tele-Communications, Inc.). Although *Tennessee* flopped, they financed *Precious* and their risky investment paid off.[34] The film grossed $47.5 million domestically.

Daniels's interactions with the Magnesses demonstrate that white financiers do not require full creative control for such a film to succeed, as implied by the Hollywood plantation arrangement Haile Gerima describes in the introduction. Paternalistic attitudes and the historical tradition of ownership and responsibility in the plantation model actually limit potential for economic success. Ice Cube, the rapper/actor/screenwriter/producer who created the *Friday* and *Barbershop* franchises reiterates this point in the conclusion. Allowing filmmakers to focus on the story as opposed to privileging crossover appeal in this case contributed to creating a story that resonated with black audiences, although not without controversy.[35]

After a successful run at the Sundance Film Festival, Daniels eventually gained the support of Perry and Winfrey, two exceptional black media moguls with the power of solid, distinct, yet overlapping female audience bases. Once again, women serve as a formidable force in realizing the potential for black films, subjects, and worldviews. These titans along with distribution from Lionsgate Films (which purchased *Precious* for $5.5 million, beating out the Weinstein Company)[36] catapulted the film to the top of the box office. In general, various elements, like the filmmaker's tenacity and collaboration amongst people of color, are often overshadowed by the influence of whites on the financial success of a black film.

As with most films, key factors contribute to making culturally nuanced and economically successful African American films, which is particularly challenging due to plantation ideology and established precedent. In the case of *Precious,* Daniels's ability to identify quality material and cast, access rights, secure sound investment, recruit a talented and efficient screenwriter, and develop an extraordinary relationship with the author allowed him to successfully complete the project. His relationship with investors was particularly critical. On the set daily, the Magnesses found a way to be present without overshadowing the necessary work between Daniels, Fletcher, Sapphire, and cinematographer Andrew Dunn (who did an excellent job using camera angles and movement, lighting, and other cinematography to aid the storytelling process). This critical mix of ingredients helped to maintain the centrality of the black female protagonist and, arguably, of black audiences, repositioning crossover audiences as secondary or invisible but without undermining the film's ability to achieve economic success.

Tying the offscreen histories of the producers to the onscreen narrative proved to be a powerful marketing strategy, but with conflicting results. Daniels publicly shared his personal experience of domestic abuse at the hands of his father, which may have contributed to the film's sensitive portrayal of the issue. Likewise, producers Winfrey and Perry have also been public about their personal experiences with sexual abuse, which may have contributed to their promoting the film. Actor and comedian Mo'Nique, who plays Precious's mother in the film, also revealed on *Oprah* that she drew inspiration for her monstrous character from her experience of sexual abuse at the hands of her brother. This shared history of abuse and the common denominator of African ancestry led some critics to express concern that cultural outsiders might consider the film and offscreen abuse narratives as evidence of pathology specific to African Americans.[37] Understandably, this danger discourages many black performers and audiences from supporting or participating in films or plays dealing with such controversial subject matter.

In his adaptation, Daniels confronts the challenge of exposing dirty laundry. Daniels has asserted that he made the film for the author and his family, who he knew would recognize and appreciate the language and experiences of the protagonist, however unlikely the character may be as a leading lady in Hollywood. Daniels finds a happy medium between portrayals of sexuality, abuse, and violence depicted in *The Color Purple* and the gratuitous sex scenes and multiple altercations between black men and women in *Waiting to Exhale.* He capitalizes on film's ability to transport the viewer into and out of pornographic moments by providing snapshots of the violence Precious experiences. The visual language used to articulate Precious's experience tries to avoid voyeurism and mostly succeeds. When she escapes through her fantasies, the viewer goes with her rather than being subjected to witnessing the graphic rape while the character zones out. Offering viewers an alternative to voyeurism of the sexual violence by providing instead an opportunity to experience Precious's coping mechanism allows for a more intimate relationship with Precious and her psychological process.

Whatever its flaws, *Precious* is not solely responsible for the perception that black people and their culture are pathological. Plantation ideology limits consistent and broad representation of the lived experiences of people of color. It intensifies audience impressions of those themes examined in cinematic adaptations of black women's literature that have been broadly distributed. While educational pursuits, community concerns, spiritual beliefs, and more complex human interactions receive less treatment in films with predominantly black casts, films like *Precious* are more likely to reinforce existing perceptions of black pathology. The solution to this conundrum is not fewer films about incest and the abuse of black women. On the contrary, ignoring complex black experiences and the darker side of humanity can be just as limiting for black artists and audiences.[38] More varied types of films covering a broad range of issues, genres, and subject matter require consistent and frequent treatment as well as broad distribution to counteract plantation ideology.

Focusing on the imperfections of humanity instead of crossover appeal yields promising results when well executed and provided with sufficient distribution. Unlike many of the black filmmakers discussed in this book, Daniels did not attend film school.[39] Yet his informal study of the medium has enabled him to articulate his lived experiences. This is apparent in *Shadowboxer*, which is autobiographical,[40] but it is even more cleverly articulated through cinematic devices in *Precious*. For example, the opening credits use Precious's handwriting with translations in parentheses just beneath. First-person narration through voiceover preserves Sapphire's human-interest story, which she admits initially was not included in early drafts of the novel as she focused on her political agenda of exposing racism, sexism, and classism.

Daniels maintains this focus on the black female protagonist and her humanity through cinematography, mise-en-scène, and editing, especially in the rape and abuse scenes. They demonstrate how an intelligent child like Precious finds escape from mental, physical, sexual, and emotional abuse through fantasy, which is typified by associations with Hollywood glamour (e.g., her fantasy boyfriend, Tom Cruise). Scenes featuring Precious and her mother, Mary, tend to be set in their dark apartment, filmed with low-key lighting and chiaroscuro. This lighting technique is often used as shorthand in horror films to indicate danger. Yet it is also indicative of the gloom and hopelessness of Precious's reality. This visually contrasts with her fantasy world, which is filmed

Precious (2009): Mary (Mo'Nique) and Precious (Gabourey Sidibe) in dark apartment

with saturated colors and diffusion filters to create the effect of a romantic, dreamlike atmosphere. These contrasting techniques along with frequent close-ups and extreme close-ups on Precious make her a compelling, unconventional point of entry into the film. It is a calculated attempt to illuminate her internal perception of her experiences in these environments.

Possible implementation strategies for black literary adaptations and original films are creatively represented in *Precious,* demonstrating Daniels's ability to capitalize on translating literary devices into cinematic language. For example, multiple scenes strategically convey the connections between the abuse and Precious's social positioning. Specifically, when Precious takes Ms. Rain's reading exam, several images and sounds signal the connection. In addition to close-ups on Precious as she attempts to take the test (at which time pencil marks become audible and images slow to demonstrate her frustration), the scene is followed by Ms. Rain holding a book, initially sharing the frame with Precious. This transitions into extreme close-ups of Ms. Rain's mouth sounding out words, Precious's eye (reminiscent of Toni Morrison's novel *The Bluest Eye,* which also concerns issues of race, color, class, and incest), a medium-close-up of Mary (Mo'Nique), an extreme close-up of Precious's father's arm tattoo as he abuses her, and a pot of food boiling on the stove, along with sounds of Mary verbally abusing Precious as she is being sexually abused by her father. These images increase in speed and intensity as Precious tries to verbalize words on the page, ending in a close-up of Precious. This further encourages audience identification with her pain. *The Bluest Eye* also connects issues of systematic racial oppression to literacy by identifying the Dick and Jane readers as racially

Precious (2009): Precious's fantasy

motivated socializing mechanisms. Through specificity of Precious's circumstances and strategic use of the medium, the influence of her past on her present and undeniable limitations it will have on her future effectively convey
this particular representation of black experience and the effects of hegemonic
power structures.

The approach is very similar to playwright Lydia Diamond's stage adaptation of *Toni Morrison's The Bluest Eye*.[41] Originally published in 1970, the novel
takes place in Ohio in the late 1930s and early 1940s. It focuses on a dark-skinned
black girl named Pecola Breedlove, who is sexually abused and impregnated by
her father, Cholly. Morrison eloquently addresses the topic of incest by offering
significant exploration of the abuse Cholly experiences at the hands of white
men. They force him at gunpoint to commit sex acts on a black girl against
her will following the burial of his aunt/mother figure. Diamond recognized the
need to preserve the spirit of Morrison's approach but not necessarily fidelity
to the novel in regard to conveying the traumatic effect of these experiences
on the character. As such, she included a note preceding the published play
expressing the importance of sparing the audience "graphic, realistic representations of sexual violence."[42] Similar stylized staging of both scenes creates a
parallel that implies a direct connection between Cholly's abuse at the hands of
the white men and his eventual rape of Pecola.

Creating works with a focus on black audiences displaces and discourages white male perspectives that tend to distort African American experiences. Diamond, for example, revealed that she wrote the play for her son.[43]
The power of her imagined audience, as opposed to the typical, predominantly
white audience at the Steppenwolf Theatre Company in Chicago (which commissioned the adaptation and where it premiered in 2005) grounds the narrative and visual storytelling. Likewise, in the DVD commentary of *Precious*,
Daniels described a similar process in which he targeted the author, family
members, and himself as the film's audience.[44] These models speak to the
inherent intertextuality of African American film in conversation with literature and theater.

From an economic perspective, filmic representations of illicit sex and
egregious abuse can invite censorship through ratings restrictions. Such ratings
can destroy a film's chances for distribution and reduce the number of ticket
sales by limiting access to younger audiences. The objective of black filmmakers and allies is not to avoid telling these stories but to be critical and creative
in producing them, as Kasi Lemmons accomplishes with her original film and
directorial debut *Eve's Bayou* (1997). Set in 1962, the film concerns the Batistes,
a large black family in Louisiana and Eve's (Jurnee Smollett-Bell) growing disil-
lusionment with her father, Dr. Louis Batiste (Samuel L. Jackson, also the film's
producer). When Eve discovers her father committing infidelity with a local

woman, and her elder sister, Cisely (Meagan Good), accuses him of attempted rape, Eve seeks the assistance of a local witch to cast a voodoo spell that will kill him. In the process, Eve also discovers her inherited gift of second sight. Her visions are unable to prevent her father's murder when she learns Cisely's accusations may not be true or to shed light on the truth after his death. As yet another film with a predominantly black cast that happens to feature themes of incest, it is an exceptional example of the ways such issues have been represented in previous and subsequent works. Rather than focusing on incest as the central theme, the film concerns Eve's discovery of her father's tragic flaw and the unraveling of her respected family, which has little to do with their race or class. With its carefully cultivated incorporation of black culture and class in Louisiana, the film earned $14.8 million from a $5.5 million budget. Works by Lemmons, Diamond, and Daniels represent possible models, although Daniels does not acknowledge any familiarity with these works or others that can be consulted to avoid pitfalls associated with related themes. Accessibility is a key factor in the economic success of a film.

In these works, complex issues such as colorism are also apparent on- and offscreen. Colorism is a major theme in *A Soldier's Play, The Bluest Eye, Push,* and their cinematic or theatrical counterparts. Even when it is not an overt element of the narrative, the ideology gets subliminally telegraphed into casting, commentary, and visual representations. For instance, in *Precious,* Daniels cleverly uses filmic techniques to show how the abuse distorts Precious's self-image. Precious is played in the film by actress Gabourey Sidibe, a dark-skinned African American woman. In the film, Precious sees a thin white girl with blond hair when she looks at herself in the mirror. In a later scene that takes place in the waiting room for the incest-survivor meeting, Precious narrates that she has begun to recognize her own beauty after admitting to Ms. Rain that she wishes for lighter skin and a thin physique. In other words, she wants to look like Paula Patton, the actress who plays Ms. Rain in the film.

Although the narrative challenges colorism in the dialogue, it is unwittingly contradicted throughout the film and commentary surrounding it. Unconsciously, the message of the appeal of this image is reinforced by all of Precious's caretakers and mentors: they are all light-skinned blacks or white, and stand in stark contrast to Sidibe's dark skin. Daniels's choice to cast Patton as Ms. Rain, for instance, is a good example of this problem. In the novel, Ms. Rain is described as dark-skinned with dreadlocks, very different from the fair-skinned, thin Patton whom Daniels admits to casting in order to "breathe beauty" into a not-so-beautiful world. He also admits to a bias in favor of lighter-skinned people due to his upbringing. However, he does not publicly make the connection to his casting choices in the film.[45] Plantation ideology is insidious and holds a powerful sway in various ways.

Nonetheless, Daniels and his collaborators encourage audience identification with Precious through numerous close-ups, especially during painful
moments. As the titular figure, she is the center of the narrative and everyone
else is positioned in relation to her. Yet her marginal social status is reflected in
her interactions with others and her reactions to these interactions (expressed
through close-ups and narration), making audiences privy to her experience.
Precious demonstrates that a black character *can* be the point of entry of a film
that appeals to an audience beyond the indie circuit. With such a positive outcome, it might appear that, as Oprah predicted, an unknown, unconvention-
ally beautiful, dark-skinned, black actress making her acting debut would have
a bright future in Hollywood playing a range of lead and supporting roles. As
chapter 5 argues, however, this is highly unlikely due to plantation politics
embedded within industry practices.

Prominent black media moguls gave *Precious* the extra push it needed for
a broad distribution, making it possible to earn $47 million in 129 days. On the
other hand, Halle Berry's *Frankie & Alice* (2010), an examination of a black woman
with multiple personality disorder trying to reconcile her identity with one of her
white racist personalities, has not been considered economically viable enough
to broadly distribute in theaters. It deals with a brand of black pathology that
implicates white racism. The issue of selling black pathology in Hollywood is anything but simple. Still, *Precious* would have been an anomaly had it not succeeded,
given the success of its predecessors. But the film is not indicative of a shift in
mainstream Hollywood about casting and the potency of black subject matter and
worldviews, as Oprah predicted it would be. In this case, black pathology indeed
sells. In fact, the data on original films and cinematic adaptations featuring African Americans in the last three decades suggest that the major film companies
are more likely to broadly distribute films that make a spectacle of pathological behaviors and attitudes in black families and communities than films that
explore a range of black experiences and perspectives.

The Color Purple: Distinguishing Exploration from Exploitation

Waiting to Exhale, Precious, and *for colored girls* have all been cited as evidence
of Hollywood's tendency to celebrate the narrative of the abused black female,
especially when black men are the abusers. According to Spike Lee, "The quick-
est way for a black playwright, novelist or poet to get published has been to
say that black men are shit. If you say that, then you are definitely going to get
media, your book published, your play done—Ntozake Shange, Alice Walker."[46]
Lee also spoke out against *Waiting to Exhale* on similar grounds and decried all of
Tyler Perry's films as buffoonery. Nevertheless, broad distribution of these films
and their source material signals the economic viability of the subject matter.

The similar responses to *Precious* and *The Color Purple,* released decades apart, indicate ongoing divisions between black audiences in regards to black representation. Reporter Felicia R. Lee's *New York Times* article includes commentary by various cultural critics familiar with both works and the scarcity of a consistent, broad range of black representation in mainstream media. In response to *Precious,* film and music critic Armond White cautions, "Black pathology sells. It's an over-the-top political fantasy that works only because it demeans blacks, women, and poor people." In response to White, Latoya Peterson, editor of *Racialicious.com,* notes, "His review buys into the narrative that there can only be one acceptable presentation of black life. He's flattening the black experience, and in that way, he denies our humanity."[47] As Mark Anthony Neal, a professor of black popular culture, explains, the conflicting responses to *Precious* represented by White and Peterson's commentary "is *The Color Purple* all over again." The larger problem, however, stems from both the fact that black representation in broadly distributed films consistently lacks diversity and that the selective focus on black representation tends to be pathological. Conflating the two films is less productive than acknowledging the success and failures of both if we are to fully realize the potential of black films, subjects, and worldviews.

Spielberg's *The Color Purple* does not capitalize on the medium in the same way as Daniels's *Precious,* although significant challenges for filmmaking that cross racial and gender lines are apparent in both. As authors Wayne J. McMullen and Martha Solomon argue, Spielberg's adaptation selectively highlights certain elements like sexism and deflects audiences' attention away from other issues like racism. The limitations may be a matter of Spielberg being a man who "filters everything through movies," which is still problematic considering the historical treatment of black people and subject matter in movies.[48]

While Walker's novel exposes plantation ideology, Spielberg's film effectively contains it. His tendency to filter everything through movies was not lost on *Newsweek* reviewer David Ansen: "Early on, I had the disorienting sensation that I was watching the first Disney movie about incest."[49] This response suggests that the film contains the very elements of juvenile escapism that characterize Spielberg's preceding films, an attempt to avoid in-depth exploration of the issues like the role of illiteracy in maintaining oppression. Spielberg misses an opportunity to cinematically explore one of the most significant aspects of the novel, which is Celie's consistently evolving vocabulary, spelling, and conceptualization over the course of the story, a reflection of her emancipated consciousness. Instead of incorporating this in the film, Spielberg includes scenes of her learning to read Charles Dickens's *Oliver Twist,* first with Nettie and later by herself. Spielberg's perception of Walker's book as being "Dickensian"[50] is indicative of the ways in which parallels and associations to mainstream white works can overshadow the potential of black worldviews.

Spielberg's Dickens association overlooks the crucial role of race in an obvious attempt to insert crossover appeal. Displaying Celie's developing literacy when she reads about a little white boy's experience of systemic oppression replaces her act of writing herself into existence. In the novel, Celie's letters describe and analyze her circumstances as a poor, uneducated black woman in the South as well as the experiences of people in her community. The fact that there is no mention of *Oliver Twist* in the novel, yet a pivotal moment in the film depicting Celie's transition into adulthood features her reading *Oliver Twist*, is disturbing. This may be why Walker described the inclusion as "so cutesy and tired as to be alienating."[51] According to Spielberg, the book had already crossed over with a predominantly white and female audience, so the *Oliver* inclusion was primarily an attempt to appeal to a white male audience.[52]

The Color Purple also exemplifies how black culture is eroded even in films and plays with predominantly black casts through sound patterns. Music is a critical element for black representation and film due to its cultural prominence. In spite of African American musician and composer Quincy Jones's participation, the film's music falls short of its potential. As Ed Guerrero observes, while blues and gospel are prominently featured, the extradiegetic sound track features "the same tired, Eurocentric movie music heard in most Hollywood products, functioning on a commentative level, jerking tears from spectators-consumers, cuing them as to when to laugh, whom to hate, and with whom to sympathize."[53] Selectively infusing elements of black culture into traditional Hollywood narrative infrastructure that requires Eurocentric extradiegetic music to guide spectators of black narratives has major implications. It reinforces the idea that the world beyond the narrative is a white world in which black narrative is leasing space. Unquestionably taking cues from Hollywood in terms of musicality, as in the case of *A Soldier's Story*, is dangerous because it inadvertently reinforces plantation ideology.

The musical stage adaptation of *The Color Purple* provides another opportunity to recenter the cultural worldview through relevant styles of black music in live performance. The stage musical adaptation was produced with a comparatively generous $11 million budget, in part due to the success of the novel and its subsequent cinematic companion, even though powerbrokers on Broadway had previously snubbed the possibility of adapting the story into a musical. In December 2006, a year after its opening, it had already recouped its production expenses, sold $7 million for a satellite production in Chicago, sold $5 million in souvenirs, and attracted more diverse audiences than traditional Broadway plays, which tend to attract middle-aged white women.[54] The play's composer/lyricists team consisted of African Americans Brenda Russell and Stephen Bray and white American Allee Willis, experienced writers and producers of black popular music. The musical attracted an unprecedented, predominantly black audience on Broadway, yet again demonstrating the power of black audiences, black subject matter, and the potential of combined efforts in theatrical and cinematic production. The stage play's success in the 2000s also revived black-cast plays on Broadway in the same way the film renewed Hollywood studio executives' interest in African American films in the 1980s.

Varying responses to the work across media confirm that black audiences are as diverse as any other group of human beings. Celie is a viable point of entry into the novel, but many black males also reported a limited ability to empathetically identify.[55] Even in this case, Walker's cultural literacy could not generate a uniform response to her novel. However, it provided much-needed context and nuance missing in the film. For instance, several male characters, including Pa, Mister, and Harpo, engage in violent behaviors, but Walker shows their transformation. This is not adequately portrayed in the film. Spielberg ultimately fails to show how these characters are also victims of racial oppression and gender norms. Spielberg's film aligns with narrative elements that focus on Celie's literal victimization without considering the literal and metaphorical transformation of Celie and the other characters. This results in a film based on Spielberg's aligning those elements of the novel that most closely resemble and reinforce the master narrative, a common Hollywood practice.

Celie's most obvious oppression is at the hands of other blacks in her family and in her community, namely Pa and Mister. This is because most of her experiences take place in the home, the accepted space for women during this period. In the novel, Celie writes about encounters with racist whites that virtually disappear in the film adaptation. She writes about encounters with a store clerk in town, the white men who hunt with Pa, and the white mayor and prison guards who beat and imprison Sofia for defending herself against the white mayor's assault. The interracial, incestuous rape that Celie writes about in the novel but is completely omitted in the film concerns Mary Agnes, Harpo's girlfriend who goes by the name of Squeak. Squeak's white uncle rapes her even though he knows she is his biracial niece. Also in the novel, when Celie confides in Shug that she conceived two children with Pa as a result of rape, Shug responds that she thought only white people did those things.[56] The film omits these elements to avoid offending crossover audiences, but as a result they also severely minimize the perspectives and experiences of black people. The screenplay and film align with Celie's most obvious oppression, embellishing dysfunctional black male behavior. As a result, the film focuses on Celie's victimization in the private sphere rather than recognizing how racism in the public sphere contributes to the oppression she experiences at home.

Demonization of black men by black women became a significant feature of African American films, especially after the success of *The Color Purple*. This not only exemplifies the inherent intertextuality of black film but also reveals the challenges of adapting black women's literature into a marketable studio-film. Although the novel explores the power of sisterhood, this theme is mostly lost in adaptation, reflecting the cultural politics of crossover appeal. The story chronicles Celie's journey from adolescence to middle age and all of the challenges she faces being a defenseless black woman in a black community in the racist American South. Yet the film depoliticizes Walker's nuanced intercultura-tion of feminism and Black Liberation through womanist philosophy. Specifi-cally, the film redirects references to white racism to focus exclusively on the abuse that black women experience at the hands of black men. According to Jacqueline Bobo, professor of film and black feminist cultural theory, the debate over the novel affected public reception of the film, particularly with African Americans who were divided along gender and class lines due to language and subject matter.[57] Historically, minority women have faced cultural and commu-nity pressure to keep the shame of abuse quiet, at times blaming the victim. Such dysfunctional behaviors become normalized through silence.

Sexism and domestic abuse appear to be internal community problems, but they are also closely tied to racism, which Walker deconstructs in her novel. The controversy surrounding the novel and its popularity stems from a last-ing tension in some black communities concerned with external perceptions. However, when the focus on domestic abuse in the film appeared to shift to sisterhood in the musical, representing the nostalgia of youth and innocence, vocal protests against the work diminished. In stark contrast to the protests elicited by the novel and film, the musical attracted male and female audiences that were at least 50 percent black (at times over 80 percent).[58] Jamie Walker's review suggests black male audiences of the musical resolved to acknowledge the taboo subjects they protested against in the 1980s, thereby enabling them to appreciate the story.[59] The unwavering support of black and crossover audi-ences who attended the record-breaking musical on Broadway demonstrates how adaptation can be a tool for expanding audiences, even for those who felt previously alienated.

While childhood, sisterhood, and innocence are embellished in the process of adaptation to the stage, a close analysis of the recurring image of a child's hand-clapping game in the film demonstrates how these themes can inadver-tently demonize black men further. The patty-cake marker appears five times throughout the film. Viewers first see it in the tranquil opening before Celie's youthful pregnancy becomes apparent. Surrounded by purple flowers in an expansive field, Celie and her sister play patty-cake in profile, the embodiment of youthful innocence. The patty-cake motif recurs following their separation, first by Pa and later by Mister, which disrupts their happiness and threatens their well-being. In the scene in which Mister violently separates Celie and

The Color Purple (1985): The patty-cake motif with Celie (Desreta Jackson) and Nettie (Akosua Busia)

Nettie, the girls communicate their heartbreak by miming the patty-cake game while vowing to never part from one another.[60] This rigorously choreographed scene is significantly memorable for audiences, as it is much more brutal than the same scene in the novel. In the book, when Mister tells Celie that Nettie has to leave, Celie reports this to Nettie, who is happy to go but sad to leave her sister. Mister is absent when Nettie leaves the house, promising Celie that she will write.[61] In the film, Mister beats them and literally tears them apart from their embrace, throwing rocks at Nettie as though she is a stray dog trespassing on his property; the girls miming patty-cake from a distance follows. Celie and Nettie's brutal separation reflects popular perceptions of black men that suggest they are not family-oriented and abuse their families by neglect, battering, and abandonment. This is not the foundation of Walker's depiction in the novel, but the film's popularity has diminished this awareness. Increasing the drama in this way creates an imbalance between Walker's initial exploration of the intersections of racism and sexism as oppressive yet surmountable through self-love and sisterhood.

This is one of the most extreme examples of how the film severely distorts the novel's womanist philosophy. In fact, the patty-cake motif proved such a powerful image that it was used in promotional material for the musical. Borrowing from the film's patty-cake motif emphasizing the girls' youth and sisterhood, the poster reminds audiences of the film. Due to the use of the patty-cake motif during one of the film's most violent and heart-wrenching moments, the poster potentially directs the audience's focus to the violent characterizations of Mister from the film in spite of revisions in the musical. The musical and film treat

The Color Purple (2004): Broadway musical poster

Nettie's departure similarly, but Mister's evolution and redemption are more clearly established through his interactions with other characters in the play. By the end of the musical, Mister attempts to assist Sofia's sick child and helps reunite Celie with her adult children and Nettie. In stark contrast with the isolation he experiences at the end of the film, Mister joins the family at the reunion.

In comparison to the film, the play spends more time devoted to developing the men's struggle against social constructions of masculinity and its influence on their mistreatment of the women, illustrating a conscious recognition of its absence in the film. A story can increase in depth when adapted across media. Just as Lorraine Hansberry used the cinematic adaptation to correct "dramaturgical incompletions" in *A Raisin in the Sun, The Color Purple*'s creative stage team rectified some of the shortcomings in the film. The removal of the *Oliver Twist* reference, a more nuanced characterization of Mister, and the use of black female focus groups to guide adaptation and marketing of the musical exemplify an attempt to recenter black audiences.[62] Much like the film, the musical also downplays Celie and Shug's lesbian relationship in comparison to the novel. Nevertheless, the multiple versions of *The Color Purple* reveal the potential for capitalizing on the benefits of literature, film, and theater.

Waiting for Womanism

Waiting to Exhale exemplifies many of the same challenges as the other films discussed in this chapter. The film offers several important examples of how crossover appeal limits narrative potential. McMillan's novel embodies the womanist-aesthetic by adhering to Walker's three core womanist values of audaciousness, woman-centeredness, and community, as each female character contributes to the storytelling process. Each woman faces issues including but not limited to caring for an elderly parent or children and creating/maintaining positive romantic relationships. Unfortunately, each woman's connections to her extended family are severely minimized or eliminated in the film, much like the characters in *Set It Off*, a 1996 action film about four African American women who rob banks (see chapter 6). *Waiting to Exhale* instead focuses on elements that all but guarantee crossover appeal: sex, altercations between black men and women, sisterhood among black women, comic snapshots of gay/bisexual characters, and interracial interactions (which incidentally provide an opportunity to cast white actors).

Another example of how crossover appeal erodes black cultural perspectives is when James (Wesley Snipes), Bernadine's love interest, expresses his undying love and dedication for his white wife instead of pursuing a relationship with Bernadine. In the book, James and Bernadine first meet in a bar at a hotel where she is staying for the night. After sharing the most private details of their lives, they spend the night together without becoming intimate. Upon his wife's death from a terminal illness, James reunites with Bernadine and they pursue a relationship. bell hooks identifies this alteration as a ploy to reach the masses of white women consumers who might not have been interested in the film if it had really been about black women.[63] This represents a familiar pattern of narrative revisions to attract white audiences in hopes of increasing revenue potential.

The above example is just one instance of how the film narrative and editing reinforces stereotypical images of black women, which are challenged in the novel and performances in the film. In general, the film ignores some of the more complicated social issues. For example, McMillan revealed that what she thought was a brilliant scene between Robin and her father who has Alzheimer's "got thrown out because it was a minute and a half too long. But then they'll put in gratuitous sex scenes which get a laugh—and that's somehow more important."[64] By discarding Robin's loving relationship with her father and amplifying the many altercations the women have with their significant others, the film appears to be an African American woman's male-bashing film. This is fascinating considering African American men had major roles in producing the film: Forest Whitaker was the director and Kenneth "Babyface" Edmonds was the music director. Ronald Bass (who is white) served as co-screenwriter with the author.

The narrative is structured around the male voice of a radio DJ, carrying out Whitaker's directorial vision of music driving the narrative. The music, which is very seductive and primarily features black female vocalists, diverts attention away from some of the novel's central issues. The prominence of black females in every frame of the film as well as in the diegetic and nondiegetic sound creates the perception that this is a film about black women told from black women's perspectives (e.g., shared voiceover narration of main female characters). Yet the black male radio DJ's presence serves as a visual and aural reminder that black men, through the direction and music, control the perspective that is attributed to black women in this film.

The systematic racial oppression addressed in the novel is footnoted in the film's narrative, exemplifying reliance on stereotypes as opposed to human experience in producing "appealing" African American films, which often refer to films about middle- or upper-middle-class blacks. McMillan uses comic relief to address the same major concerns of black communities in the novel that the film diminishes. In the novel, Savannah's brother Pookey, recently released from prison, finds it necessary to manipulate his job application to say that he attended Penn State rather than the state penitentiary in order to obtain employment and support himself even though he lives with their mother. Although the joke does not directly address the problem of incarceration of African American men and the resultant limitations imposed upon their opportunities, it alludes to the ways these challenges affect their relationships with the women in their lives. Savannah does not speak as highly of Pookey as she does of Samuel, her brother in the military. It is clear that she cares for her family, even though she is frustrated with her role as the sole supporter of her mother whose welfare checks offer very little assistance. Instead, the film reduces references to black men and incarceration to a complaint expressed by the four drunken women who blame gay black men and black convicts for their inability to obtain successful romantic relationships. Such reduction contributes to superficial characterizations of the women as well as demonization of black men.

The problem with waiting for womanism is that the existing framework is designed to reject or absorb any deviations from established precedent. Woman-centeredness and community can be the focal point of lucrative films, but heavy reliance on elements that guarantee crossover appeal (stereotypes of black women and men, avoiding complicated social issues such as systemic racial oppression) reinforces damaging profiling of black people. In the nineties, without a notable director, studio financing, and the Oprah Effect, the likelihood that *Waiting to Exhale* would reach the broad audience that enabled its profitable box office would not have been possible. Industry structure and practices continue to negatively affect the potential of womanist aesthetics in form, content, and economic outcome. Continuing to wait for womanism is risky and needless, especially now that new technologies and social media are helping filmmakers to circumvent Hollywood's exclusionary practices.

Selling Black Film: The Business of Pathology

In each of the projects discussed in this chapter, black women are present, visible, and employed to articulate the visions of males at the helm of the projects. The visibility of black women and black people in general behind the camera as well as onscreen ultimately gives a false impression of their power and influence. In many ways, they are limited due to their location within society's hegemonic power structure and the industry practices that mirror it. Unlike Walker and McMillan, Sapphire seems to have had a greater influence on the adaptation of her story into film, but this isn't typical. Still, for this reason, *Precious* is a significant model for emulation in regard to the offscreen circumstances that helped produce it.

In addition to their creative and technical elements, each film exhibits potential for overcoming the limitations of the most common distribution models. As noted in the introduction, there are a variety of distribution agreements in Hollywood, including the Production/Finance/Distribution (PFD) Agreement, Negative Pick-Up, Pre-Sale, Rent-a-System, and Output Agreement. Not all these distribution deals are directly relevant to our present discussion. However, each film's outcome shows just how critical distribution is to the development of African American film.

Waiting to Exhale represents one of the most traditional business models. In theory, as the production and distribution company, Twentieth Century–Fox agreed to contribute money and fund unforeseen losses in exchange for obtaining creative and financial control over the project through what appears to be a PFD agreement.[65] As the direct financers of the film, the studio holds primary ownership while everyone else is basically an employee on the project, even McMillan. Her positioning mirrors Oprah's when she worked as an employee on her show (but Oprah later gained power through ownership, whereas McMillan did not have that opportunity within this arrangement). The studio had an obvious vested interest in the film—they released it on over 1,000 screens in its opening weekend and let it run over 100 days in theaters. Granting studios full ownership through PFD agreements can be lucrative, but these agreements mean giving up power and ownership. Negative Pick-Up agreements, which are similar to PFDs in some ways, offer an alternative arrangement. As a result of indirect financing, the studio does not have the same extensive creative controls as they would under a PFD.[66] This is one way of accessing studio resources yet maintaining a sense of autonomy otherwise lacking in the process.

The limitations McMillan experienced on *Waiting to Exhale* reflect the necessity for identifying other models like those associated with *The Color Purple* and *Precious.* In the case of *The Color Purple,* Amblin Entertainment, the Guber-Peters Company, and Warner Bros. jointly produced the film, with Warner Bros. serving as distributor. Warner Bros. likely financed the film by paying for distribution rights. Again, the studio is affiliated in the production of the film but this case more closely resembles the PFD agreement. Twentieth Century–Fox hired itself as the producer of *Waiting to Exhale.* The primary difference between the two is the presence of an independent film production company outside of the studio arm. Regardless, "under these agreements, the production company is little more than a dependent agent of the studio and is subject to the complete control of the studio on all aspects of production."[67] Like *Waiting to Exhale,* distribution of *The Color Purple* reflects the studio's vested interest in the film's success. Both were broadly distributed for long periods of time (see table 2 below). The primary difference here is that *The Color Purple* opened on only 192 screens before gradually increasing to 1,109, whereas *Waiting to Exhale* opened on 1,253 screens and within two weeks was playing in 1,402 theaters. *The Color Purple* and *A Soldier's Story*'s platform distribution enabled both to find their respective audiences as they played in theaters. Limited distribution with the intent to broaden over time effectively serves the needs to recoup expenses. This limited distribution strategy was also employed with *Precious,* which was distributed by Lionsgate rather than one of the five majors. Studios are willing to engage in this practice, but they tend to do it more frequently with narratives that can be manipulated to serve plantation ideology even when their source texts are more critical of hegemony.

Precious is an inspiring case in regards to distribution. The film did not have studio backing in the production process, which provided Daniels more creative and financial control. He produced the film independently, then sold it to Lionsgate for $5.5 million. As with Oprah taking ownership of her show, which eventually led to a media empire, the strategies that Daniels and his allies used behind the scenes set up a model for the possibilities of strategic empowerment of black film production and its distribution. A disagreement over claims to licensing (the Weinstein Company claimed to have "exclusive licensing and distribution rights to *Push*" based on an oral agreement;[68] their claims were dismissed in court) sheds some light on the distribution agreement the producers reached with Lionsgate. A license refers to "any limited grant of rights to a film, with the owner retaining other rights to the film. . . . [A] license encompasses a broad array of grants of rights, ranging all the way from a one-day pay-per-view television license to a grant of all worldwide rights for a term of twenty-five years."[69] In this case, the "exclusive rights" for *Push* that the Weinstein Company claimed likely refers to the latter. Distribution rights can be broken down into five basic subcategories: terms, territory, language, media, and exclusivity.[70] The power of the audience indicated by response to *Precious* at film festivals, by reviews, and by the endorsement of Perry and Winfrey repositioned Daniels for strategic negotiating. This enabled him to sell rights upon completion, as Perry initially did, in a way that can lead to Output Agreements, or rather "a license to acquire particular rights to a specified number of films produced in the future by a production company."[71] Like Perry, Daniels found a critical site for economic development that recognizes the power of distribution and the role of audiences in articulating the demand that will encourage broad and long-term distribution. Social media and new technology can further capitalize on the symbiotic relationship between audiences and filmmakers. Challenging hegemony in the narrative matters little if the strategy is not also employed in distribution negotiations. The details of *Precious*'s distribution, which are cursorily referenced here, are less significant to our conversation than what the apparent distribution agreement implies about the economic viability of black film subjects and worldviews as well as the intrinsic and economic value of black audiences.

Ultimately, black cultural production in film (and television) has been an asset that Hollywood turns to when in an economic bind. Black films and audiences helped Hollywood recover from the economic crisis in the film industry in the 1970s.[72] The success of *A Soldier's Story* and *The Color Purple* reminded Hollywood of the powerful potential of black audiences. Black television shows such as *In Living Color* and *Martin* helped establish Fox as a major network in the 1990s.[73] Perry substantially increased Lionsgate's profitability in the 2000s. The Weinstein Company fought hard for *Precious* because of its precarious economic standing at the time.[74] The negotiations of this deal are a powerful example of preparation meeting opportunity.

Each of these films exceeded Hollywood studio expectations, which can be determined based on funding. *The Color Purple* and *Waiting to Exhale* were studio films with budgets between $15 and $16 million. The standard budget for Hollywood films at the time was considerably higher ($20 to $40 million from the 1980s to 2000).[75] *The Color Purple* earned $95 million at the box office and *Waiting to Exhale* $67 million, further evidence that African American films generally outperform other films in terms of the return on investment.[76] The consistent practice of allotting African American films lower budgets is evidence of prejudiced values and expectations. The economic success of African American films like those discussed here clearly signals that such films are worthy investments, especially because of the low-risk associated with the small budget. In spite of the studios devaluing blacks through low budgets, blacks and their allies have learned how to use such limitations to gain entry and profit from the very system that historically disenfranchises blacks. This practice of resilience also evolves from the plantation.

The films discussed in this chapter represent economic successes. For every success, in spite of small budgets and limited distribution, there are films that don't make it. Films that do not have a white point of entry, crossover appeal, or an Africanist presence, or do not reinforce plantation ideology, are censored by limited distribution, as in the case of *Bopha!, Sankofa, Teza* (2008), and *Frankie & Alice*. While such films may eventually become available on DVD and VOD, they are denied major theatrical release and the cachet it provides. Their audience appeal tends not to be documented or acknowledged in the same way as films such as *Waiting to Exhale, The Color Purple,* and *Precious,* all of which proved their crossover appeal through festival awards, Academy Awards, box office earnings, and affiliation with media moguls.

As one of the only narratives in this study to be adapted to the screen and then to the stage, *The Color Purple* exemplifies the potential of gradual distribution. Both the play and film opened at a limited number of selected theaters, were allowed to find their audience, and were then given selectively wider distribution.[77] The film was released, re-released, and appeared on cable and network channels with broad distribution.[78] Although many studio films with white casts face restrictions,[79] race ideology plays a significant role in predetermining marketing and distribution. *The Color Purple's* platform distribution and marketing allowed it the opportunity to build an audience over time (a similar pattern can be found in the marketing and distribution of *A Soldier's Story*). The process frequently involves distancing the film from its blackness in order to attract crossover audiences or, as in the case of *Bopha!,* targeting a narrow segment of black audiences due to perceivable lack of crossover potential. Both approaches are racially predetermined in a way that devalues blacks and privileges whites. These race-specific marketing and film distribution strategies were commonly used in the 1980s and are continuously implemented regardless of the favorable economic performance of African American films in more recent decades. The time has come and the technology is available to make these strategies work on behalf of the development of African American film, not just the acquisition of the couple of slots available each year for filmmakers of color.[80]

There are serious consequences if a film does not fare favorably at test screenings or does not make a certain amount in its opening weekend. It may be perceived that it lacks an audience when the fact may be that the audience has been misidentified. Assuming that a "black film" will play well in an urban area without considering film content could lead to the film's flopping before it has a chance to reach an audience that will appreciate its style, structure, and content. Assuming that all black audiences in urban settings will be attracted to every black film released, or that white Americans, additional people of color, and international audiences won't find black films appealing simply due to the cast's race, severely underestimates black audiences, crossover audiences, and the films.

Debates on individual films tend to deflect attention away from the fact that black people do not control distribution, which further reinforces Hollywood's investment patterns. These patterns reinforce race ideology by stunting the growth of black film through limited distribution as well as repetitive and at times dark themes that lack the depth of inquiry they require. One need only review the budget, gross, and distribution patterns of black women's literary cinema in comparison to films based on works authored by black men (see tables 2 and 3). As indicated by these films, black literature covers a broad range of material and time periods, yet there is clearly a preference for cinematic adaptions of black women's literature considering the disparity in economic support. Films based on books by and about black women do not demonize black men by default. In fact, most of the source texts demonstrate how interlocking systems of oppression as well as women's interactions with black men contribute to black, female protagonists' experiences. As my analysis reveals, these elements are frequently manipulated in films to reinforce the master narrative.

A comparative analysis of both tables reveals that on average, films adapted from black women's literature tend to receive larger budgets and broader distribution over longer periods of time than films adapted from black men's literature, which may have resulted in the considerably lower return on investment for these films. Considering the themes in the black women's literary cinema, it appears that Hollywood is more interested in investing in narratives that focus

TABLE 2.
Budgets, Distribution, and Earnings of Cinematic Adaptations of Black Women's Literature

Film (Year)	Estimated Budget (millions)	Domestic Gross (millions)	Screens	Days
Beloved (1998)	$53–80	$22	1,571	150
The Color Purple (1985)	$15	$95	1,109	166
How Stella Got Her Groove Back (1998)	$20	$37	1,399	150
Precious (2009)	$12	$47	1,003	129
Waiting to Exhale (1996)	$16	$67	1,402	115
What's Love Got to Do with It (1993)	N/A	$39	1,100	33
Woman Thou Art Loosed (2004)	N/A	$6.9	521	52

Sources: Figures are averages of estimates from IMDB.com, The Numbers.com, and BoxOfficeMojo.com.

TABLE 3.
Budgets, Distribution, and Earnings of Cinematic Adaptations of Black Men's Literature

Film (Year)	Estimated Budget (millions)	Domestic Gross (millions)	Screens	Days
Devil in a Blue Dress (1995)	$27	$16	1,432	87
Miracle at St. Anna (2008)	$45	$7.9	1,185	60
Native Son (1986)	$2	$1.3	N/A	N/A
Once Upon a Time . . . When We Were Colored (1995)	$2.7[a]	$2.6	78	150
Panther (1995)	$6–$9[b]	$6.8	713	68
A Rage in Harlem (1991)	N/A	$10	545	52
South Central (1992)	$4	$1.3	37	N/A

Sources: Figures are averages of estimates from IMDB.com, The Numbers.com, and BoxOfficeMojo.com except as noted.

[a]Pam Lambert, "What's Wrong with This Picture? Exclusion of Minorities Has Become a Way of Life in Hollywood," People, March 18, 1996.

[b]Mario Van Peebles, Ula Y. Taylor, Tarika Lewis, and Melvin Van Peebles, Panther: A Pictorial History of the Black Panthers and the Story Behind the Film (New York: Newmarket Press, 1995), 176.

on the friction between black men and women; as a result, the pathological issues that are addressed in their source texts end up overly emphasized and superficially treated in the film adaptations. The numbers allow executives to justify their investment decisions based on profitability rather than racism, but the outcome is the same. Frequent repetition of these manipulated narratives provides an overwhelmingly negative depiction of black people and cultures. While films adapted from black men's literature, on average, have not received the same investments as films adapted from black women's literature, black male-centric hip-hop gangsta original films (discussed in chapter 6) have received funding and distribution comparable to that of cinematic adaptations of black women's literature. Under these circumstances, outcomes paradoxically support the economic viability of black film while also providing studio executives the numerical values to justify their investment in material deemed as black pathology.

For example, gross earnings of *The Color Purple* and *Waiting to Exhale* significantly exceeded their budgets, as noted. With these successes, Hollywood studios erroneously assume that these types of films ought to serve as models for emulation without considering other alternatives. But Hollywood's refusal to invest in *Precious* because of the belief that it lacked economic potential provides an interesting counterexample. The eventual battle between the Weinstein Company and Lionsgate over ownership of distribution rights and the economic success of *Precious* disrupts the fallacy that African American films lack widespread appeal.[81] The ability to convince Hollywood of a film's potential profitability plays a major role here. *Precious* accomplished this when in 2009 it became the third film in Sundance Film Festival history to win both the Grand Jury Prize and the Audience Award,[82] two highly coveted honors. Of course *Precious* no longer had to convince anyone of its potential to earn a profit once box office receipts were tallied up. The success of *Precious* may very well lead to the production of more similarly themed films, much to the chagrin of the many critics who found the film to be demeaning toward black people.

The economic strategies that propelled the film are just as noteworthy as the debatable impact of the film's form and content. *Precious* received a similar platform distribution as *The Color Purple* and *A Soldier's Story* even though the role of blacks behind the scenes has increased significantly since the 1980s. The remarkable appeal of black films across the color line is occurring more frequently as film producers and participants engage in a complex process of rebranding black film as universal.

Specifically, the "Oliver Twist strategy" has become an important tactic for marketing black films. For instance, Sapphire has been able to capitalize on the similarities between white poverty and black experience by referring to the title character as "a positive 'Oliver Twist-like' figure that grew out of the stories of young people she met in New York in the late 1980s, when crack and AIDS emerged."[83] The problem with framing the experiences of young black women in reference to that of a little white boy reinforces the false universal of white experience in order to placate white audiences. To achieve this kind of universalism often requires the diminishing or reframing of key issues for black communities, in this case illiteracy and its historical role in the oppression of African Americans.

The economic success of *The Color Purple* and *Precious* was due in part to their ability to sell the universality of their stories, in spite of their black female protagonists. Each example in this chapter exhibits signs of this appeal for universalism, which tends to privilege whiteness. Such universal claims feature prominently in marketing strategies for African American films (for example, the distancing from black culture used to market and distribute *A Soldier's Story* in 1984). Progress lies in acknowledging and promoting the universality of black subjects and worldviews without being compelled to link them to dominant narratives and associations just to placate white audiences.

In sum, the mainstream entertainment industry only regards the perspectives of black audiences when they align with white audiences, either through similar class values or dominant cultural perceptions. Aligning values to appeal to black and white audiences is believed to increase revenue potential. This is not always the case. Regardless, this perspective has the potential to distort African American culture as well as internal and external perceptions of black culture due to frequent, consistent, and highly selective representations that reinforce hegemonic ideals. This is especially the case when other films such as those discussed in chapter 4 fail to achieve notable profits at the box office due to limited distribution.

The films discussed here provide clear evidence that cultural nuance from black women's literature is transferable to film. While perceivably pathological themes like those in these films have proven to be marketable, it is important to remember the strength of black and female audiences. They have been discounted via patterns of distribution that suppress films which counter the master narrative by juxtaposing history with more nuanced portrayals of black culture. Black female audiences represent a diversity of cultures, nationalities, classes, religions, and sexualities, and they can serve a powerful role in developing African American film in spite of the fact that this power has been misappropriated for mainstream purposes.

Like theater, literature can effectively inform film production and help address the problem of cultural amnesia. More specifically, the selected alterations in each of these lucrative examples and the relationship between the filmmakers, authors, and financiers illustrate the importance of contractual agreements and creative control. Lee Daniels and Sapphire's collaboration on

Precious offers an effective model for productive interaction and broad distribution in the existing framework. Digital technology and new media's role in self-publishing, e-book publication, filmmaking, and marketing provide much-needed alternative routes to production and distribution. With these resources, strategic adaptation can help simultaneously develop audiences across media while also correcting flaws in subsequent works. The hazards of overlooking intersectionality and intertextuality as well as hybrid distribution and horizontal integration become even more apparent among historical dramas. In chapter 4, the focus shifts to cultural trauma and the challenges of filming history.

4

Breaking the Chains of History and Genre

But culture, a true culture, a democratic culture can heal society by jux-taposing two histories of a people. That's why African Americans are continually struggling now to have their sense of history, their own his-tory, told to their own children. Because they realize their children cannot transform or go forward without this fundamental requirement of human nature, the history of a people.

                                                                    —Haile Gerima, 1994

Considering the influence of early novels on historical films such as *The Birth of a Nation* and the various film versions of *Uncle Tom's Cabin*, translating writ-ten language for private consumption into a publicly consumed visual language historically limits black representation. It also inspires intertextual discourse between African American novelists and filmmakers. As theater and perfor-mance studies scholar Peggy Phelan explains, "Performance implicates the real through the presence of living bodies. In spectatorship there is an element of consumption: there are no left-overs, the gazing spectator must try to take everything in. Without a copy, live performance plunges into visibility—in a maniacally charged present—and disappears into memory, into the realm of invisibility and unconscious where it eludes regulation and control."[1] In the-ater and cinema, literary master narratives become completely overpowering because of their perceived reality, particularly with historical narratives.

Performative indigenization presents various possibilities for challenging the authenticity of the historical master narrative, especially in theater. As an act of protest and agency, performative indigenization infuses counteractive memories into the unconscious memory where they also "elude regulation and control." Performative indigenization is particularly potent when unspoiled by containment strategies: requisite master narrative form and content, cinematography and editing to shift focus away from the typically isolated black character to the white character (usually the male hero), and censorship through limited distribution. Performative indigenization on and off the set can also challenge the status quo, which is so frequently reinforced by period films that feature critical moments of black history.

This chapter focuses on three films that challenge the limitations imposed by the master narrative upon African American films. These black literary adaptations failed economically in comparison to higher grossing master narratives, cinematic adaptations of black women's literature, and original films, yet they offer important lessons for African American filmmaking. Like the examples in previous chapters, stylistic devices in source texts have the potential to resolve apparent problems in cinematic versions of each story. The offscreen circumstances surrounding their perceived failures also reinforce the necessity of proactive, collective strategies for representing history in African American adaptations and original films through targeted, consistent use of intersectionality and intertextuality.

Toni Morrison's *Beloved,* Melvin Van Peebles's *Panther,* and Clifton Taulbert's *Once Upon a Time . . . When We Were Colored* succeed as literature, confronting cultural trauma and the collective memory of slavery for black Americans.[2] But the cinematic adaptations of these works failed to produce competitive film revenues in spite of their cultural resonance. Such noncommercial genre films typically earn lower box office revenues than commercial genre films regardless of the cast's racial composition. In general, historical dramas don't tend to yield the huge box office of popular commercial genres such as action, adventure, thriller, science fiction, horror, comedy, and romantic comedy. As screenwriter and author Stephen V. Duncan observes, "The list of produced films between 2000 to 2007 reveals that nearly all fell under the categories of popular genres; few were pure dramas."[3] As in the case of *Precious* and *The Color Purple*, dramas tend to fare better with festival and Academy nominations and awards.

These and other noncommercial African American films with similar economic outcomes further contribute to the perceived failure of African American film even though predominantly black casts are less a factor than genre. Genres generally refer to classes or types of films categorized according to shared narrative, visual, and/or sound conventions. Racial genre labels only apply to films with nonwhite casts, thereby reinforcing whiteness as the norm. In other words, "black" is treated as a genre while white is not. The examples discussed in this chapter help demonstrate how black perspectives are revising and reformulating existing genres to create ones that significantly contribute to cinematic vocabulary, particularly in regard to historical dramas.

Holding History Hostage through Distribution

Cultural trauma significantly influences representations of history in all media. It is particularly potent in black historical dramas on stage and screen. The trauma of revisiting stories about slavery and other horrors can trigger unresolved, negative emotions. Historian George M. Fredrickson identifies slavery as the skeleton in America's closet one hundred and thirty-five years after its abolition. As he notes, "Among the African-American descendants of its victims there is a difference of opinion about whether the memory of it should be suppressed as unpleasant and dispiriting or commemorated in the ways that Jews remember the Holocaust. There is no national museum of slavery and any attempt to establish one would be controversial."[4] Elaborating on Fredrickson's observation, sociologist Ron Eyerman further recognizes that black Americans, frequently divided in their opinions regarding the commemoration of slavery, starkly contrast with most white Americans, who "see no reason to accept responsibility for slavery or its effects on American blacks."[5]

Black professional theater plays an important role in confronting cultural trauma. August Wilson's ten-play cycle of history plays exemplifies this even though the narrative structure of his plays does not deviate from traditional standards as much as Robert O'Hara's play *Insurrection: Holding History.* This may explain mixed reviews of the latter. *Insurrection* examines intangibles, the politics of having a history. Described as a "comic fantasia," the play fuses contemporary concerns of a young, gay, black man who travels back in time with his great-great-grandfather in search of the past, which leads them to Nat Turner's rebellion.[6] Both Wilson's and O'Hara's works typify black professional theater's depiction of history, specifically representations of slavery since the 1980s. They echo Gerima's interpretation of history, laying claim to it in order to empower future generations to "transform or go forward." Wilson's history plays and their mainstream acceptance is an exceptional example, often cited as evidence of equitable racial treatment in mainstream, white American theater. Suzan-Lori Parks, Robert O'Hara, Lydia Diamond, Lynn Nottage, and others also represent the potential of black-authored historical dramas, many of which are staged in mainstream white institutions. In contrast, contemporary urban circuit plays are being adapted more frequently and consistently into films, thereby overshadowing counter-narratives about slavery and other historical moments.

Black writers' explorations of slavery have historically been more accepted and profitable in print than on the big screen. This is due in part to the fact that cinematic adaptations of such historical narratives are not provided the same competitive distribution as hip-hop gangsta films, Tyler Perry's films, or cinematic adaptations of black women's literature. The limited treatment of black history in visual media and limited dissemination of this material is problematic because cinematic and other techniques that cater to crossover audiences frequently end up corrupting or eroding the positive development of African American film's form and content. Without careful consideration, the resulting pressure to appeal to crossover audiences can trigger effects of cultural trauma for black audiences. Encounters with everyday racism, institutionalized racism, and other oppressions have often been cited as the reason black audiences are more drawn to comedies.[7] While comedies may momentarily suspend feelings of trauma, they frequently lack the sophistication or depth to fully explore the complexities of black culture in theatrical and cinematic performances.

In addition to noncommercial genre films, these predominantly black historical dramas are perceived as being a tough sell in comparison to the films discussed in chapter 1. Filmmakers are pressured to abide by the unwritten rule that a film must incorporate a white point of entry regardless of historical time period or context, a practice that ends up rewriting history in a way that minimizes the accomplishments of people of color, thereby reinforcing master narratives. Historical dramas from black perspectives that do not have a traditional white point of entry are relatively uncommon, but they do exist. *Sankofa* and *Bamboozled* are two excellent examples. Both films received comparatively limited distribution, if any at all. As such, distribution deals are vehicles for censorship, making African American historical dramas a battleground in cultural warfare. African American historical dramas have the potential to disrupt hegemonic perceptions of the past and present. *Beloved, Panther*, and *Once Upon a Time* illuminate evolving narrative and visual techniques that demonstrate this potential.

Historical dramas have appeared in the form of television miniseries such as *Roots, Queen*, and *Mama Flora's Family*. Historical dramas rarely achieve major theatrical release without a white director, as in the case of Edward Zwick's *Glory* (1989), which concerns a white general leading the first all-black volunteer company in the Civil War, or Steven Spielberg's *Amistad* (1997), a courtroom drama in which a white lawyer defends Africans who are charged with mutiny after taking over a slave ship in 1839. In the case of *Red Tails* (discussed in the introduction), major theatrical release was helped along by having George Lucas on board as executive producer. But unlike *Glory* and *Amistad, Red Tails* is not about slavery and does not have a white point of entry, although Lucas arguably serves that purpose as the film's spokesman on the press junket. When black films such as John Singleton's *Rosewood* (1997), in which a racist lynch mob attacks a black Florida community in 1923, Mario Van Peebles's *Posse* (1993), a western focusing on black infantrymen from the Spanish American War in pursuit of gold and the men who lynched their leader's father, and other black-themed historical dramas do not achieve a competitive box office, the results can negatively affect the production and distribution of subsequent films with similar themes or casting. Censorship through limited or lack of distribution of works that contradict dominant historical perceptions reinforces race ideology. The distribution game exposes plantation politics at play. Historical dramas featuring black subject matter are more likely to receive larger budgets as well as broader and longer theatrical release when produced by a predominantly white creative and production team, thereby increasing the likelihood of larger gross receipts for these films (see table 4). Paradoxically, effective stories without substantial distribution are counterproductive: without audience access, there is little opportunity for cultural growth in cinematic storytelling. Substantial distribution for an ineffective storytelling approach is even more detrimental because the circulating material continues to define African American film.

Establishing culturally nuanced aesthetics for historical dramas not only becomes theoretically possible with the films discussed in this chapter, it becomes necessary. Specifically, African American contributions to American cinema such as *Beloved* and *Sankofa* emerge as a manifestation of cultural trauma. These films contain examples of a translatable literary device informing technique and genre, influencing shape, structure, and visual tone. Culturally nuanced translations demonstrate the potential of black film subjects and worldviews. They also expose the limitations of existing genres and generic conventions, as well as filmmakers' methods for counteracting these challenges.

Historical dramas are not the only examples in which limited distribution serves to censor black films and to reinforce racial stereotypes. A closer look at particular genres reveals the connections between genre, distribution, and racial representation. The American Film Institute (AFI) ranks John Ford's *The Searchers* (1956) as the best western film of all time.[8] Based on a novel by Alan Le May, it follows the search of a Civil War veteran (John Wayne) for his niece (Natalie Wood), who has been abducted by Comanches, depicted in the film as a tribe of bloodthirsty Indians. Many westerns incorporate such depictions of Native Americans. Indeed, the western's use of race ideology is more overt than other genres that also reinforce hegemony.

Westerns have inspired several important revisions. For example, Kevin Willmott's *The Only Good Indian* (2009) directly challenges *The Searchers*' narrative, cinematography, mise-en-scène, sound, and editing. Set in early 1900s, the film focuses on the abduction of a Native American boy forced into a school designed to assimilate Indians into white society, even against their will. Directed by an African American, *The Only Good Indian* expands popular conceptions of black film. Revisionist genres and films like this can effectively provide alternate histories, yet censorship through limited distribution remains a problem. The film premiered at the 2009 Sundance Film Festival and had subsequent screenings at other festivals. Although Willmott won Best Director at the

TABLE 4.

African American Dramatic Films Based on History

Film (Year)	Screenplay	Creative Team (Director/Writer/ Producer)	Estimated Budget(millions)	Domestic Gross (millions)	Screens	Days
Amistad (1997)	Original	Predominantly white (1 black producer confirmed)	$39	$44	1,019	135
Beloved (1998)	Adapted from novel	Predominantly white (1 black writer, 1 black producer confirmed)	$53–80	$22	1571	150
Glory (1989)	Adapted from nonfiction books	Predominantly white	$18	$27	811	102
Night Catches Us (2010)	Original	Predominantly black (several white producers)	N/A	$0.075	9	80
Once Upon a Time (1995)	Adapted from nonfiction book	Predominantly black	$2.7[a]	$2.6	78	150
Panther (1995)	Adapted from novel	Predominantly black	$6–$9[b]	$6.8	713	68
Posse (1993)	Original	Predominantly black (1 white writer, several white producers)	N/A	$18	949	24
Red Tails (2012)	Adapted from nonfiction book	Predominantly black (1 white executive producer)	$58	$49	2,573	138
Rosewood (1997)	Original	Predominantly white (1 black director)	$25	$13	991	73
Sankofa (1993)	Original	Predominantly black	$1	$2.4	5	395

Sources: Figures are averages of estimates from IMDB.com, The Numbers.com, and BoxOfficeMojo.com except as noted.

[a]Pam Lambert, "What's Wrong With This Picture? Exclusion of Minorities Has Become a Way of Life in Hollywood," People, March 18, 1996.

[b]Mario Van Peebles, Ula Y. Taylor, Tarika Lewis, and Melvin Van Peebles, Panther: A Pictorial History of the Black Panthers and the Story Behind the Film (New York: Newmarket Press, 1995), 176.

American Indian Film Festival, he could not obtain a major theatrical release for the film, which instead went straight to DVD and VOD—another example of how distribution can be a vehicle for censorship.

The Challenges of Converging Literary and Cinematic Genres

Bringing together literary and cinematic genres is full of challenges, hidden and otherwise. Jonathan Demme's adaptation of *Beloved* represents a failed attempt to fully creolize historical fiction and the ghost story as a mediator of cultural trauma. *Panther*, adapted from historical fiction and fantasy, is less adept in its approach than *Once Upon a Time*, which is based on a memoir. Both historical dramas demonstrate the steps necessary for developing culturally nuanced variations of historical dramas that reshape, refine, and redefine African American cinematic storytelling. Each reflects the interconnectedness of past, present, and future for African Americans by returning to critical, historical moments.

It would be difficult, of course, to discuss historical dramas about slavery without some discussion of *Roots*. Although Alex Haley's book was adapted as a television miniseries, *Roots* had a significant influence on African American cinema, as evidenced by the many movies that include intertextual references to the series and its characters.[9] But if we compare the enduring influence and success of *Roots* to the reception of *Beloved, Panther*, and *Once Upon a Time*, a different story emerges. These films' reception indicates audiences consume certain stories more easily in private rather than in public. This may explain why slavery from black perspectives tends to receive more treatment on television than in theaters. While *Roots* is a good example of how television and cable outlets can significantly influence African American film development, made-for-television productions are less prestigious than theatrical releases and thus downgrade the importance of black perspectives on slavery. The reason why television may be the more productive outlet for slavery narratives is because it allows private consumption of what is, as Frederickson wrote, a skeleton in America's closet.

The threat of cultural amnesia persists when black perspectives on slavery are not treated as worthy of cinematic exploration to counter the overwhelmingly white perspectives that have populated the plantation genre since 1915. Many filmmakers are still in the process of developing a cinematic language that can articulate history's complexity and its material and metaphysical effects beyond the reconciliation narrative. They are not provided the platform to reach or broaden audiences who are either culturally literate and/or cinematically savvy enough to read between the lines.

Hollywood Slave Narrative?: Rememory and
Horror in Toni Morrison's *Beloved*

Not even the Oprah Effect could save the film adaptation of *Beloved*.[10] The film, its elusive title character, and the story of the family and community she haunts defy classification. Even the characters in the novel are unsure of what to call her: crawling already?, the baby ghost, Beloved, a demon, a ghost; no one really knows who or what she is, but she is a very real presence for all who encounter her. The novel's varied elements have been celebrated, and Morrison's visual metaphors have been particularly noted by critics and fans alike.[11] The novel fuses historical fiction with a ghost story, creating a fascinatingly complex hybrid that Demme adapted into film at Oprah's behest. Morrison praised his efforts, in spite of the fact that the intense visual language of the novel proved difficult but not impossible to translate to the screen. Most critics found the film severely lacking in communicating the depth and complexity of slavery's horrors that Morrison so eloquently accomplishes in the novel.

Literary adaptations face a host of challenges. The above example, however, exposes a limitation that is of particular relevance for African American filmmaking. Most notably, in an interview with Michael Silverblatt, Morrison identifies Demme's cinematic adaptation as an example of the "powerful difference" between media. Literature and cinema are consumed differently and each medium has a distinct artist-audience relationship.[12] While cinematic techniques such as voiceover have been an effective tool for creating intimacy with the audience, studio executives can override the author or filmmaker's decision to use such a technique in adaptation. The film production process is highly collaborative and frequently lacks racial and cultural diversity in the most empowered positions, so the cultural significance of particular devices may be disregarded for economic concerns. The historically minimal presence and token participation of culturally literate African Americans and allies throughout the film production process can pose serious drawbacks to representing diverse cultural perspectives.

The story Morrison introduces in the novel clashes with the happy slave formula embedded in the tradition of the classic Hollywood historical drama. According to Gerima, "Slavery was a scientific adventure, an attempt by industrialized society to create a robotic or mindless human being, pure labor. And there was the further idea of creating slaves who would be happy as slaves—it didn't happen in reality, but it did happen in the plantation school of literature, for example. And it happened in the plantation school of cinema."[13] This romantic notion of slavery, usually depicted from plantation owners' perspectives, relies on racial reconciliation narratives and the idea of the happy slave. Romantic notions of slavery, however, are intentionally contradicted in Gerima's *Sankofa*. In regard to the plantation school of cinema's happy slave formula,

Gerima explains, "Now, what I did was flip this. I brought out the individual identities and motives of the characters, transforming the 'happy slaves' into an African race opposed to this whole idea, by making the history of slavery full of resistance, full of rebellion. Resistance and rebellion—the plantation school of thought believed it was always provoked by outsiders, that Africans were not capable of having that human need."[14] Similarly, Morrison's novel deviates from established precedent, but the cinematic adaptation ultimately exposes the consequences of race ideology in industry practices and the power of generic cinematic conventions. The economic stakes of film production become apparent when considering her novel's journey to the silver screen.

Interestingly, *Beloved* was co-produced and distributed by what is currently known as Walt Disney Studios Motion Pictures. Historically racist depictions of African Americans have frequently appeared in animated and live action films disseminated by Disney. Their track record consists of films with predominantly white casts featuring African Americans in minor and supporting roles as the voices of animals in animated features (*Song of the South* [1946], *Dumbo* [1941], *The Jungle Book* [1967]), comic leads (*Snow Dogs* [2002], *The Haunted Mansion* [2003]), sports films (*Cool Runnings* [1993]), and racial reconciliation dramas (*Remember the Titans* [2000], *Glory Road* [2006]). Disney Pictures also produces adaptations, but nothing in their repertoire remotely resembles *Beloved* or the depth and complexity of Morrison's work. Disney's inexperience producing and marketing serious-themed African American films likely contributed to the film's economic failure (though blame has generally fallen on the film itself). Disney expected it to perform well. After all, the film had the novel's critical acclaim, the Oprah connection, and a well-regarded white director (Demme). The film was broadly marketed but unable to overcome negative word of mouth upon release. It only recouped approximately $22 million of its estimated $80 million budget ($53 million production and $30 million promotional). Indeed, the film's budget was considerably larger than the budget of any previous film featuring a predominantly black cast.[15] As a test case, the film failed to demonstrate mainstream appeal of expensive, serious-themed African American films.[16] Nearly fifteen years after *Beloved* was released, films continue to struggle against the perceived failure of African American films. Specifically, the effects of such outcomes resonate in Lucas's attempt to get distribution for *Red Tails*. Lucas himself expressed concerns that box office failure would negatively affect the future of African American films.[17]

Measuring all African American films on the success or failure of a single film with a predominantly black cast, regardless of genre, keeps the vicious cycle going. The privileged, independent evaluation of mainstream, white American films stands in stark contrast to the race-based assessment of African American films. This double standard is a significant part of Hollywood culture and industry practices. Hollywood's classification of black as a genre limits strategies for producing,

marketing, and distributing a film based on other patterns of established precedent. As such, *Beloved* never really had a chance. Its writers and director, production
and distribution companies, as well as the critics and the industry's target audiences, lacked sufficient literacy in black cultures and perspectives, further undermining the development of African American film.

Critics attributed the film's failure to various technical elements that are
actually in conflict with the generic categories used to market the film. The
screenplay dismisses the story's cultural context by reducing it to a generic
Hollywood genre film, which makes it easier to package for mainstream viewing and profit. The repetition and frequency of commercial master narratives,
genres, and cinematic techniques are restrictive, specifically to the detriment of
people of color, because they minimize and ignore diverse perspectives of concepts such as horror and terror. This triggers interpretations that may differ due
to historical black experience in the United States and throughout the world. An
inability to generically classify a film not only complicates its meaning for audiences but also thwarts cinematic precedent, which in turn severely reduces any
opportunity for alternative perspectives of terror or horror. Relying on established precedent to pitch or construct a film reinforces dominant perspectives
for the purpose of marketing, production, and distribution. To do otherwise is
to risk losing funding up front or distribution upon completion.

This process contributed to *Beloved*'s negative outcome. It does not fit
within the generic structures it was adapted to occupy: Hollywood historical
drama/plantation school of cinema, love story (romance and nostalgia), ghost
story (horror). The film is clearly a hybrid but was not necessarily marketed
as such. In fact, Oprah and other spokespersons compared it to the Holocaust
film *Sophie's Choice* (1982). Starring Meryl Streep as Sophie, a survivor of Nazi
concentration camps forced to choose between her two children when one is
ordered to die, the earlier film demonstrates the effect of past traumas on the
present. Comparing the two films in this way equates the Holocaust with slavery
as well as equating films on those subjects. Most films about slavery, however,
have been told from the perspective of slave owners, not the enslaved, while
many Holocaust films privilege the perspective of victims and survivors, not the
Nazi perpetrators. As discussed in chapter 6, films about slavery are also produced and distributed less frequently, especially in theaters, than films about
the Holocaust. As a result, drawing parallels between *Sophie's Choice* and *Beloved*
is a strategic approach to increasing crossover appeal, much like the Oliver
Twist strategy discussed in chapter 3. However, it does not accurately describe
the film or prepare audiences for its fusion of genres or black subject matter.

As a hybrid film, *Beloved* represents a unique contribution to American cinema from an African American perspective. It is a departure from the traditional happy slave narrative in that it confronts slavery from the perspective

of the enslaved. Morrison's narrative is an exquisite exploration of blackpain, defined by interdisciplinary scholar Debra Walker King as "the visual and verbal representation of pained black bodies that function as rhetorical devices, as instruments of socialization, and as sociopolitical strategy in American popular culture and literature."[18] Blackpain is also present in the plantation school of cinema in which black bodies are beaten, mutilated, maimed, and killed. Reactions to blackpain distinguishes benevolent white characters from openly racist white characters, thereby providing the binary opposition needed for racial melodrama and racial reconciliation. Authors like Morrison and filmmakers like Gerima use blackpain in a distinctive way that exposes its traditional use as a device that exonerates whiteness along with the happy slave formula. Like *Sankofa,* Morrison's *Beloved* explores the horrors of slavery using the supernatural to articulate physical and metaphysical wounding experienced by enslaved and emancipated individuals, families, and communities. *Beloved* is in fact a horror film that clashes with Hollywood's established horror genre and the plantation school of cinema. It represents a unique opportunity for cross-pollination, innovatively merging existing genres with an African American cultural perspective.

Ultimately, the complexity of the novel exposes the limited nature of traditional film. Hollywood's classification of the cinematic adaptation as traditional horror film was inaccurate and counterproductive in terms of narrative structure and content as well as marketing and distribution. But there was no clear mainstream model to fashion the marketing and distribution of this cinematic adaptation. Relying on established precedent undermined the film's ability to access a potential audience beyond the book's readership. Regardless of its economic failure, Demme's adaptation of Morrison's *Beloved* still helped to establish a precedent for films that merge a Hollywood genre with African American cultural sensibilities of the supernatural and of horror.

Trends in the production of horror films offer a useful window into the history of race relations and African American experiences in the United States. According to Stephen V. Duncan, horror films typically explore contemporary taboos. In *Beloved,* the taboo is slavery, a topic Hollywood tends to avoid (especially from the 1990s to 2000s). As Ed Guerrero notes, "Recognizing the postwar pressures of an intensifying black political struggle for human rights, by the late 1960s a sharp reversal of perspective in the plantation genre was expressed in such films as *Mandingo* (1975) and *Drum* (1976)."[19] Following the 1970s reversal came erasure, as films with predominantly black casts and with major theatrical release in the 1980s (such as *The Color Purple* and *A Soldier's Story*) were historical in context but did not focus on slavery. Rather than taking the reversal a step further to complicate depictions of the plantation from black perspectives, Hollywood has become stagnant and ambivalent in regards to depicting slavery. Gerima's *Sankofa* could have filled that gap had it been broadly distributed. Instead, studios have begun to revise narratives to downplay the prominence of slavery. For instance, Miramax Films avoided the issue of slavery in Anthony Minghella's adaptation of Charles Frazier's *Cold Mountain* (2003) by casting white actress Renée Zellweger in the role of Ruby, a black woman in the novel. Such casting undermines the strength and power of the relationship between Ruby and Ada, a white woman (portrayed in the film by Nicole Kidman). Spielberg's *Amistad* (1997) is the only other film prominently featuring slavery to receive a major theatrical release prior to Quentin Tarantino's controversial *Django Unchained* (2012).

In 1998, the same year as *Beloved*'s theatrical release, Hollywood unveiled *The Secret Diary of Desmond Pfeiffer*, an American television sitcom about President Abraham Lincoln's valet, a black English nobleman kidnapped by enemies and forced into American slavery. After the airing of just one episode on UPN, protests from the NAACP and other activist groups resulted in the supposedly lighthearted depiction of American slavery being canceled. Spike Lee's film *Bamboozled* parodies the consequences of slave comedies and exposes the dearth of consistent, serious treatments of the subject.

Unlike *Sankofa* and *Beloved*, previous portrayals of slavery and emancipation do not tend to use the supernatural to explore its horrors. Historically, the capture and transport of Africans into slavery, the separation of families, the violence inflicted upon them on plantations, the romantic heterosexual liaisons between slave masters and female slaves, and, occasionally, mistresses and male slaves, feature prominently. Horror, as we know it, is generally depicted in other ways: fear of the unknown, loss of free will, dread (especially at night), a stranger in a strange land, life after death (haunting), and unresolved conflict.[20] Combining elements to explore slavery using the supernatural simultaneously innovates plantation genre and horror films. Yet established precedent undermines the kind of productive cross-pollination attempted in *Beloved*. All these elements are significantly relevant to slavery, but the happy slave formula's prevalence complicates audiences' ability to suspend disbelief long enough to understand the metaphysical implications of slavery so eloquently depicted in Morrison's novel.

Hollywood horror films explore primal fears and anxieties with social taboos that either completely ignore black Americans or include them by featuring voodoo or other racial stereotypes. It was not until the 1990s that horror films with predominantly black casts or significant black characters began to appear. *Def by Temptation* (1990), *Tales from the Hood* (1995), and *Vampire in Brooklyn* (1995) are horror/comedies that received relatively decent distribution "aimed at a niche within a niche market."[21] *Queen of the Damned* (2002) and *Candyman* (1992) feature a prominent black character and are part of horror franchises. The latter actually indexes slavery as the title character, the son of a slave, haunts a black inner-city community following his gruesome murder at the hands of a white mob angered by his involvement with a white woman. The Hollywood horror conventions used in these films cannot be compared to Morrison's nuanced exploration of the concept in *Beloved*.

Beloved's deviations from established conventions contribute to its failure. This woman- and community-centered film introduces Beloved as a poltergeist, particularly in the opening scene when the dog, Hereboy, is violently thrown around the room by an invisible force. Sethe's capable hands lift the dog's motionless body, reinserting its eyeball into the socket. When Beloved appears in the flesh, portrayed by the beautiful, light-skinned Thandie Newton, she is depicted as grotesque and possibly demonically possessed, as indicated by her voice when she croaks out her name. These elements intertextually reference popular horror films such as *Poltergeist* (1982) and *The Exorcist* (1973), a tradition that continues in films such as *Paranormal Activity* (2007). All these films have white female protagonists, are set in contemporary suburban middle-class homes, and are part of a larger franchise. The horror elements of *Beloved*'s narrative, however, are more effectively aligned with *Night of the Living Dead* (1968). Shot in black and white, the film tells the story of a small group attacked in a farmhouse by hordes of flesh-eating zombies. The film's most admirable character is a black man who is shot by rescuers for no logical reason.[22] Its extremely effective rendering of the zombies socially critiques race- and class-based fears in contemporary American society. The comparison of *Beloved* to a Holocaust film such as *Sophie's Choice* and its use of techniques from horror films such as *Poltergeist* and *The Exorcist* undermine the film's ability to achieve the level of discourse of films such as *Night of the Living Dead*.

Unfortunately, *Beloved* fails to achieve an effective hybridization of horror and plantation genres. The filmmakers do not consistently recognize and utilize the novel's visual metaphors. Sethe's description of the seductive beauty of Sweet Home, the plantation from which she escaped after being dehumanized, violated, attacked, and traumatized beyond comprehension does not translate into the film. The filmmakers are unable to realize the horrors that led her to slit the throat of her baby daughter. Selective focus on the elements that emphasize formulaic conventions of horror and romance prevail when Demme privileges fear of the supernatural over the horror of slavery.

The film spends very little time visually depicting Sweet Home and its serenity in lieu of blackpain. The various flashbacks throughout the film focus on the horrors inflicted on the enslaved bodies, like Schoolteacher's boys violating Sethe and stealing her milk, as well as the hanging of the Pauls from the sycamore tree. Haunting images of Paul D, bound by chains and a metal collar and with a steel bit in his mouth, accompany flashes of Halle, Sethe's husband, smearing butter on his own face as a reenactment of Sethe's violation in the barn, which he witnessed but could not prevent. These images appear in grainy, overexposed, and saturated flashbacks that occur whenever a character encounters a moment, person, or incident that triggers their memories of these horrors. For instance, Paul D experiences such an occurrence while walking through the corridor when he first enters 124, Sethe's haunted home. Moreover, Paul D's walk down the corridor in 124 critically exemplifies the potential for African American cinematic language. This scene is one of several attempts to translate Morrison's visual metaphors into cinema.

The film is to some degree successful in its depiction of cultural trauma as a shared experience of individual and collective memory and historical haunting. The pulsing red light and sense of sadness Paul D experiences with each step in the book becomes in the film a series of increasingly fast-paced flashbacks interspersed with shots edited into the scene to convey his being haunted. In the final image, his past intersects with Sethe's. Paul D walks into the house looking straight ahead into an open kitchen doorway, moving slowly, with heavy steps, through the corridor, bathed in the red and purplish pulsing light representing the sadness Sethe and Paul D describe. He sees two bodies lying on the ground and closes his eyes. When he reopens his eyes, a closed shed door appears and begins to swing open slowly, revealing the young Sethe in the act of killing her children. The image disappears before viewers or Paul D can fully decipher it. His attempt to avoid familiar and foreign memories by walking with his eyes nearly closed reflects filmmakers' attempts to translate the novel's visual metaphors into cinematic language.

While this scene adopts a traditional use of flashbacks, the sequence's final image manifests Morrison's concept of rememory, a significant component of the novel. Morrison introduces the concept through Sethe, who describes the power of experiences and their impression upon consciousness and the external world as the lingering metaphysical remains of places and events that become visually manifest throughout time. For this reason, she warns her daughter, Denver, never to return to Sweet Home, fearing the past's potential influence.[23] This explains Paul D's experience of Sethe's memory of Beloved's death at the end of the sequence. Once he returns to the site of the trauma, it awaits him whether he invokes it or not. It is important to note that the sequence of memory flashes is not a rememory because it is part of Paul D's memory of his experiences elsewhere. However, the final image in the sequence is a rememory because it is Sethe's and the baby ghost's shared memory, not Paul D's. The memory manifests outside of Sethe and the baby ghost and Paul D witnesses it, although he was not previously present. This technique becomes cinematic shorthand for conveying the jarring and traumatic effects of the past on present individual and collective experiences. Merging these images of blackpain within this single sequence intertextually references cinematic treatment of slavery without privileging the perspective of the plantation owner. It shows how the rememory of slavery and individual traumas affect those who did not directly experience it. This is further reiterated in a later scene when Paul D and Sethe lie dreaming after making love and images of their dreams merge on the walls above them. This is not a direct reference to blood memory, a relevant phenomenon in which African Americans have reported physiologically and psychologically experiencing memories, emotions, traumas, and epiphanies of their ancestors. Blood memory is more of an individual, internal experience. Rememory is a combination of both depending on the circumstances.

Multiple challenges to visually conveying the concept and effect of blood memory and rememory persist. In this case, flashbacks are not sufficient. In the sequence, nothing distinguishes the final image from the others. Viewers familiar with the novel are more likely to recognize the tragic image as a rememory that does not belong to Paul D. Yet sound, cinematography, mise-en-scène, or editing techniques are needed to set the image apart from those that precede it. The novel offers insight into this powerful concept by referring to rememory as a noun and a verb. Sethe refers to "rememory" as something Paul D stirs up with his romantic attention to her as well as her process of coming to terms with the past through her relationship with Beloved.[24]

Rememory is not just a "thought-picture" or an image, but a process of visualizing the past's influence on the present. Cinematically, rememory is a technique and a process. As a technique, it visualizes the emergence of the past in the present and is most often used in historical films that are confrontational rather than escapist. As a process, the reception of the onscreen narrative becomes a method of confronting cultural trauma. Rememory films contain scenes of the past influencing the present. Approaching Beloved as a rememory film in form and content as opposed to a traditional Hollywood slavery or horror film may have translated into better critical and economic success. This would involve constructing the film with a commitment to engaging in a process of rememory, confronting the past rather than aligning the film with predecessors that do not accurately compare. The film's cultural influence may still outweigh its economic failure by its use of black worldviews to complicate our understanding of the consequences of slavery. As such, rememory stands as a unique contribution to American cinema's stagnated view of history, particularly in regards to slavery.

Not every film that employs rememory techniques is a rememory film. A Soldier's Story and Diary of a Mad Black Woman are specific examples of films that employ rememory techniques in critical scenes but would not be considered rememory films in the same way as Beloved and Sankofa. Unlike Demme, who only succeeds in employing rememory effectively in a few key scenes, Gerima succeeds in consistently developing rememory techniques throughout Sankofa. Both attempts expose the challenges of producing and reproducing rememory films. Gerima effectively produced the rememory film but was unable to get broad distribution, thereby contributing to a modest profit but comparatively uncompetitive box office in contrast to films with higher gross receipts ($50 million or more). Demme did not effectively produce his version of the rememory film yet received a broad distribution and failed box office. According to Demme, Disney pulled *Beloved* from theaters after four weeks in order to make room for *Waterboy* (1998), a white comedy starring Adam Sandler. Furthermore, the company did not honor its promise to re-release the film at the end of the year.[25] Both outcomes undermine the continuous development of the rememory techniques as well as reinforce white hegemony within Hollywood investment patterns. Any films that employ rememory techniques will be categorically denied major studio support according to standard practices.

Rememory, as both a technique and a process, counteracts master narratives and one-sided reconciliation narratives as well as diffuses the Africanist presence. The most effective portrayal of rememory in *Beloved* occurs in the Clearing when Sethe, Denver, and Beloved enter the woods to pay tribute to Baby Suggs, years after her death. They witness her in a past moment preaching a message of love to the newly emancipated community. In one of the most beautifully photographed scenes, Demme clearly distinguishes rememory from flashbacks as the film stock and quality change to reflect this memory of the past reemerging when they return to the site in which it occurred. At the very end of the sequence, as the men, women, and children laugh, cry, and dance in a process of conjuring up love within themselves and for one another, Baby Suggs waves at Sethe, Denver, and Beloved and they wave back. This moment visually articulates the interconnectedness and fluidity of time. Unfortunately, Demme and his collaborators do not clearly distinguish between flashbacks or sequences of memory flashes and rememories throughout the film.

Morrison's literary style closely resembles Gerima's cinematic translation of the Akan concept of *Cra*, "a belief in spirits, the belief that people who have died but are not yet settled roam the village, trying to find a living body to enter, to go back into the living world to repent their crimes or avenge injustice done to them."[26] Morrison does not describe this concept as part of her process or characterization of Beloved, but both reflect the interconnectedness of time and the coexistence of the natural and the supernatural. The terror that black people experience during and after slavery is a source of fear and unresolved conflict. Characters lacking physical descriptions in the novel are ghosts trying to reclaim their bodies and enter the living world following their bouts with slavery. This seamless coexistence of both realms is clearly delineated in the novel, as it is common knowledge that "not a house in the country ain't packed with some dead Negro's grief."[27] The baby ghost at 124 is distinct because of the terror that led to the infanticide, not the ghost itself.

Embodying horror through Beloved's grotesque portrayal reduces the potential for the audience to feel empathy while increasing the potential for repulsion. To capitalize on Beloved's ghostlike qualities, the filmmakers might have utilized shots from her perspective more consistently, revealing only fragments of her throughout. Instead we receive numerous close-ups and medium-close shots of Newton as Beloved, which does not necessarily offset the repulsion many film audiences reported. Her voice and the filming of her face and body contribute to this, particularly in the exorcism scene where she appears nude with a protruding belly and visible pubic hair while she hisses and spits. Beloved is treated like the monster in horror films, not the wounded spirit and casualty of slavery portrayed in Morrison's novel.

Film critics recognize the film's distinct style but few attribute it to cultural expression. Exploring themes of haunting is not exclusive to African Americans, but there are some identifiable cinematic patterns that reflect the ongoing evolution and development of a culturally nuanced cinematic language. Scholar Barbara Tepa Lupack recognizes the film's cinematic vocabulary but does not specify what it is.[28] She may be referring to what film critic John C. Tibbetts identifies as the way "the filmmakers unnecessarily complicate the already fractured storyline with an over-indulgent use of slow-motion effects, sudden flashbacks, a barrage of persistently recurring image motifs . . . a succession of starkly contrasting mood changes and numerous irritatingly contrived special effects."[29] The concept of haunting and other similar cinematic techniques appear in *A Soldier's Story*, *Sankofa*, and *To Sleep with Anger*. These techniques demonstrate how African descendants revisit the past in order to better understand the present as well as their individual and collective identities. Techniques used in existing commercial genres are frequently insufficient for in-depth explorations of the effects of slavery and racism.

Distribution channels and marketing campaigns are not yet prepared to promote rememory films. Existing industry practices and practitioners do not recognize this emerging genre and have not conducted research to locate its audience. Tibbetts described the film as "literal minded and arty," suggesting it targets a niche market. Primary impressions of *Beloved* in early theatrical release described it as "depressing," "brutal," "grim," and "hard to follow." Even the director referred to the film as having the odds stacked against it due to the demanding material and the length.[30] Negative word of mouth, Demme's comments, and Oprah's focus on the romance and ghost story collectively overlook the horror of slavery. *Beloved* is therefore a good example of how commercial genres can negatively affect offscreen narrative and promotion of nontraditional films. Without proper advertising and audience preparation through repetition, not even the Oprah Effect can change perceptions of African American films. Disney's overreliance on Winfrey, Demme, and the success of the novel was misguided and ultimately contributed to the economic failure of the film.

Beloved was never a fair test case, but its effects are clear. It took a decade before *Precious*, another African American novel cinematic adaptation with serious themes, received major theatrical release. Of course, it earned major release only after winning several key industry awards and gaining support from Perry and Winfrey. The collaborative efforts of these two media moguls positively influenced *Precious*'s outcome in a way that was not yet possible for *Beloved*. It takes time to build an audience, especially for emerging genres. Even Hollywood as we know it was not built overnight.

Beloved offers other important lessons for exploring new genres across media. For example, at 172 minutes Demme's cinematic adaptation proved to be inadequate for delving into the nuances of *Beloved*'s narrative, but it was still too long for the average movie theater audience. A television or web miniseries, however, screened over several days, could have offered a film such as *Beloved* a better chance at success. As noted, a miniseries offers the public a viewing experience in private. While television and web distributions do not yet currently carry the same cachet as theatrical release, they do allow more time for character development and narrative build-up. This is particularly important when dealing with the issue of slavery from black perspectives.

What about choice of director? Hollywood rarely hires black directors such as Gerima, who are positioned to articulate the complexities of a narrative such as *Beloved* due to cultural knowledge and practical filmmaking experience. Brand-name white directors such as Demme or Spielberg, who are capable filmmakers, may not possess comparable cultural literacy or willingness to accept the consultation of those who are familiar with the cultural perspectives represented by these narratives. While these two directors are no doubt talented, it is no secret that their affiliation with a project helps guarantee distribution. Conversely, films with black directors are just as economically viable as those with white directors, but they are consistently distributed on a much more limited basis. In sum, it becomes clear that industry practices relying solely on crossover appeal in lieu of cultural nuance undermine the economic and creative potential of African American films.

Panther: Black Power Fantasy, Action Films, and Hero Narratives

The Black Panthers, also known as the Black Panther Party for Self-Defense, represent a critical facet of American history not typically examined in any great depth by Hollywood cinema. In most broadly distributed films, the Black Panthers are generally presented as superficial caricatures that spout slogans and tote guns while wearing black turtlenecks and berets with serious afros, an extreme militant group that hates white people. Before 1995, the Black Panthers were featured only briefly in mainstream white Hollywood narrative feature films such as *Forrest Gump* (1994). They are also featured in *Dead Presidents* (1995), a heist film with a predominantly black cast in which the sole female of the crew is a member of the Black Panthers. Outside of several documentaries, Mario Van Peebles's *Panther* (1995), a cinematic adaptation of a novel by his father Melvin, who also wrote the screenplay and helped produce the film, represents the first narrative feature-film treatment of the Black Panthers. Released three years before *Beloved*, it is a historical drama with commercial potential that strategically utilizes generic conventions to make an onscreen and offscreen political statement. The lack of any serious treatment of the Black Panthers before 1995 is indicative of the racist cultural politics that pervade the entertainment industry.

The Black Panther is a multi-layered and contentious symbol. Founded in 1966, the group remained active until 1982. Huey P. Newton and Bobby Seale, the cofounders of the Black Panther Party, adopted the name and symbol for their organization from the Lowndes County Freedom Organization (LCFO), an independent political party in Alabama. John Hulett, LCFO chairman, explains, "The black panther is an animal that when it is pressured it moves back until it is cornered, then it comes out fighting for life or death. We felt we had been pushed back long enough and that it was time for Negroes to come out and take over."[31]

Black Panther was also the name of a comic book superhero introduced by Marvel Comics in 1966, the same year the Black Panther Party was formed. And yet the creators of Marvel's character—the first black hero in American comic books—did not openly acknowledge any connection to the Black Panther Party. The comic book character first appeared as an antagonist in Marvel's *The Fantastic Four*.[32] Also known as T'Challa, king of the fictional African nation of Wakanda, he eventually joins forces with the Avengers, a crew of international superheroes. In 1973, Black Panther received his own series. By 1979, "with that same sense of uncanniness and the near eclipse of the Black Power movement," Black Panther began "to fade into the background of Marvel's stable narratives."[33] The comic book narrative does not directly reference the Black Panther Party or the political landscape of the 1960s. However, T'Challa briefly resurfaced in Marvel comics in the late 1990s following the release of the Van Peebles's *Panther*. Black Entertainment Television (BET) and Marvel also produced a primetime animated series for the 2009–2010 season, and the character is expected to receive cinematic treatment in the near future.

The Marvel hero's apparent disconnect from the controversial political party with whom he shares his name exemplifies a recurring pattern of whitewashing black heroes. This practice minimizes the black hero's association with black communities and shifts the gaze from collective power for social justice to individual superpower for "universal" justice. This shift does not accurately reflect the oppressive circumstances of black people's past or present lives. Such heroes depoliticize heroism and undermine the power of hero narratives for black audiences. Like Stan Lee, the reported creator of the Black Panther comic book hero, and Christopher Priest and Reginald Hudlin, who took up the mantle of the character, Van Peebles also believes in the necessity of a black superhero. Van Peebles differs with them in how to achieve it, however, especially considering the politics of action films.

Panther has been referred to as an action film and Black Panther fantasy. Action films generally contain violence, action sequences, a male hero (most often with a female in a predicament), and an unrelenting wicked villain threatening to disrupt social stability in a contemporary plot. As a variation, *Panther* emphasizes masculine heroics and over-the-top violence, which generally serve as vehicles for character development. The film most closely fits the paranoid conspiracy subgenre, although Mario Van Peebles describes it as a political thriller, exploiting the reality that particularities of daily activities and interactions may unleash a wave of chaotic and life-threatening consequences. Alfred Hitchcock's *North by Northwest* (1959) exemplifies this in its story of foreign spies pursuing a white New York advertising executive when he is mistaken for a government agent. A more recent and noteworthy example is *Enemy of the State* (1998). Will Smith, a prominent African American film star, portrays a lawyer being pursued by a corrupt politician and a team of National Security Agents when he unwittingly obtains evidence of a politically motivated murder. Action films do not typically feature African Americans in lead roles or examine conspiracy from black perspectives. As a culturally specific hybrid of the action film (paranoid conspiracy subgenre) and historical drama, *Panther* exposes the dearth of African American hero narratives. This was also Lucas's motivating factor for *Red Tails*.

Filmmakers can use commercial genres and subgenres to make more nuanced and creative films that educate and entertain, not just for the sake of crossover appeal, marketing, and distribution. Paranoid conspiracy films focus on innocent individuals who become ensnared in devious plots. Their formulaic conventions provide fascinating tools for exploring the rise and fall of the Black Panther Party. The daily routine of an average citizen, who arbitrarily gets entangled in the conspiracy, occurs in *Panther* when the fictional character Judge, a young African American army veteran and college student, grows increasingly aware of the volatile political climate in his community. Torn between material aspirations and political consciousness, Judge observes the founding of the Black Panther Party for Self-Defense and eventually joins.

The Van Peebleses employ several devices that fuse action film with historical drama, merging fiction and nonfiction. Before the film begins, the following caption appears: "This film is a dramatization, which depicts some real persons and historical events to tell its story. As such, the film uses fictionalized events and dialogue for dramatic purposes. The depiction of any real persons as part of this story should therefore not be taken as accurate representation of historical facts. Any similarity between fictional characters and actual persons, living or dead, is unintended and coincidental." This disclaimer was lost on critics of the film who challenged its veracity.

The opening sequence's fusion of fact and fiction occurs throughout the film. The opening sequence also demonstrates how filmmakers effectively translate Melvin Van Peebles's research for the novel by using documentary footage to situate the fictional onscreen narrative. Credits run throughout the sequence, which begins with the song "We Shall Overcome" while archival footage of 1960s protests and Dr. Martin Luther King Jr. is shown. Footage also contrasts Dr. King speaking on nonviolence as a powerful weapon with Malcolm X, who asserts, "We are nonviolent with those who are nonviolent with us." As the sequence continues, police attack unarmed protestors and violence escalates, thereby dramatizing black people's lack of protection under the law. To complicate the images, the sequence cuts to President John F. Kennedy stating, "Race has no place in American life nor law." Following a freeze-frame, the scene cuts to black, with the sounds of a shotgun being cocked and a gunshot. The black screen then transitions into archival footage of police and firefighters spraying African Americans with water hoses and attacking them with dogs and clubs. A voiceover of Malcolm X citing the law and insisting upon the necessity of self-defense plays. Eventually an image of Malcolm X appears as his voiceover continues to emphasize that those without equal protection under the law are "justified to resort to any means necessary to bring about justice where the government cannot give them justice." The sequence cuts back to archival footage of police brutality against nonviolent black protestors before returning to Malcolm X in freeze-frame as the gunshot and black-screen motif repeats. Zooming in slowly, the graphic of the title increases in size, appearing to slowly stalk toward the viewer. This dramatizes the symbolic impetus of the Panther slogan, "To come out fighting for life or death," as the voiceover begins. Opening narration about the Black Panthers coincides with the yellow and orange flickering of the Black Panther emblem accentuated by subtle sounds of flames. The growing title eventually morphs into the Black Panther emblem underscored by an ominous growl as the narration of the origins of the organization continues. As the sound of the growl increases, the emblem continues to approach viewers at an increasingly faster pace. The graphic's movement creates the illusion of the audience entering the panther's body only to emerge in a black-and-white image of Bobby Seale (Courtney B. Vance) and Huey P. Newton (Marcus Chong) standing before a sign that reads "Black Panther Party for Self-Defense." Holding a rifle, Newton looks in the camera while Seale, also armed, looks straight ahead. The closing sequence of the film reveals that this image is a reenactment of an actual photo of the Black Panther's co-founders. The voiceover continues by identifying them and telling the story of the Panthers. The camera zooms in, ending with a medium close-up two-shot of the men. This sequence, along with the closing sequence and several scenes throughout, merges fact with fiction, exposing the malleability of history and need to intervene in the master narrative's version of history. The film's first two minutes set the historical context of the national and local politics that led to the Black Panther Party's formation and growth on a national level. In the process the power of the people to reenact history from alternative vantage points is exposed.

The disclaimer, combined with the opening and closing sequences, articulates the filmmakers' core objective: to use a historical moment as a strategic device for developing a hero narrative, counteracting the damage of contemporary hip-hop gangsta films in which heroes are often criminalized. Several scenes demonstrate this, especially one of the earliest scenes in the movie when the Panthers are out on patrol observing the police officers that patrol their community. They witness an act of police brutality against an unarmed black man outside of a nightclub. Newton, Seale, and several other Panthers intervene. Armed and in full uniform, the Panthers challenge the police in front of a crowd of black onlookers. The shotguns they carry are less intimidating than their knowledge of the law. Many crowd members appear anxious and prepared to flee a potential gun battle. The Panthers' knowledge of the law prevents the violence from escalating even as Newton calls a policeman a "pig," insulting him within the law's parameters. They display prowess in this standoff and again later when they storm the capital to protest the changing gun laws. These demonstrations make the Panthers look heroic in front of Judge and the fictional community in the film. Together, they serve as a collective protagonist and a point of entry for film audiences. This approach creates a hero narrative that emphasizes the prowess of heroes and elucidates the historical context in which heroes have emerged for blacks in the United States. The novel and film accomplish what Marvel's superhero originally failed to do: explore contemporary relevance for the emergence of the hero and establish the hero's relationship with the black community.

In this film, the blurring of fact with fiction serves an important strategic role. The story is told from Judge's perspective to avoid privileging any of the leaders' points of view while also allowing the audience to follow the story of the party as opposed to any major individuals within the party. Huey enlists Judge to act as a double agent for the Panthers and the FBI in order to counteract FBI infiltration of the Black Panther Party. Melvin Van Peebles based the novel's conspiracy theory on actual documents regarding the FBI's investigation of the Panthers. He suggests that the FBI flooded black communities with drugs to kill the people's emerging political consciousness and activism, maintaining the shackles of oppression through debilitating drug abuse and incarceration. The narrative effectively ties the film's historical moment to contemporary events, including the beating of Rodney King by Los Angeles police officers in 1991, the subsequent trial, acquittals, and riots, as well as the frequent criminalization of blacks in the media at the time of the film's release.

Onscreen and off, *Panther* exposes the cultural politics that control film production and reception. The genre encourages examination of interlocking systems of oppression and unraveling webs of deceit. The device is intended to mobilize young African American males to challenge stereotypes of innate corruption and violence within black communities depicted in the hip-hop gangsta films. Judge, an unwilling hero, becomes increasingly entrenched in the plot and realizes the truth about the conspiracy to flood the community with drugs. He has difficulty convincing the Panthers and authorities of police corruption in collaboration with the FBI. Judge, along with some of the Panthers, fight the police in a gun battle and set the warehouse containing the drugs on fire.

Panther represents the potential of black filmmakers and allies to revise existing genres through effective translation of literary devices and more strategic use of the five elements of cinema. *Panther* advances the paranoid conspiracy subgenre by including black perspectives while rethinking the hip-hop gangsta film formula. Mario Van Peebles became a leading filmmaker of hip-hop gangsta films with *New Jack City* (1991), nearly twenty years after his father's success with *Sweet Sweetback's Baadasssss Song* (1971), a film about a hustler who becomes a revolutionary. In fact, *New Jack City* was the most profitable movie for Warner Bros. in 1991.[34] Because of Mario's success with *New Jack City* and *Posse*, the latter a revisionist western with a predominantly black cast, he had the freedom to choose his next project. (Like Mario Van Peebles, John Singleton and the Hughes Brothers received Hollywood resources to produce narrative fiction films about African American history only after they produced films in the "sports driven, inner-city ethnic region.")[35] Against the advice of many, he selected *Panther*. Like Melvin Van Peebles's other works, the novel is male- and community-centered, contrasting the womanist aesthetic depicted in popular 1990s novels such as *Waiting to Exhale* and *Push*. This version of the story of the development of the Black Panther Party via a male-centered perspective marginalizes women's perspectives.

The novel's cinematic quality is particularly intriguing as it suggests possibilities for cross-medium innovations. *Kirkus Reviews* describes the novel as "the Hollywood version of Panther history—characters are reduced to good guys and bad guys, their struggles into the stuff of action-adventure flics; the imaginary incendiary ending comes right from the brutish heroics of Bruce Willis or Eddie Murphy."[36] While the novel lacks the literary complexity of Morrison's works, the adaptation of the novel to film provides an important model for understanding the inherent intertextuality of African American literature, theater, and film. It would be imprudent to dismiss it.

Like Perry, the Van Peebleses used branding and methods of horizontal integration to expand the project's reach and combat negative implications of the complex "nigga identity" associated with urban youth depicted in the hip-hop gangsta films. A history book entitled *Panther: A Pictorial History of the Black Panthers and the Story Behind the Film* was published to coincide with the film release. The book was intended to help situate the film as "edutainment." Other related merchandise went on sale as well, including hats and T-shirts. The commodification of black revolutionary images, as argued by William Lyne, reflects the decline of African American progressive politics.[37] However, it has become an effective strategy for generating revenue for filmmakers and their subsequent projects. Filmmaking is still a capitalist enterprise, which complicates the matter of progressive politics. As Mario Van Peebles explains, the primary objective was "to reach the gang members who inherited the bravado of the Panthers without the political ideology to understand that their own behavior is often counterrevolutionary."[38] Their mission is particularly fascinating considering their previous contributions. In cinema, Melvin Van Peebles created the "ghettocentric identity in which the specific race, class and gendered experiences in late capitalist urban centers coalesce to create a new identity—Nigga."[39] But taking *Sweetback* out of its revolutionary context has had a detrimental effect. The formulaic conventions that created Blaxploitation films foreground the inhumanity of black people and degrade black women. Through *Panther* and *Posse*, the Van Peebleses intervene to break the cycle of counterrevolutionary ideology and behavior in hip-hop gangsta films. Their collaboration represents a cross-generational link.

Melvin Van Peebles's connection to the Black Panther Party creates additional linkages across time and space. Although he was never a member of the Black Panthers, *Sweetback* was mandatory viewing for Panther members. Newton also wrote an article about the film in the Panther paper, noting the significance of the scene in which a boy (played by the young Mario Van Peebles) engages in a sexual encounter with a woman, which he interprets as the catalyst for Sweetback's developing revolutionary consciousness. The scene opens with a black woman in a whorehouse. She sees young Sweetback entering a hallway to deliver newspapers and beckons him. As he enters the room she undresses him and places him on top of her, instructing him to "move, you ain't getting your picture taken." Their sexual encounter is mostly captured with a medium-long two-shot so that the focus remains primarily on his back and the woman's face as she clearly enjoys the encounter. Using a dissolve, young Mario becomes adult Melvin, thereby establishing the name and purpose of Sweetback as a character, but also positioning black women as vehicles for Sweetback's heterosexual virility. While *Sweetback* is not without problems or controversy, it is symbolic of the father/son team's first collaboration. Onscreen and off, *Panther* complicates several elements from *Sweetback* and its successors, including how black women and the community are represented.

Adapting the FBI files into *Panther*, the novel and narrative fiction film, as opposed to a documentary such as *Classified X* (1998), reflects an attempt to reach an audience that has been conditioned to receive information in a generic format that is easily accessible. This male-centered narrative with its black male hero and requisite action sequences attracted black male audiences, a previously invisible readership. The book's first printing consisted of 50,000 copies and Gramercy Pictures purchased the film rights. After numerous challenges and significant controversy, the film earned $6.8 million with a budget ranging from $6 to $9 million, significantly lower than the $20 million of a typical low-budget Hollywood film at the time. The pattern of inequitable budgets persists.

The Van Peebleses' financial sacrifices for creative control of the cultural integrity of the film are noteworthy. Several studios were in the process of developing Panther projects but all insisted on a white point of entry for crossover appeal. Mario Van Peebles refused on the grounds that there were "no white Panthers per se in the Black Panther Party," although they later collaborated with white radicals such as David Horowitz. The film also focuses more on the party's origins than on the more controversial later years. The Van Peebleses' refusal to insert a white point of entry into the film and their insistence on retaining the power of the final cut proved to be a turn-off for many of the studios they approached.[40] However, they were able to proceed with foreign financing. Additionally, actors Dick Gregory and Angela Bassett agreed to work for scale.[41] Although a white point of entry appears to reflect an economic necessity in the filmmaking process, to rearrange a narrative about the Black Panther Party around a white character would have been insulting and extremely dangerous. The Black Panthers were founded on the belief of the psychological importance of black people liberating themselves.[42] Standard Hollywood practice suggests that no matter how involved black people are in the making of history, even if it is their own, they are simply irrelevant outside of the presence of whites.

In spite of the film's opening disclaimer, various critics denounced its inaccuracies rather than examining larger political, cultural, and creative implications. The Van Peebleses' position as outsiders within the industry was less a subject of interest during heated debates about the film than the film's apparent inaccuracies, which Seale and Eldridge Cleaver (both depicted in the film) criticized, as did Horowitz (who is not depicted in the film). Horowitz, a white conservative American writer, political advocate, founder of the David Horowitz Freedom Center, and one of the film's loudest dissenters, was initially an ally of the Panthers. In the 1970s, he befriended Newton and the Black Panthers, help-ing to run a school for children of party members. He recommended that New-ton hire a bookkeeper, a white woman named Betty Van Patter. She eventually disappeared after allegedly discovering the organization's misappropriation of funds. Her body was discovered with a massive head wound in the San Francisco Bay, reinforcing Horowitz's suspicions regarding the criminality of the party. In turn, the Panthers suggested that Horowitz's recommendation was an attempt to spy on the organization.[43]

Horowitz's animosity toward the Panthers manifested in various ways over the decades following Van Patter's murder, but it intensified with the film's release pending. He launched a campaign against the film and the filmmak-ers, accusing the Panthers of being "cocaine-addicted gangsters who turned out their own women as prostitutes and committed hundreds of felonies."[44] The filmmakers do not directly address these charges, which former Panther Elaine Brown finds racist and inaccurate. She and David Hilliard, another former mem-ber, were involved in the production process and endorsed the film.[45] The Van Peebleses maintain that the Panthers never claimed to be saints, although they were not necessarily the thugs Horowitz and the media had made them out to be. Omission of the darker side of the Panther narrative results in part from the filmmakers' choice to focus on the genesis of the organization.

In spite of their omissions, the film is remarkable. A star in his own right, Mario Van Peebles nevertheless avoids playing a major role in the film in order to maintain the focus on the Panther organization and the surrounding commu-nity as collective protagonists. Like *Sweetback*, the film situates the black com-munity as the star, which is exemplified by one of the vigil scenes when older members of the community peacefully protest the city's refusal to put a stop-light at a busy intersection where several black children had been killed. While church members carry lit candles and hold marches, younger men, recruited by Panthers, observe and document badge numbers of disorderly policemen. This image of intergenerational collaboration effectively establishes the community as a character and collective protagonist. Throughout the film, they suffer bru-talities together, get arrested together, and get released together. Promoting collective empowerment and heroism through strategic use of cinematogra-phy, editing, and mise-en-scène offers an effective model for subsequent films. Such African American cultural values stand in stark contrast to the nihilism depicted in hip-hop gangsta films as well as the industry's reliance on the star system (see chapters 5 and 6).

Throughout the film, civil rights and Black Power iconography are linked with Martin Luther King Jr. and Malcolm X. Linking these revolutionary figures and their associated ideology through images dispersed throughout the film simultaneously resurrects memories of African American heroes from the past while making a significant association with the present. *Panther* also connects Panther ideology to Malcolm X via direct intertextual reference to Spike Lee's *Malcolm X* (1992), with Angela Bassett playing Betty Shabazz, Malcolm's widow, in both films. This and similar strategies attempt to bridge the gaps of cultural memory that the filmmakers discovered among black youths who, during test screenings, admitted that they thought Huey Newton was a cookie, not a political figure and co-founder of the Black Panther Party. *Panther* is a strong example of how historical dramas resurrecting the past can heal cultural trauma and counteract cultural amnesia.

The offscreen controversy, however, reflects the challenges of producing African American historical dramas and hero narratives. Racial double standards for mythmaking, hero worship, and revisionist history persist. Industry patterns assume the master narrative is objective, as though history has not privileged a particular political stance. Such blinkered approaches maintain the unrestricted use of cinema to produce and reproduce racial reconciliation narratives targeted at crossover audiences. This double standard is painfully apparent in Oliver Stone's *JFK* (1991). Also a paranoid conspiracy film, it selectively focuses on the conspiracy theory behind the Kennedy assassination rather than the personal or political life of the president. Roger Donaldson's *Thirteen Days* (2000) looks at the Kennedy presidency but focuses strictly on the Cuban Missile Crisis. Neither film was criticized for selective treatment of their subjects. In fact, Stone's film has been celebrated as an exemplar of the new school of cinema while *Panther* has been dismissed as a lie.[46] As a result, the controversy surrounding *Panther* and its dismissal raises important questions about inequality, accountability, and artistry that have significant implications for African Americans. They are disadvantaged by having to measure up to a different standard than historical films made by white directors such as Stone or Donaldson, especially if told from the perspective of a black protagonist.

As it stands, *Panther* represents a necessary step in telling the Panther story. Due to persistent, historically damaging black images in American cinema, a black film about a multifaceted individual, a controversial group, or a disputed historical moment requires careful consideration. This includes building or maintaining the self-esteem of its most vulnerable audiences. In this case, the target audiences were still children and young adults, no matter how hardened they may have become in communities under siege of violence, drugs, and poverty. Introducing their collective heroic potential is necessary to counteract and contradict the nihilism depicted in films from the 1990s. The Van Peebleses succeed in introducing black heroes to a black community with sensitivity and nuance. However, such an approach is most successful when the subject is treated in-depth, repeatedly, in a series of films covering a broad range of genres, characterizations, narratives, and visual strategies. Black subject matter is less likely to receive such treatment due to industry practices for two reasons. First, the treatment of black subject matter from a black perspective tends to be equated with all black perspectives. When a film featuring black subject matter, especially if directed by a black director, fails at the box office, it is perceived as the failure of all black films regardless of genre, historical period, or offscreen circumstances. As Mario Van Peebles observed, "If Hollywood makes several Vietnam films that eventually don't perform financially, no one says white films aren't making money. They attribute this economic failure to the theme or the genre of pictures but not the race of the actors or the filmmakers involved."[47]

In spite of *Panther*'s failure at box office, the film provided the Van Peebleses with valuable information about their target audience. Lively responses from the film's core demographic at test screenings helped the filmmakers identify potentially insightful elements to develop in the future. Their responses indicated what kinds of visual language resonated most. The film scored an approval rating of 98 out of 100 with the test audience, but gross receipts of $6.8 million just barely recouped the estimated budget, further reinforcing the negative assumption that black-themed films are failures. The comparatively limited distribution of the film once again thwarts the potential for paralleling its cultural success with its economic success.

Black female writer and director Tanya Hamilton revisited the subject of the Black Panthers in her 2010 film *Night Catches Us*. The film received limited distribution through Magnolia Pictures. Starring Kerry Washington and Anthony Mackie, it explores the legacy of the Panthers with great depth and sensitivity. It is set in Philadelphia in 1976, several years following the deterioration of the Black Panther Party, and focuses on Marcus Washington's (Mackie) return to his neighborhood following his controversial departure several years earlier, after the shooting death of a prominent party leader at the hands of the police. Upon his return, he reunites with the slain leader's widow, and the complexity of their past and the Panthers' role in the neighborhood is revealed. Hamilton's film illustrates how the limitations of one film's version of historical events can be signified and improved upon in subsequent films. The film's limited theatrical release kept it from reaching a broad audience. However, its availability through Netflix offers a noteworthy example of alternative revenue streams and audience accessibility. In spite of lacking the cachet of a major theatrical release and the economic benefits of building an audience through a long run in theaters, online and cable outlets are becoming increasingly viable for the long-term success of African American films.

In sum, *Panther*'s onscreen narrative and offscreen circumstances expose how a feature film about black history attempts to adapt master narratives and existing genres for the purposes of disseminating Afrocentric worldviews. The complex circumstances surrounding production, distribution, and reception of *Panther* reveals the need for the development of African American film through strategic use of genre, history, and deep awareness of the racial ideologies that guide Hollywood investment decisions.

Reversing the Africanist Presence: *Once Upon a Time . . . When We Were Colored*

Like *Beloved* and *Panther, Once Upon a Time . . . When We Were Colored* (1995) appears to be a failure when compared to more lucrative films with predominantly black casts. In fact, *Once Upon a Time* is in many ways an antidote to films such as *Convicts* and *Driving Miss Daisy.* Accomplishing two critical feats, it counteracts the master narrative by focusing on traditionally marginalized characters and exemplifies methods for using nostalgia to combat nihilism, thereby distinguishing the master narrative for black and crossover audiences. It exemplifies careful articulation of the complexity of African American experiences by challenging established precedent of the Africanist presence. The on- and offscreen narrative of this film and the adaptation process offer striking solutions to several major challenges that African Americans and their allies continue to face in Hollywood.

Once Upon a Time is based on Clifton Taulbert's 1989 memoir of the same title. Motivated by fear of cultural amnesia, similarly to the Van Peebleses and Gerima, Taulbert authored what has been described as a memoir, an autobiography, and a memory novel. It recovers the cultural legacy of a southern black community from the pre–civil rights era depicted in *Driving Miss Daisy.* It is part of a long tradition of African American autobiographies about the South. Those written during and about the 1940s through the 1960s often chronicle the alienation, oppression, and terror that led African Americans to flee. Maya Angelou's 1969 autobiography, *I Know Why the Caged Bird Sings*, represents an important shift away from the terrors of the South and toward the autonomy of the black community. Like Taulbert's book, it reflects social and literary change, the soul-searching shaped by the segregated South so characteristic of works of the 1980s and 1990s.[48] The parallels between past and present in Taulbert's and Angelou's respective works illuminate the oppression and terror inflicted upon black communities, whether at the hands of whites or other blacks. These works also distinguish individual experience from the Africanist presence, reminding black audiences how individuals, families, and communities remained intact in spite of external terror and oppression. In this case, Taulbert's departure from his community in pursuit of education and social mobility uplifts and serves his community. The story encompasses a variety of cultural values under threat of being forgotten in a cycle of films that perpetuate nihilistic images and interactions among blacks in urban communities.

Taulbert's approach to merging fact and fiction is much more literal than those of Van Peebles and Morrison. He includes actual photographs and documents in his text. While these don't make an appearance in the film, they do provide a guide for the filmmaker's dramatization of black people and their more complicated perceptions of one another and white people. Taulbert's success highlights an absence of black male authors in the publishing industry (that is, until the recent flood of black erotica novels on the market). According to the American Bookseller's Association, of the 9.9 million black adults who are regular book buyers, more than 75 percent are women.[49] These numbers have significantly affected black male authors, who were scaled back in the 1980s and 1990s due to a lack of a discernible black male book-buying public. As a result, black men received fewer publishing opportunities than black women.[50] This is yet another example of how competition between black women and men was encouraged. Representations of black cultures that consistently privilege the upper or middle class over the working class, men over women, and heterosexuals over homosexuals, also function as divisive politics that ultimately reinforce the master narrative and a one-sided view of blacks.

Taulbert's memoir-novel promotes African American cinematic language. Prioritizing values that do not rely on materialism, the film starkly contradicts many of the films of the decade that emphasize wealth and individualism to the detriment of family and community. According to psychologist Linda James Myers, the greed and materialism embedded in western-based cultures negatively influence people of color in terms of self-perception and collective identity. Black families' adoption of the dominant culture's nuclear family results in semi-isolation from extended family, increases the likelihood of domestic violence, and contributes to a cycle of brutality and impoverishment that fragments black families and communities.[51] Adopting dominant definitions of family structure is detrimental for a group whose families have been historically disrupted and scattered due to slavery, migration, oppression, and other institutional forces. Taulbert's story reveals that dominant white American norms are not the only definitions of functionality and effectiveness. This is especially pertinent for families who may have to rely more on extended family.

Taulbert's story also demonstrates the importance of counteracting cultural amnesia and facing cultural trauma regardless of the medium. As he explains,

I had been taught to respect the owners of the large plantations. In the agrarian South, land ownership more than any other factor decided who had status; the more land a person owned the more he was worth. The realization that I was the descendant of black plantation owners gave me a sudden sense of pride. At the same time I felt cheated. . . . On further reflection, I realized that many of the values of the Southern culture had been illegitimate, even, perhaps the value placed on land ownership. . . . If land ownership is not a legitimate measure of a people's worth, I wondered, what is? I began to think about my childhood and other values I'd learned as I grew up in an environment much like that experienced by thousands of other colored Americans.[52]

The book's exploration of African American cultural values makes the film a fascinating document for exploring the dramatizing of such values in cinema.

The 1995 film adaptation of *Once Upon a Time* was directed by Tim Reid, an African American actor making his directorial debut. Similar to Charles Fuller's *A Soldier's Play*, Reid's film dramatizes the interconnectedness of time. Unlike Fuller's more stylized use of lighting and overlapping dialogue to achieve this effect onstage and in the film, Reid uses narration. This strategy also reflects African American worldviews regarding the interconnectedness of self and the community. In the film, Taulbert (voiced by Phill Lewis) narrates, beginning with his birth and ending with his departure from the Delta for school. The film privileges the experiences of community over individual by combining voiceover narration that recounts the author's perceptions of events with dialogue and action focusing on the family and community. Much like *Panther*, this film's community is also a collective protagonist.

Once Upon a Time challenges the superficial treatment of African Americans in mainstream Hollywood films such as *Driving Miss Daisy*, as well as the one-sided treatment in hip-hop gangsta films such as *Boyz N the Hood*. Collectively analyzing the representative body of work during this time period, each of the films, with the exception of *Driving Miss Daisy*, offers insight into aspects of black experiences in America. Unfortunately, films such as *Once Upon a Time* that do not sell the master narrative or black pathology are less likely to receive studio support or comparable distribution. *Once Upon a Time* opened on fourteen screens. After 150 days in theaters, it closed after appearing on seventy-seven screens, earning $2.3 million on a $2.7 million budget.[53] The film earned considerably less than black women's literary adaptations or hip-hop gangsta films, had a lower budget, was shown on fewer screens, and, in some cases, was in theaters for a fewer number of days. These numbers expose how industry patterns of investment and distribution undermine the potential of African American filmmaking, favoring one particular representation of blackness over others.

Once Upon a Time's narrative redefines African American values depicted in mainstream films and much of contemporary literature by emphasizing strong kinship bonds, religious orientation, adaptability of family roles, and an achievement-oriented work ethic. The cultural nuance and sensitivity Reid displays in the filmmaking process and product reflects the problems and potential of historical dramas for African Americans. To avoid the formulaic conventions established in the plantation school of cinema, Reid mixes generic conventions of nostalgia with rememory. In other words, he combines the escapist elements of nostalgia with the confrontational nature of rememory. As a result, *Once Upon a Time* is not a typical rememory film but utilizes rememory techniques in its onscreen and offscreen narrative. The combination of escapism and nostalgia allows the story to flourish in spite of the limitations stemming from the historical drama's reliance on the master narrative.

Starkly contrasting mainstream films featuring African Americans, the film's mise en scène and cinematography reflects an oppositional perception of segregation. Most of the scenes in *Once Upon a Time* take place in a black neighborhood. When scenes shift to the white side of town, the narrative continues from the perspective of the black characters. Unlike conventional master narratives, the characters are not depicted as subservient, timid, or comical. At around age six, young Clifton sees the Klan for the first time in a parade after his grandfather takes him into "town" for the day. He notes that crossing the railroad track leads him into another world, a world that the black characters do not revere or express a desire to live in. In fact, they are unimpressed with the white people they encounter, which is articulated in relevant medium close-ups and reaction shots of black characters. Their dialogue communicates agreement but their facial expressions, body language, and interactions with one another clearly demonstrate their disapproval or disregard for white characters expressing racist ideas or engaging in racist behavior. Cinematography, mise-en-scène, and editing allow these actors' performances to convey the characters' double consciousness, a display of performative indigenization that is nurtured and explored rather than repressed as in *Driving Miss Daisy*.

Reid's film dramatizes what bell hooks documents in her study of representations of whiteness in the black imagination.[54] A specific example of this occurs early in the film when three black women pick cotton as the overseer approaches. They immediately change the conversation and begin to compliment the overseer on the wonderful crop produced last year. He selfishly takes credit as they smile at him, speaking in exaggerated black southern dialect. As he turns his back and arrogantly walks away, they continue to smile at one another, acknowledging that the crop was abundant due to their labor, not his. They comment that the overseer "ain't nothin' but a redneck tryin' to be a white man" as they laugh. These southern women and the way they are filmed in this scene—with a collective medium-long shot, individual medium close-ups, and two-shots—contradict the stereotypical images that viewers may have become accustomed to with mainstream films such as *Driving Miss Daisy.* The medium-long shots purposefully include the women in the frame, further acknowledging their kinship. The medium close-ups represents them as individuals and two-shots indicate their more intimate relationships with one another as distinct members of the collective. As a result, this scene challenges the facile depictions of racial reconciliation depicted in previous films. Other scenes depicting positive interactions between blacks and whites who genuinely recognize black people's humanity create a more nuanced portrayal of interracial interaction and race reconciliation founded on social justice, not on an inexplicable process of forgiving and forgetting.

Further complicating the master narrative, the film shows that the black community is fully aware of their exploitation. Over the course of the film they devise methods of resistance in accordance with the actual civil rights movement. Cleve (Richard Roundtree) has owned an ice delivery business for nearly thirty years. With customers in black and white communities, his success threatens a white newcomer who offers to purchase Cleve's business. When Cleve refuses, a common intimidation technique of threatening the lives and livelihoods of black residents ensues. One woman quits her domestic job in protest. The white supplier of Cleve's ice business and other white residents continue to intimidate the black community. The black residents eventually orchestrate a collective protest by leaving their jobs, successfully ending the insurrection without bloodshed.

Roundtree, well known for portraying Shaft, a black protagonist in 1970s Blaxploitation films, offers another example of ghosting on a subliminal level. Audiences familiar with Shaft may also link the heroics of Cleve's generation with those of Shaft, a symbolic predecessor to the protagonists in hip-hop gangsta films. Using ghosting as a strategic device, three generations of varying degrees of heroism are depicted in the casting of a single actor.

Unlike other films that include pre–civil rights black characterizations, *Once Upon a Time* revises rather than reinforces perceptions of black subservience and reconciliation. He accomplishes this by including dialogue and images that allow black actors to communicate with audiences via the characters' perceptions of white racism and segregation. Unlike Morgan Freeman in *Driving Miss Daisy* or James Earl Jones and Starletta DuPois in *Convicts* or even Wolfgang Bodison in *A Few Good Men,* African Americans in this film occupy the frame frequently enough to combat the popular representations of the past. The film does not include a single moment in which the black community embraces false premises of white superiority, which strengthens them individually and collectively. As the collective protagonist and point of entry into the film, the black community is well poised to empower black audiences.

Similarly, in the scene in which Clifton and Grandpa encounter the Klan, the sequence focuses less on the interracial conflict as opposed to the healthy self-perception Clifton develops in the process. Taulbert's objective is to identify those values that helped determine his self-worth and that of the thousands of African Americans with similar experiences. Reid successfully dramatizes Taulbert's objective throughout the film. The sequence begins with a wide-angle shot in which Grandpa and young Clifton appear in the frame followed by a wide-shot of the Klan parade as they pass. The Klan leader confronts Grandpa, who holds Clifton's hand with one hand and an ice cream cone in the other. Grandpa maintains eye contact with the Klansman in a shot-reverse-shot sequence. As the Klansman walks away, a close-up on Grandpa's face suggests that he has been unaffected by the encounter. The close-up on Grandpa's hand crushing the ice cream cone as he calmly tells Clifton that it's time for more ice cream tells another story. These contrasting visual elements complicate traditional representations of black people in the presence of the Klan. Rather than cowering, Grandpa stands firm, displaying a reserved anger. In these ways, Reid's sophisticated technical elements enhance this complex coming-of-age story. He acknowledges racism but refuses to dwell on it in ways that make African Americans appear to be passive victims relying on the mercy and friendship of whites. This stands in stark contrast to the master narrative so frequently disseminated by Hollywood studios and with the powerlessness and nihilism associated with the hip-hop gangsta film, which received greater distribution and thereby higher gross receipts.

Once Upon a Time was released during a decline in the hip-hop gangsta film's popularity. Attempting to fill the void, the adaptation of Taulbert's narrative tries to counteract the cultural damage inflicted by gangsta films. *Once Upon a Time* reminds audiences of the humanity of black people often diminished in hip-hop gangsta films. Violence, promiscuity, drug use, and incarceration end up being glorified, often overshadowing the characters' humanity. *Once Upon a Time* starkly contrasts with the nihilism and eroded values that hip-hop gangsta films represent. It documents life experiences, cultural values, and struggles that preceded the contemporary era. Due to limitations imposed by industry practices, however, the film did not make much of an impact in the short term. Still, like *Bamboozled*, its post-theatrical life suggests that the success of African American films may require long-term evaluation as opposed to the opening weekend box office, which can be deceptive in terms of interest and potential. Cultural traditions of the past, such as the passing of information through coded songs and dialect, are predecessors to the word-of-mouth campaigns often used to market African American films. Such practices may take more time and a different allocation of resources than those typically employed by Hollywood studios. Twitter, a real-time online information network, is now expediting such messaging.

Studios' inability to see *cultural* distinctions in favor of *race* gets manifested not only in their investment decisions, but also in the producing, marketing, and distribution of African American films. As a result, African American film production remains marginal to Hollywood studio films with predominantly white casts. Alternatives emerge in the independent film industry where some of the most empowering and nuanced representations of black people are developed in stark contrast to mainstream films. Unfortunately, limited availability remains a problem. The economic viability of *Once Upon a Time* was not readily apparent, leading every studio to reject it because it was considered "too soft" or, as Reid noted, "too human." This kind of coded discourse makes it difficult to expose the race ideology driving studio investment decisions. In spite of these challenges, Reid raised a $2.7 million budget from BET Pictures (a joint venture between the black television network and Blockbuster Entertainment), and the movie opened to enthusiastic reviews.[55] Currently, BET Pictures is ranked at 138 out of 574 on The-Numbers.com Top-Grossing Distributors List 1995–2012.[56] In other words, BET Pictures could not offer the same widespread distribution as organizations like Warner Bros. The film recouped most if not all production costs in movie houses, and quite possibly through distribution on video and television. For this reason, film-life post-theatrical release may also contribute to McKenzie's promotion of the economic viability of African American films, revealing that black independent film is still a viable option in spite of the barriers imposed by Hollywood. Reid's tenacious opposition to Hollywood's glum prospects for the film provides hope that nostalgia films can thwart master narratives and be economically successful.

Conclusion

Directors Reid and Van Peebles both understand the potential for cinema to diminish cultural memory and erode cultural values. When we take the long view, we can see important links across genres and media. For example, often set in urban areas, many of the characters in hip-hop gangsta films are from families who migrated from the South. The industrial jobs that initially attracted black families to urban areas eventually disappeared. As jobs vanished, economic problems in black neighborhoods increased. Like the Van Peebleses' film, Taulbert and Reid's project also bridges a gap in cultural memory for "the boyz n the hood" test audience who knew little about the historical struggle of their predecessors. Collectively, these projects show how certain literary styles and visual techniques can help to positively develop more culturally nuanced cinematic language, especially using hybrid genres. Their box office outcomes may appear to be failed attempts in comparison to other ventures, yet they all succeed in exposing the limitations of conventional Hollywood genres and reception due to established precedent as well as distribution and marketing or lack thereof.

The star system also plays a major role in the fate of these films and an even greater role in the distribution and development of African American film generally. While the screenplay mediates the novel and the film, trained actors with black cultural experience are often invaluable resources. The legendary Phylicia Rashad recognized the characters in the script for *Once Upon a Time* as similar to family and friends like her own great-aunt Fanny.[57] A recurring problem with many Hollywood scripts depicting African American experience concerns characterizations based on established precedents in mainstream works or prototypes developed by writers who do not interact with people of color. Scripts that resonate with actors—such as the way *Once Upon a Time* resonated for Rashad—could serve as a model for screenwriters and inspire greater collaboration between actors, actresses, and various industry insiders developing more culturally nuanced portrayals of black experience in film. As chapter 5 reveals, many are denied the opportunity due to the industry's star system.

PART THREE

It's Not Just Business

Color-Coded Economics and Original Films

They never knew exactly what they had. They approach these things with precedent. You know, "Well this is the way *Menace II Society* was marketed." But *Bamboozled* is not like *Menace II Society* or *Set It Off* or *Friday*. They tried to do niche marketing but our film is a hybrid.

—Spike Lee, 2001

5

The Paradox of Branding, Black Star Power, and Box Office Politics

Really, there is a scale—I think it's called The Ulmer Scale, I'm not sure—there's been a scale that's been created where you stick in an actor's name and it generates a percentage. . . . And that's how a lot of these guys overseas make money. They're like, we need 90%. Now if that means Don Cheadle and Gabriel Byrne and Kathleen Turner, fine. As long as it equals 90%. . . . Well, this is a scale that I have seen one time that someone pulled out of a briefcase and showed me, and that I've never seen again. . . . And I've been looking for it ever since.

—Don Cheadle, 2004

The Ulmer Scale, developed by James Ulmer, a film analyst, journalist, and contributing writer to the *New York Times*, in 1997, tracks and scores star bankability, which refers to "the degree to which an actor's name alone can raise full or majority financing up front for a motion picture."[1] The higher the score, the greater the actor's bankability. Don Cheadle's discovery of the Ulmer Scale parallels an incident in Morrison's *Beloved* when a former slave recounts the moment he discovered his economic value in the slave market. While the Ulmer Scale tracks the value of actors from all races, the commodification of black bodies has persisted since slavery. In 1787, the Three-fifths Compromise determined that three-fifths of the slave population in southern states would be counted for the purposes of taxation and representation.[2] This remained the practice until slavery was abolished with the adoption of the Thirteenth Amendment to the Constitution in 1865. A few years later, in 1868, the Fourteenth Amendment was passed, providing representation and equal protection to all people under the law. African Americans had no representation or protection as human beings under the law prior to these amendments, which had to be reinforced by the civil rights movement of the 1950s and 1960s.

The treatment of blacks under the Three-fifths Compromise is symbolically similar to the valuation of black stars on the Ulmer Scale, regardless of intention.

Under the Three-fifths Compromise, the black population served to benefit the very states that exploited them, yet black people could not reap the benefits of their contributions. This chapter considers the similarly liminal status of black stars in the current star system in Hollywood and its horizontal integration with professional theater. While all are measured according to their ability to generate revenue, this practice is particularly harmful for black actors, actresses, and audiences. Film and theater are the only industries in American society where one can legally use racial criteria in hiring practices. Casting notices frequently include the race, color, age, and other physical characteristics that actors must possess to even be considered. Plantation ideology is insidiously reinforced by such practices. The economic and cultural consequences for black Americans and women are, on close inspection, detrimental to the future of African American film.

It would be inaccurate and disrespectful to equate the experiences of current African American actors and actresses in Hollywood to enslaved Africans' positioning on plantations without acknowledging the vast differences between them. Enslaved Africans not only experienced limitations on their freedom but also death, maiming, sexual assault, and other violence and threats of violence that whites could inflict upon them with impunity. Unlike their ancestors, Cheadle and his colleagues can choose their professions and, in many cases, the roles they play. In comparison to their white counterparts, however, black actors still experience significant disparities. Although contemporary black actors and actresses may appear to have more options than their predecessors in the field, industry practices and established precedent significantly influences their careers and complicates their selections.

There are eerie parallels between the plantation scheme and the star system, especially in regard to branding, patterns of typecasting, and the path to stardom. Branding, discussed in greater detail in this chapter, is closely tied to typecasting and star power. Performers of any race who successfully execute a particular character type are more likely to be cast in similar roles. Through these roles and careful cultivation, the performer becomes a recognizable brand with symbolic and economic potential. Through ghosting, the performer infuses meaning from previous roles into the film while simultaneously attracting familiar audiences, which increases the film's earning potential. Typecasting limits all actors, but African Americans are at a particular disadvantage. Historically, casting patterns in mainstream Hollywood films are particularly challenging for black actors and actresses. They are considered for fewer roles and are often perceived as being a strain on revenue potential just because of their race. The cause for the sluggish growth in the number of the select few rising black stars becomes clear. As actor Samuel L. Jackson explains, if the power brokers in Hollywood can't sign a known black star, "they say, 'Well, we'll wait till we can.' They're not looking for the next us."[3] The visible presence of the best-known black stars such as Jackson and others discussed throughout this chapter gives the impression of progress and equality, while at the same time Hollywood studios' tunnel vision is significantly narrowing the path to stardom for women and people of color. The select few black stars with proven bankability achieved by successful branding through particular character types become commodities frequently used to serve the master narrative—albeit in often very subtle ways.

During slavery, black bodies were commodities, listed in the slave ledgers that documented their monetary value based on age, ability, appearance, and temperament. Today, we have the Ulmer Scale, which substantially influences all actors, especially individual black actors' and actresses' careers through casting and distribution. Fewer blacks are likely to make inroads in Hollywood in comparison to white actors. However, black actors and actresses that achieve significant star power have greater opportunities than lesser known blacks to play against type and challenge the master narrative in the process. This chapter divulges the paradox of black star power as a key factor shaping the future of African American film.

Stardom and the star system have been the subject of several scholarly projects. Film studies scholar Richard Dyer's analyses of stars and the culture of celebrity in *Stars* (1979) distinguishes between an actor, actress, and star in terms of the offscreen power dynamic, while his later works, *The Matter of Images: Essays on Representation* (1993) and *White* (1997), address matters of race and sexuality. Black actors' and actresses' historical struggle for visibility and autonomy has been chronicled in countless biographies as well as several academic studies, including Charlene Regester's *African American Actresses: The Struggle for Visibility 1900–1960* and Wendy Sung's "Mainstream African American Cinema: The Struggle for Black Images in Hollywood," which chronicles more recent phenomena since 2000. These works offer much needed exploration of individual and collective experiences of black actors and actresses on and offscreen, yet they do not include an economic perspective.

Randy A. Nelson and Robert Glotfelty, however, offer a constructive analysis in their article "Movie Stars and Box Office Revenues: An Empirical Analysis," which appeared in the *Journal of Cultural Economics* in 2012. Nelson and Glotfelty's core criticism concerns previous studies of movie stars and box office revenues that focus on a single star rather than the potential effect of multiple stars.[4] They examine relationships between star power and box office revenues with data from nine different countries as well as the continuous measure of star power based on the number of hits on a star's webpage on IMDB.com.[5] Defining star power as "an actor's ability to increase the number of movie goers who wish to see a given film"[6] or play, they examine a range of studies that found a positive relationship between star power and a film's success or no relationship between stars and box office revenues.[7] Nelson and Glotfelty reject the use of Oscar nominations and an actor's appearance in films ranked in the top ten at the box office, given that Oscar nominations limit the number of stars to twenty in any given year and the most successful films are franchises cast with actors who would not be considered true stars in the traditional sense.[8] But the authors do not interrogate the racial implication of this system of evaluation, nor do they acknowledge that black stars tend to receive fewer Oscar nominations than white actors and are cast less frequently in blockbuster franchises, especially in lead roles. They find that the Oscar standard "treats all nominated stars as if they are equal," even when some nominees have limited box office success in comparison to others.[9] On the other hand, several big box office stars such as Ben Stiller, Will Ferrell, Bruce Willis, Arnold Schwarzenegger, and Jim Carrey have never received Oscar nominations.[10] Of the few black stars mentioned in the article, top box office earners Eddie Murphy, Will Smith, and Denzel Washington have been nominated for Oscars.

Unlike McKenzie's study of the economic viability of African American films (discussed in the introduction), Nelson and Glotfelty do not consider the racial categorization of films, nor do they consider the race of the casts in the films they discuss. This chapter addresses the heretofore overlooked intersection of race, culture, and economics, elucidating how the location of black actors and actresses in the plantation scheme encroaches on the development of African American film.

The Making of a Black Star in Hollywood

Strategically creating stars to meet economic objectives has cultural conse-quences that are not altogether divorced from race. There are distinguish-able differences between actors, actresses, and stars. The primary distinction between star and celebrity is magnetism, which can be natural or constructed. Even an actor or actress with natural allure needs studio system support to gain traction. Many celebrities are not considered stars because they lack bankabil-ity, which "varies depending on the budget level of a movie. Generally, the lower the budget, the higher an actor's bankable value in that project."[11] Considering that films with predominantly black casts tend to have lower budgets, the bank-able value of actors on these projects should be higher. As discussed in greater detail below, the bankability of black stars is on average much lower than that of their white counterparts.

Bankability determines power. In *Stars*, Dyer uses biographer Patrick McGil-ligan's application of the auteur theory to actors (as opposed to directors) in order to explain that one has more power as a star than as merely an actor or actress that is "a semi-passive icon, a symbol that is manipulated by writers and directors."[12] Not all stars proactively develop their iconic status, but those auteurs can influence artistic decisions (e.g., casting, writing, directing) and demand certain limitations on the basis of their screen personas.[13] Some stars become so important to a production they can "change lines, adlib, shift meaning, influence the narrative and style of a film and altogether [signify] something clear-cut to audiences despite the intent of writers and directors."[14] Stars thus assume the privileges black performers have historically and covertly employed through indigenization. Morgan Freeman took liberties in his performance in *Driving Miss Daisy* even though he was not the star he has since become. The primary difference between the actor, actress, and star is not only the pay scale but also the power to influence representation and production outcome, which is intricately tied to economics.

Plantation ideology has historically positioned any black star in Hollywood as an anomaly, at least until Dorothy Dandridge. Dandridge's stardom in the 1950s was a contradictory improvement compared to several notable black actors and actresses that preceded her, including but not limited to Evelyn Preer, Bert Williams, Paul Robeson, Hattie McDaniel, and countless others.[15] Dandridge was able to obtain leading roles and star opposite white male stars. However, she was used primarily to reinforce race and gender hierarchies. In *The Decks Ran Red* (1958), Dandridge portrays Mahia, a Polynesian woman and wife of a black Polynesian cook. She is the object of desire of the captain and others on the ship, which leaves her in a precarious position as the only female on the freighter when a mutiny occurs. Around 1958, Dandridge was known as a black actress, although Hollywood frequently manipulated her complexion (she wore lighter makeup to portray nonblack racial Others and darker makeup to portray black women).[16] In *The Decks Ran Red*, Dandridge's Mahia embodies the same sense of hypersexuality as many of her other characters; she becomes the object of desire for multiple men across racial lines. In her posthumously published autobiography, Dandridge lamented, "America was not geared to make [a black woman] into a Liz Taylor, a Monroe or a Gardner. . . . My sex symbolism was as a wanton, a prostitute, not as a woman seeking love and a husband, the same as other women."[17] As Charlene Regester further commented, "Her hypersexuality and in consequence her husband's emasculation in *The Decks Ran Red* demonstrate how the cinema industry used black bodies to affirm the power and privilege of white males."[18]

The emergence of stars such as Dandridge, Sydney Poitier, and Harry Belafonte helped pave the way for contemporary black stars. For instance, Halle Berry has claimed Dandridge as her predecessor and in doing so obtained leading roles opposite white male stars. She even served as executive producer of and starred in the television movie *Introducing Dorothy Dandridge* (1999), for which she won an Emmy for Outstanding Lead Actress. Berry is part of a growing group of black stars. Black star power (the power of an actor or actress of African descent to significantly influence the production and outcome of a film through financing, performance, marketing, and/or distribution) has also been on the rise. The path to stardom frequently involves cultivating one's craft in stage and/or film productions with predominantly black casts before taking on roles in mainstream master narratives. Predominantly black cast productions such as *A Soldier's Play* introduced audiences to Denzel Washington and Samuel L. Jackson. Yet these actors' real star power on stage and screen stems from their crossover appeal to white audiences. Washington's apartheid film *Cry Freedom* (1987) and Jackson's appearance in the comedy franchise *National Lampoon's Loaded Weapon 1* (1993) helped them become stars around the same time that Morgan Freeman's stardom was on the rise as a result of his role in *Driving Miss Daisy*. Generally appearing in supporting roles to white males, these actors became iconic via international and crossover appeal that minimized predominantly black audiences. White American actors and actresses do not face the same challenge of crossing over (except in regard to Hollywood's international market, which is mostly populated by people of European and Asian descent).

But while black star power has grown significantly in the past few decades in comparison to previous eras, it remains restricted by precedent. Studio executives use tools such as the Ulmer Scale to assess risk based on the cast of a film. Although they insist their primary evaluation is based on money and not race, investment patterns suggest otherwise. Race and gender ideologies are deeply embedded in the formulas and patterns of production that produce them. The Ulmer Scale's risk assessment stems from surveying dozens of dealmakers "directly involved in the business of buying, selling, producing, financing and distributing talent and negotiating the deals" in Hollywood and key international territories.[19] This sounds very technical and devoid of any bias, but the result is the same. A star's bankability relies on their ability to cross over as a consumable product in markets that tend to exclude or minimize people of color. Therefore, black stars who can transcend the industry practice of using stars as brands to sell movies as products and instead use their star status as a business to create their own products are the key to the future of African American film.

Breaking Down the Ulmer Scale

James Ulmer, the creator of the Ulmer Scale, has been measuring star power for the *Hollywood Reporter* for over twenty years and has numerous well-known publications to his credit, including *James Ulmer's Hollywood Hot List: The Complete Guide to Star Ranking*, which has been dubbed "the industry bible of star power." His qualifications lend him a great deal of credibility. While he maintains that his ratings and methodologies are not foolproof, he does recommend that they can help manage risk. According to his website:

> The Ulmer Scale is the film industry's premier series of powerbases for tracking, measuring, and ranking the star power of more than 1,400 actors worldwide. Polling dozens of leading deal-makers from Hollywood and key international territories, the Scale uses a 100-point ranking system to measure bankability, the key component of star power. . . . Often it is the most critical factor in determining whether an actor is hired for a project. . . . The Ulmer Scale tracks [bankability] exclusively for all three film budget levels: art house, mid-range, and studio-level features.[20]

The Ulmer List tracks other critical factors, including stars' willingness to travel and promote a film, career management, level of professionalism, acting talent, and acting range, which are noticeably listed last. Star power and bankability determine whether a film gets distribution as well as how broadly and how long it will be circulated. Powerbrokers and professionals in the American filmmaking industry and abroad continue to consult the Ulmer Scale as a reliable tool for determining a project's economic viability.

The Ulmer Scale attempts to minimize risk by ranking bankability at three budget levels: low ($1–$8 million), medium ($8–$30 million), and high (more than $30 million). As noted, most films with predominantly black casts fall within the low or medium range. The tendency of films in the low and medium range to break even or exceed their budgets in receipts reinforces McKenzie's findings (see the introduction). While medium and low budget levels increases the bankability of the actors and actresses on the project, the smaller budget films tend to receive less distribution with reverberating consequences.

This ambiguously neutral process for assessing risk is more exclusive than studio executives and Ulmer may realize. Ulmer bases his outcome on interviews with a large sampling of international film buyers, financiers, sales agents, producers, and company executives. It is unclear if any of the power brokers he consults include African Americans or people of African descent in other parts of the world. To be sure, there are more power brokers of African descent than ever in Hollywood, including Marvet Britto (producer and founder of the Britto Agency), Tracey Edmonds (president and COO of Our Stories Films as well as president and CEO of Edmonds Entertainment), Kasi Lemmons (director, screenwriter, and actress), Suzanne de Passe (CEO of de Passe Entertainment Group, LLC), Andrea Nelson Meigs (motion picture talent agent for International Creative Management), James Lassiter (Will Smith's partner at Overbrook Entertainment), Jonathan Rodgers (president and CEO of TV One), and Charles King (senior vice-president and motion picture agent for William Morris Agency). Unfortunately, it is unclear if any of these people have any influence on the Ulmer ratings. The process is not exactly transparent in this regard and it is unknown if poll participants reflect the range of diversity that benefits all cultural backgrounds.

This is similar to the Motion Picture Association of America's (MPAA) ratings board, "which has been accused of being secretive, inconsistent and out of touch with American mores."[21] Ulmer ratings generated without representation of people of color are unquestionably problematic, regardless of intent. The Ulmer firm asserts that they are relying on global industry professionals who are at the intersection of the deal points.[22] As described, the Ulmer Scale's approach suggests a colorblind analysis of previous films and outcomes. However, a colorblind analysis of films that are not at all colorblind in form or content makes such claims suspect. Some critics voice additional concerns. According to film columnist Patrick Goldstein, the most recent list seems to be lagging behind contemporary public opinion.[23] Most top-ranking stars are white males over the age of thirty-five, whereas American audiences tend to appreciate younger stars like Zac Efron (who earns a score of 206 out of 300 on the Ulmer Scale), Shia LaBeouf (226), and Jamie Foxx (231). The list, however, reads more in favor of actors such as Al Pacino (242), Harrison Ford (253), and Robert Redford (226), especially for buyers who prefer name recognition of stars with longevity.

As Ulmer's trends reveal, establishing name recognition in the international market is tricky for all actors and actresses. It is particularly challenging for blacks that are significantly outnumbered in the industry and on the Ulmer Scale. This lag in name recognition suggests that outdated films and narratives dominate the international market. In other words, the international market lacks exposure to more varied recent films, narratives, and visual languages. The system reinforces this problem by manufacturing existing audience expectations rather than expanding them through consistent distribution of a broader range of films over a long period of time in order to build the requisite, competitive name recognition.

The Ulmer Scale's reliance on the international market is particularly complicated for black actors, actresses, and black film in general. It is especially difficult for black stars to establish name recognition abroad when films with predominantly black casts are less likely to be distributed internationally and the select few black stars that appear in the more widely distributed white-cast films occupy marginal roles. While black stars can transcend race through bankability, racial transcendence is flimsy and most effective when keeping the number and visibility of black bodies onscreen to a minimum. In other words, black stars are more visible and bankable when they occupy the screen with whites. These patterns of casting and distribution hamstring the development of black film.

Collectively, African American actors are perceived as less valuable than their white American counterparts. Industry practices of creating, calculating, and utilizing star power affects both the emergence and the lifespan of black stars. Close inspection of the Ulmer Scale ratings helps to illuminate the racial and gender disparities in casting and distribution practices. The scale includes categories for women and for actors and actresses of color, but whiteness and maleness remain unmarked. The bulk of the scale categorizes performers according to "The World's Top Actors" ranging from A+ to the D list, where the majority of black actors appear. This is followed by the same list arranged alphabetically, an uppers and downers list (tracking stars who have significantly increased or decreased their bankability since the previous scale), and graphs charting the progression or regression of select actors and actresses. Categories of the Top 50 Female Stars, Top 50 Black Stars, Top 50 Hispanic Stars, Top 50 Asian Stars (listing only 28), and the Top 50 South Asian Stars (listing only 14) conclude the scale. Although racial categories are used, the Ulmer Scale does not address the racial disparities reflected in its numbers. While the Ulmer Scale tracks data that industry insiders can use to determine a project's economic viability, it also provides useful evidence exposing the racial and gender disparities perpetuated in industry practices (see table 5).

The Ulmer Scale's authority in Hollywood necessitates an exploration of its potentially positive and negative influences on the development of African American film. The scale simultaneously epitomizes and exposes problems with so-called neutral data. At first glance, the 2009–2010 list appears very promising for African Americans because Will Smith tops the list as most bankable star in the world. But a closer look at the racially stratified catalog reveals several problems. Smith is the only African American and Reese Witherspoon the only woman who appear on the top ten list of the World's Top Actors, a list that will significantly influence films produced in the coming years. According to this list, white men will dominate the films that are most likely to gain a broad distribution. Relying on the Ulmer Scale increases the likelihood that more films like those discussed in chapter 1 are going to be produced and distributed by Hollywood studios in the domestic and international market. This is how the master narrative maintains its authority.

Moreover, while the bankability of an actor or actress may not be solely based on race or gender, the fact that African Americans and women in general score much lower on the scale than white males is problematic. Blacks fare better than Latino/as, Asians, and South Asians, but the ratings nevertheless expose a racial component that cannot be ignored. The current system ensures that a white actor of a particular caliber must be included in nonwhite, studio-produced films in order to secure competitive financing and distribution. Unless it has a relatively well known white director, a bankable black director,

TABLE 5.

The Ulmer Scale in Black

Star Rating	Definition	No. Black Stars/Total	Examples
A+ (300–291)	"Fireproof" stars that can nearly always guarantee upfront sale, regardless of script, cast, director, or producer. Their names alone assure studios a strong opening weekend.	1 of 2	Will Smith
A (290–251)	Stars that may not trigger an automatic upfront sale, but are an excellent bet if director and budget is right and material is consistent with actor's past work. Like A+, they can virtually guarantee a wide studio release for their films.	1 of 26	Denzel Washington
B+ (250–201)	Actors that can nearly boast the same clout as A stars, but elements in film package (budget and co-stars) may weigh heavier. Can usually guarantee studio distribution.	5 of 84	Jamie Foxx, Morgan Freeman, Eddie Murphy, Halle Berry, and Beyoncé Knowles
B (200–151)	Can sometimes trigger upfront sale but other factors such as script, genre, director, co-stars, and budget are all the more important. Their name value sometimes guarantees territorial sales in ancillary markets such as free and pay TV, cable, video, and DVD.	11 of 122	Samuel L. Jackson, Forest Whitaker, Laurence Fishburne, Vin Diesel, Chris Tucker, Chris Rock, Cuba Gooding Jr., Don Cheadle, Queen Latifah, Whoopi Goldberg, and Danny Glover
C (150–101)	These actors have little, if any, ability to trigger a presale based on their names alone. With the right co-stars, directors, and budgets, however, they can occasionally enhance territorial sales in the ancillary markets.	18 of 327	Martin Lawrence, Dave Chappelle, Angela Bassett, Jada Pinkett Smith, Ice Cube, Thandie Newton, Alfre Woodard (and eleven others)
D (0–100)	Actors with little or no traction in pre-sales or in the ancillary markets.	60 of 841	Vivica A. Fox, Viola Davis, Taraji P. Henson, Ice T, Morris Chestnutt, Mario Van Peebles, Eve, Wanda Sykes, Regina King, Lela Rochon, Omar Epps, Larenz Tate, Nia Long, Kimberly Elise, Zoë Saldaña (and forty-five others)

or multiple bankable black actors whose influence can match that of a single white star, African American film must include roles for white males. With the exception of those few at the very top, a single black actor does not equal the numerical value associated with a white actor in the same category. These valuations are eerily reminiscent of the Three-fifths Compromise. The racial and gender disparities in the Ulmer Scale ratings are reflected through studios' support of films featuring predominantly white casts with male leads. These films can exclude people of color with impunity, facing no limitations in distribution due to lack of diversity in a film. On the contrary, films featuring a predominantly black or Latino/a cast are often unable to secure competitive budgets and distribution in comparison to a film with a predominantly white cast. These are some of the consequences of relying on the Ulmer Scale's racially and gender-stratified ratings to assess and manage economic risk without considering the ideological implications.

Moreover, as Cheadle found, the scale itself is difficult to access. One copy of the Actor's *Hot List* 2009–2010 costs $199, a steep price for the average consumer. Not only is the publication protected by copyright laws, there is a clause stating that "no part of this publication may be reproduced, stored in a retrieval system, or transmitted in any form, transmitted by any means—electronic, mechanical, photocopying, recording or otherwise—without prior permission of the copyright proprietor thereof" (Ulmer 1997–2010). Understandably, the consulting firm would like to maintain ownership and economic control over its intellectual property, products, and services. Yet Hollywood's reliance on these figures and the lack of transparency involved in identifying the global industry professionals participating in the data collection suggests a deliberate, clandestine operation.[24]

Cheadle's comments about the Ulmer Scale appeared in a PBS series entitled *America Beyond the Color Line*. In the series, Henry Louis Gates Jr. talks with several industry insiders about whether Hollywood is institutionally racist or if it is becoming increasingly color-blind in pursuit of the box office dollar. When the Ulmer Scale group caught wind of Cheadle's comments, they found a way to use them as a marketing tool. Under the press and media section on their website, they include a partial transcript of Cheadle's conversation with Gates. Below the transcript, they posted the following: "We deeply appreciate your subversive tone in describing the Scale. From the sound of it we are The Bearers of an Opus-Dei-ish Secret Code, stashing our stats in underground caverns and unveiling them only during Dark of the Moon Initiation Ceremonies for Commie Producers at Ed Asner's House. Nicely done, Don."[25] The tone of the response and the fact that the group advertised their decision to send Cheadle a free copy of the scale so "he won't have to look for it anymore," as well as putting him on its cover, suggests that a cynical view guides these methodologies. The group's willingness to use his image (along with those of several other performers) and comments further reinforces plantation ideology. It is unclear if the consultancy compensated Cheadle beyond giving him a free copy of the $199 publication. The consultancy closes the page with this statement: "May he win his Oscar (and raise his score) soon"—further insinuating that the Ulmer Scale has a unique authority to determine his worth. Regardless of intent, this exchange exhibits the very plantation ideology plaguing the development of African American film because it overlooks how race, color, and gender influence investment decisions. Notably, Ulmer's eagerness to comply with the use of his numerical data to clarify the racial implications of star power for this study is promising in spite of the Ulmer Scale group's published response to Cheadle.

Employing the Ulmer Scale without acknowledging the plantation ideology embedded within it is hazardous. Although Will Smith's bankability exceeds Johnny Depp's by one point, the disparity between white stars and black stars is clear (see Figure 5 and appendix). Following Smith, all of the top ten white stars and several others precede Denzel Washington, the second black actor on the list of black stars. In other words, only one black star scores above any of the top ten white stars. Smith and Washington are the only black stars that score within twenty points of their white counterparts. The Ulmer Scale recognizes that no one can predict box office success, but the consultancy emphasizes the validity and reliability of their data collection and analysis of trends in the careers of actors and actresses. Yet these trends devalue black actors and actresses by relying heavily on established precedent. Such standards do not acknowledge that African American films consistently achieve comparatively greater economic success than other films in the domestic box office. This limited perspective is driven by the promise of excessive profits in the international market, in which Hollywood has cultivated a taste for films with predominantly white casts, rendering black, Latina/o, Asian, South Asian, and Native Americans virtually invisible. The Ulmer Scale Risk Consultancy and the Hollywood studio system do not openly subscribe to the racial or gender ideology reflected in these valuations. Yet these patterns have real consequences.

Casting Patterns, Narratives, Distribution, and the Future

Since casting patterns are intricately tied to narrative, producers attempting to manage risk are more likely to adopt master narratives and hire white actors in spite of black film's positive economic trends. In the case of nonwhite narratives, a white point of entry becomes an economic necessity if filmmakers want to secure studio financing or distribution. Some have transcended these challenges while others have been unable to navigate the treacherous terrain of the Hollywood studio system and financial grids used to manage risk,

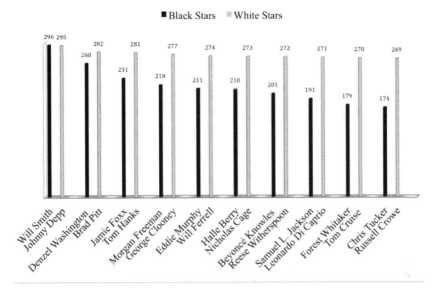

FIGURE 5: Comparison of Ulmer Ratings of the Top 10 Black Stars and Top 10 White Stars, 2009–2010

Source: James Ulmer, *The Ulmer Scale* (Los Angeles: Ulmer Scale, 1997–2010), 39–66.

create products and audiences, and develop or diminish star power. While the white point of entry is problematic for many black narratives and filmmakers exploring black subject matter, it has been used strategically and subversively onscreen and off. As revealed in chapters 2 and 4, the white point of entry can negatively influence African American storytelling by promoting superficial racial reconciliation narratives.

A white character proved necessary in Spike Lee's *Do the Right Thing* (1989), a film depicting increasing racial tension in a Brooklyn neighborhood during the hottest day of the summer. Lee originally asked Robert De Niro to play the role of Sal, the Italian American pizzeria owner, which aligns with studio practices of enlisting a major white star in films with predominantly black casts. De Niro declined, however. This decision ultimately benefitted the film's ensemble dynamic.[26] Casting a star such as De Niro may have ensured broad distribution, but, as Lee later recognized, having a major white star in a predominantly black ensemble cast could have undermined the narrative's focus on the community. The role of Sal went instead to Danny Aiello. Spike Lee portrayed Mookie, an African American who worked for Sal delivering pizzas. Throughout the film, racial tensions build to a boiling point. The film ends the way Lee envisioned, with Mookie aligning with the community protestors that burn down Sal's shop after the police murder his friend, Radio Raheem (Bill Nunn).[27] However, the film's significance would have been dramatically changed had Paramount had its way. Three days before shooting began, the studio asked Lee to change the ending, to instead have Mookie and Sal (in Lee's words) "hug and be friends and sing 'We Are the World.'"[28] While creative control can also be an issue for white directors, this example clearly demonstrates how the ramifications of cultural representation can be particularly challenging for black directors. Changes made in the struggle for creative control can modify story dynamics and undermine honest explorations of black subject matter. Casting a major white star as a white point of entry and superficially resolving racial conflict between Italian Americans, African Americans, and a predominantly white police force would have disrupted and depoliticized Lee's narrative.[29]

Filmmakers asked to make alterations do not have to comply, though they risk losing funding. When Paramount presented Lee with the option to change the ending and keep the $8–10 million budget, Lee pitched the project to Universal in time to secure a $6.3 million budget instead. As previously established, films with lower budgets receive less distribution. This film is just one example of how more creative control affects distribution. Since smaller budget films receive less distribution, alternative distribution strategies are crucial.

In spite of Lee's skillful filmmaking and savvy negotiation for creative control, the film was noticeably absent from the Academy Awards. The honor for Best Picture that year was bestowed upon *Driving Miss Daisy*, thereby reinforcing the master narrative and limiting Lee's ability at the time to increase his score on the *Hot List* of Directors. Lee and other African American directors have yet to win an Academy Award for their efforts. Still, Lee has achieved a level of credibility and celebrity thanks in part to the unprecedented relationship he established between African American directors and major studios with *Do the Right Thing*. The film's subject matter, cinematic style, and the compromises Lee made in the process offer a model for African American filmmaking quite different from that of Tyler Perry.

Guaranteed distribution through casting inherently limits development of more nuanced narratives. As indicated by the Ulmer Scale, a "fireproof star" is the only sure way "to guarantee an upfront sale, regardless of script, cast, director or producer" on the project.[30] At present, Will Smith and Johnny Depp are the only actors with this status. This means that only narratives with a male lead are guaranteed distribution. For his part, Smith has established crossover appeal, and it is significant that his only film that addresses racial politics, the biopic *Ali* (2005)—for which he was nominated for an Academy Award—is his lowest grossing film to date. He has since avoided films that evoke any kind of overt racial discourse, appearing instead primarily in action films (the *Men in Black* franchise), romantic comedies (*Hitch*), and biopics (*The Pursuit of Happyness*, for which he earned an additional Academy Award nomination). In short, with such few highly bankable actors in Hollywood, the range of narratives and characters guaranteed distribution is severely limited.

Maintaining the cultural perspective of a project does not always doom a film to economic failure. *Do the Right Thing* earned $27 million on its $6.3 million budget. The film secured competitive distribution with two out of the five majors, Paramount and then Universal, with Universal subsequently distributing several of Lee's films.[31] The director has a history of securing major distributors for his work.

As a renowned director, Lee can positively influence his films' distribution. As an African American director, his unprecedented relationship with major distributors such as Universal, Warner Bros., and Twentieth Century–Fox has also influenced the emergence of black stars in Hollywood. Lee's celebrity and studio support enables him to enlist the most bankable actors for his projects, which usually encourages studio distribution. However, Lee regularly reserves roles for talented newcomers. This practice has significantly affected the development of African American film and the emergence of black stars. Lee was the first to cast Halle Berry, Queen Latifah, Martin Lawrence, and Mekhi Phifer. Lee also worked with prominent actors such as Samuel L. Jackson before they became noteworthy in mainstream Hollywood.

The paradoxical nature of black stardom in Hollywood can be seen in the high number of films featuring predominantly white casts with blacks in minor and supporting roles that get produced in Hollywood in comparison to films with predominantly black casts. The definition of success for black stars and directors often requires successful crossover into mainstream films or television shows with predominantly white casts. Actors who have achieved this include Halle Berry (*Father Hood* [1993], *Losing Isaiah* [1995]), Queen Latifah (*Living Out Loud* [1998], *Chicago* [2002], with an Academy Award nomination), and Mekhi Phifer (*Hell's Kitchen* [1998], *I Still Know What You Did Last Summer* [1998]). Black stars attempting to increase bankability are essentially required to court white audiences. By doing so, they increase their Ulmer Scale ratings but not the overall production of African American films with broad distribution. Their higher ratings may enhance their ability to "guarantee studio distribution" or "sometimes trigger an upfront sale," but the improved rating is less often used in conjunction with films featuring predominantly black casts. Instead, it lends greater support to production of films with predominantly white casts in which black actors must now appear in order to maintain their ratings.

On occasion, first-rate black star power is used to boost the careers of other rising stars. Martin Lawrence's crossover stardom followed his co-starring with more bankable crossover black stars such as Eddie Murphy (*Boomerang* [1992]) and Will Smith (*Bad Boys* [1995]) while also starring in *Martin*, his Fox television series featuring a predominantly black cast (1992–1997). He has since become a household name, although he still straddles the Ulmer Scale's B and C lists. Black crossover stars such as Freeman are also used to further the careers of lesser-known white actors. In *Safe House* (2012), a rogue CIA operative (Denzel Washington, who also served as executive producer), evades, manipulates, mentors, and eventually succumbs to a rising CIA agent (white actor Ryan Reynolds) whose values of patriotism overcome Washington's conniving character. This film in particular reveals how the limitations imposed by established precedent influence narratives even when black star power carries the film.

With strategic planning, black star power can positively influence distribution, profitability, and the development of rising stars across racial categories. In other words, cross-racial casting can potentially work both ways. Under ideal circumstances, blacks, Latina/os, Native Americans, Asians, South Asians, and whites can combine star power to attract diverse audiences. Interculturation as opposed to acculturation can empower and enrich participants and products, thereby establishing potential for new standards, some of which are discussed in chapter 6. Unfortunately, when black stars crossover to white audiences through minor and supporting roles in films with predominantly white casts, they are absorbed into the mainstream and are frequently unable to maintain the connection with the core audience that catapulted them to stardom in the first place. They rarely appear in films with predominantly black casts again.

Black Star Ratings in Context

Currently, as a result of the Ulmer Scale and related matrices, African American stars occupy a unique position in Hollywood. Specifically, more black stars appear on the Ulmer Hot List than stars from any other nonwhite ethnic group. New "bonus sections," as the Ulmer website refers to them, also reflect disconcerting statistics for women and other minorities. Of the top ten female stars (in studio-level movies), Penelope Cruz and Cameron Diaz, listed at number ten and number four, respectively, are the only Hispanic actresses listed. The list of the top ten female stars has no African American, Asian, or South Asian stars. Moreover, both Cruz and Diaz are phenotypically white. The heightened status of phenotypically white Hispanic women in studio-level films parallels preferences for mulatta-type or light-skinned black actresses (discussed later in this chapter). Such casting patterns simultaneously reinforce gender hierarchies.

The Ulmer Scale, as noted, consistently privileges white men. The plantation ideology embedded in this rating system is laid bare by the scale's gender and race valuations. The master narrative almost always uses a black-white binary (apparent in films such as *Convicts* and *Driving Miss Daisy*) to the exclusion of other ethnicities. Dependence upon the white point of entry in this paradigm also makes it less likely that films with predominantly black casts can include Native American, Latino, Asian and Asian American, and South Asian performers in their films without negatively influencing distribution. All this ultimately affects the Ulmer Scale ratings of people of color.

The *Rush Hour* franchise, however, sets an unusual precedent. A mainstream variation of the black/white buddy formula as seen in the *Lethal Weapon* franchise, it features an Asian and an African American, Jackie Chan and Chris Tucker. This cross-racial casting is made possible due to Chan's exceptionally high ranking on the scale and international superstar status—he carries a rating of 236 out of 300. As a comedy and action hybrid, the films rarely investigate the complex relationship of African Americans and Asian Americans in depth. Cultural differences are humorously observed and interspersed throughout action sequences. Such pairings represent another strategy for reinforcing the master narrative. Both characters are marked by racial stereotypes, the very stereotypes that reinforce white supremacy even in the absence of a major white character or actor. Chan also stars in the remake *The Karate Kid* (2010) with Will Smith's son, Jaden Smith. Successful narrative and casting formulas, such as pairing African American and Asian stars in buddy films, are likely to be repeated when proven economically viable through multiple films.

The structure and frequency of producing and reproducing master narratives inadvertently limits opportunities for black, Latina/o, Asian, South Asian, and Native American stars, most of whom do not appear on the Ulmer Scale. Without frequent opportunities to perform, or having to rely primarily upon minor or supporting roles, the likelihood these stars will increase their Ulmer rating is slim. Additionally, the possibility of introducing new stars of similar ethnicities severely decreases. Paradoxically, in the black-white racial reconciliation narrative, black stars possess an element of privilege denied stars of other ethnicities. Nonetheless, white stars maintain a monopoly on roles in studio-level films. The complex history and visible struggle of African Americans in the United States complicates their status and condition as one of the most bankable nonwhite ethnic groups in Hollywood.

"When and Where I Enter": Black Women and Stardom

In her book *A Voice from the South* (1892), Anna Julia Cooper identifies the dual oppression black women experience due to racism and sexism: "Only the Black woman can say, when and where I enter, in the quiet, undisputed dignity of my womanhood, without violence and without suing or special patronage, then and there the whole Negro race enters with me."[32] Considering the unique position African American women occupy in society generally and in Hollywood specifically, the role of black actresses in shaping the future of African American film requires careful consideration. As discussed in chapter 3, Oprah Winfrey's success can be misleading in terms of the overall standing of black women in Hollywood. A closer look at the careers of a group of black actresses reveals major problems at the intersections of race, color, and gender. Black men, regardless of complexion, and light-skinned black women tend to have greater star power than black women with darker complexions. Acknowledging "when and where [and how]" the black actress enters the paradigm exposes several disconcerting patterns bound to influence future film production if they are not actively challenged.

Star power for black women is a precious commodity closely tied to race and color. The only two black women to appear on the Top Ten Black Actors list are Halle Berry (with a score of 210) and Beyoncé Knowles (201). Along with Thandie Newton (116) and Vanessa L. Williams (58), these actresses represent a mulatta type popularized in the minstrel tradition and the Tom Shows of the late nineteenth and early twentieth centuries and exemplified for nearly a century in actresses such as Evelyn Preer, Nina Mae McKinney, Fredi Washington, Lena Horne, and Dorothy Dandridge. The roles they play have a complex history and continue to haunt African American actresses striving to attain star power in Hollywood. Even in films with predominantly black casts and black directors, actresses who embody the mulatta type are most often cast in leading lady roles but only as the love interest of white and black male stars. As a result, African American women with lighter skin are more likely to attain star power in Hollywood than those with darker complexions.

Women with darker complexions or more varied body types have made inroads in Hollywood, but rarely as leading ladies, which makes a difference in terms of star power. In mainstream films with predominantly white casts they are more likely to receive minor or supporting roles as the sidekick, best friend, nurse, or servant for the white or lighter-skinned lead—in other words, they primarily serve the role of the Other. Yet some darker-skinned actresses have had opportunities to play interracial love interests. Mo'Nique has a minor role as a woman in an interracial relationship in *Shadowboxer* (2005). Tyra Ferrell portrays John Turturro's interracial love interest in *Jungle Fever* (1991), which primarily focuses on the interracial relationship between a married black man (Wesley Snipes) and his Italian American co-worker (Annabella Sciorra). Whoopi Goldberg engages in an interracial relationship in *Sister Act* (1992), a film in which she starred as a lounge singer who hides out in a convent after witnessing her lover (Harvey Keitel) commit a murder. N'Bushe Wright co-stars as white American actor Michael Rappaport's love interest in *Zebra Head* (1992). Taraji P. Henson is the love interest of Adam Rodriguez, a Latino, love interest in Tyler Perry's *I Can Do Bad All By Myself* (2009). With the exception of Henson and Wright, these actresses are not often portrayed as desirable to white or black men. As a result, lighter-skinned black actresses who fit the mulatta type are afforded more opportunities to play leading ladies and love interests alongside prominent white male leads. Consider the following examples: Halle Berry and Bruce Willis (Ulmer score of 244) in *Perfect Stranger* (2007), Beyoncé Knowles and Mike Myers (231) in *Austin Powers: Goldmember* (2002), Thandie Newton and Mark Wahlberg (241) in *The Truth about Charlie* (2002), and Vanessa L. Williams with Arnold Schwarzenegger (237) in *Eraser* (1996). Here again we see how plantation ideology values whiteness, maleness, and light complexions.

The Ulmer Scale emphasizes the importance of name recognition. For the mulatta type, desirability is often the primary way of achieving this. The offscreen personas of light-skinned actresses can become just as important as their onscreen roles. Berry's desirability initially as a pageant contestant, model, and actress exemplifies the mainstream appeal of her look, which almost worked against her desire to be taken seriously as an actress. She had to prove to the director and producers of *Monster's Ball* that she could believably portray Leticia Musgrove, an impoverished black woman who is married to a black death-row inmate and is mother to their obese son. Musgrove eventually becomes the love interest of the white racist prison guard (Billy Bob Thornton) who helps execute her husband. This role earned her an Oscar. Berry has since obtained a level of name recognition that clearly influenced her rising score in spite of the turmoil in her personal life: two very public divorces (from David Justice and Eric Benét), a failed interracial relationship with Gabriel Aubrey (also the father of her first child) followed by a nasty custody dispute with charges of racism, and her more recent marriage to French actor Olivier Martinez.

Berry's career has survived box office flops only to face other challenges. She starred in *Catwoman* (2004), a Hollywood experiment featuring a biack female lead in an action film that earned a reputation as the worst picture of the year, taking down with it the likelihood for similar innovations in casting. Following the debacle, Berry returned to her marginal status as Storm in the *X-Men* franchise, co-starred in films with (phenotypically) white male leads (*Things We Lost in the Fire* [2007]), and appeared in predominantly white ensembles (*New Year's Eve* [2011]). The only films with predominantly black casts she has starred in since *Why Do Fools Fall in Love* (1998) are not theatrical releases but the television dramas *Introducing Dorothy Dandridge* (1999) and *Their Eyes Were Watching God* (2005). In fact, Berry's progression as a movie star perfectly exemplifies how Hollywood tends to draw black stars away from films with predominantly black casts. *Catwoman* also reiterates how black individuals and single films featuring a black protagonist become representative of all black films when they fail economically. Films with predominantly white casts and white performers do not endure this type of scrutiny. Nonetheless, Berry has maintained her career in spite of these challenges, and her desirability persists.

Berry has also parlayed her star power into producing. She was the executive producer of *Introducing Dorothy Dandridge* and *Lackawana Blues* (2005) and the producer of *Frankie & Alice* (2010). While the first two films were television dramas, the latter's failed theatrical release suggests even Berry's name with her Oscar-pedigree and desirability could not guarantee distribution. This is bad news for African American film. In *Frankie & Alice*, Berry plays a black woman with multiple personality disorder who is in danger of succumbing to her racist alter-personality. Freestyle Releasing distributed the film, which played in one theater for three days, grossing approximately $9,000. Considering Berry's evolution, the outcome of this film strongly suggests that an actress who fits the mulatta type only wields star power when she occupies the designated position within a plantation scheme (i.e., as the white or black male's object of desire). Venturing out of this location to examine more in-depth human experiences from black or biracial perspectives, particularly in a woman-centered narrative, invites censorship through limited or no distribution. Even the careers of stars such as Berry, who persists in being recognized for her beauty and sex appeal by black and crossover audiences, are thwarted by industry practices.

Beyoncé Knowles, the only other woman on the Top Ten Black Actors list, exemplifies how horizontal integration reinforces plantation ideology across media. As a singer, Knowles does not have the same tenure or credentials as Berry or the other actresses mentioned here. However, her Ulmer Scale ratings speak volumes about the power of branding. Her path is similar to Queen Latifah, Will Smith, Ice Cube, and many other black recording artists past and present who have successfully transitioned their brand from music to movies. Her sex symbol persona is mutually reinforced by her L'Oreal endorsements. Over the years her complexion has become increasingly lighter on album covers and ads, reinforcing the narrative of her Creole heritage while simultaneously deemphasizing her blackness.[33] Intentionally or not, her rise has relied on branding that flourishes by creating distance from her blackness and instead staking claims of mixed heritage. This translates into bankability for black actors and actresses in the industry, especially if the physical features are there.

Knowles has numerous Grammys and music awards to her credit, in spite of questions concerning her credibility as an actress.[34] She starred in the television film *Carmen: A Hip Hopera* (2001) and theatrical releases *Austin Powers in Goldmember* (2002), *The Fighting Temptations* (2003), *Dreamgirls* (2006), *Cadillac Records* (2008), and *Obsessed* (2009). Each role embodies her sex appeal, vocal talents, or some combination of the two. Her name recognition is inextricably tied to her desirability as well as her combined wealth with rapper mogul and husband Jay-Z, also known as Shawn Carter. The rise of a black star such as

Knowles is inevitable in an industry with an insatiable appetite for profit, especially since Dandridge cemented the precedent set by Lena Horne and Hazel Scott. These actresses grew increasingly political, which ultimately damaged their careers. For her part, Knowles rarely makes any direct comments regarding race or politics, although she endorsed President Barack Obama's reelection campaign and his support for gay marriage, and she called for a moment of silence for Trayvon Martin during a concert and appeared but did not speak at a Justice for Trayvon rally with her husband following the controversial verdict in the high-profile 2013 murder case. In general, however, Knowles treads carefully, accessing privilege historically denied to actresses of darker hue or with more overt political opinions.

Emphasis on the bottom line ensures blacks in comedic and musical roles dominate black representation. As a consequence, there is less opportunity for more serious themed films that might feature a broader range of black representation, especially in regard to images of black female desirability. Like Berry, Thandie Newton established her onscreen image of allure as a leading lady to white male stars by repeatedly appearing in interracial relationships in films such as *Jefferson in Paris* (1995), *The Journey of August King* (1995), *The Leading Man* (1996), *Besieged* (1998), *The Truth about Charlie* (2002), *The Chronicles of Riddick* (2004), *Run, Fatboy, Run* (2007), and *Retreat* (2011). The frequency in which she appears in interracial relationships onscreen, as well as her actual interracial marriage to British writer/director/producer Ol Parker, firmly establishes her desirability and crossover appeal to white audiences. Her casting patterns exemplify Hollywood's tendency to employ light-skinned actresses who fit the mulatta type to superficially explore interracial interaction through sex and at times actual relationships.

The potential reversal of power in this casting dynamic can also be seen in Newton's career. Like Berry, she has also played opposite prominent black male stars, thereby showing how star power generated in films with predominantly white casts can be transferred to support films with predominantly black casts or related films. She has appeared in films with Academy Award nominees Terrence Howard (*Crash* [2004]), Will Smith (*The Pursuit of Happyness* [2006]), and Eddie Murphy (*Norbit* [2007]). Her more recent work in Tyler Perry's films, *for colored girls* (2010) and *Good Deeds* (2012), is mutually beneficial. Her name recognition, talent, and crossover appeal lends credibility to Perry's work. His films also provide her greater exposure to his core audiences, which have helped produce significant box office revenues. However, the economic benefits are not often redirected back to African American films. Nevertheless, Newton has distinguished herself as a credible actress. She has yet to be nominated for an Academy Award in spite of her range and talent. It is possible her severely critiqued performance as the title character in *Beloved* may have influenced her

Ulmer Scale rating, which is considerably lower than Berry's and Knowles's. However, Newton's appeal to crossover audiences and core black audiences persists in spite of this.

Although actresses who can portray the mulatta type may in general have more access to opportunities in films with predominantly white casts or with black casts than actresses with darker complexions, they are not immune to some of the challenges that all actors face. In addition to the difficulties of typecasting, age can also play a factor in star power. The fact is that few roles are available in big-budget and/or studio-produced movies for actresses who are over forty-five years old. For an actress such as Vanessa L. Williams, this greatly diminishes their star power. As a beauty pageant veteran, model, and recording artist, the majority of Williams's roles are for television rather than theatrical release. This is unlikely to change given that she has a score of 58 out of 300 on the Ulmer Scale, placing her firmly on the D-list. Williams's current status on the Ulmer Scale exemplifies the challenges of maintaining and cultivating star power in an industry that privileges actors who are young, white, and male.

There are other limitations to star power that are infused with colorism, further revealing race hierarchies. Although the African American actresses discussed above have a greater chance of achieving the highest ratings on the Ulmer Scale, they are not guaranteed roles that call for black or biracial actors. Even as recently as 2007, Angelina Jolie, a white American actress who has a score of 258, portrayed a biracial woman who loses her white husband to a terrorist execution in *A Mighty Heart* (2007). Jolie's bankability substantially exceeds that of Berry, Knowles, Newton, and Williams. Why risk casting a black woman or a woman of mixed heritage when you can cast a white woman whose star power guarantees wide distribution? Such are the consequences of putting profits over all else. Of course even with highly bankable actors, a film can still have a miserable box office performance. With a production budget of $16 million, *A Mighty Heart* grossed only $9 million domestically and an additional $9 million internationally. In other words, it took international distribution for the film to break even—in contrast with films with predominantly black casts that were not distributed abroad even though they proved their ability to make a substantial profit in the domestic market. Thus *A Mighty Heart* demonstrates the structural privilege white stars and productions receive through distribution. Yet the film's failure at the domestic box office does not mean failure for any other film with a predominantly white cast, nor has it prevented Jolie from making at least eight other films since then. But Berry's failure with *Catwoman* had much greater consequences that not only continue to affect her career, but also film productions featuring black protagonists or predominantly black casts. Whether or not African American actresses embody the mulatta type, they have comparatively limited options that still may be denied if bankability does not add up to secure investment. The playing field is not as level as studio executives and the Ulmer Scale suggest. As a result, minimal roles for African American women combined with their Ulmer Scale ratings have had a significant influence on the development of African American film.

Recurring patterns of colorism are apparent in several films examined as part of this study. Darker-skinned actresses who play love interests to black male stars tend to be comparatively lighter in complexion than their male lovers (Robin Givens, Nia Long, Gabrielle Union, Meagan Good, Angela Bassett, Taraji P. Henson, Kerry Washington, Regina King, Kimberly Elise, Vivica A. Fox). Consistently casting lighter-skinned actresses in these roles inevitably reinforces mainstream standards of beauty. Darker-skinned actresses such as Whoopi Goldberg, Viola Davis, Mo'Nique, Octavia Spencer, Alfre Woodard, CCH Pounder, and Irma P. Hall tend to play more character roles in the supporting category. Such positioning severely decreases the likelihood of having a narrative film built around these actresses, unless they are portraying the traditional roles associated with their type. Davis's first leading role in a studio-produced film was in *The Help*, in which she played a maid to white families in 1960s Mississippi. Mo'Nique has yet to play a lead role in a studio-produced film, but she has starred in a sitcom with a predominantly black cast, *The Parkers*, and served as executive producer of *Phat Girlz* (2006). Billed as a comedy, the film is more of a dramedy focusing on her character's professional goals of becoming a plus-size fashion designer while also struggling with self-esteem issues resulting from her weight. Goldberg's first starring role was as Celie in *The Color Purple* (1985). In Woodard's first prominently featured role in *Extremities* (1986), she plays a roommate of Farah Fawcett's character. Pounder also mostly takes on supporting film and television roles since she initially starred in *Bagdad Café* (1987) as a truck stop café owner who befriends a white German tourist who eventually works there. The fact that the majority of these women rarely play leading characters in film and television (even early in their careers) decreases the circulation of their names and also reinforces the types they physically represent as marginal. Such practices reinforce the devaluing of blackness.

When working behind the camera, these actresses afford new opportunities to other black actors. Berry's work as an executive producer later provided Newton an opportunity to appear in *Lackawana Blues*. Woodard, Goldberg, and others have also produced or executive produced films, some of which feature predominantly black casts. However limited by plantation ideology, the star power of these actresses indicates the untapped potential of black star power in Hollywood to further develop African American film.

Black Star Power: Will Smith, Jamie Foxx, and Eddie Murphy

With bankable white male stars outweighing racially diverse and female actors and actresses, the master narrative reigns. It serves as the star vehicle for white men (*A Few Good Men*) and white women (*Extremities*) while ethnic minorities are consistently marginalized in the category of supporting characters that are only significant in relation to whites or whiteness. The star system and the master narrative have a symbiotic relationship that reinforces the vicious cycle of perceived failure for African Americans and other people of color as well as women. In spite of these challenges, more black actors and actresses are becoming increasingly strategic in terms of boosting their star power in front of and behind the camera.

In addition to his privileged status as the world's biggest star, Will Smith also exemplifies the dual influence of onscreen and offscreen star power. Smith and partners James Lassiter and Ken Stovitz own Overbrook Entertainment, which has become one of the most lucrative production companies in Hollywood. Not only did they invest in an off-Broadway production of Wilson's *Jitney*, they also produced a dozen films that have performed well at the box office (see table 6). Smith starred in seven of those films, which were distributed by Sony, Twentieth Century–Fox, and Warner Bros., three of the top five distribution companies. Source material for the films was either literary or based on real-life events with the exception of *Hitch, Seven Pounds*, and *Hancock*. Notably, even the comparatively low-grossing *Seven Pounds* turned a profit, unlike *Ali*, the film in which Smith shares the screen with the most blacks and which actually had a negative return on investment. The films that are not based on books or real-life events that have done extremely well are commercial genre films such as the action film *Hancock* and the romantic comedy *Hitch*. Smith became the most bankable star in the world by playing lead roles in a variety of commercial genre films generally targeted at crossover audiences.

In the case of *Hitch*, Smith became the first African American male lead to star in a studio-level romantic comedy. He initially wanted Oscar winner Halle Berry to co-star in the film, but that would have made it a black film and limited its worldwide distribution. This is yet another example in which plantation ideology denies a black actress employment. Thus while Overbrook's cross-racial casting represents a positive example of developing star power amongst people of color and challenges the black-white binary so frequently reproduced in the master narrative, it also further reinforces narrative patterns of colorism and racism. By casting Eva Mendes, a Latina actress with a score of 136 on the Ulmer Scale, as his love interest, Smith was able to simultaneously avoid the controversy of an interracial romance with a white woman and the devaluation that would come with the casting of a black woman in the lead female role. With Mendes in the cast, *Hitch* opened at number one and grossed

TABLE 6.

Films Produced by Will Smith's Overbrook Entertainment

Title (year)	Distributor	Budget (millions)	Domestic Gross (millions)	Percent Return on Investment
Ali (2001)	Sony	$108	$58	(46.30%)
Showtime (2002)	Warner Bros.	$85	$38	(55.29%)
I, Robot (2004)	Twentieth Century Fox	$115	$145	26.09%
Saving Face (2004)	Sony	N/A	$1.2	N/A
Hitch (2005)	Sony	$65	$178	173.85%
ATL (2006)	Warner Bros.	$18	$21	16.67%
The Pursuit of Happyness (2006)	Sony	$55	$163	196.36%
I Am Legend (2007)	Warner Bros.	$150	$256	70.67%
Hancock (2008)	Sony	$150	$227	51.33%
Lakeview Terrace (2008)	Sony/Screen Gems	$21	$39	85.71%
The Secret Life of Bees (2008)	Fox Searchlight	$11	$37	236.36%
Seven Pounds (2008)	Sony	$55	$69	25.45%

Sources: Figures are averages of estimates from IMDB.com, TheNumbers.com, and BoxOfficeMojo.com.

$179 million domestically. Mendes is a Cuban American actress who gained access into mainstream films by playing the love interest of black male stars such as Denzel Washington in *Training Day* (2001) and *Out of Time* (2003) and Mike Epps in *All about the Benjamins* (2002). In fact, the frequent pairing of black males and Latinas has become something of a trend in Hollywood. One of the earliest examples is Jim Brown and Raquel Welch in *100 Rifles* (1969). More contemporary examples include Spike Lee and Rosie Perez in *Do the Right Thing*, Wesley Snipes and Jennifer Lopez in *Money Train* (1995), Laurence Fishburne and Salma Hayek in *Fled* (1996), Rosalyn Sanchez and Chris Tucker in *Rush Hour 2*, and Sanchez and Cuba Gooding Jr. in *Boat Trip* (2002).[35] This trend means that ethnic minorities are often positioned to compete for the same roles while the bulk of Hollywood narratives are designed to employ white actors and actresses.

The Overbrook films in which Smith does not star still display patterns of distribution with outcomes that illuminate Smith's significant star power. All of Overbrook's films except *Lakeview Terrace* and *The Secret Life of Bees* were distributed by one of the top five distributors in Hollywood. *Lakeview Terrace* features an interracial couple (Patrick Wilson and Kerry Washington) who are harassed by their neighbor (Samuel L. Jackson) who also happens to be a black cop. *The Secret Life of Bees* also features a predominantly black cast. *Saving Face*, starring Michelle Krusiec and Joan Chen, Asian actresses in a gay/lesbian comedy, received the least distribution and therefore the worst box office (it earned only $1.2 million). Classified as an original comedy, *ATL* also features a predominantly African American cast and was distributed by Sony. The film stars notable rappers T.I. and Big Boi. Curiously, the films Smith has helped produce represent more ethnic diversity than the films in which he stars.

Smith's star power is strengthened by films that reinforce the master narrative, as he portrays the only or the primary black person onscreen in a predominantly white cast. He may be the leading character in these films, but he often serves as a model minority, a stereotype that disregards inequalities and maintains the dominance of whites by reinforcing the belief that all groups can achieve the American Dream through hard work. Guerrero defines the model minority as typical immigrants "with personal initiative and self-discipline, whereas Afro-Americans, Indians and Chicanos lack this 'human capital.'"[36] Smith has played a pilot and aspiring astronaut in *Independence Day* (1996), a handsome detective endowed with a trust fund in the *Bad Boys* franchise, a homeless single father who becomes a successful businessman in *The Pursuit of Happyness*, and a dysfunctional superhero who turns his life around with a white family's help in *Hancock*. From these a pattern emerges: Smith stars as the lone black man with exceptional capabilities that so distinguish him from other blacks that they have been rendered invisible or minimized to the point of insignificance. In this way, Smith's success works against the future development of African American film because it implies that the most profitable way to sell blackness onscreen is with a minimal, nonthreatening black presence. The economic outcome for *Ali* reinforces this perception. Smith's star power relies squarely on this paradigm: Smith and Lassiter's approach to identifying the most lucrative genres (action films with special effects) and securing such roles for Smith has resulted in Smith's becoming the biggest star in the world. The future of African American film depends upon such careful strategizing, but not necessarily and exclusively within the Hollywood framework.

Overbrook's creative choices and investment patterns demonstrate one way of adapting to Hollywood's color-coded economics. Consider their collaboration with filmmakers such as Gina Prince-Bythewood on the cinematic adaptation of *The Secret Life of Bees* (a novel by Sue Monk Kidd). Prince-Bythewood made her directorial debut with *Love & Basketball* in 2000. That film grossed $27 million on a $17 million budget through Spike Lee's production company, 40 Acres & A Mule Filmworks. Eight years later, *The Secret Life of Bees* earned $37 million on an $11 million budget.[37] The film stars Dakota Fanning, a young white American actress. She portrays Lily Owens, a fourteen-year-old girl who runs away with her African American caretaker (Jennifer Hudson) to a South Carolina town where they stay with the Boatwright sisters (Queen Latifah, Alicia Keys, and Sophie Okonedo). Casting black women in the role of caretakers is a predictable pattern dating back to *Uncle Tom's Cabin* and *The Birth of a Nation*. *The Secret Life of Bees* superficially supports the current patterns, ensuring that a white female star is more likely to be cast in a studio-level film while black actresses are less likely to have studio funding for narratives with black female protagonists. Furthermore, three out of the four black actresses in this film are crossover stars from the music industry. And like Knowles, Keys and Okonedo embody physical attributes of the mulatta type. In this film, Keys and Fanning portray the only characters with love interests, both of whom are black males. Collectively and individually, these elements further reinforce the mainstream master narrative in spite of Prince-Bythewood's insightful adaptation of the novel and direction of the film.

While Overbrook's general filmography in many ways disregards the dangers of plantation ideology and the devaluation of black people, it also reflects progress. Patterns of investment in directors such as Prince-Bythewood and the diverse range of films starring other actors of color and not just Smith suggest Overbrook may be moving in new directions. It is possible to create new formulas that will employ more African Americans and other people of color without forcing them to compete for the same limited roles, while also featuring a broader range of lifestyles onscreen. Black star power can be redirected to shape future possibilities for African American films.

It is difficult for any actor to become a star in Hollywood. It is even more challenging for people of color due to racial precedent, even if this remains unacknowledged. Because people of color are less likely to have leading roles in studio-produced, high-budget films, especially commercial genre films, the only way to increase bankability is with parallel progression in the music industry or stand-up comedy, which brings us to the venerable Jamie Foxx. Foxx began his career as a stand-up comedian and actor on the television series *In Living Color*. He successfully carried films with predominantly black casts early in his career (*Booty Call* [1997] and *The Player's Club* [1998]). In 2000, he starred in *Bait*, an action film about an ex-con who unwittingly helps police catch a criminal. In 2004, he played the title role in the biopic *Ray* (2004), portraying the legendary musician Ray Charles. Foxx won an Oscar for this performance. He now appears as the singularly significant African American man in a world of whites. In Quentin Tarantino's *Django Unchained* (2012), Foxx portrays a slave-turned-bounty hunter attempting to rescue his wife (Kerry Washington) from "a brutal Mississippi plantation owner" played by Leonardo DiCaprio. Smith turned down the role, which would have been a major divergence from previous roles, in order to focus on *Men in Black 3* (2012).

Because role choice and box office affects future ratings, many black stars on the A+, A, B+, and B lists avoid films with predominantly black casts unless other major black stars are involved (e.g., Foxx co-starred in *Ali* with Will Smith). As previously noted, such casting negatively affects distribution and therefore outcome. Occasionally black stars join forces with black directors and white stars in order to reverse this trend (e.g., Foxx stars in F. Gary Gray's *Law Abiding Citizen* [2009]), but these projects may also include white stars or more whites than blacks in supporting roles. Jamie Foxx is a multifaceted star in terms of his background in comedy and music. His career exemplifies patterns that are similar to yet distinct from Will Smith as rapper/actor and Eddie Murphy as an actor/comedian. Each of these stars access a range of roles, thereby exemplifying the influence a background in comedy and music can have on developing black star power.

Foxx persists in doing action films, comedic roles and character roles in serious dramas, while also integrating music into his work. Not unlike Smith's, Foxx's filmography includes a range of roles not frequently available to black actors. Yet Foxx's television producing credits for his own projects are much more conservative investments in comparison to Smith's production of theatrical releases. The television documentaries, specials, and series (including reality television) Foxx produces do not reflect the range in Overbrook's catalog. As one of the only films dealing with serious themes in Foxx's producing credits, *Life Support* (2007), a television movie starring Queen Latifah as a recovering crack addict who becomes an AIDS activist due to her HIV positive status, is the outlier in his work as a producer. Due to his background in comedy and music and the strides he has made as a character actor in serious roles, Foxx has a pliable brand with serious potential that he has yet to fully exploit.

The model for Foxx's brand as an actor/producer is still in development, especially when considering his most prominent predecessor, Eddie Murphy, with whom he shares several commonalities. Foxx and Eddie Murphy are the only two comedians on the Top Ten Black Actors list. Both actor/comedians have expanded their repertoire to include music recordings, and both appeared in the hit film *Dreamgirls* (2006), for which Murphy received an Academy Award nomination for Best Supporting Actor. Both actor/comedians exemplify a trending path to star power for black performers. Murphy has continued to appear in films with predominantly black casts even as his star power has increased, although admittedly he plays multiple roles in many of these films and thereby serves as the primary representation of blacks.

Murphy paved the way for performers like Foxx, and his progression exemplifies the relationship between developing and maintaining star power and attempting to produce films featuring African Americans. Consider his trajectory toward stardom through stand-up and television. Murphy's success in television (*Saturday Night Live*—sixty-seven episodes from 1980 to 1984) translated into opportunities to star in theatrical releases as the Africanist presence in productions with predominantly white casts: *48 Hours* (1982), *Trading Places* (1983), *Beverly Hills Cop* (1984), *The Golden Child* (1986), and *Beverly Hills Cop 2* (1987). His breakout role in *Coming to America* (1989), one of the highest-grossing African American films of all time with grosses of $128 million domestically and a reported $350 million internationally, continues to influence perceptions regarding the profitability of black film (see chapter 6).[38] Like Smith, Murphy has made significant profits for the studios with these projects that have earned a combined $629 million domestically (plus another $200 million internationally), even before he was provided the opportunity to carry a film like *Coming to America*. Murphy and his films exemplify the paradox of black box office success, as the majority of his projects began to feature fewer roles for other black actors. However, in order to reverse this trend, Murphy produced seven theatrical releases, six of which are films with predominantly black casts: *Eddie Murphy Raw* (1987), *Harlem Nights* (1989), *Vampire in Brooklyn* (1995), *Life* (1999), *Nutty Professor II: The Klumps* (2000), *Norbit* (2007), and *Tower Heist* (2011). Murphy plays multiple roles in half of these films. *Tower Heist* (2011) is a mixed-cast film that also stars Ben Stiller as the central protagonist with Eddie Murphy in a supporting role. While the comedies Murphy produced are not as lucrative as those films he appeared in before *Coming to America*, only *Life* and *Tower Heist* failed to generate a profit in the domestic market. Overall, the films with predominantly black casts that Murphy produced have earned a total of $411 million and are generally profitable. As a result, the theatrical releases Murphy has produced and starred in contribute to the economic viability of black film even though they do not reflect the diversity or range of films Smith has produced with Overbrook entertainment.

Over the past several decades, Murphy has continued to work steadily, releasing a film every year with the exception of 2005. His films have ranged from major successes (e.g., the *Shrek* franchise with Mike Myers) to major failures (*Holy Man* [1998]), making his box office difficult to predict. Further proving the economic viability of black stars, Murphy has made billions for the studios and holds his spot as number seven on the 2009/2010 Top Ten Black Actors list. Meanwhile, Jamie Foxx, Martin Lawrence, Dave Chappelle, Chris Tucker, and Chris Rock, among others, continue to benefit from the success of iconic figures such as Richard Pryor and Murphy. The influence of *Coming to America* along with Murphy's overall contribution to the development of African American film is discussed in greater detail in chapter 6.

Maximizing Star Power

While black women have less star power than black men, Halle Berry, Queen Latifah, and Jada Pinkett Smith are making significant strides behind the camera as producers with greater creative control. These practices can effectively reunite black stars with the black audiences they are encouraged to disregard in pursuit of crossover appeal, while accessing broader audiences for economic viability. Queen Latifah went from her first minor role in *Jungle Fever* (1991) to a major role in *Set It Off* (1996), soon expanding her repertoire to include comedies, musicals, and dramas such as *The Secret Life of Bees*. As of 2013, she served as executive producer for six television shows (e.g., *Let's Stay Together* [2011–2013]) and four theatrical releases (*Bringing Down the House* [2003]), and also as producer for five theatrical releases (*Just Wright* [2010]). As a rapper-turned-actor she follows in Will Smith's footsteps, not unlike other recording artists that take ownership of their brand and create their own star vehicles. Two other examples of this trend are Beyoncé Knowles and Alicia Keys. Knowles has served as executive producer of two of her films, *Cadillac Records* (2008) and *Obsessed* (2009), in addition to producing concert and documentary videos of her live shows. In 2012 she also inked an unconventional, multi-year $50 million deal with Pepsi to fund her chosen creative projects.[39] For her part, Keys produced Diamond's *Stick Fly* on Broadway, financially supporting black talent that would otherwise have considerably fewer opportunities.

As for directing films, black actors venture into this territory more frequently than black actresses, thereby mirroring gender disparities throughout the industry. Denzel Washington's directing credits include *Antwone Fisher* (2002) and *The Great Debaters* (2007), produced with $12 million to $15 million budgets while earning upward of $20 million to $30 million, respectively. Both feature predominantly black casts and address themes that resonate for black audiences even though they also have crossover appeal. Directing these films has not adversely affected Washington's Ulmer score, which is usually the case as survey respondents express concern that an actor's "directorial interests" will "shift focus from pursuing studio-driven roles."[40] Washington also performed in the films he directed and appeared in several successful commercial films since, thereby alleviating such concerns. Washington's approach suggests the way to maintain star power and promote development of African American film is to remain active in both acting and directing in black and mainstream films. Since he appears more frequently in commercial genre films as the lone black character in a world of whites, much like Smith, this strategy alone may slow the progression of African American films being produced. On the other hand, Washington's approach is one of many that can help counteract the damage caused by plantation ideology. Black stars in Hollywood are under a great deal of pressure from black and cross-over audiences to use their star power to shape perceptions of black people and culture with every project they direct, produce, or perform.

Conclusion

Understanding how the Ulmer Scale influences casting and distribution is critical to understanding the challenges African Americans face in cinema today. Of the 2,000 films I examined for this study, many of those with poor box office receipts were negatively affected by poor distribution and a cast featuring actors and actresses on the D list or lower. Most African American actors have low Ulmer scores because their films have poor distribution, which leads to low box office and low Ulmer scores. It is not just business when the valuation of the highest-rated black stars diminishes simply because they are accompanied by other blacks, even in commercial genre films. This institutionalized racism facilitates the everyday racism that people of color face while trying to work in and outside of Hollywood.

Horizontal integration and past precedents continue to reinforce stereotypes of blacks as entertainers and clowns, impeding the growth of African American filmmaking. Based on the Ulmer Scale, singers/rappers and stand-up comedians who become actors or actresses are more likely to become stars than those whose initial acting credits are in television and/or theater, the least likely avenues for becoming a major star. Filmmakers that can accommodate the character types generally played by B+ actors and above have the greatest chance of obtaining financial support to produce the film and a significant box office return. By definition, their films will have better distribution than films with actors and actresses on the C and D lists, especially if they include white actors. Because most of the black stars on the Ulmer Scale appear on the C and D list, the future of studio-produced films featuring African Americans is bleak. Stars positioned higher on the scale may be out of the budget range for many independent or low-budget filmmakers, so unless black stars and their agents agree to work for scale, there is little likelihood of making alternative narratives accessible and changing standard Hollywood patterns. Otherwise, African Americans and allies are left to rely on C and D list actors and reputable directors, which still do not translate into competitive distribution.

Ultimately, established precedent continues to limit the potential of black film, subjects, and worldviews. At the same time, however, black stars that are able to transcend the industry practice of using stars as brands to sell movies and instead use their star status as a business to create their own products are the key to the future of African American film. These possibilities are being explored and realized by a variety of filmmakers discussed in chapter 6, many of whom are thwarted by the censorship that occurs when a film receives limited or no distribution.

While the Ulmer Scale plays a significant role in determining investment choices, there are other modes of evaluation, such as the IMDB.com StarMeter ratings, used by Nelson and Glotfelty. They find that its inclusion of general audience feedback and the number of hits on stars' pages on the site to be more timely and reliable than the Ulmer Scale's tracking process. Using StarMeter can give underrepresented audiences more control over identifying stars beyond actual ticket sales.

Although African American actors and actresses featured in this chapter hold a certain cachet of star power that can absorb some of the risk involved when deviating from standard Hollywood practices, precedent continues to have a powerful influence. One need only trace the paths to stardom of a handful of black actors who managed to make the Ulmer list to see that African Americans with entrepreneurial inclinations are making great strides. Filmmakers who use the Ulmer Scale but are also conscious of the drawbacks of the master narrative's form, content, characterizations, and technical and visual elements will be more empowered to make culturally nuanced, economically viable films. Alternative modes of distribution through new media and technology can also assist in centering a diverse range of black subjects, performers, and audiences, which is imperative for reversing damage caused by industry practices. Such practices allow actresses such as Halle Berry, the first African American to win a Best Actress Academy Award, for *Monster's Ball* (2001), to reach a pinnacle of success and yet face a paucity of quality roles afterward. On the contrary, the white actress Charlize Theron, winner in the same category for *Monster* (2003), has since played a plethora of roles. The fact that the current system privileges whites and males cannot be denied in spite of increasing black star power. Black stars achieving the requisite star power for broad distribution does not necessarily mean erasing all considerations of crossover appeal. As the next chapter reveals, making films with stories and performances that resonate first and foremost for black audiences can also have the economic benefits that come with crossover appeal without the baggage of the same old plantation ideology.

6

Big Business

Hip-Hop Gangsta Films and Black Comedies

[Studio executives are] cognizant of what doesn't work internationally. Black baseball movies, period dramas about football, rap, inner-city films–most countries can't relate to that. Americana seems to be desired by international markets, but there comes a point where even they will resist and say, "We don't get it," and it's generally in that ethnic, inner-city, sports-driven region. We can't give 'em what they don't want.

–Duncan Clark, head of the international theatrical department at Sony, 1998

From 1995 to 2012, there have been more films produced from original screenplays than any other source material. Novels run a close second, while stage plays are far less frequently adapted, even among African American films.[1] While the preceding chapters have used adaptation to expose plantation ideology within theater, publishing, and film, this chapter examines the influence of plantation ideology on films with original screenplays.

Among African American films, the most economically successful genres that feature original screenplays are hip-hop gangsta films and comedies. The latter is one of the most accessible commercial genres, as evidenced by the prevalence of African American or rather black comedy franchises. Historically, whites have used blacks in comedy for economic gain, moral authority, or political clout, thereby maintaining the hegemonic social order.[2] Black comedy franchises as well as hip-hop gangsta films support McKenzie's findings (discussed in the introduction) that African American films generate significant revenues. The films, filmmakers, and film franchises within these two genres demonstrate the struggle and success as well as the creative possibilities and systemic limitations of original, economically viable, studio-produced films with predominantly black casts. This chapter examines both genres up close, further highlighting the racial and gender disparities that influence the development of cinematic language and economic outcomes.

The Magic Formula: Standard Hollywood Screenplays

Black film franchises are big business, and those who direct them are important people in Hollywood. Those films that subscribe to the standard screenplay format are especially well poised for success. Studio-affiliated filmmakers such as Spike Lee and controversial Hollywood outsiders such as Tyler Perry continue to fare better than independent filmmakers such as Haile Gerima for this reason. The standard screenplay format is thus significant for the evolution of African American cinematic language. While alternative screenplay formats exist, standard Hollywood screenplays utilize a three-act structure.[3] In addition to the narrative structure, the presentation of the screenplay also has several physical criteria including a fixed-pitched font (12 point Courier), standard margins, white paper, black ink, a simple title page, and a preferred length of 100–110 pages.[4] Like the Ulmer Scale, Hollywood's standard screenplay criteria are used to calculate critical elements of production value and costs. Using a consistent, homogeneous format with a relatively uniform amount of content per page (one minute equals one page) enables film producers to estimate cost, set production schedules, and determine scene cuts. However, the superficial structural requirements of the Hollywood screenplay have a direct influence on storytelling models. In short, the use of or disregard for this homogenized approach to storytelling can make or break a project, even down to the size of the margins. "Altering a script's format or margins or even paper size . . . upsets all the calculations" and can instantly brand a script as unprofessional.[5] Adhering to this standardized structure is critical for gaining financial support and other resources, including a bankable cast.

Understandably, a uniform format facilitates the necessary economic projections that have to be run with any project. However, cinematic language, like any other language, requires variation in pronunciation, grammatical structure, and meaning to express ideas. As discussed in chapter 4, standard formats and popular generic formulas may not always be the most productive approach to film language and filmmaking. My comparative analysis of the unpublished shooting script and the post-production script of Gerima's *Sankofa* revealed that many of the film's most complex concepts (e.g., rememory), discussed later in the chapter, were achieved through on-set improvisation and a much longer and more detailed script that reads almost like a novel rather than a standard screenplay. Historically, regardless of genre, this standardized format enables the master narrative as well as racial reconciliation narratives. It promotes white protagonists accompanied by an Africanist presence and problematic female and nonwhite ethnic group characterization. Using the standard format without variation can pose great challenges to cultural storytelling. Hollywood's underuse of viable screenplay alternatives has contributed to its stagnation. Standard screenplay format is yet another aspect of established precedent that poses challenges for developing African American film.

Cycles, Franchises, and Genres

Studio executives concede that some black films are able to translate to an international audience, but they suggest this is the exception rather than the rule.[6] Ironically, successful commercial genres such as African American comedy reinforce the cycle of perceived failure. Their success suggests that they are the only types of films worthy of broad distribution, consequently increasing earning potential. Similarly, film cycles and franchises emerge when one film performs unexpectedly well. As film scholar Amanda Ann Klein explains, film cycles are distinguishable from genres although both are "a series of films associated with each other through shared images, characters, settings, plots and themes. However, while film genres are primarily defined by the repetition of key images (their semantics) and themes (their syntax), film cycles are primarily defined by how they are used (their pragmatics)."[7] Financial viability and public discourse drive film cycles, which tend to last five to ten years.[8] Film cycles are also distinguishable from franchises or known brands consisting of three or more movies. Whether they are part of a cycle, a genre, or a franchise, studio executives frequently evaluate African American films using double standards.

Race ideology contributes to this tunnel vision, which ultimately undermines the future development of films, genres, and cycles. For instance, grouping together all black films from the 1990s under the label of the hip-hop gangsta film genre overlooks their inter-genre distinctions. Media scholar Beretta E. Smith-Shomade identifies the hip-hop gangsta film as a genre that differs from the traditional urban-crime movie due to distinct representations of black women and crime.[9] She distinguishes *Set It Off* (1996) as a hip-hop gangsta film that "centers crime as a business and defers to black cultural norms by including black women in critical roles."[10] This contrasts with films such as *Boyz N the Hood*, which "focus on crime not as an organized systematic business but as a sociological pathological problem, expressly confined to and defined by a homogenous black (male) community."[11] Although these films represent two distinct genres, Klein describes these types of films as part of a cycle.[12] For this reason, I consider these films to be part of the hip-hop gangsta film cycle. Like the Blaxploitation films of the 1970s, this cycle differs from the Tyler Perry franchise (2005 to present) that consists of similarly themed morality tales promoting Perry's brand including but not limited to the *Madea* franchise. As Klein explains, all cycles decline due to changing industry currents. Yet the decline of black film cycles contributes to the perceived failure of black film.

Black Comedy, Not a Laughing Matter: *Coming to America*

Both sides in the NAACP-versus-Hollywood debate reference *Coming to America* (1988) to justify concerns regarding the success or failure of African American films. The film played on 2,064 screens and earned approximately $128 million domestically in less than three months (as well as $350 million internationally).[13] The film's financial success is proof of African American film's economic viability. Additionally, the film earned an NAACP Image Award, an honor reserved for progressive representations of people of color. There are some arguments, however, that *Coming to America*'s economic performance is not quite what it seems when measured in terms of net profits as opposed to gross profits. Net profits refers to gross receipts after subtracting all related, conceivable costs for the motion picture. Such costs include negative cost (and interest), distribution fees, residuals, distribution costs, and, typically, participations. Gross profits, on the other hand, include all motion picture earnings.[14] The difference between net profits and gross profits lies at the heart of economic success. According to law and economics professor Victor P. Goldberg, Paramount had cleared $125 million by the end of 1989, but negative costs (including gross participations)[15] were $47 million, distribution costs $36 million, distribution fees $42 million, and the gross points[16] for Eddie Murphy and the director John Landis $10 million and $1 million, respectively. With interest of $6 million on the negative costs, the accounts showed the movie to be approximately $18 million in the red. Of each additional dollar of revenue received at that point, about one-third would go to reducing the deficit. Goldberg maintains that even if Murphy and Landis had received only their fixed fees, there still would have been no net profits.[17] However, Goldberg does not explain how the $350 million the film grossed internationally factors into this failure to recoup production costs. This is especially intriguing considering international markets' established role in overall profitability. The mystery of Hollywood accounting affects all films but is particularly troubling for evaluating black films when the process has been used to suggest that the highest-grossing African American film to date was an economic failure in Hollywood.

To be sure, a seemingly successful box office may not necessarily equal a successful economic outcome for any project. Oliver Stone's *JFK* (1991) and Tim Burton's *Batman* (1989) failed to yield net profits, but their economic failure was never ascribed to the cast's whiteness. In fact, the *Star Wars* franchise carries on with seven of the nine films produced as of 2008. *The Return of the Jedi*'s (1983) inability to produce net profits likely contributed to the sixteen-year stall in production preceding *The Phantom Menace* (1999). The interruption occurred in spite of the fact that *Jedi* earned $475 million at the box office on a $32 million budget and ranks fifteenth in American box office history.[18] That these and many other films, such as *Coming to America*, did not turn a net profit exposes the lack of transparency in Hollywood accounting.

In the film, Murphy portrays an African prince named Akeem who comes to America in search of a bride. He leaves his luxurious palace in the fictional Zamunda, where tradition requires him to marry a woman who has been trained since birth to walk, talk, and behave as his queen. He and his sidekick Semi (Arsenio Hall) relocate to Queens, New York, where they encounter a series of dysfunctional women and colorful characters. He finally meets Lisa (Shari Headley), daughter of the owner of McDowell's restaurant, clearly a stand-in for McDonald's. Triumphing over tradition and Lisa's mean-spirited and wealthy black American boyfriend, Darryl, the couple eventually weds in Zamunda.

According to the film's credits, writers David Sheffield and Barry W. Blaustein adapted their screenplay from Murphy's own story. However, soon after the film's release, white humorist Art Buchwald sued Paramount for $6.2 million, claiming that the story idea was originally his and that the studio stole it.[19] The judge awarded Buchwald $150,000 and his producing partner, Alan Bernheim, $750,000 in spite of Paramount's claims that the film failed to produce net profits.[20] The lawsuit required the studio to disclose earnings and calculations, thereby exposing the general lack of transparency in Hollywood accounting. Racial double standards compound the problem further when studio executives use the highest-grossing African American film to date as an example of the perceived failure of African American film.

Film and media studies scholar Bambi Haggins, while not resolving the various claims, suggests that the film adapts a concept Murphy introduced in *Eddie Murphy Raw* (1987), a live recording of one of his stand-up comedy performances. Murphy complains that he has become so rich and famous that "if I ever want to get married I have to go off to the woods of Africa and find me some crazy, naked, zebra bitch, that knows nothing about money." He describes this imaginary woman, Umfufu, as being "butt-naked on a zebra, with a big bone in her nose and a big plate lip, and a big fucked up afro." Regardless of the story's genesis, the film incorporates negative representations of black women as well as the complex relationship between Africans and African Americans.

The film has been categorized as "black comedy," defined by Mark A. Reid as "any black-oriented comedy whose laughter is not evoked through the objectified *racial* other but might objectify other groups, such as women, homosexuals, and certain social classes, within and outside this community. In black comedy, laughter rises from an *inventive* narrative structure that does not retain the racially tendentious quality of blackface, hybrid and satiric hybrid minstrel forms."[21] Similarly, the master narrative's formulaic conventions rely on patterns of positioning women and other nonwhite groups at the margins. By definition, the wit and satire of black humor are complex, varied, and fundamental components of black comedy.

Black comedy, initially developed and performed in front of predominantly black audiences, faces several challenges when crossing over to white audiences. As Murphy's description of the African female construct suggests, historical mainstream representations of Africa as underdeveloped persist in spite of centuries of African civilizations and contemporary urban cities in countries throughout the continent. In front of a predominantly black audience, such jokes can be regarded as intra-ethnic humor generated to come to terms with outmoded perceptions of Africa and the other class-based and gender ideologies apparent in the film. They also serve as effective, yet dangerous strategies for crossover appeal, thereby exemplifying the complications of black comedy as one of the most accessible commercial genres for African Americans.

Coming to America's use of black comedic conventions establishes an important precedent for subsequent films and franchises. In the film, Murphy portrays several characters, including the lead role of Akeem and several supporting roles (most memorably, the barbershop owner). Black comedians now commonly play multiple roles in their films, occasionally cross-dressing. Tyler Perry's *Madea* franchise, which to date has grossed over $307 million domestically, is an obvious example.[22] Ice Cube's *Barbershop* franchise, which has grossed $141 million domestically,[23] also uses ethnic humor incorporating Africans or distinguishable nonwhites. Franchises base their success on repeating themes and characters, many of which incorporate negative stereotypes and, as a consequence, further reinforce plantation ideology.

Plantation ideology is, as discussed previously, not simply a form of racial oppression but includes the stratification of genders. Women are primarily significant in relation to the male protagonist, and the heroine is generally a petite mulatta type. In keeping with Murphy's apparent distaste for the African female Other construct in his stand-up, women with darker complexions or diverse body types are used in the film for comic relief. This is primarily the case in all of Murphy's films but the trend is apparent in others as well, including the *Big Momma's House, Friday*, and *Madea* franchises. Even if the love interest has a darker complexion, she is generally lighter in comparison to the male protagonist, thereby reinforcing colorism. This creates a black variation of a master narrative that mirrors the dominant worldview but in terms of color rather than race. Paradoxically, black master narratives with formulaic narrative conventions that reinforce mainstream perceptions of blackness may also simultaneously challenge those perceptions in subtle ways such as strategic casting and nuanced characterizations in performance.

Including certain kinds of representations of Africa, Africans, and African Americans has become a strategy for attracting African American and crossover audiences to African American films. Mixing popular perceptions with updated representations, *Coming to America* alternatively represents African royalty in place of Murphy's underdeveloped depiction of Africa. Images of black African royalty and black American bourgeoisie defy dominant perceptions of race and class.[24] The film simultaneously supports popular conceptions of lower-class blacks who primarily serve as a backdrop for interactions between upper classes. Historically, people of African descent are disadvantaged in the plantation scheme, and Africans are most vulnerable due to their marginalization within the global framework. Africans are an "invisible audience" in Hollywood's definition of the global market and, as this film exemplifies, are frequently erased. The film maintains the Hollywood tradition of using Africa as a backdrop for Americans.[25] This is most obvious in the black American cast's portrayal of Africans. As discussed in part I, this practice is rooted in minstrelsy. Blackface minstrelsy performed by whites, argues social historian Eric Lott, simultaneously serves to express love for black culture and theft of its identity.[26] According to Cedric J. Robinson, black performers often engaged in the practice as an act of resistance and reversal, reclaiming ownership and economic access to the performance traditions whites appropriated through minstrelsy.[27] This is apparent in the careers of Ira Aldridge, Bert Williams, and George Walker, as well as in the characterization of Asagai in Lorraine Hansberry's *A Raisin in the Sun* and films such as *Bopha!* and *Sankofa.*

Recent controversies concerning black British performers Idris Elba as Nelson Mandela in *Long Walk to Freedom* (2014) and Thandie Newton in *Half of a Yellow Sun* (2013) further illustrate the complexity of onscreen representations of Africa in American films.[28] Native South Africans have rarely portrayed the legendary Mandela or other leading roles in broadly distributed, mainstream studio-produced films. Similarly, casting the biracial Newton as a Nigerian Igbo woman (not to mention a lighter-skinned Zoë Saldaña using prosthetics, dark make-up, and fake teeth to portray black American jazz singer/songwriter/pianist and civil rights activist Nina Simone in a 2013 biopic) further exposes the problems of casting according to colorism. Inaccurate film representation of heroes, nations, and ethnicities reinforces plantation ideology on a global scale, especially when capable actors with the physical characteristics are overlooked for the sake of distribution. The master narrative and the influence of standard industry practices paradoxically privileges black Americans and black British actors in ways that black Africans and other ethnicities that cannot pass as white are not afforded. There have been several protests by African actors regarding their exclusion from major roles in broadly distributed, mainstream films like these.[29]

Many black American and black British performers have successfully and strategically subverted the misappropriation of blackness. As discussed in chapter 2, Freeman, Glover, and Woodard subverted the misappropriation of blackness with *Bopha!*, but the film suffered limited distribution. Others such as Don Cheadle have used their star power to bring attention to the genocides in Rwanda and Sudan (*Hotel Rwanda* [2004]), as well as the treatment of Muslims post-9/11 (*Traitor* [2008]). Per common industry practices, black American and black British performers cast as Africans increase potential profitability.

Unfortunately, these practices also limit opportunities for African performers and frequently present distorted representations of African cultures. In many ways, this makes black British and American actors accomplices in Hollywood's plantation scheme. The double bind for black performers extends across genres but is of particular import for black comedy such as *Coming to America*.

Murphy uses genre, improvisation, and various characterizations exemplifying the traditional wit and satire of black humor that critiques slavery and racism to modulate the film's representations of Africans. While *A Raisin in the Sun* openly recognizes obstacles of racism and discrimination, *Coming to America*'s comic narrative, characterizations, and themes overlook these issues. Standard screenplay format suggests that *Coming to America* is a fairy tale investigating the American Dream from a black perspective. The script's black narrator begins the tale about a prince in "a land far, far away . . ." and invites the viewer to join the fantasy by suggesting the prince is "much like you and me . . . except that he lived helluva lot better."[30] Its racial and gender constructions continue with a black man being serviced primarily by black women who clean "his royal penis," obey his every command, and throw petals at his feet when he walks. The script contains strong whiffs of patriarchal capitalism with a racial twist. Excepting voiceover narration, the film maintains the basic structure of a romantic comedy, which generally consists of three durable plot types: ensemble, marriage, and love triangle.[31] According to Stephen V. Duncan, the underlying plot for nearly every romantic comedy is "boy meets girl, boy loses girl, boy gets girl back, and they live happily ever after."[32] Since *Coming to America*, this heteronormative commercial genre has been expanded to effectively incorporate black Americans and ethnically diverse casts (*Love Jones* [1997], *The Best Man* [1999], *The Wood* [1999], *Love & Basketball* [2000], *Hav Plenty* [2002]), as well as interracial pairings (*Hitch* and *Something New* [2006]).[33] Yet the marginal positioning of black women, doubly affected by patriarchal capitalism and racist ideologies embedded in industry practices, continues to inform the genre. Overall, the film exemplifies an infusion of colorism and class into the heteronormative romantic comedy plot that is in alignment with plantation ideology.

Despite its superficiality, *Coming to America* is also subversive in its portrayal of a black fairy tale that repositions black people in a racialized patriarchal capitalist system. This variation of the black American Dream indexes slavery by intertextually referencing the television miniseries *Roots* (1977), arguably the first historical drama about slavery from the perspective of the enslaved, based on Alex Haley's book of the same name. For example, the American barbers in Queens refer to Akeem as Kunta Kinte, the lead character in *Roots*.[34] Kunta, Haley's first African ancestor on American soil, fights to regain his freedom and maintain his sense of autonomy. American Studies professor Leslie Fishbein attributed the miniseries's success to its catering to white middle-class sensibility.[35] In general, middle class refers to income levels ranging from $40,000 to $95,000 and associated attitudes believing in "hard work, a self-governing disposition, and controlled impulses."[36] While other groups also hold these beliefs, they have been historically treated as exclusive white property or, less frequently, attributed to the model minority. The myth of meritocracy supported by the American Dream—"the premise that one can achieve success and prosperity through determination, hard work and courage—an open system for mobility"[37]—too frequently overlooks racial and gender disparities.

Coming to America successfully maintains black vantage points while catering to so-called white middle-class sensibilities. Murphy's film engages in its own brand of mythmaking that extends beyond the myth of meritocracy. Akeem's inherited wealth exceeds that of the upper- and middle-class Americans (depicted in the film by the McDowells and Darryl's family, who have achieved property ownership and economic success as entrepreneurs of a food franchise and hair product empire). Akeem serves as an important counterpoint to the black Americans in the film as he comes to America by choice rather than force, excessively wealthy as opposed to impoverished (although he pretends to be poor to find a wife).

Murphy's signifying repetition and reversal are recognizable formulaic devices apparent in many African American films that offer intertextual references to slavery and racism. Repetition and reversal of the joke in *Raw* about the African woman in many ways serves as an organizing feature of the narrative and motivation for characterization. Instead of going to Africa to find a wife in the bush who knows nothing of Murphy's wealth as an entertainer, he embodies the African coming to America seeking a woman with no knowledge of his royalty. This reversal counteracts the negative associations of Africa that Murphy introduced in *Raw*.

Coming to America and *Sankofa* both represent Africans, albeit in distinct ways. Murphy reverses "the savage, uneducated, impoverished African" while Gerima reverses "the happy slave." They both strategically subvert comedies and plantation films. However, complications are unavoidable. In Murphy's characterization of Akeem, according to Victor Dugga, he is a less sympathetic representation of the African in America in comparison to Kunta. Nonetheless, the subversive underpinnings of these representations allow for multiple interpretations.

In the film, geographic locations that delineate class point to the dangers of black comedy crossing over to white American and international audiences. The royal palace of Zamunda in Africa is set in juxtaposition with urban Queens in the United States. The film also contrasts the low-income neighborhood where McDowell's business is located with the middle-class neighborhood where he lives. Akeem's movement through these spaces symbolizes the limitations of crossing over. Various stereotypes about Africa are shattered, yet they are replaced with images that reinforce sexism, colorism, and other perceptions of desirability.

Communication with black audiences in scripted films is often coded out of economic necessity, much like survival strategies on literal plantations. Films such as *Coming to America* are "rooted in a history where commentary and critique had to be coded for *the folks* (to borrow Zora Neale Hurston's oft-repeated moniker for African American communities), black comedy is tied inextricably to the African American community."[38] While the black performer recognizes black (meta-)communities, in comedy or otherwise, Hollywood privileges crossover (white and nonblack international) audiences. As a result, Haggins writes, "The process of crossover—and the extension of both humor and influence beyond black communal spaces—adds a problematic twist to the already Byzantine task faced by the African American comic: to be funny, accessible, and topical while retaining his or her *authentic* black voice."[39] The authentic black voice Haggins refers to is most often represented by the folk, the spaces they reside in, and the cultural symbols that represent them.

The relationship between jokes and folkloric spaces typify the dangers of crossover appeal. American Studies scholar Ben Chappell defines folkloric space as a carnivalesque space of folkloric performance where portrayal of a set of social relations and performance constitute a *way of speaking* and seeing that is characteristic of the culture.[40] The folk are commonly represented as rural in literature, theater, and film. In his musical *Simply Heavenly* (1959), Langston Hughes depicts them as common, rural, and urban people frequently dismissed as stereotypes. Historically, in order to avoid associations of all blacks with folk culture, some blacks reject or distance themselves by adopting bourgeois attitudes. Commonly associated with lower-class status and paradoxically perceived as profound and simple, the folk are idealistically unencumbered by the accoutrements of the black middle class. According to sociologist E. Franklin Frazier, "Black bourgeoisie [that] had 'escape[d] into a world of make-believe' and by putting on the 'masks' of the white middle class, its members had found a 'sham society' that could only leave them with feelings of 'emptiness and futility' [*sic*]."[41] Robert Gregg finds this popular assertion inaccurate, suggesting that the black upper and middle class have always been tied to lower classes by race and a sense of responsibility. The folk and their worlds tend to represent a space where "the mask" worn in the presence of whites and upper classes can be comfortably removed.

Many mainstream films, including *Coming to America*, use folkloric spaces to speak directly or in code to "invisible" black audiences. Haggins identifies "safe, communal black spaces—whether Granny's front porch or center stage at the Apollo" that speak to black experiences.[42] *Coming to America* uses urban settings and folklore to explore economic and political issues with jokes that are clearly targeted at black audiences yet also resonate with crossover audiences (though not necessarily for the same reason). Whereas black audiences, who are admittedly diverse, may be "laughin' to keep from crying," crossover audiences may be laughing for very different reasons. According to Haggins and reporter and author Wil Haygood, in regards to crossover audiences, "sometimes the laughter is of a confused sort, owing to misinterpretation, the joke merged with history and the ears of whites placed at awkward angles."[43] This film shows how staging a scene in folkloric space acknowledges black audiences in ways that may be lost on cultural outsiders. It is often a strategic device in which ethnic humor presents undiluted representations of black perspectives that tend to be whitewashed in other locations to avoid offending crossover audiences.

Class ideology infused with racial undertones further exposes the complications that stem from crossover appeal through ethnic humor. In *Coming to America*, the folk are the barbers. They recognize Akeem's difference but tend to embrace him rather than ridicule him as Darryl does. Darryl's interactions with Akeem, Semi, and lower-class blacks echo Amiri Baraka's stinging criticism that the black middle class internalizes white mainstream values, blaming other blacks for their condition rather than acknowledging the limitations imposed by a racist power structure.[44] In moments when the folk comment on Akeem's difference and background, it is done in ignorance or jest and not necessarily to humiliate him, although both can be harmful. To be sure, the class-based alliances between black Americans and white Americans appear throughout the film.

Crossover audiences can laugh comfortably at racist jokes coming from members of the black middle and upper class. In an interview with Spike Lee by Gary Crowdus and Dan Georgakas, Lee suggests that white audiences look to blacks to determine when and where it is appropriate to laugh at black ethnic jokes.[45] African American laughter at jokes targeting black Africans reinforces racial and ethnic stereotypes and gives free license to black and white filmmakers to continue making these jokes.[46] Yet Lee's insightful assertion does not account for black audiences' oppositional gaze and subversive laughter, nor does it acknowledge the potential effects of normalized representations. However, Lee's very public reprimand of Tyler Perry's films nuances his concerns about such powerful images. Silencing black audiences and performers to avoid white stereotyping takes away their power and becomes yet another form of censorship that could have a devastating effect on audiences who laugh to keep from crying. Lee's *The Original Kings of Comedy* (2000) and *Bamboozled* further exemplify his nuanced understanding of the empowering performer/audience relationship in stand-up and the complicated politics that surround black comedy in Hollywood.

Coming to America exemplifies both the limitations and the possibilities of signifying on black film tropes. Crossover audiences are led to believe that

Akeem does not fit black stereotypes because of his class status, not his cultural heritage. A wealthy African prince is already an oxymoron in Hollywood's white American imagination. Jokes in the film generate communal laughter among African Americans while establishing bonds between African Americans, white Americans, and the foreign market. These jokes are at the expense of Africans, who may also find the film humorous and less overtly racist or hurtful due to intra-racial exchange reminiscent of signifying traditions.[47] Without interracial conflict between blacks and whites, the film becomes more appealing to cross-over audiences in domestic and international markets.

Black comedy's political economy resides in folkloric spaces where ethnic humor simultaneously questions and reinforces African American cultural values. Two prominent American folkloric spaces in *Coming to America* are the barbershop and the Black Awareness Rally. In the midst of a variety of improvised ethnic jokes, the barbers educate Akeem about American identity. When Akeem wants to change his hair to resemble Darryl's in hopes of attracting Lisa, Clarence (Eddie Murphy) tells him not to process his hair, suggesting more young people wear their hair natural like "Martin Luther 'the' King Jr." Clarence then brags about meeting Dr. King, a story that all his friends contest. Through their humor they teach Akeem about the civil rights movement while interrogating the consistency of Dr. King's nonviolent beliefs, with Clarence insisting that Dr. King punched him in the chest. Nevertheless, Clarence cuts off Akeem's prince's lock, a long braid grown since birth. Symbolically, this suggests there are distinct differences between the African and African American that Akeem must and can reconcile in order to develop an American identity.

Black comedies such as *Coming to America* tend to downplay racism while upholding colorism. *Coming to America* reinforces colorism for women in particular. Akeem meets Lisa at the Black Awareness Rally, a folkloric space, where she appears in stark contrast to her dark-skinned sister, Patrice (Allison Dean). Patrice's fast-food uniform stands in direct opposition to Lisa's business suit, further equating color with class and all but guaranteeing that Akeem will find Lisa more attractive than Patrice. She is represented as above Patrice, as well as Imani Izzi (Vanessa Bell Calloway), the dark-skinned, beautiful princess Akeem rejected in Zamunda after having her jump up and down and bark like a "big dog" on his command. Imani is characterized as a beautiful idiot while Patrice is demonized as a hypersexual gold-digger. In contrast, Lisa's virtue and good nature makes her more appealing, thereby reinforcing mainstream standards of beauty, crossover audience expectations, and preference for the mulatta type (especially considering Vanessa L. Williams was originally slated to portray Lisa).

More recent comedies contain other promising yet problematic reversals. *Tyler Perry's Diary of a Mad Black Woman* pits the beautiful Helen (Kimberly

Elise) against Brenda (Lisa Marcos), the sexy Latina who steals Helen's husband, Charles (Steve Harris). Elise appears darker in comparison to the white-Hispanic Marcos. Charles's adultery with Brenda reinforces colorism and racism. But his eventual return to Helen, following Brenda's rejection, tentatively challenges the position of dark-skinned black women as undesirable in comparison to lighter-skinned women. Helen's love interest, Orlando (Shemar Moore, who is biracial), helps establish her desirability in contrast. In addition to Perry's film, Elise has also played the love interest of Oscar winners Denzel Washington, Jamie Foxx, and Forest Whitaker. These minor reversals exemplify visual alternatives to standard practices. Full-figured, "brown-skinned" Queen Latifah also reverses some of these patterns by producing films in which she stars as the love interest opposite rapper-actors LL Cool J (*Last Holiday* [2006]) and Common (*Just Wright* [2010]). These opportunities arose after playing a comedic variation of the mammy-type in *Bringing Down the House* (2003), opposite Steve Martin. Her desirability was introduced in her leading role on the television series *Living Single* (1993–1998) and supporting roles in films such as *Brown Sugar* (2002). These examples demonstrate strategies for counteracting colorism and stereotyping in black comedy and various other sub-genres. Yet conventions that guarantee good profit margins end up undermining any opportunity for broad distribution and adequate funding of films with more serious themes (until and unless a particular commercial film performs unexpectedly well, sparking the emergence of a cycle).

Coming to America paved the way for various black comedy franchises including the Wayans brothers' *Scary Movie*, Tyler Perry's *Madea*, Ice Cube's *Friday* and *Barbershop*, and Martin Lawrence's *Big Momma's House*, among others. These comedies capitalize on established black comedy formulas and innovate them with the power of their brands. The films' economic viability paradoxically influences the progress of serious-themed films, which becomes painfully apparent with the emergence of the hip-hop gangsta film cycle in the 1990s.

Boyz N the Hood and *Set It Off:* The Trouble with Success

Numerous black directors who found success creating commercial hip-hop gangsta films initially suggested that Spike Lee's *Do the Right Thing* set the precedent.[48] Indeed, hip-hop gangsta films expose how racist ideology can both limit and encourage African American cinematic development. *Boyz N the Hood* (1991) uses formulaic conventions to explore contemporary urban phenomena such as crime, poverty, and violence. *Boyz*'s economic success established it as a model for emulation. In *Set It Off* (1996), screenwriters Takashi Bufford and Kate Lanier riff off the *Boyz* model, exemplifying strategies for evolving genres and stimulating cinematic development.

Unfortunately, industry practices continue to restrict representations of African Americans, women, and people of color. Films that follow in the spirit of the *Boyz* model situate black women as "bitches" and "ho's" while foregrounding the inhumanity of blacks and crime.[49] While illuminating an unknown yet profitable target audience, the expectations established by the genre caused a backlash, which is dangerous for a community that historically relies on women to maintain families and communities in the absence of black men due to systemic oppression.

Set in Los Angeles, *Boyz N the Hood* is a coming-of-age story starring Cuba Gooding Jr. as Tre, a seventeen-year-old African American living in South Central Los Angeles. The black folkloric spaces in this film have morphed into warzones, places that often overlook the remnants of community and culture that sustain those who stay. The film focuses on Tre's relationship with his father, Furious (Laurence Fishburne), who raises him from age ten to seventeen while his mother, Reva (Angela Bassett), earns an advanced degree. The film also features Tre's friendship with Ricky (Morris Chestnutt) and Doughboy (Ice Cube), two brothers raised by a single mother, Brenda Baker (Tyra Ferrell). As the boys grow into men they face various dangers that lead to Ricky's and Doughboy's deaths. Tre eventually escapes to Morehouse College in Atlanta along with his girlfriend Brandi (Nia Long), who attends nearby Spelman College.

The escape narrative historically serves a critical function in theater, literature, and film. African American autobiographies about the South tend to chronicle black flight from oppression and terrorism.[50] Similarly, Gregg finds "the idea of 'escaping the ghetto' has been a powerful one ever since modern black ghettos made their first appearance at the beginning of this century."[51] From the South to the ghetto, an escape from oppressive and dangerous circumstances drives the very narratives that studio executives have suggested do not sell overseas. Several films with predominantly black casts across genres, including *Boyz N the Hood* and *Set It Off*, share escape themes as ongoing solutions to black Americans' challenges in American society. Like the Younger family in *A Raisin in the Sun*, blacks moving from one location to another remain connected whether they want to or not, often through familial relationships or by association. As Gregg explains, "In a racially divided society, members of the African American middle class are constantly pressured to see themselves in relation to poorer African Americans. They have managed to 'escape' (even when, in fact, many of them never actually lived in the ghetto), and they must consider the plight of those less fortunate than themselves."[52] The escape narratives in hip-hop gangsta films, especially in *Boyz N the Hood* and *Set It Off*, send a compelling message about individualism, escape, class mobility, meritocracy, and the American Dream. International audiences reject "the ethnic, inner-city" films, possibly because they violently expose the illusions and exclusivity of the American Dream in comparison to other film genres. Notably, these very same escape narratives are directly contested in historical films such as *Panther, Beloved,* and *Once Upon a Time.* Nonetheless, hip-hop gangsta films demonstrate the need for more films, regardless of genre, that complicate the escape narrative as well as race and class ideologies embedded within it.

The hip-hop gangsta film cycle also exemplifies the potential offscreen influence of black film on future outcomes. Considered to be the best the genre has to offer, *Boyz N the Hood* inspired numerous studies, conferences, and reports that investigate poverty, despair, disease, and death driving black men toward social apocalypse.[53] With a budget of $6.3 million, the film earned $57 million after approximately fifty-nine days on 928 screens. As the most economically successful film of the hip-hop gangsta film cycle, it also has some of the most limited constructions of black women. Their constrained representations are apparent in the film's narrative patterns and cinematic devices. The few hip-hop gangsta films that focus on women, *Set It Off* and *Just Another Girl on the IRT,* have not generated nearly as much investigation of the black female experience. Degradation of black women in black film becomes marketable in much the same way that the master narrative's treatment of black people and culture has become marketable.

Repetition of narratives, cinematic devices, and economic outcomes negatively influences subsequent films. Flat characterizations and filming techniques of black women become standard. For instance, Henry Louis Gates Jr. has noted the ways in which *Boyz* resorts to stereotyping upper-middle-class black women.[54] This potentially encourages the idea that upward social mobility not obtained through criminal activity is just seen as "acting white." Tre and Brandi's eventual escape to historically black colleges counteracts this. Nuanced depictions of the intersections of race, gender, and class distinguish the escape narrative not as a departure from black people and culture but the quest to be a part of another aspect of black culture and experience. Other films addressing similar themes include *School Daze* (1988), *Higher Learning* (1995), and *Stomp the Yard* (2007).

Patriarchal capitalism presents several hazards for black cinematic storytelling. Representing black males as primarily unsupervised except by law enforcement and correctional institutions does not reflect the historical survival of black families and African American communities that have depended upon single mothers and the black church, which is noticeably absent from *Boyz N the Hood.* Convention maintains that only the black man can fix what has been broken in the black community. This assertion becomes particularly significant when considering the race and gender of the screenwriters and director of *Set It Off.* Director F. Gary Gray and screenwriter Takashi Bufford are, in fact, African American males. The fact that co-writer Kate Lanier is a white female who has penned scripts for several films about black women is also noteworthy: *What's Love Got to Do with It?* (1993), *Glitter* (2001), and *Beauty Shop* (2005).[55] Gray directed hip-hop music videos,[56] a genre of videos that was becoming increasingly misogynistic and hyper-sexualized through groups such as 2Live Crew and N.W.A., among others. Since none of the filmmakers on this project are black women, their only intervention is through performance, much like black Americans in early mainstream theater and film.

Hip-hop gangsta filmic conventions tend to privilege masculine perspectives stemming from ghettocentric ideology, often at the expense of African American women. Hip-hop gangsta films' flat and stereotypical characterizations of black women stand in stark contrast to more developed black male characters that occupy the frame more frequently. Women receive fewer facial close-ups. They are filmed instead with medium and long shots, allowing for more focus on the body or close-ups on body parts such as cleavage, buttocks, and lips. These filmic techniques resemble music videos of the 1990s, a trend that continues to enable music and film to mutually subjugate black women. Black women are silenced while a segment of the black male population gets a voice. Encouraging degradation of one group by another reinforces the master narrative. The economic success of films that perpetuate the same ideologies that appeared in *Boyz* thus decreases the likelihood that overt departures from these narratives will ever receive studio funding or broad distribution.

Some have argued that *Boyz* has a more diverse array of black women than other films in this cycle and more positive and realistic models for both sexes.[57] These differing opinions reflect the complexity of the cycle and its ongoing influence. There are numerous complications exemplified by Doughboy's blaming the spread of HIV/AIDS on dirty, dangerous women. Singleton initiates a necessary discussion about AIDS, but demonizes black women in the process, allowing black men to continuously call them "hootchies," "bitches," and "ho's." Overall, the film depicts a nihilistic and immoral culture that needs to change.

In *Boyz*, several black actresses subvert their limited characterizations through a tradition of performative indigenization. Reva, the ideal mother, sets the stage for the failures of the other women in the film. She and the other mothers are framed as the cause of their children's psychological suffering. For example, the audience is meant to believe that Brenda's favoritism toward Ricky is the cause of Doughboy's misogynistic disposition toward women. In *Boyz* and hip-hop gangsta films in general, women are provided little opportunity to counteract these representations as supporting or minor characters to male protagonists. However, one exception is Reva's response to Tre's father's accusations:

> It's my turn to talk. Of course you took your son, my son, our son and you
> taught him what he needed to be a man. I'll give you that, because most
> men ain't man enough to do what you did. But that gives you no reason,

do you hear me, no reason to tell me that I can't be a mother to my son. What you did is no different from what mothers have been doing from the beginning of time. It's just too bad more brothers won't do the same. But don't think you're special. (Maybe cute, but not special. Drink your café au lait. It's on me.)[58]

This last part is not in the script and appears to have been improvised, softening the tone of the speech. Such empowered performances counteract the script's limitations. This occurs in another scene when the men show a lack of consideration at Doughboy's welcome-back party by serving themselves before the women. Although the script does not prescribe their response, the actresses improvise both facial expressions and dialogue. The most outspoken female character, Shalika (Regina King), raises her hand, leans back in a pose filled with attitude, and, as she begins to walk forward with the rest of the girls, says, "Sorry-assed niggas." Although director John Singleton may have influenced these performances (including the facial expressions) to account for what was missing in his script, the structure of the overall narrative and filming techniques privileges the men. This pattern of silencing black women to assert black masculinity is a problematic trend throughout this film cycle.

As noted in chapter 1, performative indigenization effectively challenges dominant narratives. But it isn't always enough. In the climactic moment in *Boyz N the Hood*, when a gang murders Ricky, Brenda and his girlfriend weep over his body as Brandi weeps in fear of Tre's retribution. Yet the women completely disappear, their grief unarticulated. Instead, the film focuses on the men's revenge killing, removing any possibility for a more complex investigation of black associations with crime and poverty. Commercial genres including comedy and action may enable economic success and draw attention to relevant issues, yet these films often lack critical nuance.

Developing African American cinema as a collective body of work rather than relying on a single film is a viable strategy for addressing the shortcomings of past films and enhancing the cultural and economic potential of future films. *Set It Off*, a necessary departure from the established gangsta formula, is most powerful when it is considered as a variation within a larger body of work. *New Jack City* (1991), *Juice* (1992), *South Central* (1992), and *Menace II Society* (1993), among others, all focus on black men. Only *Straight Out of Brooklyn* (1991), which tells the story of a young man struggling against poverty in an urban setting, provides women with the dialogue and screen time denied to them in other films.[59]

Leveraging black women's position at the intersection of race, gender, and class is an effective yet restrained method for distinguishing the potential of black subject matter in commercial genre films. Mark A. Reid's study of black feminism and independent film is particularly useful for illuminating the significance of infusing womanism or the womanist aesthetic into hip-hop gangsta films. Reid refers to "black womanist film" as "narrative constructions as well as viewing positions that permit 'womanish' as opposed to 'girlish,' processes of female subjectivity. Films belonging to this category dramatize the shared experiences of black women."[60] His work also examines black women's instrumental pioneering of "creative processes for the reception and production of racialized, sexualized, and engendered black subjectivities."[61] *Set It Off* exemplifies the infusion of a womanist aesthetic into a commercial genre as a necessary and viable strategy for contesting and reforming genre. Repetition strengthens reformation, which is less likely to happen for African American films that have to rely on studio funding.

Bufford and Lanier's *Set It Off* evolves the category of hip-hop gangsta films, pushing the cycle in new directions and (re)forming African American cinematic language in a way that is specific to working-class and poor African American women. Unfortunately, its economic outcome made it impossible to fully complete the process of utilizing the inherent intertextuality of black film to directly respond to problematic precedents. Intersectionality is a powerful tool for creating commercial yet culturally nuanced black representations. *Set It Off* is an anomaly that exposes the limitations of traditional Hollywood genres and filmmaking formulas.

As actress Alfre Woodard notes in the epigraph to chapter 1, reliance on screenplays rather than a broader range of source material can be a liability. This is especially the case for films seeking to subvert the limitations established by existing works. *Set It Off* has been identified as a hip-hop gangsta film similar to *Boyz N the Hood* except that it expresses feminist frustrations (much like the 1991 film *Thelma and Louise*, which focuses on two white women on a crime spree). In this case, however, the screenwriter's reliance on standard screenplay models limited the film's ability to fully communicate the perspectives it tried to represent. There's a fine line between relying on the established success of existing models and subverting those models. A film risks following the pitfalls of established convention.

Set It Off exposes the racial and gender disparities in Hollywood's Ulmer Scale as well as the reverberating effects of these disparities both on- and off-screen. Employing black people and women, either for behind-the-scenes roles or as actors, does not guarantee a fair or honest representation of black culture or women. However, continuous domination by white men (particularly those who avoid discussion of Hollywood's racial politics), in front of and behind the camera, certainly decreases the opportunity of any kind of deviation from mainstream representations that have been established as economically successful. African Americans and women screenwriters are still a minority in Hollywood, though both African Americans and women are not without some notable successes (Geoffrey Fletcher, an African American, wrote the screenplay for *Precious*, which earned him an Oscar for Best Adapted Screenplay; Shonda Rhimes, an African American woman, is the award-winning creator, head writer, and executive producer of the hit television series *Grey's Anatomy;* Kathryn Bigelow, a white American, was the first woman to win an Academy Award for Best Director for *The Hurt Locker* [2008]). However, the year that *Set It Off* was released, only 2.6 percent of the 8,500 Writers Guild of America members were African American.[62] Action-adventure films are the highest-grossing films and hold the most international appeal, but African Americans and women are the least likely to write (or be hired to write), direct, or star in these types of films. As a result, they will never be competitive in the industry that measures success by international box office receipts. "No one wants to be the first to develop a script from a woman writer for a big-budget action-adventure film," due to a widely held belief that a female star cannot successfully carry a big budget film.[63] Gender-bias makes *Set It Off* a significant deviation from established precedent even though it is not an action-adventure film. Queen Latifah, Jada Pinkett Smith, Vivica A. Fox, and Kimberly Elise were uniquely poised to combat these perceptions and dismal statistics. Their continued success thereafter, as indicated by their Ulmer Scale ratings, suggests that it worked—to a degree. All except Elise, a newcomer at the time, are on The World's Top 50 Black Stars list.[64]

Set It Off was not a failure per se. It earned $36 million at the box office off a $9 million budget, but it did not meet expectations considering it played on 1,016 screens for 117 days, as compared to *Boyz N the Hood*, which played on 928 screens for 59 days and returned $50 million on its investment. *Set It Off* 's budget and distribution suggest that studio executives believed in the film's box office potential. Yet its inability to generate as much gross profits or critical acclaim as either *Boyz N the Hood* or *Thelma and Louise* (which earned $45 million with a $16.5 million budget) overshadows the fact that the film earned four times its budget, more than sufficient in an industry that regards breaking even as a positive outcome.

According to Bufford, *Set It Off* 's economic potential was not completely lost on New Line when they agreed to a sequel. Because sequels and prequels to comedies such as *Dumb and Dumber* (1995) and *The Mask* (1994) failed to meet expectations without their original stars, New Line abandoned the project when Jada Pinkett Smith declined to participate.[65] Still, *Set It Off* 's offscreen circumstances should not overshadow its innovation within the genre through strategic reversals.

In the film, four African American women, Frankie (Vivica A. Fox), Stony (Jada Pinkett Smith), Tisean (Kimberly Elise), and Cleo (Queen Latifah), all childhood friends, pull off several bank heists before tragedy strikes. Following her humiliating, erroneous dismissal from her bank teller job after a deadly robbery at the bank where she worked, Frankie shares her knowledge of bank protocol with her friends. Lacking sustainable employment options and experiencing a series of tragic losses, the women come to believe the money from the bank robberies can help them escape poverty. Their final heist goes terribly wrong, leading to the deaths of all except Stony, who escapes across the border. *Set It Off*'s reversals primarily occur by foregrounding the women in their homes and community as well as in public and private locations outside of their neighborhood, illuminating their experiences with racism, sexism, and classism. This starkly contrasts with films such as *A Soldier's Story*, which shifts the focus to whites and interracial interactions. By self-consciously straddling two mainstream cinematic genres, *Set It Off* illuminates the potential for hybrid forms to articulate black experiences within the confines of existing genres. Bufford and Lanier's film introduces the possibilities of a commercially viable new genre that does not render women and children silent or invisible. For example, there are two small children in *Boyz N the Hood* and *Set It Off*, respectively, who suffer due to the unnecessary, violent death of a parent. In *Boyz N the Hood* the child of a dead father is left in the hands of a single mother, whose experiences are never fully examined. In contrast, *Set It Off* exemplifies the substantial affect of the mother's death on the child, which is lost to the system. Furthermore, *Boyz N the Hood* emphasizes the grim statistics regarding black male homicides without noting that homicide is the leading cause of death for African American women between the ages of fifteen and twenty-four.[66] The hybrid genre inspires new possibilities for infusing black subject matter into commercial genres and using commercial genres to articulate black experiences without succumbing to the pitfalls of established precedents. *Set It Off* demonstrates that it is possible to create more nuanced models that are also economically viable by identifying and utilizing culturally resonant subject matter and storytelling techniques. Careful study of the failures of preceding films can guide the process.

Taking concepts such as sisterhood out of cultural and historical context can defeat the purpose of making such alterations. For example, sisterhood in *Set It Off* disconnects the women in the film from their extended families and community, which the final film emphasizes more than the screenplay. Tisean's grandfather and cousin are in the script but completely disappear in the film, and Stony's loss of her parents and her brother's murder are the only explained familial absences. The women's isolation from their extended family depoliticizes their motivation for robbing banks. Their crimes appear to be only for material gain as opposed to an act of resistance in response to their poor, black community having been negatively affected by the closing of the local plant or by police brutality. Sisterhood in *Set It Off* replaces the brotherhood of *Boyz N the Hood*, emphasizing loyalty as the significant feature of the cycle. Trying to emulate its predecessors, the film misses an important opportunity to make critical connections between concepts of sisterhood, for example, and organized crime as social protest. Nevertheless, dismissing *Boyz N the Hood*, *Set It Off*, and other films of the hip-hop gangsta cycle would be a critical mistake in developing and distributing films with predominantly black casts. As a distinct genre, hip-hop gangsta films provide an indispensable model for commercially viable black-themed films.

Black Directors: Haile Gerima, Spike Lee, Tyler Perry, and the Future

Filmmakers who create films with black subject matter do not always take a politically conscious or socially aware approach to their representations of black experiences. The choice to feature black subject matter in film can align with commercial aspirations even though the films are less likely to achieve broad distribution, thereby fulfilling Hollywood's goal for excessive profits. Entertainment value, commercial potential, and political or social motivation do not have to be treated as mutually exclusive. The careers and films of Haile Gerima, Spike Lee, Tyler Perry, and others demonstrate this.

As already established, the patterns determined in directors' filmographies have a direct influence on the films that get made. For example, before *Set It Off*, F. Gary Gray directed *Friday* (1995), a comedy about a day in the life of Craig (rapper/actor Ice Cube) and Smokey (comedian Chris Tucker) in which they smoke, drink, and get into various situations. Made on a $3.5 million budget, the film earned $27 million at the box office. *Friday* eventually became a film franchise, further reinforcing McKenzie's argument that African American films generally outperform other types of films at the box office. In addition to several music videos and television shows, Gray has since directed *The Negotiator* (1998), starring Samuel L. Jackson and Kevin Spacey; *A Man Apart* (2003), starring Vin Diesel and Lorenz Tate; *The Italian Job* (2003), starring Mark Wahlberg; and *Be Cool* (2005), starring John Travolta. The latter two feature a predominantly white all-star cast. In 2009, Gray directed *Law Abiding Citizen*, starring Jamie Foxx and Gerard Butler. In Gray's case, his success with hip-hop gangsta films yielded additional opportunities, including projects with white male leads and predominantly white casts. Gray is a great example of an economically successful black filmmaker who no longer exclusively produces films with predominantly black casts. Filmmakers such as Gray are rewarded with larger budgets and greater distribution for making this transition. In this way, the plight of black filmmakers is not unlike that of black actors and actresses in terms of Hollywood marketability and distancing. Gray's trajectory, representative of hip-hop gangsta filmmakers generally, contrasts with that of black independent filmmakers such as Gerima.

Gerima's filmography spans four decades. As an independent filmmaker, he has directed only nine feature-length films, far fewer than Lee's thirty-six (including narrative and documentary films for television) over three decades.[67] Nor does it compare to the ten films Tyler Perry has directed in the past four

years (in addition to the numerous videos of his stage plays). Still, as a pioneer
for developing African American cinematic language, Gerima's work challenges
established precedent by providing new models that privilege cultural values
above commercial appeal. Unlike hip-hop gangsta films, black comedy franchises, or black women's literary adaptations, his films have not received the
broad distribution needed for commercial success. Gerima's cinematic storytelling tests the limits of the medium, articulating the past's influence on the
present, particularly for characters of African descent. The limited distribution
(and consequently limited access) of works like Gerima's has a profoundly negative effect on the development of African American cinematic language and
black cultural cinematic literacy.

His commitment to developing this cinematic language is apparent
throughout his filmography, especially *Teza* (2008), which is about an Ethiopian
intellectual's homecoming under a tyrannical government. It won the Grand
Prize at the Ouagadougou Pan African Film and Television festival and numerous other international awards.[68] Reviews of *Teza* suggest that Gerima perfected
earlier techniques exemplified in *Sankofa*'s structure and content. However, the
offscreen narrative has not improved, as patterns of censorship through limited
or no distribution persists.

It took Gerima twenty years and one million dollars to produce *Sankofa*.[69]
It appeared on five screens for 395 days,[70] earning approximately $2.4 million
in a decade when films in the hip-hop gangsta cycle were earning much more.
It may not have had Hollywood marketability, but *Sankofa* is a successful film
by definition because it was able to at least break even in spite of having been
censored through limited distribution. Gerima rented theaters in urban areas
and relied on word-of-mouth advertising. His perseverance made it possible
to recoup production expenses and make a profit. Author and educator Haki
Madhubuti praises the filmmaker's ingenuity as an artist and as a distributor,
saying that the film's limited distribution was attributable to it having been
considered "too black."[71] In this, *Sankofa* is similar to *Bopha!* and *Teza*, the latter of which earned $30,071 domestically from being shown on one screen for
twenty-one days. The box office outcomes of these films reflect a recurring pattern of limited distribution for films located in or focused on Africa that do not
rely on a white point of entry and do not feature a racial reconciliation narrative
as a means of legitimizing the story's black characters.

But Gerima is not without his critics. Francophone scholar Sylvie Kandé
finds Gerima's approach to slavery in *Sankofa* just as inaccurate and nostalgic as
the plantation school he critiques. Kandé points to the film's numerous awards
as well as its availability on video, chastising Gerima for persisting with the
offscreen narrative of limited distribution. Yet neither *Sankofa* nor *Teza* received
a major theatrical release in the United States, nor did they receive all the

accoutrements that come with such a release, including substantial advertising, press junkets, and a significant run in multiple movie theaters. These films represent important models for creating more nuanced articulations of black experiences, especially if their shortcomings are addressed in subsequent films' narrative patterns and correlated distribution.

Sankofa is about the identity revolution of female protagonist Mona/Shola (Oyafunmike Ogunlano), an African American fashion model shooting on location with a white photographer. While provocatively posing on the beach in front of Cape Coast castle, Mona is reprimanded by Sankofa (Kofi Ghanaba), its self-appointed guardian. His words induce her possession and backward time-travel in order to help her remember her history and identity. Mona becomes Shola, a loyal slave on a plantation who eventually leads a rebellion that returns her to the present forever changed. Needless to say, the subject matter proved too subversive for studio executives to imagine an identifiable audience. Their inability to see beyond white American and exclusive international audiences led them to ignore potential black audiences at home and abroad. These invisible black audiences supported the independently distributed film. Like the hip-hop gangsta film cycle, Sankofa illuminated a heretofore untapped market that continues to be ignored (as demonstrated by the master narrative films with predominantly white casts that almost always receive broad distribution).

Mona/Shola's transformation exemplifies the metaphysical implications of confronting slavery and cultural trauma, enabling the film to transcend the plantation school of cinema through rememory. Gerima's film and filmmaking process illustrates the politics of the sublime,[72] in which an oppositional gaze induces cultural memory, reconnecting individuals and collectives to their divinity, forgotten due to oppression. The sublime has intellectual, spiritual, and political connotations that are rarely associated with people of color. To claim the sublime is to engage in a political act that negates the dehumanization of black people and asserts higher levels of intellect and spiritual transcendence typically denied by racism. Rememory genre films and techniques can further facilitate this process. Gerima never refers to Sankofa as a rememory film, but it embodies several elements that echo this genre and its techniques.

Even major criticisms of the film cannot reverse culturally and politically empowering narrative elements and cinematic techniques. The film repositions and complicates theatrical conventions of the "happy slave"[73] popularized by Hollywood. By placing archetypes and stereotypes in binary opposition throughout the film, Gerima exposes the fallacy of the plantation school of cinema's stereotypes. He first places Mona, "the best example of a Negro, a sorry white invention, who hates herself and who has lost history only to be re-enslaved in a twentieth-century lifestyle that is embarrassing and degrading," in binary opposition to Sankofa.[74] Gerima continues to expose and resolve the tensions between archetypes and stereotypes through specific relationships: Shango (the symbolic Yoruban god of war) and Shola's (house slave) romantic relationship, Nunu (Mother Africa) and Joe's (mulatto son) familial relationship, the People in the Hills (maroons) and the plantation slaves (a complex representation of collective groups). In direct resistance, Gerima continuously exposes and resolves the tensions until Mona/Shola's transformations are complete. Her return to the Cape Coast castle to sit among other Africans and tourists of African descent embodies the history circulating in their blood and memories.

Sankofa offers useful examples and definitions of the rememory film as both a genre and a technique, as well as the potency of the politics of the sublime to nuance black representation. For example, Mona's tour of the castle sets the tone for rememory to achieve the politics of the sublime. Following Sankofa's second reprimand, Mona enters the castle for a tour that inspires her to rememory when she faces a rememory. In the beginning she is led by a Ghanaian tour guide who explains the castle's history. Separated from the group following the loud sound of a door closing, all that is visible is Mona with her back against the wall and a tunnel of darkness to her right. Visibly alarmed, she turns to look back into the dark tunnel twice, and on the second look it becomes a room full of Africans chained together around a small fire. At first they appear not to see Mona, gazing straight ahead or off in the distance, silently contemplating their predicament. As Mona screams and runs about, their gaze rests on her. They appear to recognize her, unsurprised that she wants nothing to do with them. She runs from each room, all filled to capacity with chained Africans. They approach Mona with outstretched hands, frightening her even more. She sees no resemblance between them and herself. She believes they intend to hurt her, but the audience can see they are merely reaching out to her. Yet the sheer number of them and the spectacle they create is horrifying. Running through the castle Mona reaches the locked door, which again resembles a deep, dark tunnel. After she screams and bangs on the door it swings open, revealing to Mona white slavers from the past. She is relieved to see them and asks them to save her from the Africans in the dark castle. They grab Mona and drag her back into the castle, seeing no difference between her and the others. Mona is obviously traumatized by this lack of recognition and fights to escape. Finally, slavers strip Mona naked before the gaze of the enslaved Africans and brand her. This is the catalyst that begins her journey to the past. The power of the gaze is implicit throughout this scene. The way Mona looks at the Africans, the way that the Africans gaze at her, and the way Mona and the slavers see one another expose the ways that slavery has been filmed prior to Gerima's project. Through the use of the cinematic apparatus, he attempts to combat the ways we see people of African descent and their relationship to the history of slavery, not merely as helpless victims but as human beings in horrific circumstances.

The project's focus on these ways of seeing reflects the transcendent qualities of survival and resistance as well as the complexities of reenacting cultural trauma by filming slavery.

Gerima's technique of filming people with histories of oppression in empowering ways is particularly noteworthy. This is best exemplified in *Sankofa* in one of the most disturbing scenes in the film, when the pregnant Kuta is returned after her escape and beaten to death in front of the others. Under the command of the overseer, Joe counts the headman's lashes while Nunu unrelentingly stares at Joe. The power of her stare cripples the overseer and makes Joe lose count. Nunu eventually intervenes in order to save Kuta's unborn child. As the merciless beating persists, the nameless enslaved Africans watching the beating are individually filmed looking directly into the camera, returning the audience's gaze and engaging the concept of the power of looking. Here Gerima intentionally creates an oppositional gaze between the enslaved and the audience. This oppositional gaze technique subverts the way in which slaves in groups are typically filmed as being looked at or overlooked, but never looking back.

Teza reinforces the concept of the gaze fifteen years later. This film also uses the eyes of the movie's hero, Anberber, to refract and reflect the "confused, vicious, sprawling world" depicted on screen.[75] Gerima successfully merges twentieth-century European and African history through Anberber's struggle as a displaced African intellectual. Film critic Matt Zoller Seitz praises Gerima's approach to contrasting Anberber's nightmares and hallucinations with meditative landscape shots as evidence that *Teza* has "all the hallmarks of a career summation" that soars rather than collapses under the weight of its ambition.[76] But distribution was worse for *Teza* than *Sankofa*, suggesting a bleak future for films with predominantly black casts that do not follow mainstream traditions.

Films about slavery have been less frequently produced in Hollywood in the latter half of the twentieth century and the beginning of the twenty-first than in previous decades. Nearly fifty feature-length narrative films about the Holocaust, the most comparable type of mainstream film to rememory films, have been produced in the United States since 1980. The prevalence and frequency of Holocaust films suggest that audiences are capable of processing trauma, genocide, and inhumanity onscreen. However, any depictions that do not allow for the United States to appear heroic or constructs it as the perpetrator of an atrocity are frequently censored through limited distribution. This problem did not begin with Gerima, nor is he the only filmmaker to experience this challenge.

Regardless of the filmmaker's race, many independent films do not receive major theatrical release; however, the lack of major theatrical distribution for films with predominantly black casts is an ongoing and serious problem. A few recent examples include *Frankie & Alice* and *Dark Tide*, both starring the Oscar winner Halle Berry; *Winnie*, starring the Oscar-winning singer/actress Jennifer

Hudson and the Oscar nominee Terrence Howard; *Pastor Brown* and *Black Water Transit*, starring Laurence Fishburne; *Mama I Want to Sing*, starring the singer/ actress Ciara; *Bolden!*, starring Anthony Mackie; *All Things Fall Apart*, starring Mario Van Peebles and the rapper/actor 50 Cent; and *The Discarded Boys/In the Hive*, among others. Festival films lacking preliminary distribution deals take longer to get distributed in theaters or on home video.[77]

Recognizing these limitations, several black independent filmmakers have devised alternatives. Gerima and his wife/producer, Shirikiana Aina, established their own distribution company, Mypeduh Films, Inc., in 1982. They describe the creation of Mypeduh Films as a way to "humbly construct a means of independently telling our stories through film and video."[78] The distribution company primarily focuses on African and African American films and other works from the global African Diaspora. Distribution markets include nontheatrical, educational, and institutional venues and private retailers. Products can be purchased at the Sankofa Video and Bookstore in Washington, D.C., or online. In addition, Gerima runs Negod Gwad Productions and Elimu Productions, which produce dramatic and documentary film and videos. He also has a nonprofit organization called Positive Productions, Inc., which provides film services for independent filmmakers. Gerima's work as a filmmaker extends beyond the creative into the business and philanthropic because he recognizes that the challenges black filmmakers face within the industry are multiple and complex. His distribution strategies and revolt against established precedent expose how difficult it can be to penetrate the interlocking systems of oppression created by vertical and horizontal integration, even on a comparatively small scale.

Filmmaker Ava DuVernay developed a model for distributing films with predominantly black casts through the African American Film Festival Releasing Movement, demonstrating the effectiveness of collective strategies. With the support of an alliance of ethnic film festival resources, social networks, and mailing lists, DuVernay's organization plans to use the independent film program recently begun by the AMC theater chain to release black-themed films in commercial theaters for a two-week run.[79] Limited theatrical release promoted by institutions and supporters that recognize the cultural value and the commercial potential of a work does not compare to the broad distribution that studio-level films receive. Yet this significant intervention takes the burden off a single filmmaker to create content, produce, market, and distribute a film that is already perceived as an economic risk due to the race ideologies that drive the filmmaking economy. These filmmakers carry on the tradition of entrepreneurship and cultural politics established by Oscar Micheaux, who took his films directly to theaters in order to ensure distribution. From Micheaux to DuVernay, many black filmmakers and allies recognize how the combined challenges of production and distribution shape the future of black film.

Spike Lee and the Future for Blacks in the Studio System

Spike Lee's politicized filmmaking and technical savvy have made him famous. Part of his celebrity stems from his publicly subversive tactics, which in many ways build on the legacy of UCLA's independent black filmmakers.[80] Inspired by the political and social struggles of the 1960s, African and African American students in the UCLA Theater Arts department began making films that combined political ideology and techniques from Micheaux's family dramas to counter Hollywood films' inability to speak to black experiences around the world. The first wave of students to emerge from this group included Gerima, Charles Burnett, and Larry Clark. A second wave of filmmakers from UCLA included Bill Woodberry, Julie Dash, and Alile Sharon Larkin.[81] Their collective resistance is reminiscent of The Frogs, an early twentieth-century group of black American stage performers that included George Walker and Bert Williams.

The UCLA film school tended to focus on adapting Micheaux's creative rather than his entrepreneurial legacy. As Ntongela Masilela explains, "The revolutionary breakthrough of the UCLA school was to draw on Micheaux's work yet shift its social subject matter from a middle-class to a working-class milieu in which black labor struggled against White capital."[82] Nevertheless, Micheaux's work exemplifies the necessity of revision, reversal, and repetition. He introduced one of the first deliberate attempts to truly reflect the internal thoughts of an African American character, especially in regards to racism, in *Within Our Gates* (1919). Ephraim, the servant responsible for inciting a white mob to track down and murder a black sharecropper suspected of killing the plantation owner, finds himself alone in the midst of the crowd. To illustrate his discomfort, Micheaux goes beyond offering a close-up of the actor's face and medium shot of his shifting from foot to foot. Unlike the filming of black characters in *The Birth of a Nation*, Micheaux redirects the gaze to black experiences. Following the close-up, Micheaux superimposes an image of Ephraim hanging from a rope, dissolving into a close-up of Ephraim as he gasps at the white mob surrounding him. Micheaux's visual articulation of a black character's internal thoughts reflects the fundamental role that technique plays in the cultural and political economy of African American filmmaking. Humanizing black characters through dialogue, close-ups, and other elements is apparent in the work and techniques devised by Lee, Gerima, and other African American filmmakers. They exemplify a developing African American cinematic language that can aid the development of film in general.

Similarly, Lee's double-dolly shot, which has been primarily used on black protagonists, also communicates characters' internal state. The double-dolly shot is achieved when the camera is on a dolly moving backward and the actor being filmed is on another dolly moving forward. It creates the illusion of being suspended, floating over the scene. Lee began using this technique in *Mo' Better*

Blues (1990) as a way of showing off his technical savvy, but it has since been incorporated only in scenes where it has a particular significance. For example, he uses it in one of the most memorable moments of *Malcolm X* (1992). Malcolm (Denzel Washington) approaches the Audubon Ballroom on the day of his assassination as the sound track plays Sam Cooke's "A Change Is Gonna Come." The technique illustrates a transported or alienated feeling, representative of the character's awareness that he will be assassinated. Lee developed the technique with former classmate and longtime director of photography Ernest Dickerson (Dickerson directed the hip-hop gangsta film *Juice* and numerous other projects for film and television). Artistic evolution of the craft represented in the work of Micheaux, Van Peebles, Gerima, and Lee has received more attention than the recurring problems of distribution. Lee benefits from their artistic influence along with the access granted by studio affiliation. He therefore serves as a critical model for emulation for many black filmmakers and allies currently working in the industry.

As Lee accomplishes his objective of being one of the most consistently produced and distributed filmmakers in the industry, other African American directors face a paradox. For years Lee has represented the standard for African American film. This is particularly problematic considering his films are frequently classified as "niche films." They mediate between the more artistic and politicized films of the Los Angeles School of Black Filmmakers and the mass market hip-hop gangsta films. By capitalizing on both, Lee is afforded privileges denied directors like Gerima. As a result, subsequent filmmakers are more likely to emulate Lee's model, competing for the couple of slots per year because the primary objective of film production, however political, is to make a profit, especially given the high cost of filmmaking.

In *Bamboozled*, Lee uses his outsider-within location to examine blacks' double bind as writers, directors, actors, and powerbrokers in the entertainment industry. This film sophisticatedly combines production, distribution, and exhibition issues that Jesse Rhines examines in *Black Film/White Money* and that Melvin Van Peebles explores in *Classified X*. Countless scholars from the 1970s to the present have been trying to reconcile the double bind in order to revolutionize black film content as well as modes of production and distribution. As a result, Lee provides a contemporary visual document of black experiences in entertainment that tells the story behind the numbers and the color-coded economics that produce them.

Bamboozled is a cautionary tale about Pierre Delacroix, also known as Pierless Dothan (Damon Wayans), a young African American television writer. Due to pressure from his boss, Thomas Dunwitty (Michael Rappaport), Delacroix creates a modern blackface minstrel show featuring the misadventures of Mantan and Sleep'n Eat, entitled *Mantan: The New Millennium Minstrel Show*, to prove that the Continental Network Station (CNS) prefers to represent African Americans as buffoons. Sloan (Jada Pinkett Smith), Delacroix's assistant, and the show's stars, Manray/Mantan (Savion Glover) and Womack/Sleep'n Eat (Tommy Davidson), are all affected by its success and tragic outcome. The Mau Maus, a pseudo-revolutionary group of hip-hop artists, stage a violent protest against the show's degrading imagery by kidnapping and murdering Manray and streaming the murder live online. The events surrounding Delacroix's experience convey Lee's argument that racism is embedded in the fabric of American society and disseminated throughout the media.

Lee depicts interlocking systems of oppression working against black artists, activists, and audiences through vertical integration. The film traces the show's development from conception, production, distribution, and exhibition on the network. It exposes a distortion of Delacroix's original ideas, which can only be expressed and broadly distributed as an employee of a major network. Lee's dramatization of creative centralization in television through conglomeration can be easily applied to the film industry. According to film studies professors Maria Pramaggiore and Tom Wallis, "The expenditures of six media companies account for three-quarters of the total spending on screenwriting in the United States," which has led the Writer's Guild of America to contend that the existing marketplace "stifles creativity" either by "absorbing new, creative talent into impersonal conglomerates that churn out standardized product, or by ignoring this talent altogether."[83] Delacroix experiences both extremes when the network rejects his shows, rebuffing a broader range of black representation in favor of one that pushes the envelope. He goes from being completely ignored to being acculturated into the system through work that reinforces the very ideology that demeans him, his family, and scores of blacks. Many of them become accomplices in the soul murder the show executes by embracing it through viewership or merchandising. The network's and the public's enthusiasm mutually reinforces the same plantation ideology apparent in nineteenth-century minstrel shows, further suggesting that works which reinforce dominant racial paradigms are more likely to be broadly distributed than those that challenge it.[84]

Lee also dramatizes the overwhelming effects of market synergy through horizontal integration. Audiences are powerless to stop the show through protests or even reasoning with Delacroix or the network. Refusal to watch the show is undermined when they are assailed by public television displays, advertising, and merchandising. The plantation ideology the show reinforces becomes more deeply entrenched in popular culture through merchandising and budding trends, like the resurgence of blackface and the casual adoption of the term "nigger." As the show's popularity increases, Delacroix receives compensation and various awards for his efforts. The combination of dramatized vertical and horizontal integration and the symbiotic relationship between black artists and audiences exposes economically structured processes that coerce them into collaborating in their dehumanization.

Lee had big hopes for the film. He wrote the part of Delacroix for Will Smith, who opted to do *The Legend of Bagger Vance* (2000) instead. Casting an A+ list film star in the role would have guaranteed broad distribution and exposed audiences less familiar with the particular details of black experience in the entertainment industry. Such casting may also have introduced domestic and international audiences to another representation of African American film, and been a profound test case for strategic use of crossover appeal to benefit the evolution of African American film and cinematic language. Nonetheless, Smith declined the offer, allowing Wayans to stretch his range beyond comedy to tell Delacroix's story.

Numerous elements in the film are worthy of discussion, but the most relevant for our purposes concerns Lee's characterization of the audience of *Mantan: The New Millennium Minstrel Show*. This depiction dramatizes the problems of crossover appeal for African American writers, performers, and audiences. Lee shows the stages of development of growing an audience for a work prominently featuring African Americans. In doing so, the film illuminates the exchange of power between storyteller and audience, and Lee ends up dramatizing processes of cultural amnesia that develop in such an audience and among performers and practitioners. Patterns of using black audiences to launch stars, directors, and their works are apparent in this staging of the audience's progression. The evolution begins with a live performance of the show taped for a predominantly African American studio audience, with some mixing. The growing audience base reflects the contagious mania of coonery and buffoonery that continues to plague commercial viability of diverse African American narratives. Black audiences are selectively consulted to review works that contain predominantly black casts or feature blacks in minor or supporting roles. Their opinions of films with predominantly white or other ethnic casts are rarely sought.

The complexity and depth of Lee's film was lost on the New Line Cinema executives who engage the common practice of categorizing the film according to race as opposed to genre. Like *Beloved*, the film is not easy to classify according to existing commercial genres. Writer, music producer, and cultural critic Greg Tate refers to it as a science-fiction film about how mainstream media has failed to address where African Americans figure into the American scheme except as slaves.[85] The inability to classify films such as *Bamboozled* and *Beloved* continues to be a major problem for African American filmmaking. Major and minor studios clearly have difficulty understanding these films and identifying audiences, which ultimately affects box office outcomes. Established as a film distributor in 1967 by Robert Shaye and Michael Lynne, New Line Cinema became an independent film studio before merging with Time Warner in 1996 and Warner Bros. in 2008. When distributing *Bamboozled*, New Line had already merged with a major media conglomerate, which further illuminates creative centralization in which independents are absorbed and acculturated into the mainstream. New Line's treatment of black themes preceding the merger was not necessarily distinct. Yet their distribution of art house and cult films on college campuses clearly catered to a niche market that yielded lucrative returns over time.

New Line's first venture into production and distribution of films with predominantly black casts did not occur until Reginald Hudlin's directorial debut, *House Party* (1990). In this commercial-genre crossover hit about teenagers— starring the rap duo Christopher "Kid" Harris and Peter "Play" Martin as Kid and Play, and a young Martin Lawrence as Bilal—Play invites Kid to a house party but Kid's father forbids him to attend. Tapping into the growing urban market, the film earned $26 million on a $2.5 million budget. Its success ushered into production and distribution more studio films with predominantly black casts. In the following decade, New Line distributed twelve more such films: *Hangin' with the Homeboys* (1991), *House Party 2* (1991), *Who's the Man?* (1993), *Menace II Society* (1993), *House Party 3* (1994), *Above the Rim* (1994), *Friday* (1995), *Set It Off* (1996), *B.A.P.S* (1997), *The Player's Club* (1998), *Next Friday* (2000), and *Turn It Up* (2000). Unfortunately, these films do not represent a broad range of genres or representations of blacks. Most are comedies, with the exception of the hip-hop gangsta cycle films *Menace II Society* and *Set It Off*. *The Player's Club* is a dramedy featuring prominent comedians Jamie Foxx and Bernie Mac in addition to Ice Cube, the film's writer/director. All the films fit into that "ethnic, inner-city," region described by studio executives negating economic viability of black-themed films.

The Los Angeles School of Black Filmmakers was also active at this time, representing a broader range of blackness without comparable mainstream distribution. Julie Dash's *Daughters of the Dust* (1991) became the first feature-length film by an African American woman to receive general theatrical release in the United States. Dash paved the way for Kasi Lemmons, writer/director of *Eve's Bayou*. Utilizing avant-garde techniques, *Daughters of the Dust* features a predominantly black cast and earned $1.6 million on an $800,000 budget, as well as critical acclaim.[86] Yet it could not initiate the production of similar films. The preference for comedies and hip-hop gangsta films limits implementation of a cinematic vocabulary that communicates complexity and humanity through black experiences.

Ideologies that privilege white over black clearly influence the executives at New Line, who overlooked *Bamboozled*'s complex themes and considered the film more akin to the hip-hop gangsta cycle (and comedies) due to its cast.

To Lee, however, his film was a hybrid that could not be marketed the same way as *Menace II Society* or *Set It Off*. New Line's refusal to reconsider ultimately undermined the film's box office. The film's unconventional techniques are more similar to the art house and cult films that New Line initially distributed on American college campuses. Since its theatrical release, *Bamboozled* has found an extended life in this very market, serving as a pedagogical tool for theater, film, cultural studies, and communication and media studies scholars and students. The studio's limited perspective of genre and race overlooked this potential market. The concept of supplying foreign and art films for college campuses is an approach to distribution that has the potential to counteract current limitations.

Bamboozled appears to prophesy the struggles of artists such as Dave Chappelle. Much like Delacroix, in 2003 Chappelle developed a project called *Chappelle's Show*, a variation of sketch comedy that Chappelle referred to as "hip-hop Masterpiece Theater."[87] It pushes the envelope, and in this way appears to be the type of show that Dunwitty asked Delacroix to produce. In *Bamboozled*, Dunwitty calls contemporary shows about middle-class blacks "too clean" and "too whitebread," saying that people want to be entertained and that black people set the consumer trends. He calls for "a show that will make headlines. I want millions and millions of viewers tuned in and glued to their fucking televisions every week saying did you see what the fuck they were doing on CNS last night? I want advertisers sucking my dick to buy on this show." Ultimately, this is what *Chappelle's Show* became for Comedy Central, a basic cable network.

The framework of sketch comedy contributed to the show's edginess, unlike what is seen in situation comedy and its stifling structure.[88] By taking less money, Chappelle and his white co-creator, Neal Brennan, maintained the creative control denied Delacroix. In 2004, Chappelle signed a $50 million, two-year contract with Comedy Central and found himself in a predicament not unlike Delacroix's. Chappelle realized that some of his skits could be socially irresponsible when his white employee laughed heartily at Chappelle's blackface performance in a sketch. *Chappelle's Show* received three Emmy nominations and was the highest-rated cable program for the 18–34-year-old demographic, with an average of 3.1 million total viewers in its second season.[89] *Chappelle's Show: Season 2 Uncensored* DVD sold 500,000 copies in one day and 1.2 million copies in a week, ultimately creating an entirely new revenue stream for the network. The show's economic and critical achievements further reiterate the economic viability of black-themed subject matter in film and television. Its success also exemplifies economics as a critical factor for developing black star power. Significantly, rather than the show appearing on Black Entertainment Television, Chappelle developed his star power on Comedy Central, which promotes the crossover appeal necessary to create star power. The show's reruns continue to have a large fan base, as does Chappelle, who left the show and his $50 million deal after a critical incident that exposes the complications of black artists in Hollywood.

Chappelle appeared on *Oprah* and *Inside the Actor's Studio* to clarify his reasons for breaking the lucrative deal. The *Oprah* website explains:

> During his third season, Dave began questioning his work on the show. From the very first episode, Dave's sketches sparked controversy. But, over time, he says some of his sketches started to make him feel "socially irresponsible." One particular sketch still disturbs Dave today. The skit was about a pixie (played by Dave) who appeared in black face, which Dave describes as the "visual personification of the n-word." "There was a good-spirited intention behind it," Dave says. "So then when I'm on the set, and we're finally taping the sketch, somebody on the set [who] was white laughed in such a way—I know the difference of people laughing with me and people laughing at me—and it was the first time I had ever gotten a laugh that I was uncomfortable with. Not just uncomfortable, but like, should I fire this person?" After this incident, Dave began thinking about the message he was sending to millions of viewers. Dave says some people understood exactly what he was trying to say with his racially charged comedy . . . while others got the wrong idea. "That concerned me," he says. "I don't want black people to be disappointed in me for putting that [message] out there. . . . It's a complete moral dilemma."[90]

Several accounts suggest that Chappelle walked off the set without explanation when he completed filming the season, setting off rumors that he had gone crazy or was on drugs. He went to South Africa for two weeks to gather his thoughts and reassess his work, something Delacroix never does in the film. Chappelle said he needed to get away from the "circumstances that were coming with the new-found plateau of fame" that comes when those with a vested interest in controlling "the guy who generates money" try to get in his pockets.[91] Plantation ideology is played out in multiple ways with similar results.

Chappelle's departure ended up allowing him the freedom to identify other career possibilities. His story offers solutions not initially apparent in Lee's nihilistic ending of *Bamboozled*. On *Oprah*, he expressed conflicted emotions about whether to return to the show, suggesting that if he continued he would donate his earnings to charity. He felt this would absolve him should he say or do something socially irresponsible. Chappelle did not return to the show, however, and reruns from the first three seasons continue to be shown on the network.

While it may appear that Comedy Central won by continuing to profit from Chappelle's work in spite of his departure, this is not the case. Copycat programs such as *Chocolate News*, *Mind of Mencia*, and *Key and Peele* have not generated the excitement or the revenue of Chappelle's show. In contrast, Chappelle uses his star power for live stand-up comedy in venues where he maintains direct connection with the audience and creative control of the material in a way he feels comfortable managing. Unlike in *Bamboozled*, where his comedian father, Junebug (Paul Mooney), rejects crossover success in favor of a low-key career on the stand-up circuit, Delacroix never comes to such a realization. Delacroix's outlook seemingly reflects Lee's reliance on studio support due to his position within the studio system.

The power of the major studios and the limited access of African Americans within the system resonate in *Bamboozled*'s nihilistic ending. All the major black characters die, with the exception of Sloan, who still has blood on her hands. The alternative routes Chappelle chose are not presented as viable options for Delacroix. Delacroix disdains what he perceives as a lack of ambition in his alcoholic father's refusal to pursue mainstream success rather than an act of protest and self-respect. Delacroix lacks entrepreneurial motivation. He plans to get fired from one network so that he can work for another without breaking his contract, rather than working independently. The film's nihilistic ending and its failed box office both portend a bleak future for African American film. The film's ending and economic outcome questions whether assimilation (at a cost) is the only path to economic success. This is only the case, however, if one sees the existing studio system as the sole outlet for the production and distribution of African American films. Lee's recent decision to use Kickstarter, a fundraising website for creative projects, to raise $1.25 million to independently produce a film in 2013 suggests that he is now seeking alternatives and finding freedom beyond the studio system over a decade after *Bamboozled*'s release.[92] In fact, the studio system offers a limited and outmoded approach to African American films moving forward.

While Lee's bleak assessment of the industry in *Bamboozled* overlooks various possibilities for overcoming the industry's interlocking systems of oppression, he continues to grow in notable ways as a filmmaker. *Bamboozled* and *Miracle at St. Anna* reflects this growth as well as the complicated position he occupies in Hollywood as one of the most consistently produced and distributed African American filmmakers, with weaker box office statistics than many of his black and white peers. Similar to August Wilson, Lee is privileged and frequently cited as proof that the system is not racist but inclusive and open to black themes and subject matter.

Historically, whites in Hollywood and on Broadway have more frequently treated critical moments like slavery (1619–1865), World War II (1939–1945), and the civil rights era (1955–1968) by minimizing or erasing black experiences. This is particularly true in regard to treatment of World War II films, which makes Fuller's *A Soldier's Play* and its cinematic companion such a significant contribution. There have been approximately fifty-eight films about World War II produced by the United States from 1980 to 2008. Of these, the only ones that focus on African Americans include *A Soldier's Story* (1984), distributed by Columbia Pictures, HBO's *The Tuskegee Airmen* (1995), and Lee's comparatively epic *Miracle at St. Anna* (2008), distributed by Touchstone Pictures. *Red Tails* (2012) also focuses on this era.

The posters for *Miracle at St. Anna* feature a white child clinging to a black soldier whose uniformed arm returns the embrace, clearly indicating that a significant relationship between blacks and whites will be examined. This cinematic adaptation of James McBride's novel of the same name allowed Lee to illuminate African American contributions in World War II that had been summarily ignored in the fifty-six preceding World War II films, including Clint Eastwood's contemporary treatments.[93] *Miracle at St. Anna*'s estimated $45 million budget clearly demonstrates Lee's access to substantial film financing even after *Bamboozled* fared so poorly at the box office, having recouped only $2.2 million of its $10 million budget after playing on 243 screens for forty-five days. Likewise, *Miracle at St. Anna* earned only $7.9 million after appearing on approximately 1,185 screens for fifty-nine days. This is a major failure in comparison to Clint Eastwood's *Flags of Our Fathers* (2006)[94] and *Letters from Iwo Jima* (2006).[95] The latter tells the story of the battle of Iwo Jima from the perspective of Japanese soldiers. Lee's ability to secure $45 million in financing for *Miracle at St. Anna* following such a drastic loss of revenue suggests his position within the Hollywood framework is quite secure. Yet Lee's inability to recoup more than one-fifth of the production expenses with such a large budget also illuminates the harsh role numbers can play in reinforcing the perceived economic failures of African American films. Even George Lucas acknowledged this when expressing his fear that the failure of *Red Tails* at the box office could be a crucial blow for the future of African American films.

Lee and Perry represent two extremes of the debate regarding the future of African American film through major studio distribution, minor studio distribution, or independent distribution. Lee's celebrity and successive failed box office are just as paradoxical as Perry's economic success and lack of critical acclaim. As Lee observes, Perry's success creates a paradox of perception that is extremely problematic. However, it is important to acknowledge Lee's privileged position within the system he critiques, as well as Perry's initial exclusion and more recent absorption into that same system. As an entrepreneur, Perry represents alternative approaches that Lee appears unwilling to explore until recently. While Lee maintains his celebrity status as one of the best-known black directors in Hollywood, Perry's bankability cannot be ignored: he is now the second wealthiest director on the *Forbes* list, behind only James Cameron. Like Will Smith's coveted bankability as the biggest movie star in the world and

Oprah's power to influence audiences, Perry's success leads to the perception that African Americans are improving their position and power in Hollywood. This is only partially true.

Lee, Perry, and Smith are among the few African Americans who can influence those with the power to greenlight films. The race-based competition for the couple of African American distribution slots per year is no longer a viable solution to distribution problems. Nevertheless, many are working inside the studio system following Lee's model, further illuminating the limitations of the existing paradigm. Even with NAACP protests and press conferences commenting on the existing framework's racial underpinnings, a major boycott from studio-produced films has not been realized, perhaps in part because a traditional boycott may undermine gains made by those continuing to work within the system to promote change. Then there is the matter of the technological revolution, which is in full swing and can help exploit Hollywood's structural imperfections to introduce change.

But black artists working in the system without deviation will continue to experience its negative effects. Lee Daniels, Antoine Fuqua, and Tim Story are recent economic success stories. Daniels directed two films whose combined box office totaled approximately $47.9 million. His Oscar nomination and track record of working with Oscar-winning actors (Cuba Gooding Jr., Mo'Nique, Halle Berry, and Helen Mirren) should have made it easier to pursue any project he wanted. He chose *Selma*, which focuses on marches during the civil rights era, but he abandoned the project due to insufficient funds. Instead, his follow-up project to *Precious* turned out to be *The Paperboy* (2012), also set in the South in the 1960s but starring a predominantly white cast including Matthew McConaughey, Nicole Kidman, John Cusack, and Zac Efron.[96] For the film Daniels was able to secure $12.5 million, further illustrating the complex position of black directors as they shift away from films with predominantly black casts in the mainstream market.

Fortunately, Daniels was able to secure a $30 million budget to produce *The Butler* (2013) starring Forest Whitaker and Oprah Winfrey. The film's lead character occupies a subservient role, not unlike Morgan Freeman's character in *Driving Miss Daisy*. Yet the film maintains the focus on black cultural perspectives through the use of various elements Daniels also used in *Precious*. The film's $115 million box office and critical acclaim further reinforces the economic viability of African American film as well as the resonating power of the Oprah Effect. Similarly, black British filmmaker Steve McQueen managed to obtain a major theatrical release for his independent film *12 Years a Slave* (2013), starring Chiwetel Ejiofor and produced in collaboration with Brad Pitt. As of this writing, the film earned approximately $33 million in the box office along with numerous festival awards. Like Quentin Tarantino's western, *Django Unchained*, which earned $162 million on a $100 million budget, McQueen's historical drama is set during slavery. Although each of these films deserves greater examination than I can provide here, their outcomes will notably affect the future of African American films. I hope their economic success and critical acclaim will encourage more consistent investment in a range of black films directed by black filmmakers and allies, especially films that challenge the master narrative. Historically, this has not been the case, thereby necessitating the ongoing exploration of alternative production and distribution strategies.

Daniels's work is considerably less commercial than Antoine Fuqua's action films and music videos. The total domestic box office from all of Fuqua's projects to date is approximately $380 million. His top earner was *Training Day* (2001), for which Denzel Washington won an Oscar for Best Actor. Fuqua recognizes the value placed on box office returns and the restrictions imposed upon black filmmakers when they try to gain studio support. But like Daniels, Fuqua focuses more on the projects than racial politics in order to meet the demands of his economic criteria and the action film genre. As the examples throughout this book reveal, racial politics cannot be completely divorced from the equation because ideologies that permit racial discrimination are so deeply embedded in the system.

Tim Story has made even greater strides than Lee in the studio system and is gaining recognition with films like *Think Like a Man*. As director of the *Fantastic Four* franchise (in 2005 and 2007), he is the king of the box office compared to other black filmmakers.[97] His box office totaled approximately $900 million as of May 2012, placing him ahead of Perry as the top-earning black director.[98] Story's breakout hit was the 2002 film *Barbershop*, an African American film (and eventual franchise) considered to be a huge crossover success with $76 million in earnings. *Taxi* (2004) was his next film. It starred Queen Latifah and Jimmy Fallon and grossed $36.6 million on a $25 million budget. Story is one of the few African American film directors chosen to direct mainstream blockbuster hits such as the *Fantastic Four* franchise. This illustrious honor did not, however, prevent problems with subsequent films. His 2012 film *Think Like a Man* suffered from poor international distribution (as discussed in the introduction) and his 2009 film *Hurricane Season* went straight to DVD. The latter film is about a reassembled high school basketball team in post-Katrina Louisiana that goes on to win a state championship. The film did not recoup its $15 million budget before going straight to DVD due to financial problems (it eventually aired on BET). Clearly the current system relies too heavily on theatrical release for measuring success.

Prominent directors such as Story and Lee represent a wide range of progress and struggle for African Americans within the studio system. Existing alternatives that can expand accessibility and capitalize on the supposed niche market of films exploring black themes, subjects, and worldviews are available. Indeed, contemporary infrastructure can be used to support African American film. Examples include DuVernay's theatrical release of independent black films in commercial theaters, Gerima's nontheatrical, educational distribution (and philanthropic work), and Jeff Friday's Film Life, Inc.'s collaboration with Hollywood studios to promote film and television releases (and his NFL Pro Hollywood Football Camp program, which helps train pro-athletes to become producers), as well as Earvin "Magic" Johnson's movie theaters and television network. Other forward-thinking options such as implementing a global African diasporic distribution network can also circumvent the existing system and its exclusionary practices through the use of new media.

Conclusion

Despite a lack of consistent and open acknowledgment in Hollywood, black films, subjects, and worldviews are big business. Black directors and performers are developing successful offscreen methods to support the narrative and visual formulas that have yielded big profits. The filmmakers, films cycles, and franchises discussed in this chapter are establishing new precedents of black bankability that can be used to take greater risks onscreen and off. This is critical in order to counteract the effects of film cycles, with their one-dimensional view of black culture considered to represent all black film.

While Hollywood studios have been increasingly willing to tap black talent in light of the success of certain film cycles, some are still used to support the same stagnant master narrative. For instance, contemporary black directors receive subtle studio incentives to move away from films with predominantly black casts, thereby reinforcing the racial double standard that makes either working within the studio system or competing for the same couple of slots per year so limiting. Employing strategies such as hybrid distribution and strategic horizontal integration to support works that integrate intertextuality and intersectionality into narratives that can speak to black and global audiences through new media and technology is critical to the undoing of the double standards and, most importantly, to the ongoing development of African American film. Indeed, the changes being heralded by the digital revolution promise more opportunities for intercultural exchange, to the mutual benefit of film and culture.

Conclusion

The Story Behind the Numbers

> People who are smart kind of let us do our thing. I keep saying that
> because I want studio executives to read this. The ones that are smart
> let us *do our thing.* We bring back a great movie and never go over bud-
> get, and everyone's happy at the end of the day.
>
> —Ice Cube, 2008

Black cultural producers continue to occupy a precarious position in Hollywood, but there are promising indicators that suggest change is afoot. On July
1, 2012, *Beasts of the Southern Wild*, Benh Zeitlin's cinematic adaptation of southerner Lucy Alibar's play, opened on four screens in the United States. Produced
in collaboration with Court 13 and the playwright, the film focuses on a little
black girl named Hushpuppy (Quvenzhané Wallis) and her relationship with
her ailing father, Wink (Dwight Henry), in a fictional southern Louisiana town
known as "the Bathtub," where they are constantly under threat of flooding.
Less than a year after its initial release, the film earned box office profits almost
twelve times its budget in addition to numerous high-profile accolades (including four Academy Award nominations). The film's onscreen narrative and offscreen successes conjure both hope and concern for the future.

The film included a number of significant alterations from the source text.
Hushpuppy evolves from an eleven-year-old boy into a six-year-old girl, while
the setting shifts from the clay hills of Georgia to the bayous of Louisiana, more
specifically an area made famous by disasters such as Hurricane Katrina and
the BP oil spill. The filmmakers rely on ghosting to convey the environmental
dangers visualized through Hushpuppy's fantastical imagination. They forgo
the typical casting of big-name stars that would have guaranteed broad distribution of the film. As a result of their choices, they introduced new black talent to Hollywood (Wallis was a nominee for Best Actress, the youngest ever in
this category). But race ideology continues to influence outcomes, economic

and otherwise. While the filmmakers for *Beasts* have been vocal about their highly collaborative filmmaking process, they have been less clear about the role of race in the casting process. Photographs of the original stage play's cast are not included in the press kits or commentary about the film, and the characters' races are not specified in the play's cast list. In fact, the only racially marked character in the play's cast list is a Japanese woman. Frequently, the lack of a racial description infers the character is white, just as lack of gender frequently reads as male. There is no playwright's note indicating otherwise. In this case, there appears to be a deliberate choice to change the race of the lead characters from white to black, although they appear in a mixed community. The film's notable lack of a traditional white point of entry presents a very promising deviation from established precedent. Through these characters, the filmmakers index the racial underpinnings of socioeconomic class exposed by the disasters in the Gulf region. This was not accidental. Court 13, a predominantly white group of filmmakers, and white American playwright Alibar recognized the potential of black film subjects, worldviews, and characterizations.

Like earlier films, *Beasts of the Southern Wild* provides us with an important example of the limitations and possibilities for exploring black subjects on film. The characters refer to themselves as "beasts" to articulate their strength and determination to survive, though their humanity is the focal point of the story. The filmmakers even refer to Hushpuppy as "a little beast" in the press kit, which, considering the history of black representation in the United States, could be considered problematic, potentially reinforcing old stereotypes if taken out of context or if one ignores the way "beast" has been used as positive slang within some communities. Recall from chapter 1 Barnum's museum and carnival displays that portrayed Africans as animalistic. *Beasts of the Southern Wild* illustrates the importance of cultural literacy, which is not racially predetermined. Filmmakers crossing the color line can and should become culturally literate in order to transcend the race ideology that has historically undermined stories such as Hushpuppy's. Still, Alibar's southern background and Zeitlin's permanent relocation to the Gulf region places both in close proximity to the people and culture they attempt to represent in the film. They collaborated with actors and actresses from the area to ensure cultural resonance, enabling them to breathe life into the characters. Their process sanctioned the sort of indigenization that normally occurs in secret, as performers were not required to imitate what has become established precedent for representing blacks on screen. These filmmakers relied on their black performers for the film's success.

Court 13's production process, especially given this film's exploration of black film subjects without a white point of entry, is reminiscent of black filmmakers such as Haile Gerima. Such similarities suggest that culturally nuanced cinematic language is being carried out across racial lines, thereby enhancing cultural literacy for filmmakers and audiences. Enhanced cultural literacy is an important and necessary ingredient for the positive development of black film-making. On the other hand, some cite the success of *Beasts* as an example of Hollywood's appropriation of the very themes, narrative forms, and aesthetics they claim are less marketable.[1] Zeitlin and his collaborators produced the film outside Hollywood, which suggests there was no conspiracy to benefit from the film at the expense of blacks. Yet the film industry's organizational structure increased Zeitlin's, Court 13's, and Alibar's chances to receive high-profile recognitions for their significant contributions to American film and even black representation onscreen. In addition to Wallis's nomination for Best Actress, the film was nominated for Best Picture, Best Director (Zeitlin), and Best Adapted Screenplay (Alibar and Zeitlin). Meanwhile, filmmakers such as Gerima continue to struggle for distribution beyond one screen in the United States despite their contributions to self-financing or fundraising. Even as filmmakers like Gerima influence independent distribution and elevate black representation onscreen, thereby improving the medium's overall quality, their work is overlooked in Hollywood. The paradox of this outcome has gone largely unnoticed by those who have showered the film with praise.

Beasts of the Southern Wild is not a commercial genre film, although it uses commercial elements such as special effects to achieve its goal. Along with commercial genre films such as *Think Like a Man* and *Red Tails*, it rounds out a fairly broad range of black representation in a small number of films with predominantly black casts released in the first half of 2012. Yet each film's economic and cultural success shines light on future challenges. Specifically, the power to control content and distribution remains in the hands of whites, even when blacks make significant contributions through performance and production. For instance, *Beasts of the Southern Wild* received broader international distribution than *Think Like a Man* and *Red Tails* combined. More blacks were involved behind the scenes in the latter two films than in *Beasts*, and both were comparatively overlooked in terms of accolades. While there is no hard evidence that a filmmaker's race determines the accolades a film receives, outcomes certainly matter with regard to funding and distributing future projects.

Like its predecessors, *Beasts* further demonstrates how films with predominantly black casts continue to be assigned low budgets and yet how these same films can be economically viable in spite of claims to the contrary. Of course, a smaller budget also means fewer expenses to recoup and so a bigger profit stands to be made. In this case, the film overcame the constraints of limited distribution typical of low-budget films by earning critical acclaim at the Sundance Film Festival. As of March 2013, the film had already earned $12 million dollars, easily recouping its $1.8 million budget.

McKenzie's economic assessment of African American films (discussed in the introduction) as viable investments as well as the recognition that small budgets carry some important benefits are both critical for understanding the development of African American film in cultural, creative, and economic terms. *Beasts of the Southern Wild* is an anomaly in terms of what its narrative and production process achieved. However, the absorption and acculturation of the film, filmmakers, and performers into the mainstream framework that followed allowed for the wide dissemination of arguably alternative perceptions of blackness (much like what occurred with Lee Daniels and *Precious*). If not absorbed, films tend to be marginalized and denied the resources or distribution outlets to carry out their work.

In addition to the positive economic trends McKenzie identifies and the benefits of a small budget, other profitable trends are also apparent in the films discussed in this study. As noted, black women's literary adaptations, hip-hop gangsta films, black comedy franchises, and the Tyler Perry film cycle have all proven profitable. But they all share the danger of potentially aligning with Hollywood's disturbing tendency to either pathologize blackness and black people or engage in superficial portrayals of black experience that align with mainstream expectations in order to achieve crossover appeal. As the many examples discussed throughout this book reveal, avoiding subject matter that could be perceived as pathological is less effective for future development than (1) increasing the range, frequency, and accessibility of a variety of genres and narratives that explore black subject matter, worldviews, and characterizations, and (2) continuously evolving cinematic language by adapting successful cultural storytelling devices across media, particularly from theater and literature. While the most economically viable narratives tend to reinforce the master narrative and elements of black pathology (in spite of the efforts of performers and many directors), other films such as historical narratives have not fared as well economically, also implicating distribution or lack thereof as a key factor. In some cases, such as *Beloved*, film narratives simply fail to speak to broad audiences. Regardless, the simultaneous development of cinematic language, distribution, and exhibition outlets is necessary to increase cultural literacy for current and future filmmakers and audiences.

Another positive trend that is less overtly connected to box office statistics yet still has a great deal of influence on the economics of black film is entrepreneurship both within and outside the industry. Black stars engaging as entrepreneurs can change their relationship to the organizations that support the existing power structure in Hollywood by becoming owners of their brands. In this way, they are able to access and create opportunities for themselves and others that would otherwise be unavailable. Oprah Winfrey, Tyler Perry, Will Smith, and Spike Lee occupy powerful positions that have been historically withheld from people of color within Hollywood's matrix of domination. Their success exemplifies areas of progress as well as ongoing challenges.

Significant revisions and reversals onscreen and off are also indicative of the promise and problems facing the future of African American film. For instance, *The Karate Kid* (2010), starring Jackie Chan and Jaden Smith, the son of Will Smith, outperformed expectations by earning $55 million in its opening weekend.[2] Other films in the original *Karate Kid* (1984) franchise featured a white male lead and, later, a white female lead. The 2010 version was the first film in the franchise to feature an African American in a lead role, thereby demonstrating the potential for innovation through more diverse casting. Smith co-stars with Chan, an international Asian star whose partnership with Chris Tucker (an African American actor) in the *Rush Hour* franchise has also proven lucrative. Cross-cultural casting may help get a film broader international distribution and potentially change the dynamics of the narrative to make race relations and ideology appear to be more progressive, but continuous vigilance is necessary to ensure that this represents an improvement. Based on trends seen in other films, the latest *Karate Kid*, which is set in Beijing and depicts Smith defending himself against Chinese bullies, might not have been as successful had it been set in the United States with an African American defending himself against white bullies. Such a narrative would have made the film less likely to receive broad distribution and thus to achieve such a successful box office. Like the other films discussed here, this film reveals how investment decisions are infused with race ideology. Again and again, crossover appeal to white and nonblack international audiences becomes the priority. As a result, a potentially more subversive version of the underdog story, one that challenges the everyday racism African Americans experience in the United States, would probably not have received a $40 million budget or the same production, financing, and distribution agreements.[3] Still, the film's economic success and Overbrook Entertainment's patterns of production are indicative of a potentially bright future for African American films as more empowering strategies are consistently employed. Overbrook Entertainment and other powerbrokers recognized throughout this book are finding new ways to speak to black and nonblack audiences. While blacks now occupy more powerful positions in Hollywood than ever before, they are not gatekeepers to the major studios. The dangers of marginalizing black audiences in the interests of crossover appeal are still very real in spite of their success, but these powerbrokers have made significant strides within the existing framework, helping to lay the groundwork for change.

Structural and ideological imperfections continue to negatively affect black film production and distribution, but all is not lost. Over the past several decades, filmmakers, performers, and their allies who have explored black subject matter and worldviews have made significant discoveries that can now be strategically exploited through new media. Using small budgets to their advantage, many have made quality films in spite of a lack of access to expensive equipment. Digital technology in production, distribution, and exhibition has provided alternative (and often affordable) pathways to the creation of adapted and original films that explore a range of black subject matter and worldviews, effectively leveling the playing field and making expensive film equipment unnecessary. Furthermore, filmmakers are successfully translating theatrical and literary devices into cinematic language. These innovative filmmakers are providing new ways to convey complex ideas, concepts, and worldviews, pioneering new forms of cinema and revising traditional storylines, particularly the stagnant historical narrative. When thwarted by distribution, filmmakers such as the Van Peebleses, Gerima, Perry, and DuVernay have found alternative routes to get their films to black audiences, while Lee, Story, Fuqua, Daniels, and others continue to work primarily within the studio system. Allies including Zeitlin and Alibar and their predecessors, such as John Sayles, have capitalized on cross-racial collaboration, providing additional models for success that can include international collaboration. Out of necessity, these filmmakers, performers, and entrepreneurs exploit Hollywood's structural imperfections by engaging in performative indigenization on- and offscreen. However, as *Driving Miss Daisy, Boyz N the Hood*, and other films reveal, performative indigenization by the actor alone is not enough to make black subject matter literally and figuratively accessible to black and nonblack audiences. Black artists located in more empowering roles in front of and behind the camera are just as critical. In this way, the past three decades have served as the foundation for pursuing viable economic and cultural alternatives that will shape future creative endeavors.

Perpetuating the plantation arrangement within the system without acknowledging areas of freedom and empowerment makes future progress less likely and limits possibilities for innovation. While some may settle for the existing system, modeling their success on that of their predecessors, others may give up altogether. Likewise, the refusal to acknowledge that racial and cultural politics continue to influence various stages of the process has harmful consequences. Even worse, by mistakenly assuming the industry and its products have transcended these oppressive circumstances, current and future works are less likely to be interrogated. A balanced viewpoint that acknowledges subjugation and empowerment is the key to imagining and implementing new models that will improve future outcomes for black film. The creole model exposes the pitfalls of continuing to vie for the same couple of production and/ or distribution slots per year, ensuring that the master narrative will continue to be a priority for studio executives due to their adherence to the bottom line.

Renewed perspectives and the new vocabulary of a revitalized discourse offer hope for the future.

Plantation ideology, the engine of the master narrative, persists in the overwhelming majority of mainstream films with predominantly white casts no matter how progressive they appear to be and regardless of studio executives' claims. Relying on crossover appeal is misguided and devalues blackness. Many films that outright challenge the master narrative lack crossover appeal and as a result tend to be censored by limited distribution. Although Hollywood's vertical integration had been dismantled and then reestablished through conglomeration in the 1980s,[4] the system that enabled it has never fundamentally changed. In fact, it remains strong even after adding a comparatively small number of ethnic minorities in less empowering positions throughout the industry. The system and its gatekeepers are not adjusting to empower blacks and other people of color out of any sense of moral obligation or desire, but changes are on the horizon.

New technology is forcing the gatekeepers of major organizations to reevaluate the system's structure as they realize that it is becoming increasingly difficult to maintain control. The sheer number of distribution outlets made possible by the internet and other digital technologies are wreaking havoc on the status quo. The various devices people use to access entertainment from computers and televisions to cell phones and other devices and the various services that allow individuals to stream videos on demand are quickly upending the traditional Hollywood power structure. Video on Demand services and digital cable are now competing with traditional theatrical release. Filmmakers can now reach investors directly through web-based venues such as Kickstarter and Indiegogo.com. They can also reach audiences directly through social media such as Facebook. New technologies give directors, actors, actresses, writers, and producers fairly inexpensive ways to not only produce high quality commercial genre and noncommercial genre films that explore a range of themes, but to get those films out to heretofore untapped domestic and international markets.

But not all new technologies are so readily accessible. Still, while 3-D technology is costly, it stands as an important example of future possibilities. It currently represents one of the most competitive elements of contemporary Hollywood films, and narratives about people of color that prominently feature 3-D technology have the potential to effectively compete within the existing paradigm. Specifically, 3-D technology, as demonstrated by *Avatar* (2009), can be used to promote an anti-imperialist message. However, 3-D films are most effective when screened in theaters that can show the films in 3-D; for the most part, only large commercial theaters have the technological requirements necessary. Additionally, while 3-D technology cannot be duplicated or bootlegged, the production costs are high, making it difficult to find investors for such ventures.

Nevertheless, filmmakers of all races that produce black subject matter and films that feature black worldviews are poised to take full advantage of this technological insurrection. This historical moment is not unlike the advent of television in competition with film. This time, however (and with very few exceptions), the playing field is leveling out in terms of the tools used to create the work and the outlets used to disseminate it. Gatekeepers cannot use traditional methods to control these outlets, nor can they control the new technology. They will have to instead adjust to meet the demands of audiences. Even the use of the Ulmer Scale may have to be reevaluated since it does not currently measure cyber audiences. Continuing to rely on the same couple of slots per year and the established precedent this practice reinforces is not only regressive, but foolhardy considering the entire industry will have to shift in order to survive.

Historically, at moments of such structural uncertainty, black audiences have become more visible as Hollywood recognizes them as viable markets in order to rejuvenate itself. This may be the reason for what some filmmakers are calling a cultural rebirth with the 2013 mainstream release of multiple black films varying in theme and genre. Even Oprah's OWN network began strategically targeting black viewers once they realized black audiences were sustaining the troubled enterprise (and Tyler Perry is now producing content for OWN). The economic viability of black subject matter, worldviews, and characterizations is better known now, but the uncertainty created in the industry by new technologies combined with the proven profitability of black film increases the likelihood that black film will be acculturated and absorbed to help sustain the existing paradigm. Historically, this leads to marginalization, as exemplified by Freeman's performance in *Driving Miss Daisy* and the altered narratives in *The Color Purple, Waiting to Exhale*, and *A Soldier's Story*.

The relationship between blacks and Hollywood in general requires substantial revision in order to overcome the impediments of existing practices. For instance, black filmmakers have appeared to be jumping ship, directing films with predominantly white rather than black casts. This enables them to gain funding and distribution more easily. However, black filmmakers directing films with predominantly white casts have opportunities to redefine black subject matter, worldviews, and characterizations rather than repressing them. Such films are beyond the scope of this study but are productive sites for exploration in the future.

For the past three decades, several artists exploring black subject matter and worldviews have found freedom and empowerment in the creole model, inspiring economically viable alternatives to existing paradigms. In addition to strategic use of small budgets, the creole model features hybrid distribution, adaptation and intertextuality, strategic use of horizontal integration, and prioritizing intersectionality as opposed to crossover appeal. Innovative narratives and distribution strategies have in many cases been developed independently, but they are proving most effective when developed together. These strategies have even evolved into organized movements that are directly challenging current paradigms across media. DuVernay's African American Film Festival Releasing Movement and the strides made by Gerima with Mypeduh Films both represent viable solutions as much as they illuminate the necessity for ongoing strategic evolution (though DuVernay's model is a short-term solution to a long-term problem that will require follow-up in order to remain effective).

Beyond the festival network and the system of theaters that exhibit independent films, more black ownership of movie theaters could further empower black audiences and provide much-needed forums for the dissemination of black film. Magic Johnson has made some strides in this area.[5] Such strategies are necessary considering vertical integration can make it difficult for theaters that screen independent films to survive outside of the studio system. Alternative strategies might include the installation of movie screening capabilities in theater houses that typically stage plays, especially those that cater to audiences that appreciate a diversity of representation on stage and screen. Also, more strategic use of the college and university market can further enable the ongoing development of black film. Many classrooms now have screening capabilities, especially using digital formats. In the 1960s and 1970s, New Line Cinema made a strategic decision to focus on screening independent films in the college and university market. This proved to be a successful strategy for building audiences and provides an important example going forward.

As mentioned, new technologies are morphing the traditional Hollywood power structure in drastic ways. Non-mainstream filmmakers are constantly innovating ways to use technology to make and distribute their work. Online streaming options such as YouTube, Hulu, Netflix, and digital cable channels are more accessible than ever before. AspireTV is one such channel that has emerged to feature television shows with predominantly black casts, narrative feature films, shorts, and documentary films. Social media including YouTube, Facebook, Twitter, Flickr, and other outlets are now important marketing channels being used by big studios and individual filmmakers alike. These media channels not only provide a system for promoting films but are increasingly becoming a vehicle for viewing films both in public and in private. Diverse options also exist in terms of funding. The NFL Pro Hollywood Boot Camp of Film Life founder and CEO Jeff Friday, in association with the American Black Film Festival, is a promising step in this direction.[6] Some filmmakers continue to pursue studio production and distribution while others rely on the independent film network where alternatives to the standard practices can be further developed rather than allowing black film to become absorbed in Hollywood's paradigm.

There are multiple pathways for developing culturally nuanced cinematic language and narratives that are also economically viable and accessible to broad audiences, including but not limited to blacks throughout the diaspora. Foremost among these pathways are horizontal integration and hybrid distribution that capitalize on intersectionality rather than crossover appeal, and the use of intertextuality as opposed to the unrevised, formulaic master narrative. Hybrid distribution deals make horizontal integration possible. Retaining ownership rights gives filmmakers the freedom to transform the story across media and use merchandising to support both the current project and future endeavors. Producing, promoting, and packaging sensitive material to market a film requires just as much careful handling as the filmmaking process. The Weinstein Company became aware of the problems of "packaging slavery," for instance, when the action figures of characters, including slaves, from Quentin Tarantino's *Django Unchained* (2012) sparked major protests against the company.[7] Developing marketable brands and merchandising controversial historical heroes, moments, and events are complex matters that deserve greater exploration in future studies of black film. To be sure, organized efforts can encourage more productive strategies for accomplishing and understanding how capitalism intersects with black cultural production. The key is to understand how this intersection can advance the objectives of black film in a way that speaks to black audiences first and foremost while also resonating with nonblack audiences domestically and abroad.

Within Hollywood, broader recognition of potential international markets could open up new opportunities for African American films. As noted in the introduction, standard Hollywood business practices ignore African diasporic audiences in Europe and the Americas. They also overlook the potential audiences for diverse films in Africa and Latin America. Considering Hollywood's thirst for profits, it would seem that these markets would be a higher priority. Unfortunately, Hollywood is apparently making no plans to cross over to these markets (which have comparably larger populations of people of color) by producing films that feature representative narratives or characters with any frequency rather than continuing to distribute the master narrative.

Nevertheless, digital technology puts these markets within reach, enabling filmmakers to circumvent Hollywood and the influence of crossover audiences. Tyler Perry uses the existing infrastructure to reach audiences in Afro-Caribbean countries.[8] It is possible for other filmmakers to do the same. Over the past decade, advancements in digital technology and internet access have created cyber audiences, which consist of a broad range of people from around the world. In addition, there is a robust bootleg network that illegally distributes studio films on DVD and online. While this network is unlawful, it represents an alternative distribution network. Perhaps this illegitimate network can be adapted into a legitimate enterprise supporting black film in the United States and abroad. Like India's Bollywood films, Nigeria's Nollywood films and Ghanaian films are accessible to South Asian and African diasporic audiences in the United States through street vendors in major cities, as well as barber shops, hair salons, and other nontraditional outlets. New media and technology can function more deliberately to track the lawful sales of films in adapted networks like these, thereby providing a complementary means for achieving and measuring economic success for black films as well as measuring and acknowledging cyber audiences. Unconventional modes of conception, production, marketing, distribution, and exhibition as well as diverse methods for measuring success are critical for the future of African American films.

Also critical are productive approaches to black cultural production, whether in film, theater, or literature. As playwright Suzan-Lori Parks explains, "There are many ways of defining blackness and there are many ways of presenting blackness onstage. The Klan does not have to be outside the door for black people to have lives worthy of dramatic literature. . . . And what happens when we choose a concern other than race to focus on? What kind of drama do we get? Let's do the math . . . Black people + x = New Dramatic Conflict (New Territory)."[9] The same is true of film. As Parks suggests and as many black directors of films with predominantly white casts and black stars have demonstrated, one does not have to completely abandon blackness in order to embark upon new territory. Intersectionality makes it possible to explore new territory, as exemplified by *Beasts of the Southern Wild* and Dee Rees's *Pariah* (2012), a film about a black teenage girl trying to reconcile her gay identity with her family's black middle-class values.

Adaptation continues to develop as a tool for advancing black theater, film, and literature, all of which are vulnerable under the current system. Literary devices offer useful, translatable prescriptions to articulate some of the more complex worldviews expressed in black literature. Rather than solely using screenplays to guide a project, artists and filmmakers are looking at the ways a particular theme has been treated across media. The interplay of media opens up opportunities for a more nuanced narrative that avoids promoting black pathology and does not undermine the humanity of the characters. Moreover, by developing these works for specifically black audiences and soliciting feedback in real time through stage productions, focus groups, and social media, filmmakers are better able to assess their progress. Black theater, in particular, can be used more strategically and consistently to develop a visual language that is in concert with black audiences before a project reaches crossover audiences. Similarly, black literary devices will benefit from more conscious and consistent development. The current white-dominated power structure is in flux, and now is the time to implement these strategies.

Various initiatives are underway to create a stronger network among black filmmakers with the objective of creating spaces for developing ideas and strategies. Collective organizing and strategizing is possible through the independent-film circuit that has supported black film even as it remained on the margins in Hollywood. Events such as the American Black Film Festival could also benefit further if scholars were included in the discussion with practicing filmmakers and industry insiders to reflect on the history, practice, and future of African American film. The National Black Theatre Festival and the Black Theatre Network Conference also offer ideal spaces for developing ideas and strategies for bridging the divide between black professional theater and the urban circuit, combining craft and resources to better communicate and build audiences in order to sustain the culture. All these projects have websites, databases, and/or social networks that can be combined and expanded upon to identify the range of diversity among black audiences around the world. Developing a stronger voice and larger audiences in black theater can directly and immediately benefit the development of African American film, especially given the recent reliance on adaptation to sustain economic relevance. Even the Ulmer Scale and films with predominantly white casts can be used to benefit African American film. Specifically, black star power gained through appearances in crossover films can also be invested back into the development of black film. The individual efforts of a select few offer a great start, but a more targeted approach to actively strategizing in this area is still needed. Rather than simply pointing out how the system works and how to function within it, we need more serious discussion of how to change the system or create a new one.

Although it is impossible to cover every aspect of the intersection of race, economics, and culture in this study, my objective is to enlighten studio executives, film scholars, teachers, students, and general audiences about the promise and potential of black film subjects and worldviews, and how myopic and unsubstantiated economic claims over the past thirty years have restricted black film. As I have argued, black film is an economically viable investment and a cultural necessity. Black film is at its most successful when narrative, visual, and aural strategies actively incorporate black cultural perspectives and use intersectionality with the understanding that through specificity we recognize the universal. Capitalizing on the inherent intertextuality of black film via creative content and distribution strategies can effectively undermine existing formulas that ultimately distort black cultural worldviews. It's not just business. The story behind the numbers is a complex tale of race ideology, color-coded economics, and established precedent in a now unpredictable and highly technological landscape. The films produced over the past three decades reveal possibilities for seizing opportunities to explore new territory. Economics, race, culture, and technology are shaping African American film, and only critical intervention in the present climate can offer hope for the future.

APPENDIX

Ulmer Ratings of Selected Actors		
Name	*Ulmer Rating out of 300*	*Letter Rating*
Danny Aiello	91	D
Angela Bassett	113	C
Halle Berry	210	B+
Big Boi	unlisted	—
Jim Brown	unlisted	—
Jim Carrey	251	A
Jackie Chan	236	B+
Dave Chappelle	119	C
Don Cheadle	163	B
Tom Cruise	270	A
Penelope Cruz	242	B+
Viola Davis	89	D
Robert De Niro	245	B+
Johnny Depp	295	A+
Cameron Diaz	261	A
Zac Efron	206	B+
Kimberly Elise	36	D
Mike Epps	unlisted	—
Dakota Fanning	184	B
Tyra Ferrell	unlisted	—
Will Ferrell	274	A
Harrison Ford	253	A
Jamie Foxx	231	B+
Morgan Freeman	218	B+
Robin Givens	52	D

(continued)

Ulmer Ratings of Selected Actors (*continued*)

Name	Ulmer Rating out of 300	Letter Rating
Vivica A. Fox	100	D
Meagan Good	56	D
Cuba Gooding Jr.	163	B
Irma P. Hall	26	D
Salma Hayek	212	B+
Taraji P. Henson	74	D
Jennifer Hudson	unlisted	—
Ice Cube	106	C
Samuel L. Jackson	191	B
Angelina Jolie	258	A
Harvey Keitel	144	C
Alicia Keys	124	C
Nicole Kidman	250	A
Regina King	57	D
Beyoncé Knowles	201	B
Martin Lawrence	150	C
Shia LeBeouf	226	B+
Spike Lee	unlisted	—
Nia Long	42	D
Jennifer Lopez	203	B+
Eva Mendes	136	C
Mo'Nique	unlisted	—
Eddie Murphy	211	B+
Mike Myers	231	B+
Thandie Newton	116	C
Bill Nunn	unlisted	—
Sophie Okonedo	unlisted	—
Al Pacino	242	B+
Rosie Perez	87	D
Mekhi Phifer	64	D
Sidney Poitier	unlisted	—
CCH Pounder	49	D
Queen Latifah	161	B
Michael Rappaport	69	D
Robert Redford	226	B+

(*continued*)

Ulmer Ratings of Selected Actors (*continued*)

Name	Ulmer Rating out of 300	Letter Rating
Ryan Reynolds	145	C
Chris Rock	171	B
Adam Rodriguez	unlisted	—
Rosalyn Sanchez	unlisted	—
Arnold Schwarzenegger	237	B+
Annabella Sciorra	71	D
Jada Pinkett Smith	115	C
Jayden Smith	unlisted	—
Will Smith	296	A+
Wesley Snipes	128	C
Octavia Spencer	unlisted	—
Ben Stiller	228	B+
Charlize Theron	223	B+
Billy Bob Thornton	156	B
T.I.	unlisted	—
Chris Tucker	174	B
John Turturro	142	C
Gabrielle Union	unlisted	—
Mark Wahlberg	241	B+
Denzel Washington	260	A
Kerry Washington	68	D
Raquel Welch	unlisted	—
Vanessa L. Williams	58	D
Bruce Willis	244	B+
Patrick Wilson	101	C
Reese Witherspoon	272	A
Alfre Woodard	103	C
N'Bushe Wright	unlisted	—

Source: James Ulmer, *The Ulmer Scale.*

NOTES

INTRODUCTION: THE COLOR OF HOLLYWOOD–BLACK, WHITE, OR GREEN?

1. All in-text numerical references to budgets, number of screens and days, and box office receipts are based on averages taken from IMDB.com, The-Numbers.com, and BoxOfficeMojo.com, unless otherwise noted. In most cases, these sources provide the production budget but not necessarily the marketing budget as distinct from production costs, so the discussion of most examples in this book will not include or specify the marketing costs unless it is relevant for the specific case study.

2. Marcus Reeves, "Tim Story is the Highest Grossing Black Director," Bet.com, May 16, 2012, http://www.bet.com/news/celebrities/2012/05/16/tim-story-now-the-highest-grossing -black-director.html. Also see Chris Witherspoon, "*Think Like a Man* Banned in France Due to 'Lack of Diversity,'" The Grio.com, May 22, 2012, http://thegrio.com/2012/05/22/ think-like-a-man-is-banned-in-france-for-lack-of-diversity/.

3. Frank Segers, "Foreign Box Office: 'Django Unchained' Unleashed Overseas, No. 1 with $49.4 Million," Hollywood Reporter.com, January 20, 2013, http://www.hollywood reporter.com/news/foreign-box-office-django-unchained-413998.

4. "Company Credits for *Red Tails* (2012)," IMDB.com, accessed March 19, 2013, http:// www.imdb.com/title/tt0485985/companycredits?ref_=tt_dt_co.

5. "Red Tails (Foreign)," BoxOfficeMojo.com, accessed March 19, 2013, http://boxoffice mojo.com/movies/?page=intl&country=00&id=redtails.htm.

6. Colin Moreshead, "Hollywood Is Now Making Films for Foreign Markets, and Their Taste in Movies Is Awful," BusinessInsider.com, September 18, 2012, http://www.business insider.com/hollywood-is-making-films-for-foreign-markets-2012-9.

7. "George Lucas Says Hollywood Won't Support Black Films," BBC.com, January 12, 2012, http://www.bbc.co.uk/news/entertainment-arts-16525977.

8. Pamela Woolford, "Filming Slavery: A Conversation with Haile Gerima," *Transition,* no. 64 (1994): 103.

9. Sylvie Kande, "Look Homeward Angel: Maroons, and Mulattos in Haile Gerima's Sankofa," in *African Cinema: Postcolonial and Feminist Readings*, ed. Kenneth W. Harrow (Trenton, NJ: Africa World Press, 1999), 91.

10. Sharon Waxman, "Hollywood Attuned to World Markets," *Washington Post,* October 26, 1998, http://www.washingtonpost.com/wp-srv/inatl/longterm/mia/part2.htm.

11. Jordi McKenzie, "Do 'African American' Films Perform Better or Worse at the Box Office? An Empirical Analysis of Motion Picture Revenues and Profits," *Applied Economics Letters* 17, no. 16 (2010): 1559–1564.

12. "Corporate Fact Sheet," SonyPictures.com, last updated August 2012, http://www .sonypictures.com/corp/corporatefact.html.

13. "Screen Gems [us]," IMDB.com, accessed March 19, 2013, http://www.imdb.com/company/c00010568/.

14. Mark A. Reid, *Redefining Black Film* (Berkeley: University of California Press, 1993); S. Craig Watkins, *Representing: Hip Hop Culture and the Production of Black Cinema* (Chicago: University of Chicago Press, 1998); Sheril D. Antonio, *Contemporary African American Cinema* (New York: Peter Lang, 2002); Ed Guerrero, *Framing Blackness: The African American Image in Film* (Philadelphia: Temple University Press, 1993); Jacqueline Bobo, "'The Subject Is Money': Reconsidering the Black Film Audience as a Theoretical Paradigm," *Black American Literature Forum* 25, no. 2 (Black Film Issue) (Summer 1991): 421–432.

15. Jesse Algeron Rhines, *Black Film/White Money* (New Brunswick, NJ: Rutgers University Press, 1996), 13.

16. Patricia Hill Collins, *Black Feminist Thought: Knowledge, Consciousness, and the Politics of Empowerment* (New York: Routledge, 2000), 18.

17. Darnell M. Hunt, "The 2009 Hollywood Writer's Report: Rewriting an All-Too-Familiar Story?" *Writer's Guild of America, West*, May 2009, 12, http://www.wga.org/uploadedFiles/who_we_are/HWR09.pdf.

18. Gina Prince-Bythewood, quoted by Stephanie Goldberg, "'Think Like a Man' and the Legacy of 'Love Jones,'" CNN.com, April 27, 2012, http://www.cnn.com/2012/04/27/showbiz/movies/love-jones-think-like-a-man/index.html.

19. Richard Barsam and Dave Monahan, *Looking at Movies: An Introduction to Film* (New York: W. W. Norton, 2010), 545.

20. In addition to Mark A. Reid's *Redefining Black Film*, also see Thomas Cripps, *Black Film as Genre* (Bloomington: Indiana University Press, 1978); Phyllis Klotman and Gloria J. Gibson, *Frame by Frame II: A Filmography of the African American Image 1978–1994* (Bloomington: Indiana University Press, 1997); and Gladstone Yearwood, *Black Film as a Signifying Practice: Cinema, Narration, and the African American Aesthetic Tradition* (Trenton, NJ: Africa World Press, 2000).

21. Kamau Brathwaite, *Contradictory Omens* (Mona, Jamaica: Savacou Publication, 1974), 10.

22. Ibid.

23. Brooks Barnes, "Race and the Safe Hollywood Bet," *New York Times*, October 18, 2008, http://www.nytimes.com/2008/10/19/weekinreview/19barnes.html.

24. Rhines, *Black Film*, 70.

25. August Wilson, "The Ground on Which I Stand," *Callaloo* 20, no. 3 (1998): 495.

26. Woolford, "Filming Slavery," 102.

27. Guerrero, *Framing Blackness*, 9–40.

28. These studies include Edward Mapp, *Blacks in American Films: Today and Yesterday* (Metuchen, NJ: Scarecrow Press, 1972); Donald Bogle, *Toms, Coons, Mulattoes, Mammies, and Bucks: An Interpretive History of Blacks in American Films* (New York: Viking Press, 1973); James P. Murray, *To Find an Image: Black Films from Uncle Tom to Superfly* (Indianapolis: Bobbs-Merrill, 1973); Gary Null, *Black Hollywood: The Negro in Motion Pictures* (Secaucus, NJ: Citadel Press, 1975); Daniel Leab, *From Sambo to Superspade: The Black Experience in Motion Pictures* (Boston: Houghton Mifflin, 1975); Thomas Cripps, *Slow Fade to Black: The Negro in American Film 1900–1942* (New York: Oxford University Press, 1977).

29. Toni Morrison, *Playing in the Dark: Whiteness and the Literary Imagination* (New York: Vintage Books, 1993).

30. Robert Perrucci and Earl Wysong, *The New Class Society* (Lanham, MD: Rowman & Littlefield, 1999), 6.

31. Ibid., 6–7.

32. Ibid., 7.
33. Ibid., 8.
34. Ibid.
35. Ibid., 9–10.
36. Patricia Hill Collins, *Fighting Words: Black Women and the Search for Justice* (Minneapolis: University of Minnesota Press, 1998), 278.
37. Nsenga K. Burton, "Hollywood's Black Movers and Shakers," TheRoot.com, May 31, 2011, http://www.theroot.com/views/hollywoods-black-movers-and-shakers.
38. Maria Pramaggiore and Tom Wallis, *Film: A Critical Introduction* (Boston: Pearson, 2008), 431.
39. Ibid., 432.
40. Ibid.
41. Although studies by James Naremore, Dudley Andrew, Robert Stam, and Julie Sanders provide significant exploration of the concept of adaptation, Hutcheon's three-part definition of the term is most relevant to our discussion. Barbara Tepa Lupack's *Literary Adaptations in Black American Cinema* (2002) is one of the few book-length studies exclusively devoted to examining black contributions. James Naremore, ed., *Film Adaptation* (New Brunswick, NJ: Rutgers University Press, 2000); Robert Stam and Alessandro Raengo, *Literature and Film: A Guide to the Theory and Practice of Adaptation* (New York: John Wiley & Sons, 2005); Julie Sanders, *Adaptation and Appropriation* (New York: Routledge, 2006); Linda Hutcheon, *A Theory of Adaptation* (New York: Routledge, 2006); Barbara Tepa Lupack, *Literary Adaptations in Black American Cinema: From Micheaux to Morrison* (Rochester, NY: University of Rochester Press, 2002).
42. Hutcheon, *Theory of Adaptation*, 7–8.
43. Anuradha Gobin, "Technologies of Control: Visual Arts and the African Slave Body from the 18th Century to the Present," *Research and Practice in Social Sciences* 2, no. 2 (February 2007): 124–150.
44. "American Marketing Association Resource Library," Marketing Power.com, accessed March 19, 2013, http://www.marketingpower.com/_layouts/Dictionary.aspx?dLetter=B.
45. Aljean Harmetz, "Strategies of Selling 'Soldier's,'" *New York Times*, October 29, 1984.
46. Stephanie Goldberg, "'Think Like a Man' and the Legacy of 'Love Jones,'" CNN.com, April 27, 2012, http://www.cnn.com/2012/04/27/showbiz/movies/love-jones-think -like-a-man/index.html.
47. Collins, *Fighting Words*, 278.
48. Watkins, *Representing*, 26.
49. "NAACP Speaks on Minorities in Television," CNN.com, August 15, 2001, http:// transcripts.cnn.com/TRANSCRIPTS/0108/15/se.01.html.
50. Wahneema Lubiano, "But Compared to What? Reading Realism, Representation, and Essentialism in *School Daze, Do the Right Thing*, and the Spike Lee Discourse," in *Representing Blackness: Issues in Film and Video*, ed. Valerie Smith (New Brunswick, NJ: Rutgers University Press, 1997), 102.
51. Studio executive Duncan Clark, quoted in Waxman, "Hollywood Attuned."
52. "Cultural Production as 'Society in the Making': Architecture as an Exemplar of the Social Construction of Cultural Artifacts," in *The Sociology of Culture: Emerging Theoretical Perspectives*, ed. Diana Crane (Cambridge, MA: Blackwell, 1994), 192.
53. Ron Eyerman, *Cultural Trauma: Slavery and the Formation of American Identity* (Cambridge: Cambridge University Press, 2001), 1.
54. Stephen Bertman, *Cultural Amnesia: America's Future and the Crisis of Memory* (Westport, CT: Greenwood Publishing Group, 2000), 14.

258 NOTES TO PAGES 16-26

55. Stratos Constantinidis, *Modern Greek Theatre: A Quest for Hellenism* (Jefferson, NC: McFarland & Company, 2001), 14.
56. Tyler Cohen, "Cinema: Ticket for One?" *Forbes*, April 28, 2003.
57. Henry Louis Gates Jr., "Black Hollywood," *America Beyond the Color Line with Henry Louis Gates* (VHS). Four-part series, directed by Daniel Percival and Mary Crisp (Alexandria, VA: PBS Home Video, 2002–2004).
58. Woolford, "Filming Slavery," 102.
59. Jeanne Dubino refers to patriarchal capitalism as an economy in which women are denied a place and are only able to advance through their interaction with men, typically marriage. Jeanne Dubino, "The Cinderella Complex: Romance Fiction, Patriarchy and Capitalism," *Journal of Popular Culture* 27, no. 3 (Winter 1993): 104.
60. Collins, *Fighting Words*, 277.
61. Shulyer M. Moore, *The Biz* (Los Angeles: Silman-James Press), 87.
62. Gary Crowdus and Dan Georgakas, "Thinking about the Power of Images: An Interview with Spike Lee," *Cineaste* 26, no. 2 (March 2001): 8.
63. Derek Thompson, "How Hollywood Accounting Can Make a $450 Million Movie 'Unprofitable,'" Atlantic.com, September 14, 2011, http://www.theatlantic.com/business/archive/2011/09/how-hollywood-accounting-can-make-a-450-million-movie-unprofitable/245134/.
64. Ibid.
65. Peter Broderick, "Hybrid Distribution: Maximizing Audience and Revenue" (keynote address, Steed Symposium, Loyola Marymount University, April 9, 2010).
66. Moore, *The Biz*, 87. Emphasis added.
67. Ibid., 88-89, 94.
68. Ibid., 89–90.
69. Ibid., 88–89.
70. Ibid., 19.
71. Ibid., 11.
72. Antonio, *Contemporary African American Cinema*, 3.
73. Carrie Rickey, "The Oscars: Racism in Hollywood? Only One African American Received a Nomination for This Year's Academy Awards," *Virginia-Pilot*, March 25, 1996, http://scholar.lib.vt.edu/VA-news/VA-Pilot/issues/1996/vp960325/03240281.htm.
74. Reid, *Redefining Black Film*, 100.
75. Ibid., 133.
76. Zeinabu Irene Davis, "The Future of Black Film," in *Cinemas of the Black Diaspora: Diversity, Dependence and Oppositionality*, ed. Michael T. Martin (Detroit: Wayne State University, 1995), 450; Manthia Diawara, "Black American Cinema: The New Realism," in *Cinemas of the Black Diaspora: Diversity, Dependence, and Oppositionality*, ed. Michael T. Martin (Detroit: Wayne State University, 1995), 406–407.
77. Shirley Brice Heath, *Ways with Words: Language, Life, and Work in Communities and Classrooms* (Cambridge: Cambridge University Press, 1983), 184–185.
78. James A. Snead, "Images of Blacks in Independent Films: A Brief Survey," in *Cinemas of the Black Diaspora: Diversity, Dependence and Oppositionality*, ed. Michael T. Martin (Detroit: Wayne State University, 1995), 373.
79. Michael Cieply, "A Breakout Year for Black Films," *New York Times*, June 1, 2013, http://www.nytimes.com/2013/06/02/movies/coming-soon-a-breakout-for-black-filmmakers.html?pagewanted=all&_r=0.

CHAPTER 1   THE PLANTATION LIVES!

1. "Top-Grossing Movie Sources 1995–2012," The Numbers.com, accessed March 19, 2013, http://www.the-numbers.com/market/Sources/.

2. Maria Pramaggiore and Tom Wallis, *Film: A Critical Introduction* (Boston: Pearson, 2008), 70–71.

3. Clyde Taylor, "The Paradox of Black Independent Cinema," in *Cinemas of the Black Diaspora: Diversity, Dependence, and Oppositionality,* ed. Michael T. Martin (Detroit: Wayne State University Press, 1995), 138.

4. Toni Morrison, *Playing in the Dark: Whiteness and the Literary Imagination* (New York: Vintage Books, 1993), 6.

5. Clyde Taylor, *The Mask of Art: Breaking the Aesthetic Contract—Film and Literature* (Bloomington: Indiana University Press, 1998), 138.

6. Ed Guerrero, *Framing Blackness: The African American Image in Film* (Philadelphia: Temple University Press, 1993), 10.

7. bell hooks, *Black Looks: Race and Representation* (Boston: South End Press, 1992), 16.

8. Stephen Railton, "Readapting *Uncle Tom's Cabin,*" in *Nineteenth-Century American Fiction on Screen* (New York: Cambridge University Press, 2007), 67.

9. Cedric J. Robinson, *Forgeries of Memory and Meaning: Blacks and the Regimes of Race in American Theater and Film before World War II* (Chapel Hill: University of North Carolina Press, 2007), 188.

10. Ibid., 87.

11. Linda Williams, *Playing the Race Card: Melodramas of Black and White from Uncle Tom to O. J. Simpson* (Princeton, NJ: Princeton University Press, 2001), 42.

12. Judith Williams, "Uncle Tom's Women," in *African American Performance and Theater History: A Reader,* ed. Harry J. Elam Jr. and David Krasner (Oxford: Oxford University Press, 2001), 20.

13. Christopher G. Diller, "Introduction," in *Uncle Tom's Cabin* by Harriet Beecher Stowe (Buffalo: Broadview Press, 2009), 14.

14. "The First Uncle Tom's Cabin Film: Edison-Porter's *Slavery Days* (1903)," Uncle Tom's Cabin and American Culture, a Multi-Media Archive, University of Virginia, accessed July 11, 2012, http://utc.iath.virginia.edu/onstage/films/mv03hp.html.

15. "A decided innovation": The 3-Reel Vitagraph Production (1910), Uncle Tom's Cabin and American Culture, a Multi-Media Archive, University of Virginia, accessed July 11, 2012, http://utc.iath.virginia.edu/onstage/films/mv10hp1.html.

16. Peter Noble, *The Negro in Films* (London: Skelton Robinson, 1948), 32.

17. Thomas Cripps, *Slow Fade to Black: The Negro in American Film 1900–1942* (New York: Oxford University Press, 1977), 158.

18. Thomas Postlewait, "The Hieroglyphic Stage: American Theatre and Society, Post-Civil War to 1945," in *The Cambridge History of American Theatre: 1870–1945,* ed. Don B. Wilmeth and C.W.E. Bigsby (Cambridge: Cambridge University Press, 1999), 158.

19. Ibid., 161.

20. James W. Cook Jr., "Of Men, Missing Links, and Nondescripts: The Strange Career of P. T. Barnum's 'What Is It?' Exhibition," in *Freakery: Cultural Spectacles of the Extraordinary Body,* ed. Rosemarie Garland Thomson (New York: New York University Press, 1996), 139–157; Bernth Lindfors, "Circus Africans," *Journal of American Culture* 6, no. 2 (Summer 1983): 9–14.

21. Lindfors, "Circus Africans," 9.

22. Neil Harris, *Humbug: The Art of P. T. Barnum* (Chicago: University of Chicago Press, 1973), 4.

23. George Walker, "The Real 'Coon' on the American Stage," *Theatre Magazine* (August 1906), reprinted in liner notes to Bert Williams, *The Early Years, 1901–1909*, audio recording (Champaign, IL: Archeophone Records, 2004), 16–19, 18.

24. Felicia Hardison Londré and Daniel J. Watermeier, *The History of North American Theater: The United States, Canada and Mexico: From Pre-Columbian Times to the Present* (New York: Continuum International Publishing Group, 1998), 223.

25. Novid Parsi and Christopher Piatt, "Color-bind," *Time Out Chicago*, July 27–August 3, 2006, 13.

26. Ibid.

27. Ibid., 18.

28. "Table PL-P2A NYC: Total Population by Mutually Exclusive Race and Hispanic Origin New York City and Burroughs, 1990–2000," prepared by Population Division—NYC Department of City Planning (May 2011), *U.S. Census Bureau 2010 and 2000 Census Public Law 94–171 Files and 1990 STF1*, NYC.gov, accessed March 20, 2013, http://www.nyc.gov/ html/dcp/html/census/demo_tables_2010.shtml.

29. Parsi and Piatt, "Color-bind," 18.

30. Ibid., 20.

31. Patricia Hill Collins, *Fighting Words: Black Women and the Search for Justice* (Minneapolis: University of Minnesota Press, 1998), 277.

32. August Wilson, "The Ground on Which I Stand," *Callaloo* 20, no. 3 (1998): 493–503.

33. Todd McCarthy, "A Few Good Men," *Daily Variety*, November 13, 1992.

34. Duane Byrge, "'Men' Musters $15.5 Mil Bow," *Hollywood Reporter*, December 15, 1992.

35. Laura Mulvey, *Visual and Other Pleasures* (Bloomington: Indiana University Press, 1989), 16–17.

36. Aaron Sorkin, "A Few Good Men: A Screenplay" (unpublished manuscript, 1991), Popular Entertainment Collections, Ray and Pat Browne Library for Popular Culture Studies, Bowling Green State University, 6.

37. Ibid., 22.

38. Ibid., 59.

39. Aaron Sorkin, *A Few Good Men* (Garden City, NY: Fireside Theatre, 1990), 101; Sorkin, "A Few Good Men," 101.

40. Sorkin, "A Few Good Men," 76.

41. William Glaberson, "A Surplus of 'A Few Good Men,'" *New York Times*, September 15, 2011, http://www.nytimes.com/2011/09/16/nyregion/4-lawyers-claim-to-be-the-hero-in-a-few-good-men.html, accessed July 12, 2012.

42. Robert Varley, "Book Will Focus on Area Man's Military Trial History," *New Haven Register*, June 12, 2006. http://www.nhregister.com/articles/2006/06/12/import/16775229 .txt?viewmode=fullstory, accessed July 12, 2012.

43. "Ex-Marine Is Found Slain," *New York Times*, April 5, 1994, http://www.nytimes .com/1994/04/05/us/ex-marine-is-found-slain.html, accessed July 12, 2012. David Cox, one of the defendants in the case, was mysteriously murdered soon after he joined a lawsuit against the filmmakers for appropriating and distorting the story.

44. Phil Powrie, *French Cinema in the 1980s: Nostalgia and the Crisis of Masculinity* (New York: Clarendon Press, 1997), 3.

45. Sven Birkerts, *American Energies: Essays on Fiction* (New York: William Morrow, 1992), 36.

46. Laurence G. Avery, "Horton Foote and the American Theater," *Mississippi Quarterly* 58, no. 1/2 (Winter 2004/2005): 387–395.

47. Horton Foote, "Introduction," in *4 Plays from the Orphans' Home Cycle* (New York: Grove Press, 1988), xiii.

48. Roy Hoffman, "Brash New South Is Still a Stranger to Its Dramatists," *New York Times*, July 2, 1989, http://www.nytimes.com/1989/07/02/theater/theater-brash-new-south -is-still-a-stranger-to-its-dramatists.html?pagewanted=all&src=pm, accessed March 15, 2013.

49. Ibid.

50. Guerrero, *Framing Blackness*, 10.

51. Arnold Hauser, *The Social History of Art: Naturalism, Impressionism, the Film Age* (London: Routledge & Kegan Paul, 1977), 238.

52. Horton Foote, "Convicts," in *4 Plays from the Orphans' Home Cycle* (New York: Grove Press, 1988), 126.

53. James V. Hatch and Ted Shine, *Black Theatre USA: The Early Period 1847–1938* (New York: Free Press, 1996), 232.

54. Marvin Carlson, *The Haunted Stage: The Theatre as Memory Machine* (Ann Arbor: University of Michigan Press, 2003), 2.

55. Ibid., 6–7.

56. Alfred Uhry, *Driving Miss Daisy: A Screenplay* (Hollywood, CA: Script City, 1988), 70.

57. John Russell Rickford and Russell John Rickford, *Spoken Soul: The Story of Black English* (New York: John Wiley & Sons, 2000), 153–154.

58. Geneva Smitherman, *Talkin and Testifyin: The Language of Black America* (Detroit: Wayne State University Press, 1977), 96.

59. Rickford and Rickford, *Spoken Soul*, 153.

60. Richard Jobson, "The Guardian/NFT interview: Morgan Freeman (I)," Guardian.co.uk, July 14, 2000, http://film.guardian.co.uk/interview/interviewpages/0,6737,344698,00 .html, accessed January 8, 2007.

61. Helen Dudar, "For Morgan Freeman, Stardom Wasn't Sudden," *New York Times*, December 10, 1989, http://www.nytimes.com/packages/html/movies/bestpictures/daisy-ar2 .html, accessed March 15, 2013.

CHAPTER 2   INSURRECTION! AFRICAN AMERICAN FILM'S
REVOLUTIONARY POTENTIAL THROUGH BLACK THEATER

1. Matthew Bernstein, "Oscar Micheaux and Leo Frank: Cinematic Justice across the Color Line," *Film Quarterly* 57, no. 4 (Summer 2004): 8.

2. Jesse Algeron Rhines, *Black Film/White Money* (New Brunswick, NJ: Rutgers University Press, 1996), 23.

3. Ibid., 24.

4. J. Ronald Green, "Twoness in the Style of Oscar Micheaux," in *Black American Cinema* ed. Manthia Diawara (New York: Routledge), 34.

5. Ibid.

6. Rhines, *Black Film*, 24.

7. Race films targeting a black movie-going market were frequently released in segregated theaters. Cedric J. Robinson, *Forgeries of Memory and Meaning: Blacks and the Regimes of Race in American Theater and Film before World War II* (Chapel Hill: University of North Carolina Press, 2007), 225.

8. Roger Fristoe, "The Blood of Jesus," TCM.com, http://www.tcm.com/this-month/ article/87405|0/The-Blood-of-Jesus.html, accessed March 20, 2013.

9. Margaret B. Wilkerson, "*A Raisin in the Sun,*" in *The Concise Oxford Companion to African American Literature,* ed. William L. Andrews, Frances Smith Foster, and Trudier Harris (Oxford: Oxford University Press, 2001), 340.

10. Margaret B. Wilkerson, "Political Radicalism and Artistic Innovation in the Works of Lorraine Hansberry," in *African American Theatre and Performance History,* ed. Harry J. Elam Jr. and David Krasner (Oxford: Oxford University Press, 2001), 41–42. Original Baraka quotes come from Amiri Baraka, "A Critical Reevaluation: *A Raisin in the Sun'*s Enduring Passion," in *Lorraine Hansberry, "A Raisin in the Sun" and "The Sign in Sidney Brustein's Window"* (New York: Vintage, 1995), 19.

11. Wilkerson, "Political Radicalism," 43. Originally stated in Lorraine Hansberry, "Willy Loman, Walter Lee Younger, and He Who Must Live," *Village Voice,* August 12, 1959, 7.

12. Wilkerson, "Political Radicalism," 46.

13. Ibid., 44–45.

14. Jill Cox-Cordova, "Shange's 'for colored girls' Has Lasting Power," CNN.com, July 21, 2009, http://www.cnn.com/2009/SHOWBIZ/books/07/21/for.colored.girls.shange/index.html?_s=PM:SHOWBIZ#cnnSTCText. Shange coined the term "choreopoem" in 1975 to describe the dramatic structure of *for colored girls,* which consists of twenty poems, music, song, and dance.

15. Felicia R. Lee, "New Funds Help Revive a Theater in St. Paul," *New York Times,* January 7, 2013, http://theater.nytimes.com/2013/01/08/theater/penumbra-theater-to-resume-programs-after-fund-raising.html; "Marion McClinton has Advice for Congo Square," *Chicago Tribune,* March 28, 2010, http://leisureblogs.chicago tribune.com/the_theater_loop/2010/03/marion-mcclinton-has-advice-for-congo-square.html.

16. Tim Donahue and Jim Patterson, *Stage Money: The Business of the Professional Theater* (Columbia: University of South Carolina Press, 2010), 1–2.

17. "Negro Ensemble Company: Mission and History," NECINC.org, http://necinc.org/about-us/mission-and-history/, accessed March 19, 2013.

18. Brandi Wilkins Catanese, *The Problem of the Color[blind]: Racial Transgression and the Politics of Black Performance* (Ann Arbor: University of Michigan Press, 2011), 69.

19. Carol Lawson, "Charles Fuller 'Stunned' on Winning Pulitzer," *New York Times,* April 13, 1982.

20. Jacqueline Bobo, "'The Subject Is Money': Reconsidering the Black Film Audience as a Theoretical Paradigm," *Black American Literature Forum* 25, no. 2 (Black Film Issue) (Summer 1991): 425. Also see H. Anthony Mapp, "A Dramatic Success," *Black Enterprise* (January 1985): 29.

21. Charles Fuller, *A Soldier's Play* (New York: Samuel L. French, 1981), 9.

22. Linda K. Hughes and Howard Faulkner, "The Role of Detection in *A Soldier's Play,*" *Clues: A Journal of Detection* 7, no. 2 (1986): 94.

23. Yvonne Shafer, "August Wilson and the Contemporary Theatre: Interview," *Journal of Dramatic Theory and Criticism* (Fall 1997): 23–38.

24. August Wilson, "The Ground on Which I Stand," *Callaloo* 20, no. 3 (1998): 493–503; August Wilson, "National Black Theater Festival (1997)," *Callaloo* 20, no. 3 (1998): 483–492.

25. Fuller, *A Soldier's Play,* 18.

26. Charles Fuller, "A Soldier's Story: A Screenplay," unpublished manuscript, 1983, Ohio University Libraries, 8.

27. Ibid., 119.

28. Ibid.

29. David Rooney, "A Soldier's Play," *Daily Variety*, October 18, 2005; Christopher Rawson, "Tensions Run High in 'Soldier's' Play," *Pittsburgh Post-Gazette*, September 15, 2005.

30. Rhonda Baraka, "On the Soundtrack Tip: Movies and Music Go Hand in Hand Creating a Win-Win Situation for Everyone Involved," *Billboard*, August 19, 2000, 42.

31. Maria Pramaggiore and Tom Wallis, *Film: A Critical Introduction* (Boston: Pearson, 2008), 227–274.

32. Ed Guerrero, *Framing Blackness: The African American Image in Film* (Philadelphia: Temple University Press, 1993), 51–52.

33. Michael Feingold, "Duel Voltage," *Village Voice*, October 11, 2005.

34. Ben Brantley, "Anatomy of the Murder of a Black Sergeant," *New York Times*, October 18, 2005, http://theater.nytimes.com/2005/10/18/theater/reviews/18sold.html?page wanted=all, accessed January 20, 2013.

35. Elyse Sommer, "Curtain Up Review: A Soldier's Play," Curtainup.com, 1997, http://www.curtainup.com/soldier.html,accessed March 20, 2013.

36. Rawson, "Tensions."

37. Rooney, "A Soldier's Play."

38. David Drake, "Taye Diggs," Broadway.com, October 24, 2005, http://www.broadway.com/gen/Buzz_Story.aspx?ci=519770&pn=1; Robert Riddell, "Gotham Soldiers On," *Daily Variety*, October 15, 2005.

39. Anne Fuchs, *Playing the Market: The Market Theatre Johannesburg 1976–1986* (London: Harwood Academic Publishers, 1990).

40. Ibid., 83.

41. Ibid., 82.

42. Desson Howe, "The Strong, Insistent Voices of 'Woza Afrika!,'" *Washington Post*, October 1, 1986.

43. Joe Brown, "New Manager for New Playwrights,'" *Washington Post*, August 17, 1987.

44. This was made possible by the support of celebrities (Paul Simon, Miriam Makeba, Harry Belafonte), fans of the play (Hamilton Fish III, a publisher, Edward Schumann, a former movie-theater executive), and commercial producers Kenneth Waissman, Robert A. Buckley, and Jane Harmon, who were brought on to help raise money for the Broadway transfer. Jeremy Gerard, "For 'Asinamali!' Backers, More Than Just a Play," *New York Times*, April 15, 1987.

45. Susan Walker, "Producer Arsenio Hall Talks Up His Movie," *Toronto Star*, September 19, 1993.

46. Duane Byrge, "Bopha!," *Hollywood Reporter*, September 17, 1993.

47. Bill Keller, "Is That Really South Africa?," *New York Times*, October 10, 1993, http://www.nytimes.com/1993/10/10/movies/film-is-that-really-south-africa.html?page wanted=all&src=pm.

48. Phillip Kakaza, "News, Documents & Commentary," *Africa News*, July 17, 1998.

49. Ibid.

50. Duma Ndlovu, ed., "Introduction," in *Woza Afrika!: An Anthology of South African Plays* (New York: George Braziller, Inc. 1986), xx.

51. Percy Mtwa, "Bopha!," in Ndlovu, *Woza Afrika: An Anthology of South African Plays*, 256–257.

52. Edward Guthmann, "Drama about a Powder Keg," *San Francisco Chronicle*, September 24, 1993.

53. Augusto Boal, "Poetics of the Oppressed," in *Modern Theories of Drama: A Selection of Writings on Drama and Theatre, 1840–1990*, ed. George W. Brandt (New York: Oxford University Press, 1998), 255, 260.

54. Walter Chaw, "A Taste of Freeman: Morgan Freeman Interview," Film Freak Central. net, December 14, 2004, http://www.filmfreakcentral.net/notes/mfreemaninterview .htm, accessed January 8, 2007.

55. *Bopha!: Handbook of Production Information* (Hollywood, CA: Paramount 1993), 8–9.

56. Keller, "South Africa?"

57. Helen Dudar, "For Morgan Freeman, Stardom Wasn't Sudden," *New York Times*, December 10, 1989, http://www.nytimes.com/packages/html/movies/bestpictures/daisy-ar2 .html, accessed March 15, 2013.

58. Keller, "South Africa?"

59. Walker, "Producer Arsenio Hall Talks Up His Movie."

60. Richard Jobson, "The Guardian/NFT interview: Morgan Freeman (I)," Guardian.co.uk, July 14, 2000, http://film.guardian.co.uk/interview/interviewpages/0,6737,344698,00 .html, accessed January 8, 2007.

61. Some examples include *Cry Freedom* and *The Power of One*. Keller, "South Africa?"

62. Guthmann, "Drama about a Powder Keg."

63. Leonard Klady, "Bopha!," *Daily Variety*, September 17, 1993.

64. Brett Pulley, "A Showbiz Whiz," Forbes.com, September 5, 2005, http://www.forbes .com/forbes/2005/1003/075.html.

65. Henry Louis Gates Jr., "The Chitlin' Circuit," in Elam and Krasner, *African American Theatre and Performance History*, 143.

66. Perry also collaborated with Jakes on *Behind Closed Doors*, the first gospel Broadway play of its kind, which equaled the success of *Woman Thou Art Loosed*.

67. Margena Christian, "Becoming Tyler," *Ebony* (October 2008): 78.

68. Gates, "The Chitlin' Circuit," 140.

69. Christian, "Becoming Tyler."

70. Gates, "The Chitlin' Circuit," 140.

71. Dorothy Pomerantz, "The Highest Paid Men in Entertainment," Forbes.com, September 12, 2011, http://www.forbes.com/sites/dorothypomerantz/2011/09/12/the -highest-paid-men-in-entertainment/.

72. Diego Arciniegas, Lydia R. Diamond, Kirsten Greenidge, Kenny Leon, Melinda Lopez, and Summer L. Williams, "The Celebration of August Wilson's Legacy," event held at Roxbury Community College, Roxbury Crossing, MA, September 14, 2009.

73. John Patterson, "Alex Cross Is Another Bad Tyler Perry Film, but the Problem Is Perry Himself," *Guardian*, November 23, 2012, http://www.guardian.co.uk/film/2012/nov/23/ tyler-perry-alex-cross.

74. Lauren Moraski, "'Alex Cross' Reviews: What the Critics Are Saying," CBSnews .com, October 19, 2012, http://www.cbsnews.com/8301-207_162-57536128/alex-cross -reviews-what-the-critics-are-saying/.

75. Richard Corliss, "God and Tyler Perry vs. Hollywood," Time.com, March 20, 2008, http://www.time.com/time/magazine/article/0,9171,1724393,00.html.

76. Roger Ebert, "Diary of a Mad Black Woman," Chicago Sun-Times, February 25, 2005, http://rogerebert.suntimes.com/apps/pbcs.dll/article?AID=/20050224/REVIEWS/ 50214001. The majority of reviews in major news outlets echo Ebert, "Diary of a Mad Black Woman Reviews," RottenTomatoes.com, http://www.rottentomatoes.com/m/ diary_of_a_mad_black_woman/reviews/?page=4, accessed March 23, 2013.

CHAPTER 3 PLAYING WITH FIRE: BLACK
WOMEN'S LITERATURE/WHITE BOX OFFICE

1. "Best Sellers List," *New York Times,* November 22, 2009, http://www.nytimes.com/best -sellers-books/2009–11–22/trade-fiction-paperback/list.html; Daniel Max, "McMillan's Millions," *New York Times,* August 9, 1992, http://www.nytimes.com/1992/08/09/ magazine/mcmillan-s-millions.html?pagewanted=all&src=pm; Evelyn C. White, *Alice Walker: A Life* (New York: W. W. Norton & Company, 2004), 362.

2. See the video "The Oprah Effect" on CNBC.com from June 9, 2009.

3. James Lou, "Oprah's Consumer Influence," CNBC.com video, May 7, 2009, http:// video.cnbc.com/gallery/?play=1&video=1117113127.

4. "Whitney and the Cast of 'Waiting to Exhale,'" *The Oprah Winfrey Show,* November 28, 1995.

5. Joe Flint, "Tyler Perry's OWN Deal Ends Plans for His Own Cable Channel," *Los Angeles Times,* October 1, 2012, http://articles.latimes.com/2012/oct/01/entertainment/ la-et-ct-tyler-perry-winfrey-20121001.

6. John O'Brien, *Interviews with Black Writers* (New York: Liveright, 1973), 192.

7. "Black Literary Agents Are Making Appearances in the Lily-White Field of Book Publishing," *Journal of Blacks in Higher Education,* no. 28 (Summer 2000): 64.

8. Henry Louis Gates Jr., *The Signifying Monkey: A Theory of African-American Literary Criticism* (New York: Oxford University Press, 1988), xxvi.

9. Steven Swann Jones, *The Fairy Tale: The Magic Mirror of Imagination* (New York: Routledge, 2002), 29.

10. Mel Watkins, "Some Letters Went to God," *New York Times,* July 25, 1982, http://www .nytimes.com/1982/07/25/books/some-letters-went-to-god-by-mel-watkins.html, accessed March 16, 2013.

11. "Columbia Journalism Review: Guide to What the Major Media Companies Own," CJR.org, last updated February 27, 2013, http://www.cjr.org/resources/?c=cbs.

12. "Columbia Journalism Review: Guide to What the Major Media Companies Own," CJR.org, last updated August 8, 2011, http://www.cjr.org/resources/?c=pearson.

13. "Columbia Journalism Review: Guide to What the Major Media Companies Own," CJR.org, last updated February 14, 2013, http://www.cjr.org/resources/?c=bertelsmann.

14. Deidra Donahue, "Self-Published Authors Find E-Success," *USA Today,* December 13, 2011, http://usatoday30.usatoday.com/life/books/news/story/2011–12–14/ self-published-authors-ebooks/51851058/1.

15. Max, "McMillan's Millions."

16. "Biography," http://www.terrymcmillan.com/view/bio, accessed February 19, 2013.

17. "Black Literary Agents Are Making Appearances in the Lily-White Field of Book Publishing," *Journal of Blacks in Higher Education,* no. 28 (Summer 2000): 64–65; Charles Whitaker, "Black Women Writers," *Ebony* (March 2000): 36.

18. Scott Edelstein, *100 Things Every Writer Needs to Know* (New York: Penguin, 1999), 196–197.

19. Paulette Richards, *Terry McMillan: A Critical Companion* (Westport, CT: Greenwood Press, 1999), 14.

20. "Review: Black Authors Rarely Have Made the Best-Seller List," *Journal of Blacks in Higher Education,* no. 34 (Winter 2001–2002): 130.

21. Thulani Davis, "Don't Worry Be Buppie: Black Novelists Head for the Mainstream," *Village Voice Literary Supplement* (May 1990): 29.

22. E. Shelley Reid, "Beyond Morrison and Walker: Looking Good and Looking Forward in Contemporary Black Women's Stories," *African American Review* 34, no. 2 (Summer 2000): 315.

23. Amy Alexander, "Terry McMillan vs. Ghetto Lit," *Nation*, October 29, 2007, http://www.thenation.com/article/terry-mcmillan-vs-ghetto-lit#axzz2XhRUTHxL, accessed March 15, 2013.

24. Nick Chiles, "Their Eyes Were Reading Smut," *New York Times*, January 4, 2006, http://www.nytimes.com/2006/01/04/opinion/04chiles.html.

25. Alexander, "Terry McMillan vs. Ghetto Lit."

26. Gates, *Signifying*, xxii.

27. Allyssa McCabe, "Cultural Background and Storytelling: A Review and Implications for Schooling," *Elementary School Journal* 97, no. 5 (1997): 460.

28. Ibid.

29. John C. Tibbetts, "So Much Is Lost in Translation: Literary Adaptations in the 1990's," *Film Genre 2000: New Critical Essays*, ed. Wheeler Winston Dixon (Albany: State University of New York, 2000), 30.

30. Whitaker, "Black Women Writers," 38.

31. Gates, *Signifying*, xxvi.

32. "From Push to Precious," DVD bonus feature, *Precious: Based on the Novel Push by Sapphire*, directed by Lee Daniels (Santa Monica, CA: Lionsgate Home Entertainment, 2009).

33. Jaqueline Bobo, "Sifting through the Controversy: Reading the Color Purple," *Callaloo*, no. 39 (Spring 1989): 332–342.

34. Lauren A. E. Shucker, "Novice Film 'Angels' Took Leap of Faith with 'Precious,'" *Wall Street Journal*, November 16, 2009, http://online.wsj.com/article/SB10001424052748704538404574537721627768260.html.

35. Lynn Hirschberg, "The Audacity of Precious," *New York Times*, October 21, 2009, http://www.nytimes.com/2009/10/25/magazine/25precious-t.html?pagewanted=1&_r=3.

36. John Horn, "Weinstein Co. Loses a Round in Its Fight Over 'Precious,'" *Los Angeles Times*, September 29, 2009, http://articles.latimes.com/2009/sep/29/business/fi-ct-precious29.

37. Felicia R. Lee, "To Blacks, Precious Is 'Demeaned' or 'Angelic,'" *New York Times*, November 20, 2009, http://www.nytimes.com/2009/11/21/movies/21precious.html?_r=1.

38. Melena Ryzik, "Viola Davis on a Mind-Set She Says Harms Black Actors," *New York Times*, February 14, 2012, http://carpetbagger.blogs.nytimes.com/2012/02/14/viola-davis-on-a-mind-set-that-harms-black-actors.

39. Hirschberg, "The Audacity of Precious."

40. Ibid.

41. Toni Morrison, *The Bluest Eye* (New York: Vintage, 2007); Lydia Diamond, *Toni Morrison's The Bluest Eye* (Woodstock, VT: Dramatic Publishing Company, 2007).

42. Diamond, *Toni Morrison's The Bluest Eye*, 5.

43. Lydia Diamond, "From Book to Stage: Lydia Diamond on Adapting the Bluest Eye" (2004–2005), http://www.steppenwolf.org/watchlisten/program-articles/detail.aspx?id=56.

44. "From Push to Precious."

45. Hirschberg, "The Audacity of Precious."

46. Marlaine Glicksman, "Lee Way," *Film Content* (October 1986): 48.

47. Lee, "To Blacks, 'Precious' Is 'Demeaned' or 'Angelic.'"

48. Wayne J. McMullen and Martha Solomon, "The Politics of Adaptation: Steven Spielberg's Appropriation of *The Color Purple*," *Text and Performance Quarterly* 14 (1994): 158–174.

49. Quoted in Joseph McBride, *Steven Spielberg: A Biography* (New York: Da Capo Press, 1999), 365.

50. Ibid., 368.

51. Alice Walker. *The Same River Twice: Honoring the Difficult* (New York: Scribner, 1996), 161.

52. Glen Collins, "Spielberg Films *The Color Purple*," in *Steven Spielberg: Interviews*, ed. Lester D. Friedman and Brent Notbohm (Jackson: University Press of Mississippi, 2000), 123.

53. Ed Guerrero, *Framing Blackness: The African American Image in Film* (Philadelphia: Temple University Press, 1993), 52.

54. Brooks Barnes, "'The Color Purple' Proves Black Themes Can Make Green on Great White Way," *Wall Street Journal*, December 1, 2006, http://online.wsj.com/article/SB116494273168237705.html.

55. Bobo, "Sifting through the Controversy," 337–338.

56. Alice Walker, *The Color Purple* (New York: Harcourt & Brace Company, 1982), 112.

57. Bobo, "Sifting through the Controversy," 332.

58. Barnes, "'The Color Purple' Proves."

59. Jamie Walker, "Broadway's 'The Color Purple' Empowers Many," http://aalbc.com/reviews/the_color_purple_on_broadway.htm, accessed March 19, 2013.

60. Menno Meyjes, *The Color Purple* (Hollywood, CA: Script City, 1985), 27.

61. Walker, *The Color Purple*, 17–18.

62. Barnes, "'The Color Purple' Proves."

63. bell hooks, *Reel to Real: Race, Sex, and Class at the Movies* (New York: Routledge,1996), 56.

64. Edward Guthmann, "Datebook," *San Francisco Chronicle*, February 8, 1998.

65. Restricted access to such agreements makes it difficult to verify. However, on IMDB.com, Twentieth Century–Fox is listed as the sole producer and distributor for the film; as such, the studio maintains full creative control as characterized by a PFD agreement. Shulyer M. Moore, *The Biz* (Los Angeles: Silman-James Press), 87.

66. Moore, *The Biz*, 87–88, 4.

67. Ibid., 87.

68. Horn, "Weinstein Co. Loses."

69. Moore, *The Biz*, 89.

70. Ibid., 90.

71. Ibid., 89.

72. Guerrero, *Framing Blackness*, 83.

73. Harry F. Waters, "Black Is Bountiful," *Newsweek* 122, no. 23 (December 6, 1993): 59.

74. Horn, "Weinstein Co. Loses."

75. Irene Zeinabu Davis, "'Beautiful-Ugly' Blackface: An Esthetic Appreciation of *Bamboozled*," *Cineaste* 26, no. 2 (2001): 16–17; "The Return of Hollywood: Fun and Profit," *Economist* (October 29, 1988): 21–24.

76. Jordi McKenzie, "Do 'African American' Films Perform Better or Worse at the Box Office? An Empirical Analysis of Motion Picture Revenues and Profits," *Applied Economics Letters* 17, no. 16 (2010): 1559–1564.

77. Nina Darnton, "'The Color Purple' to Reopen Nationwide," *New York Times*, January 9, 1987.

78. Jacqueline Bobo, "'The Subject Is Money': Reconsidering the Black Film Audience as a Theoretical Paradigm," *Black American Literature Forum* 25, no. 2 (Black Film Issue) (Summer 1991): 426.

79. Mark A. Reid, *Redefining Black Film* (Berkeley: University of California Press, 1993), 125.

80. Nsenga K. Burton, "Hollywood's Black Movers and Shakers," TheRoot.com, May 31, 2011, http://www.theroot.com/views/hollywoods-black-movers-and-shakers, accessed March 15, 2013.

81. John Horn, "'Push' Comes to Shove in Movie Rights Fight," *Los Angeles Times*, February 6, 2009, http://articles.latimes.com/2009/feb/06/business/fi-push6.

82. "2009 Sundance Film Festival," http://history.sundance.org/events/842, accessed February 24, 2013.

83. Lee, "To Blacks, 'Precious' Is 'Demeaned' or 'Angelic.'"

CHAPTER 4   BREAKING THE CHAINS OF HISTORY AND GENRE

1. Peggy Phelan, *Unmarked: The Politics of Performance* (New York: Routledge, 1993), 148.

2. Ron Eyerman, *Cultural Trauma: Slavery and the Formation of American Identity* (Cambridge: Cambridge University Press, 2001), 1.

3. Stephen V. Duncan, *Genre Screenwriting: How to Write Popular Screenplays That Sell* (New York: Continuum, 2008), xvi.

4. George Fredrickson, "The Skeleton in America's Closet," *New York Review of Books* 47, no. 17 (2000): 61.

5. Eyerman, *Cultural Trauma*, 18.

6. Peter Marks, "Of Slavery and Sex in a Time Warp," *New York Times*, December 13, 1996, http://theater.nytimes.com/mem/theater/treview.html?pagewanted=print&res=950d e3de173ef930a25751c1a960958260.

7. Darryl Littleton, *Black Comedians on Black Comedy: How African Americans Taught Us to Laugh* (New York: Applause Theatre & Cinema Books, 2006); Bambi Haggins, *Laughing Mad: The Black Comic Persona in Post-Soul America* (New Brunswick, NJ: Rutgers University Press, 2007); Glenda Carpio, *Laughing Fit to Kill: Black Humor in the Fictions of Slavery* (Oxford: Oxford University Press, 2008).

8. "America's 10 Greatest Films in 10 Classic Genres," *American Film Institute*, accessed March 23, 2013, http://www.afi.com/10top10/.

9. IMDB.com lists at least 120 films and television shows that reference the story or characters in the miniseries *Roots*. Some of the most relevant for our discussion include *Hollywood Shuffle* (1987), *Coming to America* (1988), *Do the Right Thing* (1989), *Boyz N the Hood* (1991), *House Party 2* (1991), *Sister Act 2: Back in the Habit* (1993), *The Lion King* (1994), *Romeo Must Die* (2000), *Bait* (2000), *Bamboozled* (2000), *Rush Hour 2* (2001), *Undercover Brother* (2002), *The Fighting Temptations* (2003), *Diary of a Mad Black Woman* (2005), *Madagascar 2: Escape to Africa* (2008), and *Notorious* (2009). "Roots: Did You Know?" http://www.imdb.com/title/tt0075572/trivia?tab=mc&ref_=tt_trv _cnn, accessed February 26, 2013.

10. Christopher Weems, "Winfrey Brings Human Touch to Movie 'Beloved,'" *Atlanta Inquirer*, October 17, 1998.

11. Anissa Janine Wardi, "Freak Shows, Spectacles, and Carnivals: Reading Jonathan Demme's *Beloved*," *African American Review* 39, no. 4 (2005): 513.

12. Michael Silverblatt, "The Writing Life: A Conversation between Michael Silverblatt and Toni Morrison," *Los Angeles Times*, November 1, 1998, articles.latimes.com/1998/ nov/01/books/bk-38075. Accessed January 20, 2013.

13. Gerima in Pamela Woolford, "Filming Slavery: A Conversation with Haile Gerima," *Transition*, no. 64 (1994): 92.

14. Ibid., 92.

15. George Alexander, "Fade to Black," http://www.blackenterprise.com/mag/fade-to-black-2, December 1, 2000.

16. Bernard Weinraub, "Despite Hope, 'Beloved' Generates Little Heat among Moviegoers," *New York Times*, November 9, 1998.

17. Jon Stewart, "George Lucas," *The Daily Show*, video 8:13, January 9, 2012, http://www.thedailyshow.com/watch/mon-january-9–2012/george-lucas; Jacqueline Prescott, "George Lucas Worries Hollywood Doesn't Support Black Films," *Washington Post*, January 11, 2012, http://www.washingtonpost.com/blogs/arts-post/post/george-lucas-worries-hollywood-doesnt-support-black-films/2012/01/11/gIQAbZsgrP_blog.html.

18. Debra Walker King, *African Americans and the Culture of Pain* (Charlottesville: University of Virginia Press, 2008), 16.

19. Ed Guerrero, *Framing Blackness: The African American Image in Film* (Philadelphia: Temple University Press, 1993), 10.

20. Stephen V. Duncan, "Master Class on Screenwriting" (workshop, American Black Film Festival, Miami, FL, June 25, 2010).

21. Duncan, *Genre Screenwriting*, 113.

22. Edward Buscombe, *Cinema Today* (London: Phaidon Press Limited, 2003), 89.

23. Toni Morrison, *Beloved* (New York: Plume, 1987), 36.

24. Marilyn Sanders Mobley, "A Different Remembering: Memory, History and Meaning in Toni Morrison's *Beloved*," in *Modern Critical Views: Toni Morrison*, ed. Harold Bloom (New York: Chelsea House Publishers, 1990), 195.

25. "Reelblack Talks to Jonathan Demme about New Home Movies," YouTube video, 7:49, from an interview posted by "Reelblack" September 29, 2007, http://www.youtube.com/watch?v=oK6vM8dZJyg.

26. Woolford, *Filming Slavery*, 103.

27. Morrison, *Beloved*, 5.

28. Barbara Tepa Lupack, *Literary Adaptations in Black American Cinema: From Micheaux to Morrison* (Rochester, NY: University of Rochester Press, 2002), 506.

29. John C. Tibbetts, "Oprah's Belabored Beloved," *Literature/Film Quarterly* 27, no. 1 (1999): 74–76.

30. Lupack, *Literary Adaptations*, 514.

31. Quoted in Mario Van Peebles, Ula Y. Taylor, Tarika Lewis, and Melvin Van Peebles, *Panther: A Pictorial History of the Black Panthers and the Story Behind the Film* (New York: Newmarket Press, 1995), 25–26.

32. Keith P. Feldman, "Review: *Black Panther* by Reginald Hudlin; John Romita," *MELUS* 32, no. 3, Coloring America: Multi-Ethnic Engagements with Graphic Narrative (Fall 2007): 255–258, 256, http://www.jstor.org/stable/30029802.

33. Ibid., 256.

34. Van Peebles et al., *Panther*, 159.

35. Sharon Waxman, "Hollywood Attuned to World Markets," *Washington Post*, October 26, 1998, http://www.washingtonpost.com/wp-srv/inatl/longterm/mia/part2.htm.

36. "Panther: Book Review," *Kirkus Review*, May 1, 1995.

37. William Lyne, "No Accident: From Black Power to Black Box Office," *African American Review* 34, no. 1 (Spring 2000): 39.

38. Van Peebles et al., *Panther*, 140.

39. Kara Keeling, "Ghetto Heaven: *Set It Off* and the Valorization of Black Lesbian Butch-Femme Sociality," *Black Scholar* 33, no. 1 (Spring 2003): 35.
40. Van Peebles et al., *Panther*, 138.
41. Richard Leiby, "Black Out: What a New Movie about the Black Panthers Remembers—and What It Forgets," *Washington Post*, April 30, 1995.
42. Van Peebles et al., *Panther*, 136.
43. Scott Sherman, "David Horowitz's Long March," *Nation*, June 15, 2000, http://www.thenation.com/article/david-horowitzs-long-march.
44. Michael Eric Dyson, "The Panthers, Still Untamed, Roar Back," *New York Times*, April 30, 1995.
45. Leiby, "Black Out."
46. Jeff Strickler, "'Panther' Is History with a Charge: Film Focuses More on Theory than Fact," *Star Tribune*, May 3, 1995.
47. Van Peebles et al., *Panther*, 151.
48. Onita Estes-Hicks, "The Way We Were: Precious Memories of the Black Segregated South," *African American Review* 27, no. 1 (Black South Issue, Part 1 of 2) (Spring 1993): 9–10.
49. Charles Whitaker, "What's Behind the Big Boom in Black Women Writers," *Ebony* 55, no. 5 (March 2000): 38.
50. Ibid., 38.
51. Linda James Myers, *Understanding an Afrocentric World View: Introduction to an Optimal Psychology,* 2nd ed. (Dubuque, IA: Kendall/Hunt Publishing Company, 2003), 74.
52. Clifton Taulbert, *Once Upon a Time When We Were Colored* (New York: Penguin Books, 1989), 4–5.
53. Pam Lambert, "What's Wrong with This Picture? Exclusion of Minorities Has Become a Way of Life in Hollywood," *People* 45, no. 11 (March 18, 1996), http://www.people.com/people/archive/article/0,,20103043,00.html.
54. bell hooks, *Black Looks: Race and Representation* (Boston: South End Press, 1992).
55. Lambert, "What's Wrong with This Picture?"
56. "Top-Grossing Distributors 1995–2012," http://www.the-numbers.com/market/Distributors, accessed February 26, 2013,
57. Kate Meyers, "Maternity Ward," *Entertainment Weekly*, September 20, 1996.

CHAPTER 5   THE PARADOX OF BRANDING, BLACK STAR POWER, AND BOX OFFICE POLITICS

1. James Ulmer, *The Ulmer Scale* (Los Angeles: Ulmer Scale, 1997–2010), 17.
2. U.S. Constitution, Article I, Section 2, Paragraph 3.
3. Pam Lambert, "What's Wrong with This Picture? Exclusion of Minorities Has Become a Way of Life in Hollywood," *People* 45, no. 11 (March 18, 1996), http://www.people.com/people/archive/article/0,,20103043,00.html.
4. Randy A. Nelson and Robert Glotfelty, "Movie Stars and Box Office Revenues: An Empirical Analysis," *Journal of Cultural Economics* 3, no. 2 (2012): 142–143.
5. Ibid., 141–166.
6. Ibid., 146.
7. Ibid., 142.
8. Ibid.
9. Ibid.
10. Ibid.

11. Ulmer, *Ulmer Scale*, 37.
12. Richard Dyer, "From Stars," in *Film Theory and Criticism*, 7th ed., ed. Leo Braudy and Marshall Cohen (Oxford: Oxford, University Press, 2009), 483; Patrick McGilligan, *Cagney, the Actor as Auteur* (South Brunswick, NJ: A. S. Barnes, 1975).
13. Dyer, "From Stars," 483.
14. Ibid.
15. Charlene Regester, *African American Actresses and the Struggle for Visibility 1900–1960* (Bloomington: Indiana University Press, 2010).
16. Ibid., 286–287.
17. Dorothy Dandridge and Earl Conrad, *Everything and Nothing: The Dorothy Dandridge Tragedy* (New York: HarperCollins, 2000), 196.
18. Regester, *African American Actresses*, 308. Regester further elaborates this use of Dandridge's body in *Bright Road* (1953), *Carmen Jones* (1954), *Island in the Sun* (1957), *Tamango* (1958), and *Porgy and Bess* (1959).
19. Ulmer, *Ulmer Scale*, 17.
20. "About the Ulmer Scale," http://www.ulmerscale.com/aboutUS.html, accessed February 26, 2013.
21. Scott Bowles, "Debating the MPAA's Mission," *USA Today*, April 10, 2007.
22. Ulmer, *Ulmer Scale*, 10.
23. Patrick Goldstein and James Rainey, "The Ulmer Scale: A True Test of Hollywood Star Bankability?" *Los Angeles Times*, May 22, 2009, http://latimesblogs.latimes.com/the_big_picture/2009/05/the-ulmer-scale-a-true-test-of-hollywood-star-bankability.html.
24. Fortunately, Mr. Ulmer has granted permission to report these figures for the purposes of this book. His cooperation suggests a willingness to demystify the process.
25. "PBS Moment: Don Cheadle Waxes Subversive about the Ulmer Scale," http://www.ulmerscale.com/Cheadle.html, accessed February 26, 2013,
26. Logan Hill, "How I Made It: Spike Lee on 'Do the Right Thing,'" *New York*, April 7, 2008, http://nymag.com/anniversary/40th/culture/45772/.
27. Ibid.
28. Ibid.
29. Lee actually hoped to encourage film audiences to vote and thereby oust New York mayor Ed Koch from office. In the event, David Dinkins won the fall 1989 election, becoming the first and only African American to hold the office. See Hill, "How I Made It."
30. Ulmer, *Ulmer Scale*, 17.
31. Universal distributed the following Spike Lee films: *Mo' Better Blues* (1990), *Jungle Fever* (1991), *Crooklyn* (1994), *Clockers* (1995), and *Inside Man* (2006). Other Lee films were distributed as follows: *Malcolm X* (1993), Warner Bros.; *Girl 6* (1996), Fox Searchlight Pictures; *Get on the Bus* (1996), Columbia Pictures; *He Got Game* (1996), Twentieth Century–Fox; *Summer of Sam* (1999) and *25th Hour* (2002), Buena Vista Pictures; *She Hate Me* (2004), Sony; *Bamboozled* (2000), New Line Cinema; and *Miracle at St. Anna* (2008), Touchstone Pictures.
32. Anna Julia Cooper, *A Voice from the South 1892* (Oxford: Oxford University Press, 1988), 31.
33. Jenée Desmond-Harris, "Watch This: Beyoncé Ad Raises Race Questions," TheRoot.com, February 24, 2012, http://www.theroot.com/buzz/watch-beyonc-ad-raises-race-questions.
34. Dan Zak, "Movie Review: Dan Zak on Beyoncé's Thriller 'Obsessed,'" *Washington Post*, April 25, 2009; Wesley Morris, "Movie Review: Obsessed," *Boston Globe*, April 25, 2009.

35. Vanessa Martinez, "Casting Latina Actresses/Black Actors: Revisiting the Hollywood Trend," *Shadow and Act: On Cinema and the African Diaspora*, May 8, 2012, http://blogs .indiewire.com/shadowandact/b8049250–98b7–11e1-bcc4–123138165f92.

36. Ed Guerrero, *Framing Blackness: The African American Image in Film* (Philadelphia: Temple University Press, 1993), 48.

37. Gene Seymour, "Black Directors Face Frustration, Hope and Elusive Success," *New York Times*, January 1, 2009.

38. Warrington Hudlin cites the film's economic prowess to challenge the perceived failure of African American film. See Lambert, "What's Wrong with This Picture?" and "The 10 Highest-Grossing Black Films of All Time," Black Youth Project.com, December 20, 2011, http://www.blackyouthproject.com/2011/12/the-10-highest -grossing-black-films-of-all-time/.

39. Megan Casserly, "Beyoncé's $50 million Pepsi Deal Takes Creative Cues from Jay-Z," Forbes.com, December 10, 2012, http://www.forbes.com/sites/meghancasserly/2012/12/10/ beyonce-knowles-50-million-pepsi-deal-takes-creative-cues-from-jay-z/.

40. Ulmer, *Ulmer Scale*, 24.

CHAPTER 6   BIG BUSINESS: HIP-HOP GANGSTA FILMS AND BLACK COMEDIES

1. "Top-Grossing Movie Sources 1995–2012," The Numbers.com, accessed March 18, 2013, http://www.the-numbers.com/market/Sources/. Also see Monica White Ndounou, "The Color of Hollywood" (Ph.D. diss., Ohio State University, 2007), 628–868.

2. Cedric J. Robinson, *Forgeries of Memory and Meaning: Blacks and the Regimes of Race in American Theater and Film before World War II* (Chapel Hill: University of North Carolina Press, 2007), 141–143.

3. Thompson argues that contemporary and classical Hollywood films actually use a four-part structure primarily distinguishable by its critical turning point in the "dead center" of the film. Kristin Thompson, *Storytelling in the New Hollywood: Understanding Classical Narrative Technique* (Cambridge, MA: Harvard University Press, 1999), 23–44.

4. Christopher Riley, *The Complete & Authoritative Guide to Script Format & Style*, 2nd ed. (Studio City, CA: Michael Weise Productions, 2009), 23.

5. Ibid., 24.

6. Sharon Waxman, "Hollywood Attuned to World Markets," *Washington Post*, October 26, 1998, http://www.washingtonpost.com/wp-srv/inatl/longterm/mia/part2.htm.

7. Amanda Ann Klein, *American Film Cycles: Reframing Genres, Screening Social Problems, and Defining Subcultures* (Austin: University of Texas Press, 2011), 3–4.

8. Ibid., 19.

9. Beretta E. Smith-Shomade, "Rock-a-Bye, Baby!: Black Women Disrupting Gangs and Constructing Hip-Hop Gangsta Films," *Cinema Journal* 42, no. 2 (Winter 2003): 26.

10. Ibid. Other examples include *New Jack City* (1991) and *Sugar Hill* (1993).

11. Ibid., 28. Other examples include *Straight Out of Brooklyn* (1991), *Juice* (1992), *South Central* (1992), *Menace II Society* (1993), and *Clockers* (1995).

12. Klein, *American Film Cycles*, 14–15.

13. Pam Lambert, "What's Wrong with This Picture? Exclusion of Minorities Has Become a Way of Life in Hollywood," *People* 45, no. 11 (March 18, 1996), http://www.people.com/ people/archive/article/0,,20103043,00.html.

14. Negative cost refers to "the cost of producing a motion picture, including Above-the-Line and Below-the-Line costs and certain miscellaneous costs, which include financing costs, the Completion Bond fee, and a contingency reserve—generally 10 percent

of the Above-the-Line and Below-the-Line costs"; Shulyer M. Moore, *The Biz* (Los Angeles: Silman-James Press), 7. Above-the-Line costs refer to "motion picture costs that relate to the acquisition of rights and payments to Talent and the producer" (Moore, *The Biz*, 3). Below-the-Line costs are "actual production costs (excluding Above-the-Line costs and certain miscellaneous costs described under Negative costs" (Moore, *The Biz*, 4). A completion bond is a "contractual commitment issued by a Completion Guarantor agreeing to either (a) complete and deliver a picture on time or (b) repay the bank if timely delivery is not achieved" (Moore, *The Biz*, 5). According to Moore, a distribution fee is "a retained share of profits by the Distributor, usually charged as a percentage of Gross Receipts and confusingly referred to as a 'fee'" (*The Biz*, 5). Moore defines this as "contingent payments towards Talent (writers, directors and actors) and unions pursuant to the provisions of the collective bargaining agreements entered into with the unions (e.g., DGA, WGA, SAG)" (*The Biz*, 8). Moore defines participations as "contingent payments to talent based on a percentage of gross receipts or net profits from a motion picture" (*The Biz*, 7).

15. A gross participant is "someone who is entitled to a share of Adjusted Gross Receipts, either First Dollar Gross or after a pre-defined point, such as after Actual Break-Even" (Moore, *The Biz*, 6). Actual break-even is "the point in time when a motion picture's revenues reach Net Profits based on a full Distribution Fee. . . . [Comparatively,] Cash Break-Even is 'the point in time when a motion picture's Gross Receipts reach Net Profits, but using a low Distribution Fee. There can be several levels of Cash Break-Even using progressively higher Distribution Fees until Actual Break-Even'" (Moore, *The Biz*, 3–4).

16. Gross points are a percentage of Gross receipts, which are "all gross revenues from a motion picture at a specified link in the distribution chain, such as either At-Source or received by the distributor." Gross points are "a share of the Gross Receipts, either First Dollar Gross or after a pre-defined point such as after Actual Break-Even" (Moore, *The Biz*, 6–7).

17. Victor P. Goldberg, "Net Profits Puzzle," *Columbia Law Review* 97 no. 2 (March 1997): 531.

18. Derek Thompson, "How Hollywood Accounting Can Make a $450 Million Movie 'Unprofitable,'" *Atlantic*, September 14, 2011.

19. Dennis McDougal, "Murphy Movie Made Millions But Stayed in Red, Studio Ledger Says," *Los Angeles Times*, February 4, 1990, http://articles.latimes.com/1990–02–04/news/mn-537_1_eddie-murphy-productions. Some sources report the film earned $145 million. Terry Pristin, "'Coming to America' Writer Lambastes Buchwald at Trial: Film: Barry Blaustein Challenges the Humorist's Contention That He and a Partner Created the Paramount Movie," *Los Angeles Times*, March 7, 1992, http://articles.latimes.com/1992–03–07/business/fi-3587_1_barry-blaustein, accessed July 3, 2013.

20. Bernard Weinraub, "Art Buchwald Awarded $150,000 in Suit Over Film," *New York Times*, March 17, 1992, http://www.nytimes.com/1992/03/17/movies/art-buchwald-awarded-150000-in-suit-over-film.html, accessed July 3, 2013.

21. Mark A. Reid, *Redefining Black Film* (Berkeley: University of California Press, 1993), 93.

22. "Box Office History for Madea Movies," The-Numbers.com, http://www.the-numbers.com/movies/franchise/Madea, accessed March 28, 2013.

23. "Box Office History for Barbershop Movies," The-Numbers.com, http://www.the-numbers.com/movies/franchise/Barbershop, accessed March 28, 2013.

24. Tim Arango, "Before Obama, There Was Bill Cosby," *New York Times*, November 7, 2008.

25. Victor S. Dugga, "Africa from the American Lens: A Comparative View of the Films Sheena and Coming to America," *SORAC: Journal of African Studies* 1 (April 2000): 111.

26. Eric Lott, *Love and Theft: Blackface Minstrelsy and the American Working Class* (New York: Oxford University Press, 1995), 6.

27. Robinson, *Forgeries*, 145.

28. Stuart Kemp, "Idris Elba's Nelson Mandela Pic, 'Long Walk to Freedom' Gets a Start Date," *Hollywood Reporter*, March 19, 2012.

29. Aislinn Laing, "South African Actors 'Not Tall Enough to Play Nelson Mandela,'" *The Telegraph*, March 20, 2012, http://www.telegraph.co.uk/news/worldnews/nelson-mandela/9155246/South-African-actors-not-tall-enough-to-play-Nelson-Mandela.html.

30. David Sheffield and Barry W. Blaustein, *Coming to America aka The Zamunda Project*, (Beverly Hills, CA: Creative Artists Agency, 1987), 1.

31. Stephen V. Duncan, *Genre Screenwriting: How to Write Popular Screenplays That Sell* (New York: Continuum, 2008), 158.

32. Ibid.,165.

33. Ibid., 160.

34. Leslie Fishbein, "*Roots*: Docudrama and the Interpretation of History," in *Why Docudrama? Fact-Fiction on Film and TV*, ed. Alan Rosenthal (Carbondale: Southern Illinois University Press, 1999), 271.

35. Ibid., 279.

36. Mambi Maestra Arrastia, "'Middle Class Values': A Euphemism for Whiteness in Schools," *Social Etymologies*, May 10, 2009, http://blog.lib.umn.edu/arras004/socialetymologies/2009/05/middle-class-values-a-euphemis.html.

37. Nancy E. Hill and Kathy Torres, "Negotiating the American Dream: The Paradox of Aspirations and Achievement among Latino Students and Engagement between their Families and Schools," *Journal of Social Issues* 66, no. 1 (March 2010): 95–112.

38. Bambi Haggins, *Laughing Mad: The Black Comic Persona in Post-Soul America* (New Brunswick, NJ: Rutgers University Press, 2007), 1–2.

39. Ibid., 4.

40. Ben Chappell, "Bakhtin's Barbershop: Film as Folklorist," *Western Folklore* 64, no. 3–4 (Summer–Fall 2005): 211.

41. Robert E. Gregg, "The New African American Middle Class," *Economic and Political Weekly* 33, no. 4 (November 14–20, 1998): 2938.

42. Haggins, *Laughing Mad*, 2.

43. Wil Haygood, "Why Negro Humor Is So Black," *American Prospect* 11, no. 26 (2000): 26.

44. Amiri Baraka, "The Descent of Charles Fuller into Pulitzerland and the Need for African-American Institutions," *Black American Literature Forum* 17, no. 2 (Summer 1983): 52.

45. Gary Crowdus and Dan Georgakas, "Thinking about the Power of Images: An Interview with Spike Lee," *Cineaste* 26, no. 2 (March 2001): 6.

46. Ibid.

47. Henry Louis Gates Jr., *The Signifying Monkey: A Theory of African-American Literary Criticism* (New York: Oxford University Press, 1988), 53.

48. Gene Seymour, "Black Directors Look Beyond Their Niche," *New York Times*, January 9, 2009, http://www.nytimes.com/2009/01/11/movies/11seym.html?pagewanted=all&_r=0.

49. Smith-Shomade, "'Rock-a-Bye, Baby!,'" 29.

50. Onita Estes-Hicks, "The Way We Were: Precious Memories of the Black Segregated South," *African American Review* 27, no. 1 (Black South Issue, Part 1 of 2) (Spring 1993): 9.

51. Gregg, "New African American," 2938.

52. Ibid.

53. Michael Eric Dyson, "Between Apocalypse and Redemption: John Singleton's *Boyz N the Hood*," *Cultural Critique*, no. 21 (Spring 1992): 121.

54. Henry Louis Gates Jr., "Must Buppiehood Cost Homeboy His Soul?," *New York Times*, March 1, 1992.

55. Robert W. Welkos, "Writers Cross Racial Lines in Their Films," *Seattle Times*, November 20, 1996, http://community.seattletimes.nwsource.com/archive/?date=19961120& slug=2360671.

56. Gray directed Ice Cube's *It Was a Good Day* (1992), Queen Latifah's *Black Hand Side* (1994), Outkast's *Southernplayalisticadillacmuzik* (1994), TLC's *Waterfalls* (1995), and Babyface's *How Come, How Long* (1996).

57. Dyson, "Between Apocalypse," 124; James Nadell, "*Boyz N the Hood*: A Colonial Analysis," *Journal of Black Studies* 25, no. 4 (March 1995): 462.

58. John Singleton, *Boyz N the Hood: An Original Screenplay* (Hollywood, CA: Script City, 1990), 96.

59. James P. Morris-Knower, "Homeboys and Homeplace: The Geography of Adolescence in *Straight Out of Brooklyn* and *Boyz N the Hood*," *Michigan Academician* 29, no. 2 (March 1997): 193.

60. Reid, *Redefining*, 109.

61. Ibid., 124.

62. Jesse Jackson, "A Thirty-one-Year Struggle for Fairness and Inclusion in the American Dream: An Open Letter to the Entertainment Community," *Motion Magazine*, April 10, 1996, http://www.inmotionmagazine.com/rainbow2.html.

63. Denise Bielby and William Bielby, "Women and Men in Film: Gender Inequality among Writers in a Culture Industry," *Gender & Society* 10, no. 3 (June 1996): 249, 251.

64. James Ulmer, *The Ulmer Scale* (Los Angeles: Ulmer Scale, 1997–2010), 458–462.

65. Wilson Morales, "Celebrating 'Set It Off' 15 Years Later: An Interview with Screenwriter Takashi Bufford," Blackfilm.com, November 10, 2011, http://www.blackfilm.com/read/2011/11/celebrating-set-it-off-15-years-later/.

66. James W. Messerschmidt, *Crime as Structured Action: Gender, Race, Class and Crime in the Making* (Thousand Oaks, CA: Sage Publications, 1997), 77.

67. Gerima's films are *Child of Resistance* (1973), *Harvest: 3,000 Years* (1976), *Wilmington 10— U.S.A. 10,000* (1979), *Bush Mama* (1976), *Ashes and Embers* (1972), *After Winter: Sterling Brown* (1985), *Sankofa* (1993), *Adwa* (1999), and *Teza* (2008).

68. "Awards for *Teza*," IMDB.com, http://www.imdb.com/title/tt1284592/awards?ref_=tt_awd, accessed March 18, 2013.

69. Haki Madhubuti, *Claiming Earth: Race, Rage, Rape, Redemption; Blacks Seeking a Culture of Enlightened Empowerment* (Chicago: Third World Press, 1994), 261.

70. Ndounou, "The Color of Hollywood," 828–829.

71. Madhubuti, *Claiming Earth*, 261–262.

72. Dolan Hubbard refers to the sublime as "an aesthetic value founded on the presence or suggestion of transcendent vastness or greatness in the form of power, heroism or of extent in space or time." Rhys Roberts's translation of Longinus identifies five sources of the sublime: grandeur of thought, vehement and inspired passion, elevated figures of speech, noble phrasing of diction, and elevation in the arrangement of words. Dolan Hubbard, ed., "W.E.B. DuBois and the Invention of the Sublime in *The Souls of Black Folk*," *The Souls of Black Folk One Hundred Years Later* (Columbia: University of Missouri Press, 2003), 300.

73. Pamela Woolford, "Filming Slavery: A Conversation with Haile Gerima," *Transition*, no. 64 (1994): 91.

74. Madhubuti, *Claiming Earth*, 260.

75. Matt Zoller Seitz, "Movie Review: *Teza* (2008), Lacking Shelter at Home and Abroad," *New York Times*, April 2, 2010, http://movies.nytimes.com/2010/04/02/movies/02teza.html.

76. Ibid.

77. Wilson Morales, "Ten Black Films That May Never Be Released in Theaters or on DVD," Black Film.com, August 16, 2011, http://www.blackfilm.com/read/2011/08/ten-black-films-that-may-never-be-released-in-theaters-or-on-dvd/.

78. "About Us," http://www.sankofa.com/about.php, accessed March 18, 2013.

79. Michael Cieply, "Building an Alliance to Aid Films by Blacks," *New York Times*, January 7, 2011, http://www.nytimes.com/2011/01/08/movies/08urban.html.

80. Logan Hill, "How I Made It: Spike Lee on 'Do The Right Thing,'" *New York*, April 7, 2008.

81. Ntongela Masilela, "The Los Angeles School of Black Filmmakers," in *Black American Cinema*, ed. Manthia Diawara (New York: Routledge. 1993), 107.

82. Ibid., 108.

83. Pramaggiore and Wallis, *Film*, 436. Also see "Media Conglomerates: Tangled Webs," *Economist* 363, no. 8274 (May 25–31, 2002): 81–83.

84. See the introduction, where I outline these patterns of production and illuminate the racial disparities.

85. Greg Tate, "*Bamboozled*: White Supremacy and a Black Way of Human," *Cineaste* 26, no. 2 (2001): 16.

86. Mary G. Hurd, *Women Directors and Their Films* (Westport, CT: Greenwood Publishing Group, 2007), 67.

87. Haggins, *Laughing Mad*, 206–207.

88. Ibid., 207.

89. Andrew Wallenstein, "Dave Chappelle Inks $50 million Deal," *Hollywood Reporter*, August 3, 2004.

90. "Chappelle's Story: Why Comedian Dave Chappelle Walked Away from $50 Million," *The Oprah Winfrey Show*, February 3, 2006, http://www.oprah.com/oprahshow/Chappelles-Story/1, accessed March 20, 2013.

91. Ibid.

92. Justin Maiman, "Spike Lee Wants YOU to Fund His Next Movie," *Daily Ticker*, July 25, 2013, http://finance.yahoo.com/blogs/daily-ticker/spike-lee-wants-fund-next-movie-133656599.html, accessed July 26, 2013.

93. A selected sample of World War II films released since 1980 includes *The Big Red One* (1980), *Empire of the Sun* (1980), *Biloxi Blues* (1988), *A Man Called Sarge* (1990), *For the Boys* (1991), *The English Patient* (1996), *Saving Private Ryan* (1998), and *The Thin Red Line* (1998).

94. The film had an estimated budget of $65 million with box office earnings of only $34 million domestically. After playing on 2,375 screens for fifty-two days it earned $32 million internationally, which helped recoup production expenses with a total worldwide gross of $66 million.

95. With an estimated $17 million budget and box office earnings of $13.7 million domestically, the film played on 781 screens for 124 days. It earned $61.5 million internationally for a total world gross of $75.2 million.

96. Greg Kilday, "Cannes 2012: 'Paperboy' Director Lee Daniels on His 'Precious' Follow-Up and Why Zac Efron Is 'Hungry,'" *Hollywood Reporter*, May 21, 2012.

97. "Black Directors, Their Movies, and Their Money," *Black Enterprise*, March 6, 2010.
98. Marcus Reeves, "Tim Story Is the Highest Grossing Black Director," Bet.com, May 16, 2012, http://www.bet.com/news/celebrities/2012/05/16/tim-story-now-the-highest-grossing-black-director.html.

CONCLUSION: THE STORY BEHIND THE NUMBERS

1. Zeinabu Irene Davis, "The Future of Black Film," in *Cinemas of the Black Diaspora: Diversity, Dependence and Oppositionality*, ed. Michael T. Martin (Detroit: Wayne State University Press, 1995), 450; in the same volume, Manthia Diawara, "Black American Cinema: The New Realism," 406–407.
2. Richard Corliss, "Box Office Weekend: *Karate Kid* Whups *A-Team*," Time.com, June 13, 2010, http://www.time.com/time/arts/article/0,8599,1996325,00.html.
3. Ibid.
4. Maria Pramaggiore and Tom Wallis, *Film: A Critical Introduction* (Boston: Pearson, 2008), 432; Allen John Scott, *On Hollywood: The Place, The Industry* (Princeton, NJ: Princeton University Press, 2005), 44
5. Imaeyen Ibanga, "Is There Anything Magic Johnson Doesn't Own?" HLNTV.com, March 28, 2012, http://www.hlntv.com/article/2012/03/28/magic-johnson-group-buy-mlb-los-angeles-dodgers-2-billion.
6. Randy O. Williams, "NFL Hollywood Boot Camp Teaches Players Xs and O's of Filmmaking," *Los Angeles Times*, March 31, 2012, http://articles.latimes.com/2012/mar/31/entertainment/la-et-nfl-hollywood-20120331.
7. Rahim Ali, "Django Unchained Dolls Discontinued, Jamie Foxx Responds to Spike Lee," BET.com, January 22, 2013, http://www.bet.com/news/celebrities/2013/01/22/django-unchained-dolls-discontinued-jamie-foxx-responds-to-spike-lee.html.
8. "Tyler Perry," CBSnews.com, video 12:22, July 25, 2010, http://www.cbsnews.com/video/watch/?id=6711929n.
9. Suzan-Lori Parks, "An Equation for Black People Onstage," *The America Play and Other Works* (New York: Theatre Communications Group, 1995), 19–22.

SELECTED FILMOGRAPHY

America Beyond Color Line with Henry Louis Gates. Dir. Daniel Percival and Mary Crisp. Speakers: Henry Louis Gates, Don Cheadle, Martin Luther King Jr., Reggie Rock Bythewood, Alicia Keys. PBS, 2004.

Austin Powers in Goldmember. Dir. Jay Roach. Perf. Mike Myers, Beyoncé Knowles, Seth Green. New Line Cinema, 2002.

Bamboozled. Dir. Spike Lee. Perf. Damon Wayans, Savion Glover, Michael Rappaport, Jada Pinkett Smith, Tommy Davidson, Mos Def. New Line Home Video, 2000.

Beloved. Dir. Jonathan Demme. Perf. Oprah Winfrey, Danny Glover, Thandie Newton, Beah Richards, Kimberly Elise. 1998. Buena Vista, 2002.

The Birth of a Nation. Dir. D. W. Griffith. Perf. Lillian Gish, Mae Marsh. 1915.

Birth of a Race. Dir. John W. Noble. Perf. Louis Dean, Harry Dumont, Carter B. Harkness. Birth of a Race Photoplay Corporation, 1918.

Bopha! Dir. Morgan Freeman. Perf. Danny Glover, Alfre Woodard, Malcolm McDowell. Paramount, Filmic Archives, 1992.

Boyz N the Hood. Dir. John Singleton. Perf. Laurence Fishburne, Angela Bassett, Ice Cube, Cuba Gooding Jr., Morris Chestnut, Regina King, Nia Long, Tyra Ferrell. Columbia/TriStar Pictures, 1991.

Brother from Another Planet. Dir. John Sayles. Perf. Joe Morton, Rosanna Carter, Ray Ramirez. A-Train Films and Cinecom International Films, 1984.

Classified X. Dir. Melvin Van Peebles. Perf. Melvin Van Peebles, Margaret Barker, Joanna Barnes. Centre National de la Cinématographie, 1998.

The Color Purple. Dir. Steven Spielberg. Perf. Whoopi Goldberg, Danny Glover, Adolph Caesar, Oprah Winfrey, Rae Dawn Chong. Warner Bros. and Filmic Archives, 1985.

Coming to America. Dir. John Landis. Perf. Eddie Murphy, Arsenio Hall, James Earl Jones, Madge Sinclair. Gulf & Western, Paramount, 1988.

Convicts. Dir. Peter Masterson. Perf. James Earl Jones, Robert Duvall, Lukas Haas, Starletta DuPois. Management Company Entertainment, 1991.

Cry Freedom. Dir. Richard Attenborough. Perf. Denzel Washington, Kevin Kline, Josette Simon. Universal Pictures, 1987.

Daughters of the Dust. Dir. Julie Dash. Perf. Cora Lee Day, Barbara-O, Cheryl Lynn Bruce, Tommy Hicks. 1991. Kino on Video, 1999.

Do the Right Thing. Dir. Spike Lee. Perf. Spike Lee, Joie Lee, Bill Nunn, Giancarlo Esposito, Ruby Dee, Ossie Davis. Universal Pictures, 1989.

Dreamgirls. Dir. Bill Condon. Perf. Beyoncé Knowles, Jamie Foxx, Eddie Murphy. Dreamworks SKG, 2006.

Driving Miss Daisy. Dir. Bruce Beresford. Perf. Morgan Freeman, Esther Rolle, Jessica Tandy. Warner Bros. Home Video, 1989.

A Dry White Season. Dir. Euzhan Palcy. Perf. Donald Sutherland, Janet Suzman, Zakes Mokae. Sundance Productions, 1989.

Enemy of the State. Dir. Tony Scott. Perf. Will Smith, Gene Hackman, Jon Voigt. Touchstone Pictures, 1998.

The Eraser. Dir. Chuck Russell. Perf. Arnold Schwarzenegger, Vanessa Williams, James Caan. Warner Bros. Pictures, 1996.

Eve's Bayou. Dir. Kasi Lemmons. Perf. Jurnee Smollett-Bell, Meagan Good, Samuel L. Jackson. Trimark Pictures, 1997.

The Exorcist. Dir. William Friedkin. Perf. Ellen Burstyn, Max von Sydow, Linda Blair. Warner Bros. Pictures, 1973.

A Few Good Men. Dir. Rob Reiner. Perf. Tom Cruise, Demi Moore, Jack Nicholson. Columbia/ TriStar Pictures, 1992.

For Colored Girls. Dir. Tyler Perry. Perf. Janet Jackson, Anika Noni Rose, Whoopi Goldberg. Lionsgate, 2010.

From Push to Precious. Speakers: Lee Daniels, Geoffrey Fletcher, Sapphire. Off the Cliff Productions, 2010.

Gone with the Wind. Dir. Victor Fleming. Perf. Clark Gable, Vivien Leigh, Thomas Mitchell. Metro-Goldwyn-Mayer, 1939.

Juice. Dir. Ernest Dickerson. Perf. Samuel L. Jackson, Omar Epps, Tupac Shakur, Khalil Kain, Cindy Herron. Paramount Home Video, 1992.

Just Another Girl on the IRT. Dir. Leslie Harris. Perf. Ariyan A. Johnson, Kevin Thigpen, Ebony Jerido. Miramax Films, 1992.

The Karate Kid. Dir. John G. Avildson. Perf. Ralph Macchio, Pat Morita, Elizabeth Shue. Columbia Pictures, 1884.

The Karate Kid. Dir. Harald Zwart. Perf. Jackie Chan, Jaden Smith, Taraji P. Henson. Columbia Pictures, 2010.

Main Street. Perf. Orlando Bloom, Colin Firth, Amber Tamblyn. 1984 Films, 2010.

Malcolm X. Dir. Spike Lee. Perf. Denzel Washington, Angela Bassett, Delroy Lindo. 40 Acres & a Mule, 1992.

Mandela. Dir. Ronald Harwood. Perf. Danny Glover, Alfre Woodard, Tam Mpofu, Priscilla Mundawarara. Home Box Office, 1987.

Mandingo. Dir. Richard Fleischer. Perf. James Mason, Susan George, Perry King. Paramount Pictures, 1975.

Menace II Society. Dir. Allen Hughes and Albert Hughes. Perf. Samuel L. Jackson, Bill Duke, Marilyn Coleman, Charles S. Dutton, Jada Pinkett, Larenz Tate. Facets Multimedia, Inc., New Line Cinema Home Video, 1993.

A Mighty Heart. Dir. Michael Winterbottom. Perf. Angelina Jolie, Dan Futterman, Irrfan Khan. Paramount Vantage, 2007.

Monster's Ball. Dir. Marc Forster. Perf. Billy Bob Thornton, Halle Berry, Taylor Simpson. Lionsgate Films, 2001.

New Jack City. Dir. Van Peebles, Mario. Perf. Mario Van Peebles, Bill Nunn, Wesley Snipes, Vanessa Williams, Bill Cobbs. Warner Bros. Home Video, 1991.

Night Catches Us. Dir. Tanya Hamilton. Perf. Anthony Mackie, Kerry Washington, Wendell Pierce. Magnolia Pictures, 2010.

Night of the Living Dead. Dir. George A. Romero. Perf. Duane Jones, Judith O'Dea, Karl Hardman. Image Ten, 1968.

North by Northwest. Dir. Alfred Hitchcock. Perf. Cary Grant, Eva Marie Saint, James Mason. Metro-Goldwyn-Mayer, 1959.

Of Mice and Men. Dir. Gary Sinise. Perf. John Malkovich, Gary Sinise, Ray Walston. Metro-Goldwyn-Mayer, 1992.

Once Upon a Time . . . When We Were Colored. Dir. Tim Reid. Perf. Al Freeman Jr., Phylicia Rashad, Leon, Paula Kelly. BET Pictures, 1996.

Oprah & Tyler Perry: A Project of Passion. Speakers: Lee Daniels, Tyler Perry, Oprah Winfrey. Off the Cliff Productions, 2010.

Panther. Dir. Mario Van Peebles. Perf. Kadeem Hardison, Bookeem Woodbine, Marcus Chong, Courtney B. Vance. Gramercy Pictures, 1995.

Paranormal Activity. Dir. Oren Peli. Perf. Katie Featherston, Micah Sloat, Mark Fredrichs. Blumhouse Productions, 2007.

Perfect Stranger. Dir. James Foley. Perf. Halle Berry, Bruce Willis, Giovanni Ribisi. Revolution Studios, 2007.

The Player's Club. Dir. Ice Cube. Perf. Ice Cube, LisaRaye, Dick Anthony Williams, Judyann Elder. New Line Cinema, 1998.

Poltergeist. Dir. Tobe Hooper. Perf. JoBeth Williams, Heather O'Rourke, Craig T. Nelson. Metro-Goldwyn-Mayer, 1982.

Posse. Dir. Mario Van Peebles. Perf. Mario Van Peebles, Stephen Baldwin, Charles Lane. Polygram Filmed Entertainment, 1993.

The Power of One. Dir. John G. Avildsen. Perf. Stephen Dorff, Armin Mueller-Stahl, Morgan Freeman. Warner Bros. Pictures, 1992.

Precious: Based on the Novel 'Push' by Sapphire. Dir. Lee Daniels. Perf. Gabourey Sidibe, Mo'Nique, Paula Patton, Mariah Carey. Lee Daniels Entertainment, 2009.

Ragtime. Dir. Milos Forman. Perf. James Cagney, Howard E. Rollins Jr., Elizabeth McGovern. Paramount Pictures, 1981.

Roots. Dir. Marvin J. Chomsky, John Erman. Perf. Olivia Cole, LeVar Burton, Ben Vereen. Warner Bros. Television, 1977.

Rosewood. Dir. John Singleton. Perf. Ving Rhames, Don Cheadle, Esther Rolle, Jon Voigt. Warner Bros. Pictures, 1997.

Safe House. Dir. Daniel Espinosa. Perf. Denzel Washington, Ryan Reynolds, Vera Farmiga, Universal Pictures, 2012.

Sankofa. Dir. Haile Gerima. Perf. Oyafunmike Ogunlano, Mutabaruka, Alexandra Duah, Nick Medley, Reginald Carter. Mypheduh Films, Inc., 1994.

Sarafina! Dir. Darrell Roodt. Perf. Whoopi Goldberg, Miriam Makeba, Leleti Khumalo. British Broadcasting Company, 1992.

School Daze. Dir. Spike Lee. Perf. Kadeem Hardison, Bill Nunn, James Bond III, Joie Lee, Tisha Campbell. Columbia Pictures Home Video, 1988.

The Secret Life of Bees. Dir. Gina Prince-Bythewood. Perf. Queen Latifah, Dakota Fanning, Alicia Keys, Sophie Okonedo, Jennifer Hudson. Fox Searchlight and Overbrook Entertainment, 2008.

Set It Off. Dir. F. Gary Gray. Perf. Jada Pinkett, Vivica A. Fox, Queen Latifah, Kimberly Elise. New Line Cinema, 1996.

A Soldier's Story. Dir. Norman Jewison. Perf. Howard E. Rollins Jr., Adolph Caesar, Art Evans, Denzel Washington. Columbia-Delphi Productions, 1984.

Straight Out of Brooklyn. Dir. Matty Rich. Perf. Matty Rich, George T. Odom, Mark Malone. Samuel Goldwyn Home Video, 1991.

Sweet Sweetback's Baadasssss Song. Dir. Melvin Van Peebles. Perf. Melvin Van Peebles, the black community, Brer Soul. Xenon Entertainment Group, 1971.

To Sleep with Anger. Dir. Charles Burnett. Perf. Danny Glover, Sheryl Lee Ralph, Richard Brooks, Mary Alice. Facets Multimedia, Inc., 1990.

Training Day. Dir. Antoine Fuqua. Perf. Denzel Washington, Ethan Hawke, Scott Glenn, Eva Mendes. Warner Bros. Pictures, 2001.

Traitor. Dir. Jeffrey Nachmanoff. Perf. Don Cheadle, Guy Pearce, Archie Panjabi. Overture Films, 2008.

The Truth about Charlie. Dir. Jonathan Demme. Perf. Mark Wahlberg, Thandie Newton, Tim Robbins. Universal Pictures, 2002.

Tyler Perry's Diary of a Mad Black Woman. Dir. Darren Grant. Perf. Tyler Perry, Kimberly Elise, Steve Harris. Lionsgate, 2005.

Tyler Perry's Diary of a Mad Black Woman. Dir. Tyler Perry. Perf. Tyler Perry, Curtis Blake, Marva King, Ty London. My.Te.Pe Productions, 2002.

Uncle Tom's Cabin. Dir. Harry A. Pollard. Perf. Margarita Fischer, James B. Lowe, Arthur Edmond Carewe. 1927.

Waiting to Exhale. Dir. Forest Whitaker. Perf. Whitney Houston, Angela Bassett, Loretta Devine, Lela Rochon, Gregory Hines. 1995. Twentieth Century–Fox Home Entertainment, 1999.

Within Our Gates. Dir. Oscar Micheaux. Perf. Evelyn Preer, Flo Clements, James D. Ruffin, Jack Chenault. Micheaux Book and Film Company, 1919.

The Wiz. Dir. Sidney Lumet. Perf. Diana Ross, Michael Jackson, Nipsey Russell. Universal Pictures, 1978.

Woman Thou Art Loosed. Dir. Michael Schultz. Perf. Kimberly Elise, T. D. Jakes, Michael Boatman. T. D. Jakes Ministries, 2004.

INDEX

2Live Crew, 216
3-D technology, 245
12 Years a Slave, 236; budget and gross, 236
40 Acres & A Mule Filmworks, 195
48 Hours, 197
50 Cent, 226
100 Rifles, 193

Above the Rim, 231
Abyssinia, 35
Academy Awards, nominees, 42–43, 172;
    Alfre Woodard, 29; Angela Bassett, 102;
    Beasts of the Southern Wild, 239; *The
    Color Purple*, 125; Eddie Murphy, 189,
    196; Gabourey Sidibe, 102; Lee Daniels,
    236; Mo'Nique, 102; *Precious*, 125; Queen
    Latifah, 183; Quvenzhanè Wallis, 239; *A
    Soldier's Story*, 64; Terrence Howard, 189;
    Whoopi Goldberg, 102; Will Smith, 182,
    189
Academy Awards, winners, 42–43, 172; and
    African American directors, 182; Denzel
    Washington, 237; *Driving Miss Daisy*, 182;
    Forrest Whitaker, 101; Geoffrey Fletcher,
    218; Halle Berry, 183, 200; Horton Foote,
    49; Kathryn Bigelow, 219; *Precious*, 125, 218
acculturation, 13; or absorption, 26, 100,
    235, 242; examples in films, 56; in film
    industry, 13, 74, 184, 242; *See also* creative
    centralization
acting opportunities: and branding, 12;
    casting patterns and, 6; and planta-
    tion politics, 113; playing multiple roles
    or characters, 35, 83, 197, 206; and the
    Ulmer Scale, 175, 199
action films, 148–150; *Biker Boyz*, 17; black
    female leads, 187, 219; cultural politics of,
    79, 139, 150–153, 237; economics of, 2, 11,
    219–220; and Jamie Foxx, 196; *Red Tails*,
    1–2, 17, 150; *Set It Off*, 120, 217–220; and
    Will Smith, 182, 185, 192. *See also* genre;
    genre films
Act Like a Lady, Think Like a Man (Harvey), 1.
    See also *Think Like a Man*
Actor's *Hot List* 2009–2010, 179. *See also*
    Ulmer Scale

adaptation: and acculturation, 13, 65–68;
    and African American worldviews, 159,
    161, 164; and audience building, 63, 65,
    73, 88–91, 105, 120, 148, 249–250; benefits
    of, 242; black cultural production, 12–13,
    23, 249; black literature or books, 1, 24,
    110, 138, 249; black men's literature, 127–
    128, 132–133, 149, 235; black women's
    literature, 84, 95, 99, 103–106, 110–111,
    127–128, 132–133, 137–138, 161, 222, 242;
    Broadway, 24, 29, 34–36, 49, 59–61, 115–
    117; and cultural amnesia, 69–72; and
    cultural trauma, 132–133; definition, 12,
    257n41; and distribution, 21, 139; drama-
    turgical incompletions or racial formulas,
    120, 139; and genre, 141, 149; Hollywood,
    12–13, 21–24, 29, 44, 66–68, 75, 88–89,
    138–148, 195, 239; horizontal integration,
    12, 21, 24, 34, 57, 87, 99, 130, 246; indigen-
    ization, 23, 79; intersectionality, 99, 130,
    132, 246, 249; intertextuality, 8, 12–13, 21,
    117, 130, 132, 154, 246; master narrative,
    30–31, 33, 36, 41, 44–45, 51–52, 57, 75, 114,
    159, 195, 201; pathology, 104–108, 113, 117,
    122, 128; plantation genre, 30–31, 33, 41,
    51–52, 57, 195; and poetics of liberation,
    77–78; urban circuit, 29, 83, 87
advertising, 12; crossover audiences, 85;
    early modes of, 34–35; and race ideology,
    36, 229, 232; studio, 147, 223; word-of-
    mouth, 147, 222. *See also* marketing
aesthetics of black film, 23, 104, 135, 241; and
    poor cinema, 58; womanist aesthetics,
    97–99, 101, 120–122, 153, 217–218. *See also*
    womanist aesthetics
*African American Actresses: The Struggle for
    Visibility 1900–1960* (Regester), 171
African American cinematic language:
    definition, 6, 13; examples, 67; and hybrid
    forms, 166, 218; potential of, 67, 99, 102,
    105, 144, 160; pioneers of, 218, 222, 227;
    problems of, 87, 99, 218; and screenplay
    format, 202. *See also* Afrocentric world-
    views; black Atlantic tragedy; cinematic
    language; limbo; rememory

283

African American contributions: to acting and directing, 58, 183; to American cinema, 16, 31, 135; to distribution alternatives, 21, 26, 57 58, 61, 84, 92, 107; to self-financing or fundraising, 90, 234, 241. *See also* African American cinematic language; black Atlantic tragedy; performative indigenization; rememory films

African American cultural values: cinematic language of, 6; and cultural amnesia, 16, 165; defining, 86, 162; distortion of, 101, 129; and double consciousness, 23, 65; dramatizing, 161; and economics or commercial appeal, 97, 99, 222; families and communities, 160, 212; and folklore, 212; and Hollywood, 23, 72; and materialism, 160; and nihilism, 156, 160, 164; redefining, 86, 163; and southern black, 161; and storytelling, 23. *See also* African concept of self; Afrocentric worldviews

African American English (AAE)/or black American speech, 55

African American film development: adaptation, 12, 41; audience development, 230, 238; *Beloved*, 140; and black literature, 95; black star power, 191, 193–194, 199, 250; and black theater, 29, 61, 74, 95, 250; casting, 25, 29–30, 61, 172, 176; cinematic language, 20; college and university market, 247; cultural amnesia, 16; cultural literacy, 241–242; cultural trauma, 134; distribution, 20, 123, 126, 166, 176; early films, 58; economics of, 6, 14, 57, 172; established precedent, 66, 140, 172; and form and content, 6, 12, 31, 134; and genre, 159; horizontal integration, 21, 57; hybrid distribution, 57; lessons for future, 26; past influences on, 2; and plantation ideology, 180, 203; and predominantly white cast plays or films, 41, 48; and serious themes, 196, 213; screenplays, 29; technical gloss, 51; and Ulmer Scale, 177, 180, 191; urban circuit, 85; and Will Smith, 194. *See also* collaboration in black film development; models for emulation; models influencing African American film development

African American Film Festival Releasing Movement (AAFFRM), 226, 247. *See also* distribution, film

African American films/black films: definition of, 6; limited distribution of, 9, 16–17, 24; marketing, 3, 13, 19–20, 26, 34, 72, 84, 88, 95, 108, 125–126, 128–129, 139–141, 147, 165, 167; perceived failure of 2, 24, 91, 106, 132, 139, 192, 203, 205, 272n28. *See also* films featuring African Americans

African concept of self, 60, 104

African Diasporic distribution network, 26, 238; Haile Gerima's distribution company, 226; potential markets, 15, 248–249

African Grove, 62

Africanist presence: in American theater and entertainment, 34; apartheid films, 77; *Beloved*, 146; *The Birth of a Nation*, 30, 32–34, 41; and black stars, 197; *Convicts*, 41, 49, 69; definition of, 30; and distribution, 125; *Driving Miss Daisy*, 41, 52; *A Few Good Men* 41, 44, 46; music, 69, 87; *Once Upon a Time*, 159; racial reconciliation, 41, 44, 46, 49, 52, 69, 146, 202; revisions or reversals of, 146, 159; *Uncle Tom's Cabin*, 30, 32–34, 41, 49. *See also* master narrative

Africans in American entertainment, 34; African Americans portraying, 35, 60, 77–79, 81, 89, 204–208; African female construct, 205–206, 209; black British portraying, 77–79, 207–208; circus Africans, 34–35, 240; Hollywood tradition of, 207, 211–212; reversing representations of, 207, 35, 209, 222–225, 227. *See also* South Africa

Afrocentric worldviews: in conflict with Hollywood, 16, 66–67; and cultural trauma, 16; and dramatic structure, 60, 65; in film, 16, 65–67, 70, 159; and genre, 159; in historical dramas, 16, 66–67; and the interconnectedness of time, 60, 67; in literature, 159; in storytelling, 16; in theater, 60, 65, 67, 70. *See also* African American cinematic language; African American cultural values; African concept of self; Cra

Aiello, Danny, 181, 251
Aiken, George, 33
Aina, Shirikiana, 226
Albee, E. F., 35
Aldrige, Ira, 207
Alex Cross, 86
Ali, 182, 192–194, 196
Alibar, Lucy, 239–241, 244
A list stars, 230; Ulmer Scale, 177
All About the Benjamins, 193
All Things Fall Apart, 226
Altimari, Dave, 47
Alvarado, William, 47
Amblin Entertainment, 123
America Beyond the Color Line (PBS series), 179
American Black Film Festival, 106, 247, 250
American Bookseller's Association, 160
American Dream, the, 71, 194, 208–209, 214–215; in *Coming to America*, 208–209; exposing, 214–215; and international audiences, 17, 209, 214; myth of meritocracy and model minority, 209, 214; in *Raisin in the Sun*, 59
American Film Institute (AFI), 135
American Indian Film Festival, 137
American Marketing Association, 12
Amistad, 134, 136, 142
Andrew, Dudley, 257n41
Angelou, Maya, 159

Hurston, Zora Neale, 210
Hurt Locker, The, 219
Hutcheon, Linda, 12, 257n41
hybrid distribution, 20–21, 92; and horizontal integration, 24, 57, 130, 238, 246, 248
hybrid genre, 166, 220

I Can Do Bad All By Myself, 186
Ice Cube, 107, 214, 221, 231, 239, 275n56; and black comedy, 206, 213; star power, 178, 188, 252
I Know Why the Caged Bird Sings (Angelou), 159
In Dahomey, 35
Independence Day, 194
independent film, 23, 84, 89, 123, 165, 217, 250; distribution, 26, 223, 225–226, 235, 237–238, 241, 247; filmmakers, 20–22, 58–59, 106, 199, 202, 221, 227, 231
indigenization, 17, 19, 25, 101, 173, 240; definition of, 14. *See also* oppositional gaze; performative indigenization
industry practices, 11, 16, 19, 58, 147–148, 164, 174; and race or plantation ideology, 13, 17, 25, 34, 40, 66, 113, 122, 139, 158, 170, 207–208, 214; and Ulmer Scale, 170, 174, 177, 188, 200; and urban circuit, 85, 100
In Living Color (TV series), 125, 195
Inside Man, 271n31
Inside the Actor's Studio (TV series), 233
institutionalized racism, 9, 71, 134, 199
Insurrection: Holding History (play), 133
interlocking systems of oppression, 5, 78, 126, 153, 226, 229, 234. *See also* matrix of domination
International Creative Management, 175
interracial interaction, patterns of, 68; collaboration, 73–74, 78; and distribution, 192, 194; in film, 31, 36, 41, 44, 78, 116, 120, 163–164, 208, 212, 220; and star power, 186, 187, 189; in theater, 31, 32, 41, 44, 69, 73–74
intersectionality, 218, 249–250; and crossover appeal, 99, 246, 248; definition of, 13–14; and intertextuality, 21, 130, 132, 238, 246, 248
intertextuality: and adaptation as strategy, 12–13, 21, 111, 117, 130, 132, 154, 246; and African American cinematic language, 13, 106, 218; of black film, 8, 13, 21, 98, 105, 111, 117, 154, 218, 238, 250; and intersectionality, 21, 98, 130, 132, 218, 238, 246, 248
Introducing Dorothy Dandridge, 173, 187–188
investment decisions, 3, 128; and race ideology, 4–5, 7, 15, 159, 165, 180, 243
I Still Know What You Did Last Summer, 183
Italian Job, The, 221

Jack Lawrence Theater, 74
Jackson, Samuel L., 64, 111, 183, 194, 221; star power, 170–171, 174, 178, 252
Jakes, T. D., 83, 264n66

James Ulmer's Hollywood Hot List: The Complete Guide to Star Ranking, 174, 179, 182, 184. *See also* Ulmer Scale
Jay-Z (Shawn Carter), 188
Jazz, 104
Jefferson in Paris, 189
Jewison, Norman, 64, 67
JFK, 157, 204
Jim Crow, 52
Jitney (play), 65, 192
Johnson, Earvin "Magic," 106, 238, 247
Jolie, Angelina, 190, 252
Jones, James Earl, 43, 163
Jones, Quincy, 96, 115
Jones, Steven Swann, 98
Journal of Cultural Economics, 171
Journey of August King, The, 189
Juice, 217, 228
Jungle Book, The, 139
Jungle Fever, 186, 198, 271n31
Just Another Girl on the IRT, 215
Justice, David, 187
Just Wright, 198, 213

Kandé, Sylvie, 222
Karate Kid, The: 1984 film, 243; 2010 film, 25, 185, 243
Keitel, Harvey, 186, 252
Keith, B. F., 34–35
Keller, Bill, 80
Kennedy, John F., 151, 157
Key and Peele (cable TV series), 233
Keys, Alicia, 195, 198, 252
Kidd, Sue Monk, 195
Kidman, Nicole, 142, 236, 252
Kid Rock, 17
King, Charles, 175
King, Debra Walker, 141
King, Larry L., 42, 52
King, Dr. Martin Luther, Jr., 151, 156, 212
King, Regina, 178, 191, 217, 252
King, Rodney, 153
King, Woodie, Jr., 61
Kirkus Reviews, 153
Klady, Leonard, 80
Klein, Amanda Ann, 203
Klotman, Phyllis, 8
Klumps, The, 197
Knowles, Beyoncé, 69, 195; entrepreneurship, 188–189, 198; star power, 178, 186–190, 252
Koch, Ed, 271n29
Krasner, David, 53
Krone, Gerald, 62
Krusiec, Michelle, 194

LaBelle, Patti, 69
LaBeouf, Shia, 176
Lackawana Blues, 188, 191
Lakeview Terrace, 193–194
Landis, John, 204
Lanier, Kate, 213, 215, 218, 220
Larkin, Alile Sharon, 227

Waterboy, 146
Watermelon Contest, 32
Watkins, S. Craig, 4
Waxman, Sharon, 15, 25
Wayans, Damon, 228, 230
Wayans brothers, 213
Wayne, John, 135
Weber, Max, 8
Weinstein Company, 107, 124–125, 128, 248
Welch, Raquel, 193, 253
We the Peeples, 90
Weyers, Marius, 78
What's Love Got to Do with It?, 127, 216
Whitaker, Forest, 101, 105, 121, 178, 213, 236
White (Dyer), 171
White, Armond, 114
white audiences: and black audiences, 74–75, 85, 88, 129, 211; and black comedy, 205, 211; and black star power, 183–184, 189; and black theater, 62–63, 65, 73, 111; and crossover appeal, 7, 15, 66, 77, 88–90, 97, 104, 121, 174, 184, 189, 205; and Oprah, 96; and performative indigenization, 35; and Tyler Perry, 88–90. See also crossover appeal; economic viability of black film
white cast films, predominantly, 15, 23–24, 45, 77, 132, 245–246; and African American film development, 29, 36, 56–57, 72, 165, 250; and black directors, 221, 236, 249; and broad distribution, 1, 3, 75, 81, 125, 139, 223; and star power, 179–180, 183–184, 186–187, 189–190, 190, 197
whiteness: in black imagination, 162; defined by Africanist presence, 32, 49, 69, 84, 141; as dysfunctional, 51; and plantation ideology, 187, 192; as universal norm, 129, 132; as unmarked racial category, 6, 31, 177, 204. See also master narrative; universal/universalism
white point of entry: in African American or black narratives, 40, 52, 77, 155, 181–182, 240; definition of, 17; and distribution, 125, 134, 180, 184–185, 222
white privilege in Hollywood, 82, 126, 129, 139, 184, 190, 200, 210, 231; and males, 18, 47, 173, 184, 190, 200; in narratives, 49, 51, 173
white stars, 179–182, 185, 190, 196; and star vehicles, 41. See also Ulmer Scale
white and black theater production: on Broadway, 24, 29, 31, 36, 41, 44, 48, 50, 56, 61–63, 74; in Chicago, 36, 40–41, 61–63, 83; critics, 41; organizations, 73, 62–63, 83
Who Said Watermelon, 31
Who's the Man?, 231
Why Do Fools Fall in Love, 187
Wierick, John, 76, 79

William Morris Agency, 175
Williams, Bert, 86, 173; and African characters, 35, 60, 89, 207; cultural nuance of, 40; entrepreneurship, 24, 58–59, 227; Jonah Man, 34–35; vital contrast, 35, 89
Williams, Spencer, 59
Williams, Vanessa, 186–187, 190, 212, 253
Willis, Allee, 115
Willis, Bruce, 153, 172, 187, 253
Willmott, Kevin, 135
Wilson, August, 27, 71, 84, 100, 192, 234; and Broadway, 27, 61, 65; on crossover appeal, 7, 60; on cultural imperialism, 40–41, 101; and funding black theater, 40–41, 65; strategies of empowerment, 14; ten-play cycle, 65, 133
Wilson, Patrick, 194, 253
Winfrey, Oprah, 12, 90, 102, 148, 186, 236; and strategies for developing black film, 12, 18, 26, 96, 107–108, 124, 243. See also Oprah Effect
Winnie, 225
Witherspoon, Reese, 177, 253
Within Our Gates, 227
womanism, 120, 122, 217; womanist philosophy, 117–118; womanist values, 70, 120
womanist aesthetic/womanist-centered aesthetics, 97–99, 120, 122, 153; culture and economics of, 101–105; film, definition of, 218; and hip-hop gangsta films, 217–218
Woman Thou Art Loosed, 83, 127
Wood, Natalie, 135
Wood, The, 208
Woodard, Alfre, 29, 42, 61, 79, 191, 207, 218, 253
Woodberry, Bill, 227
Wooing and Wedding a Coon, 31
World War II films, 234, 235; Flags of Our Fathers, 235; Letters from Iwo Jima, 235; Miracle at St. Anna, 235; Red Tails, 1–2; A Soldier's Play/A Soldier's Story, 63–64, 66, 71, 234–235; The Tuskegee Airmen, 235
Woza Afrika! festival, 72–75
Woza Albert!, 73
Wright, N'Bushe, 186, 253
Writer's Guild of America (WGA), 5, 219, 229
Wysong, Earl, 8–9

X-Men, 187

Zebra Head, 186
Zeitlin, Benh, 239–241, 244
Zellweger, Renée, 142
Ziegfeld, Flo, 34–35
Ziegfeld Follies, 34
Zwick, Edward, 134

ABOUT THE AUTHOR

MONICA WHITE NDOUNOU is an assistant professor of drama, American studies, and film studies at Tufts University. She directs plays and teaches interdisciplinary courses in theater, film, media, and cultural studies. She has published articles in the *Journal of Dramatic Theory and Criticism*, *Theatre Topics*, and the *New England Theatre Journal*, along with essays in *The Cambridge Companion to African American Theatre* and *Consciousness, Theatre, Literature and the Arts*. She has also presented national and international conference presentations on theater and performance, film, and popular culture.